Shopping with Allah

ECONOMIC EXPOSURES IN ASIA

Series Editor: Rebecca M. Empson, Department of Anthropology, UCL

Economic change in Asia often exceeds received models and expectations, leading to unexpected outcomes and experiences of rapid growth and sudden decline. This series seeks to capture this diversity. It places an emphasis on how people engage with volatility and flux as an omnipresent characteristic of life, and not necessarily as a passing phase. Shedding light on economic and political futures in the making, it also draws attention to the diverse ethical projects and strategies that flourish in such spaces of change.

The series publishes monographs and edited volumes that engage from a theoretical perspective with this new era of economic flux, exploring how current transformations come to shape and are being shaped by people in particular ways.

Shopping with Allah

*Muslim pilgrimage, gender and consumption
in a globalised world*

Viola Thimm

First published in 2023 by
UCL Press
University College London
Gower Street
London WC1E 6BT

Available to download free: www.uclpress.co.uk

ISBN: 978-1-80008-560-2 (Hbk)
ISBN: 978-1-80008-559-6 (Pbk)
ISBN: 978-1-80008-558-9 (PDF)
ISBN: 978-1-80008-561-9 (epub)
DOI: https://doi.org/10.14324/111.9781800085589

For 'Masjaliza', my beloved Malay friend and sister.

Contents

List of figures

List of abbreviations

BERSATU	*Parti Pribumi Bersatu Malaysia* (Malaysian United Indigenous Party)
BN	*Barisan Nasional* (National Front)
EPU	Economic Planning Unit
GBS	*Gabungan Bersatu Sabah* (United Alliance of Sabah)
GCC	Gulf Cooperation Council
GE14	14th General Election
GMTI	Global Muslim Travel Index
GPS	*Gabungan Parti Sarawak* (United Sarawak Party)
HDC	*Halal* Industry Development Corporation
ITC	Islamic Tourism Center
JAKIM	*Jabatan Kemajuan Islam Malaysia* (Department of Islamic Development Malaysia)
KKBI	*Kamus Besar Bahasa Indonesia* (Grand Dictionary of Indonesian)
KL	Kuala Lumpur
MAS	Malaysia Airlines
MIHAS	Malaysia International *Halal* Showcase
MOTAC	Ministry of Tourism and Culture
NEP	New Economic Policy
PAS	*Parti Islam Se-Malaysia* (Islamic Party of Malaysia)
PM	Prime Minister
PPBM	*Parti Pribumi Bersatu Malaysia* (United Indigenous Party)
SIS	Sisters in Islam
TH	*Tabung Haji* (the Malaysian government's pilgrim fund institution)
TTDI	*Taman Tun Dr Ismail* (a neighbourhood in Petaling Jaya)
UAE	United Arab Emirates
UMNO	United Malays National Organisation

Acknowledgements

My research interest in the religious and gender practices of Muslim Malays in Malaysia arose in the mid-2000s, when I had the opportunity to embark on an academic career as a doctoral student. I am now an associate professor and have, as a researcher, been able to return to Malaysia – and to its neighbouring country Singapore, my other main research site – on a fairly regular basis. Many of the acquaintances I made during my first long-term fieldwork in 2008–9 have become friends. Above all, I would like to thank my closest friend and 'sister' Masjaliza, whose real name I cannot disclose here for reasons of confidentiality. Without her, none of my research phases in Malaysia would have been as joyful, profound, inspiring and encouraging. She has always given me deep, often intimate, insights into her personal and family life and thereby shaped the direction of my research significantly. I dedicate this book to you, my beloved sister.

I also wish to thank Masjaliza's family – 'my Malaysian family' as they constantly emphasise – who have generously shared their everyday routines, practices, thoughts, dreams, hopes and ideas with me. Masjaliza and her close family – her husband, her two children, Ibu and Bapak, Kakak and her family – have contributed so much to my research through their never-ending conversations with me, their trust and their warmth. Your experiences have tremendously enriched my understanding of Muslim and gender practices in countless ways. I am sure you will recognise your contributions when you come across them and I hope that you find them accurately represented.

Other respondents and friends, whose names must similarly remain hidden here, have worked equally hard to guide me through my ethnographic journey. I owe all of you my deepest gratitude for sharing your stories and everyday life practices with me. This is a debt that I can never hope to repay.

I am obliged to a large number of other people and institutions without whose assistance and support this book would not have been completed or published. Professor Guido Sprenger from the University of Heidelberg guided me generously through the qualification process for which this book was originally meant – my Habilitation as the German requirement for full professorship – and gave helpful and critical comments on the manuscript based on his careful, detailed reading. While Guido Sprenger was key at the point of completing this research, Professor Monika Arnez, who was then professor at Hamburg University, was key at the beginning. She supported me in developing my original research proposal, which was ultimately successful in attracting third-party funding. I owe both of you my deepest gratitude for sharing your knowledge and your experiences with me.

Other scholars with whom I have had valuable conversations at different stages of the research include Shamsul Amri Baharuddin, Adil Johan, Yeoh Seng Guan, Sharon A. Bong, Sumit Mandal, Alicia Izharuddin, Rima Sabban, Carla Jones, Marjo Buitelaar, Nimrod Luz, Sarah J. Mahler, Mayurakshi Chaudhuri, Daromir Rudnyckyj, Johan Fischer, Melanie Wood, Tim Bunnell, Frederike Steiner, Manja Stephan-Emmrich, Claudia Derichs, Judith Schlehe, Volker Gottowik, Laila Prager, Christian Velde, Imke Moellering, Cathrine Bublatzky, Dominik Müller, Mirjam Lücking and Joan Henderson.

The research would not have been possible without institutional support from Monash Malaysia, School of Arts and Social Sciences, Malaysia, and from Zayed University, College of Humanities and Social Sciences, United Arab Emirates, during the fieldwork phases. Hosting me as a Visiting Research Fellow in both cases, the two institutions provided well-organised, inspiring and warm working environments. I especially thank Sharon A. Bong and Eswary Sivalingam from Monash Malaysia as well as Rima Sabban and Aalia AlFalasi from Zayed University for making this possible.

This book rests on research conducted with generous financial support from the German Research Foundation (Deutsche Forschungsgemeinschaft DFG), the Olympia Morata Programme in support of young female professors, and the 'Nachwuchsinitiative Universität Hamburg' (Initiative for young scholars). I would like to express my gratitude to those bodies. Without the funding and the time this allowed for concentration on research, the writing of this book would not have been possible.

I am also indebted to the editor of the *Economic Exposures in Asia* series at UCL Press, Rebecca M. Empson, and to commissioning editor for Anthropology, Chris Penfold, who organised a smooth and constructive publication process throughout. I furthermore express my thanks to the two anonymous reviewers who showed enthusiasm for this book from the outset, with their extremely positive evaluations and assessments of my manuscript.

My deepest thanks also go to my partner Harald. Without you, not only my research but also my life as an academic would not have been possible. After we had been spatially separated for a year by my field research in Southeast Asia in the course of my dissertation research from 2008 to 2009, we, and especially he, put all our energy into implementing joint field research in Malaysia and on the Arabian Peninsula from 2017 to 2018. The priority was to continue our beautiful life together and to develop myself and my career. Harald organised a one-year sabbatical in order to follow me on ethnographic fieldwork from the beginning to the end. As you know, Harry, many aha-moments and findings of this research are based on joint discussions with you in the field. Apart from the intellectual journey with you, your emotional and mental support have been essential for my path.

1
Setting the ethnographic stage for gender, mobility and religious markets

In my fourteenth month of ethnographic fieldwork, in April 2018, I followed my ninth Malaysian pilgrimage group in Dubai, the bustling city in the United Arab Emirates (UAE), and in Abu Dhabi, the UAE's smaller, calmer capital. Thirty-four pilgrims, including two children, one *mutawif* [1] (a religious tour guide from Malaysia), one Pakistani tour leader and one cultural anthropologist from Germany, spent a four-day tour together. At the very beginning of the first day, Jamil,[2] the Pakistani tour guide, announced over the tour bus microphone that the ladies of the group, who – according to him – would certainly want to get *abayas* (long, usually black coats or dresses), would be able to shop for them the next day when the group visited the *souq* (market) area of Dubai. He mentioned to me that one of the Malaysian pilgrims had asked him about shopping for *abayas* soon after her arrival at the airport. Hawa, the lady he was talking about, was undertaking her first pilgrimage journey, which incorporated this stopover in the UAE. She later told me that shopping for *abayas* was one of the main reasons for making a stopover in Dubai and not in any other place. While her main focus was on the performance of *umrah* (lesser pilgrimage) in Mecca, in today's Saudi Arabia, she had planned the whole journey according to her fashion taste as well.

Why is the *abaya* so important for Hawa? Why is it a 'must' that she gets an *abaya* in Dubai and not from anywhere else? How does she combine the shopping part with the spiritual pilgrimage journey?

Both Dubai and the Holy Land in Saudi Arabia are hotspots for buying *abayas*. Nine months earlier, while sitting with Farrah and her youngest daughter Murni at a local food stall in Kuala Lumpur (KL), Malaysia's capital city, Farrah had told me about her *abayas*. Her first *abaya* was a gift from her mother-in-law, who gave it to her on her return from pilgrimage to Mecca. She had thought, disparagingly, 'Oh, it's so black!', and she had felt uncomfortable because she imagined everyone would be able to see her body shape when wearing it. But later, when she went to Mecca herself, she discovered the way Arab women wear it. They wear jeans underneath, for example; they just throw the *abaya* over the top, and with that one move they are properly attired. She said that these days she has lots of *abayas*, which she wears for dinner or for prayer.

How does Farrah connect this garment with her communication to God, and how does she connect it to social events? Why is the style of wearing it of interest to her? Why do female family members bring *abayas* back to Malaysia from their pilgrimage trips and turn them into gifts?

A connection between the garment and the religious faith of my respondents exists; a certain type of *abaya* is saturated with religion. A month after my meal with Farrah and Murni, I met with 40-year-old[3] Sofea, an *abaya* designer and retailer from KL, in the glamorous shopping mall *Suria KLCC*, directly beneath the Petronas Twin Towers – the symbol of Malaysia's modern Islam, as I have often been told. Her philosophy regarding the *abaya* was that they as Muslims must be modest, since Allah is always watching them. This means not wearing anything too extravagant or vibrant. She explained that Dolce & Gabbana also make *abayas* – but they are not supposed to wear them, only the modest ones. Sofea said that she is close to Allah when she is modest, and that this is how the *abaya* influences her relationship with God. She remembers Him[4] when she chooses to wear something loose and modest rather than showy or shiny.

The points made by Hawa, Farrah and Sofea – the importance of buying a particular garment, the *abaya*, on the pilgrimage journey, either in Mecca or Dubai, and bringing it back home to Malaysia as a gift or for oneself; of wearing it on certain occasions and in a manner that abides by Islamic rules; and of understanding it as a means of surrendering to God – represent a small portion of the broader themes of this study: self-representation and identification, gender norms and roles, spirituality, material culture, consumption and mobility. And they all lead to the central topic of *Shopping with Allah*: the intersection of gender and faith/spirituality, focusing in particular on one significant world religion: Islam. This study investigates, in a broad sense, how this intersection develops and changes in a pilgrimage-tourism nexus as part of capitalist and *halal* consumer markets. It shows the ways in which religion is mobilised in package tourism and how spiritual, economic and gendered practices combine in a form of tourism where the goal is not purely leisure, but also ethical and spiritual cultivation. In a concrete sense, it examines how gendered and spiritual social practices and inner dispositions accrue, perpetuate and transform through Muslim pilgrimage[5] and tourism in the regional context of Malaysia and the UAE, especially Dubai. In this respect, the book sheds light on how Islam and gender frame Malaysian religious tourism and pilgrimage to the Arabian Peninsula – though it raises many further issues that are of great importance beyond these regional contexts.

This study will show that, and how, female pilgrims negotiate their identification as modern, pious Muslim women on the basis of feminised practices of shopping in Dubai (see figure 1.1), Mecca and Medina and the appropriation, integration and adaption of gendered objects purchased into their life in Malaysia. The most obvious such object that female Malaysians such as Hawa, Farrah and Sofea appropriate is the *abaya* – the long, traditionally black dress worn especially by Arab women, which they associate with 'religiosity', 'modernity' and, partially, 'sexiness'. By bringing the *religiously* connoted *abaya* into everyday life in Malaysia and, thereby, into both private and public spaces, females[6] make their spirituality visible and thereby mark their active role in religious negotiation processes. In terms of an *abaya* being *fashionable, modern* or *sexy*, females express to the outside world in local and transregional contested religious constellations that they are protagonists of a modern Islam in Malaysia.

Figure 1.1 Female Malaysian *umrah* & *ziarah* travellers shopping for *abayas* in Dubai, United Arab Emirates, 2018.

While female pilgrims embody their spiritual status by wearing an *abaya* in social private and public spaces, they also use this and other gendered clothing elements as a means of representing changing family constellations: when a wife transforms her relationship with her husband in parallel with her deeper relationship with Allah on the basis of a pilgrimage experience. These manifold constellations show how Malay Malaysian women and men involve themselves and are involved differently in reciprocally constitutive identifications, categories and practices of embodied gender and faith/spirituality regarding their privilege and marginalisation on various social scales.

The entangled perspectives, practices and identifications of the research subjects are explored in their intricacy. The *intersectional* approach has evolved as a framework to understand identities as reciprocally interrelated. Based on the intersection between gender and faith/spirituality under examination, I will make one main theoretical argument. I reconfigure both previous anthropological and intersectionality scholarship by arguing the following: gendered spirituality leads to different, mutually constitutive, gendered and religionised embodied practices of this inner disposition and of femininity or masculinity which eventually challenge gendered social hierarchical orders. In this regard, it will be argued that the spiritual relationship to the Islamic past is only possible in its fullness for males, which they express though their attire. Muslim women have a lower religious status position here (see chapter 4). Furthermore, spiritual communication with God is constituted differently by females and males: whereas males can pray to God in whatever garments they are wearing at the time, females are required to modify their bodies beforehand and thereby face specific religious restrictions (see chapter 5). Moreover, wives embody spirituality in matrimony through their garments and simultaneously reproduce submission and liberation. Men as husbands and fathers, however, express their spirituality on the level of social actions and thereby reconfigure their gendered status position, which eventually relieves their wives of parental duties (see chapter 5). Additionally, purchasing specific attire on the pilgrimage journey has developed from a gender-neutral activity to a female consumer and spiritual gift-giving experience that potentially empowers women and girls (see chapter 6).

It will be shown that the *abaya*, as the most obvious garment in all these circumstances, is itself an intersectional garment. It is the material surface where intersectionality, i.e. mutually dependent processes of gender and faith/spirituality, becomes visible. Beneath this socio-material dimension lie socio-cultural relationships, such as sacred landscaping, exchange relations, kinship and gender ideologies. This book investigates how gendered meanings and practices of spirituality and faith are redefined or reified in the process of religious travel and practices of consumption, and thereby inform wider interdisciplinary debates about intersectionality, constructions of identity, mobility and religious material culture in a globalised world.

Studying pilgrimage

The object of investigation is contemporary pilgrimage to Mecca and Medina, with a stopover in Dubai ('*umrah* & *ziarah* Dubai'), undertaken by Sunni Malay Malaysians. *Umrah* and *ziarah* are two of three forms of Muslim pilgrimage. The third form is the *hajj* – the most important form of pilgrimage – which *umrah* and (partly) *ziarah* are derived from, aligned with and measured against. The *hajj* is the fifth pillar of Sunni Islam and one of the obligatory practices of Shia Islam's Ancillaries of the Faith. Therefore, the *hajj* is compulsory for every Muslim, as long as she or he can physically and financially undertake the journey. This pilgrimage comprises determined rituals in Mecca, including circumambulating the black cube (*kaabah*), throwing pebbles and praying at Mount Arafat (see chapter 2 for details).

In contrast to the *hajj*, it is not compulsory (*wajib*) to perform *umrah*. Whereas the timeframe for the *hajj* is limited to five specific days a year, *umrah* can be performed at any time in a period of seven months. While the *hajj* lasts five days, *umrah* can be completed within a single day, as the rituals outside Mecca are not usually performed. *Ziarah* derives from the Arabian term for 'visit'. In the Malay language it can mean any form of visit, without spiritual connotation, but when it is used in connection with *umrah*, in Malaysia it is certainly understood as a religious practice (see chapter 3). *Ziarah* is an act of piety, practised in order to receive God's blessing (*barakah*) in contemporary life as well as on the day of judgment (Jamhari 2001, 1999).

The term 'pilgrimage' derives from Christian contexts and has no linguistic equivalent in the Malay (*Bahasa Melayu*) or Arabic languages. When my respondents talk in English about this phenomenon, they indeed use the term 'pilgrimage', but this remains an approximation they choose to use as a result of their exposure to English and hence of their habituation to the ways of expressing oneself in this foreign language. In *Bahasa Melayu* the expressions *mengerjakan haji* (to perform *hajj*) and *mengerjakan umrah* (to perform *umrah*) exist. The verb *mengerjakan* is commonly used for expressions related to Islamic worship when these acts of worship are regarded either as *wajib* (something Muslims must do) or as *sunat* (something that is recommended/preferred for Muslims to do). There is no Malay equivalent for the word 'pilgrim(s)'; it is expressed as *jemaah haj* (pilgrims performing *hajj*) or *jemaah umrah* (pilgrims performing *umrah*). *Jemaah* is used in the Malay language for people doing an *ibadah* (religious obligation; act of worship). Notably, neither the expression *mengerjakan ziarah* nor *jemaah ziarah* exists in *Bahasa Melayu*.

This leads to the observation that in Malaysia, only *hajj* and *umrah* are understood as 'pilgrimage' – *ziarah* is, from an emic perspective, explicitly excluded from this concept and practice. Yet in regional Muslim contexts other than Malaysia, such as Indonesia,[7] Turkey and Iran, *ziarah* certainly denotes a common form of pilgrimage (Jamhari 2001, 2000; Millie and Mayo 2019; Mohd Faizal 2013; Moufahim 2013; Prager 2013) and thus frames wider debates on pilgrimage in this research. It is mainly understood as visiting the graves of prophets or saints, which does not necessarily lead to the Arabian Peninsula but implies a visit to the shrines or graves of *local* saints (*wali*) (Jamhari 1999; Surinder 1998). The idea of 'pilgrimage' is not used for this activity by my respondents, nor do most Muslim Malays *ziarah* (i.e. visit)[8] such graves, as I have shown elsewhere (Thimm 2017).

However, I include the concept and practice of *ziarah* in this research on Muslim pilgrimage as it fulfils certain criteria my respondents apply to (their understanding of) pilgrimage. According to the Malay Malaysians in this study, these are: (1) dependence on place (it must be performed in Mecca) (see Luz 2020); (2) being bound to the spiritual moment; and (3) getting a sense for the *ummah* and for the Islamic past. Adopting these three emic criteria to more general practices of religious visits, *ziarah* can be included in an analytical understanding of Muslim pilgrimage alongside *hajj* and *umrah*. According to the three emic aspects of pilgrimage and embracing the scholarship on *ziarah* in other Muslim contexts, therefore, my etic viewpoint defines Muslim pilgrimage as reliant on the following: (1) particular places (Mecca, Medina) – but tombs/shrines of prophets or Islamic scholars or saints also count; (2) spiritual embeddedness by transforming one's inner disposition towards God – or connecting oneself and/or a dead person to God and to the afterlife (*akhirat*); and (3) a connection to the Islamic past in general, which can be achieved by commemorating particular places or figures – for example by visiting the tombs of Muslims who shaped Islamic interpretation and practice in the past and who pilgrims thus feel attached to.

Bringing Islam, gender and consumption to the fore

Based in feminist gender and intersectionality studies, this ethnography investigates the mutually influencing gendered, spiritual and religious identifications and differentiations that Malay Malaysian social actors negotiate in the framework of social, political, economic and religious dynamics. Malaysia is a multicultural society where 69.3 per cent of its citizens are classified as *Bumiputera* (Malays and native people, such as *Orang Asli* or *Kadazandusun*), 22.8 per cent of Chinese ancestry and 6.9 per cent of Indian ancestry (Department of Statistics, Malaysia 2019). According to the Malaysian Constitution, affirmative action is given in favour of Malays (article 153 [1]), but with certain limitations. Furthermore, the Constitution stipulates Sunni Islam with the Shafi'i school (*mazhab*) of jurisprudence (*fiqh*) as the religion of the state and as the compulsory religion for all Malays (article 3 [1]; article 160). So we see that Islam was established with special protection as the religion for the majority society, and this has been retained by the government today. Politicised Islam in Malaysia in particular and the socio-historical and political context in general are informed by global capitalist economies and its linkages to the *halal* industry.

The entanglements between gender, Islam and consumption are examined in this book by focusing on the perspectives of social actors. Malay Malaysian pilgrims consume religious connoted travel packages, and women in particular shop for (partly) spiritual, gender-specific souvenirs on the trip. Consumption on the religious journey becomes highly gendered. The social actors draw on the commercialisation of spirituality, driven by local and global tourism and fashion industries specialising in *Muslim(ah)*[8]-related products (see figure 1.2). These connections motivated my choice of Dubai as part of the pilgrimage study: the *ziarah* stopover in Dubai represents a grey area. On the one hand, Malaysian pilgrims consider Dubai to be an Arab and Islamic place; on the other, they see it as a modern shopping paradise. The entanglement between concepts of tourism and pilgrimage can only be observed when it comes to integrating Dubai into pilgrimage – in contrast, a *ziarah* stopover in Istanbul or Jerusalem is considered to be 'pure *ziarah*', as totally related to Islamic history, and a transit in London or Switzerland as 'holiday only'. Given the gendered character of the '*umrah* & *ziarah* Dubai' journey and its spiritual and consumerist dimensions, this form of travel naturally suggested itself as the object of investigation, even though it is not quantitatively dominant in the Malaysian context.

Figure 1.2   Studio in Dubai, where *abayas* are designed and sewn, United Arab Emirates, 2018.

Three central questions guided this research: (1) How far do Muslim forms of travel have an impact on gendered identifications and practices, and vice versa? (2) How do the consumption and distribution of objects and goods relate to religious concepts and practices and how is this relationship, in turn, connected to the category and practices of gender? (3) What meanings do female and male Muslim actors assign to the consumer goods they acquire in Dubai, Mecca and Medina and how is this meaning related to gendered and religious normative orders, discourses and social practices in Malaysia and its transregional connectivities to the Arabian Peninsula?

Consumption forms the context of this study, since it refers to broader processes of Islamisation and modernisation in Malaysia – and beyond – in which visibility is practised differently according to gender. As women are the driving force when it comes to visibly expressed transformations of gender roles, femininity and spirituality, females are thus the focus of this study. I want to clarify that in this study I am dealing with heterosexual relationships between women and men, and thereby exclude other gendered identifications (such as LGBTQI+). This is on the grounds that my respondents framed their life-images based on heteronormative conditions. The gendered notion of this study, therefore, is investigated in the sense of negotiating belonging, identification and relationships between women and men based on their respective identifications as women or men within the socio-political, cultural, economic and historical conditions in which they live. Giving priority to the emic perspective does not mean that I follow it analytically, i.e. I do not understand gender in an essentialised way of gender binarity and as exclusive relations between women and men, as the majority of my interlocutors do.

Gender and religion: mutually constitutive identifications

This study follows an approach which understands gender and Islam as identifications and cultural practices that are mutually constitutive. Whilst academic research to date has broadly dealt with either reciprocally constitutive identifications, such as gender, race, class and sexuality, or gendered perspectives of Muslim women, a systematic examination of *gender-faith intersections* is still needed. This is especially important when considering research on Muslim pilgrimage. This study will therefore contribute to three research areas. First, to anthropology, by bringing gender and faith understood as *mutually constitutive intersections from a power-critical standpoint* into anthropology. Second, to scholarship, dealing with intersectionality – which lacks investigations into relations between gender and the *Muslim religion*. Third, to research on Muslim pilgrimage, which has been neglecting gender, not to mention gender in its interrelationship with other identifications.

'Identifications' are personal and collective senses of belonging which are culturally constituted and embedded in socio-political and historical conditions; they are not something that is naturally given (Brubaker and Cooper 2000). I understand identifications (for example gendered, religious, ethnic, national, sexual, classed) as *categories of difference*, as part of human classification systems, as *social processes* which emphasise a subject's agency and various contextual dependencies, and as *structures*, in the sense of power structures, which whilst not static are still difficult to overcome. This means understanding gender and religion as systems within cultural settings which can relate to identity, social relationships, social practices and/or power (see Höpflinger *et al.* 2012).

In my theoretical understanding of gender, I follow a constructivist approach that acknowledges the lived and material body. Whereas some scholars regard constructivism and the material body as a contradiction (for example Butler 1993, 1990; Duden 2002, 1993, 1991; Landweer 1994; Lindemann 1993), this study brings the two approaches together (see Qvotrup Jensen and Elg 2010) and thereby follows the *affective turn*. According to Butler, the body is a 'surface of matter' (Butler 1993: 9) which is imposed by gender. She draws on Michel Foucault's concept of social subjects which are constantly exposed to (self-)disciplinary acts through discursively produced knowledge (see Foucault 2009a [1978], 2009b [1979], 2008, 1994, 1977). Foucault focuses on connections between body and knowledge by investigating technologies of power, control, registration and suppression of the body, especially in contexts of judicial punishment and medical inspection. He points out in his studies how bodies are made materially productive by powerful forces and that the body and sexuality are, by implication, formed by discourses rather than biology. This poststructuralist approach is directly related to structuralist approaches which pinpoint the human body as a site of materialisation of power. In this regard, Pierre Bourdieu (2010 [1979]), who owes much to structuralism, examines class-related self-formation in, on and through the body with his concept of the habitus. Bodies are structured and constituted through disciplining acts of power which are incorporated by constant bodily practices. These incorporated structures of power must, at the same time, be applied by the social subjects again and again. By drawing particularly on Foucault's research, Butler argues that processes of embodiment of gender refer to the fact that negotiations of gendered identities are normalising and (self-)disciplining acts. She states that gendered and sexual identifications are continuously discursively (re-)produced and controlled within a patrilinear heteronormative system. Hence, Butler does not investigate the category of gender but the process of categorisation itself.

While Butler explores the conditions of materialising the body, she does not explain how the constituted materiality is realised for the subject – that is, how the subject feels, senses and experiences their own body. This phenomenological void has crucial ramifications for my analytical approaches to gender. Butler's radical constructivism has been criticised, especially in German feminist thought, by bringing in the distinction between the discursively constituted body and the lived, experienced body. This is expressed with *Körper* and *Leib* respectively and refers to the condition that humans *are* a *Leib* (an experienced body with uncontrollable conditions) and *have* a *Körper* (a socio-culturally constructed body which one can access as an object).

Scholars such as Birgit Schaufler (2002), Barbara Duden (2002, 1993, 1991) and Gesa Lindemann (1993) emphasise direct, lived bodily experiences by focusing on processes and conditions – contrary to Butler – *under* the surface. Moreover, this feminist strand of research investigates rituals, gestures, gazes and words as bodily acts which are directly connected to processes of subjectification.

The practice of merging the socio-culturally constructed and the experiencing body stems from the fact that social constructivism cannot adequately explain the stability of the reproduction of gender identification and difference. It lacks explanations of the bodily-affective attachment of individuals to their gender (see Lindemann 1993). Thus, people not only perform gender but furthermore feel their gender. For example, certain body parts such as breasts or vagina structure how the body is experienced in terms of gender, as these parts are experienced as gender-relevant. The socially constructed dichotomy of gender is thus incorporated (*einverleibt*) and internalised, so that people *are* a gender, namely the gender that the body (*Körper*) signifies.

Alongside gender, religion is the other main category and practice that I focus on in this research. However, I draw more on religious faith and spirituality as theoretical concepts than on religion (see Francis 2016; Schielke 2010; van Liere 2017). 'Religion' in its common present yet narrow sense has been developed as a concept in Europe characterised by Christianity, in the context of a differentiation between religious and secular realms of life. During the Enlightenment, religion as a metaphysical sphere was separated from rational thought (Rehbein and Sprenger 2016; Tayob 2018). Based on this socio-cultural and historical development, 'religion' refers in the common – particularly – Western notion, particularly in Abrahamic traditions, to a relationship between a human and (a) divine being(s). On the level of social processes, this understanding is related in particular to institutions and institutional power. Within this context, religion evolves as an analytical category – it is understood as 'something' that can be systematised as a social realm with (clear) boundaries. In Western ways of thinking, this marks a condition for the secular–religious divide (van Liere 2017: 289).

This 'something' alone raises the question for academics (and the general public alike) of how to define or grasp it. From an anthropological perspective, by contrast, the more important question is how people act within these systems of power, how they interpret corresponding books and goods, and how they worship and submit to their God(s). In relation specifically to Islam, one of the most influential works which tries not to regard Islam as a 'thing' but as a negotiable contextualised set of meaning-making is Talal Asad's (1986) notion of Islam as a 'discursive tradition'. This has been the guiding principle in the anthropology of Islam for the last 30+ years. Asad approaches Islam as 'simply a tradition of Muslim discourse that addresses itself to conceptions of the Islamic past and future, with reference to a particular Islamic practice in the present' (Asad 1986: 14). This tradition of discourse is based on the *Qur'an* (the holy book of Islam) and the *Hadith* (the record of the sayings and deeds of the Prophet Mohamad), which is constantly debated by Islamic authorities in terms of the correctness of Islamic principles and practices.

Samuli Schielke (2010) notes that Asad still tries to *define* Islam and thereby walks away from his own goal of embedding his theoretical approach into social life. What other people consider to be Islam, he points out, depends on the question *they* ask (Schielke 2010: 2). He anticipates that Islam is part of people's lives and societies and, therefore, can have several meanings depending on the context: it can be 'a moral idiom, a practice of self-care, a discursive tradition, an aesthetic sensibility, a political ideology, a mystical quest, a source of hope, a cause of anxiety, an identity, an enemy' (Schielke 2010: 2). The problem with attaching these various meanings to Islam is, according to Schielke, that it leads to too many attempts to define Islam – 'there is too much Islam in the anthropology of Islam' (Schielke 2010: 2), which does not contribute to an understanding of concrete social actors.

From Muslim perspectives, notions of religion can be better grasped through the concept of *din* rather than through religion. *Din* includes the obligations Allah imposes on humans. *Din* is the mutual obligation between Allah and Allah's followers, who submit to Allah's authority (Sandıkcı and Jafari, A. 2013: 412). This concept includes the way of living, the mental, spiritual and intellectual attitude, and the behaviour and practices an individual or society follows. It comprises the whole of human life in its fullness but still holds a normative notion, rather than being an encompassing, vague approach. The concrete appropriation of this concept is Islam: it literally means 'submission', i.e. the submission of a person to Allah. Hence, Islam is *din* and *din* is Islam.

I prefer to use mainly religious faith and spirituality as the focal points of reference for studying the life-worlds of concrete social actors. Muslim Malaysians go on pilgrimage not only for religious purposes but also for spiritual and material reasons based on their faith. This indicates that religion, faith and spirituality denote three different conditions (see e.g. Bräunlein 2016; Chandler 2013; Kenneson 2015; Mercandante 2014; Monroe 2015; Radmacher 2015). Religion is a theological or institutional expression of certain imaginings and guiding principles, obligations or ideologies; it is a specific interpretation of social reality; and, hence, it is a socio-cultural approach to the world (Sandıkcı and Jafari, A. 2013, Schielke 2010).

Faith is a state of mind or worldview incorporating transcendent or unseen elements. Faith is what makes people turn a condition (exposing or covering skin and hair), a relationship (dressing while abiding by Islamic rules) or a material thing (veil) (see Meyer, B. and Houtman 2012) into something spiritual. Hence, spirituality indicates in certain religions, such as Islam, the inner disposition of a person. Faith and spirituality are bound to people – how they interpret and live their belief, and the meaning they attach to values. The spiritual is, therefore, non-negotiable for the individual, in contrast to things and conditions which can be steadily negotiated in daily life. However, the spiritual is a dynamic process for the individual which is subject to fluctuation on the way to enlightenment.

Holism and intersectionality

This study aims to analyse the complexity of my respondents' identifications and the interwoven social circumstances in which they operate. To make this task feasible, I focus on the intersection of two identifications – gender and religious faith/spirituality – but embed these in the myriad interwoven conditions, especially relating to ethnicity and class, that I explore in my analysis. In this sense, gender and religious faith form the stem of this research, but at certain points one or more branches emerge, develop and branch out further. While scholarship often focuses on 'identities' individually, as in the literature discussed above, identities are not lived, experienced and embodied individually. Rather, they are interwoven, as theorised by the *intersectionality* framework.

However, this understanding is not a standalone feature of the intersectionality approach. The understanding of identifications, belonging, difference and unity as entangled or even mutually constitutive is a longstanding characteristic of anthropological thought. Holistic anthropological approaches understand particular phenomena, such as identifications, in wider environments and (try to) make sense of concrete observations and encounters by putting them into larger cultural, social, political, economic and historical contexts. These contexts are, in turn, grounded in empirical ethnographic data (Bubandt and Otto 2010: 1). Both anthropology and intersectionality are encompassing frameworks that share epistemic objectives as they pinpoint the production and products of identification and power hierarchies that are part of individual lives, social practices, institutional structures and socio-cultural and political ideologies. Nonetheless, there are important differences in the characteristics of holistic and intersectional approaches, which enrich one another through engagement. As an anthropologist investigating gendered and religious conditions with a theoretical gender optic, I try to see, recognise and capture certain connectivities on the basis of a specific holistic anthropological angle. I then theorise these conditions through a certain lens – the intersectionality lens – in order to understand them. In the sections that follow, I will first discuss my understanding of holistic anthropology, then set out my theoretical intersectional approach, eventually leading to an integration of the two.

Methodological holism

The manifold relationships between various particularities and conditions in 'real life' are the objects (and subjects) of broad (mereological) debates about holism, wholes and parts in anthropology. Kapferer (2010: 187) suggests three forms of holism in anthropology: first, the discipline as such that aims to embrace all human knowledge that is somehow all connected; second, the investigation of cultures, societies and communities in the sense of wholes in which social practices are mutually dependent; and third, a form of inquiry that aims to capture assemblages and structures (see Friedman 2010: 227). Thus, on the one hand, holism is a requirement in the sense of 'a heuristic concept' (Bubandt and Otto 2010: 2) or a 'regulative ideal' (Marcus 2010: 28) that guides ethnographic modes of enquiry (Longman 2002; Thornton 1988: 291). On the other, holism is an object of study. My anthropological understanding concerning holism relates to methodological holism, which is used to investigate mutually dependent social practices that are intermingled with assemblages and structures. Thus, my form of understanding transcends the three classifications given by Kapferer.

Methodological holism interconnects subjectivity, social structures, history and social and ecological environment (see Thornton 1988: 285) with one another and thereby aims at a 'complexification of the ethnographic subject' (Marcus 1989: 8). This understanding suggests that society, individuals and the environment interpenetrate and even define one another. It stipulates that one cannot simply assign observed phenomena to a certain functional field of society, nor can one limit its explanations to that field. One response is not transparent in one single explanation, practice or attitude as a social practice invokes *various* social structures. For example, shopping for an *abaya* cannot be reduced to the field of economy. Rather, this social practice touches on economic, social, religious, gendered and classed dynamics. The single phenomenon unfolds to reveal manifold dimensions that we as social and cultural anthropologists are interested in and try to make sense of.

However, capturing the complexity of phenomena is not easy to achieve, and critiques of this encompassing claim have been ongoing since the so-called 'crisis of representation' in anthropology (Marcus and Fischer, M. 1986; see Behar and Gordon 1995 for a feminist discussion of this 'crisis'). Descriptions of one or more phenomena necessarily remain particularistic (see Holbraad 2010). As a consequence, gaps and omissions will always be part of ethnography (Marcus 1989: 10). Ethnographic studies are in fact made of unconnected parts, which turn into a holistic picture through connectivities, as Tsing (2005: 272) understands it: '[F]ragments of varied schemes and travels and encounters do create a world of global connections.'

The characteristics of the gaps, omissions, fragments and connectivities are influenced by the positionality of the researcher and by their bias. No matter how holistic the anthropological inquiry is, something will be silenced and something will be emphasised based, for example, on the researcher's experiences or schools of thought. Therefore, all research is not only inherently political (Ahmad 2018) but also partial. Given this dilemma, we need to bring some order to the manifold social phenomena and their connected structures and assemblages. In order to be able to undertake an analysis, and especially a holistic analysis, it is necessary 'to proceed from anything other than some kind of reduction of the world' (Holbraad 2010: 68). In this instance, it seems legitimate to focus on certain social phenomena and their intermingled structures in the course of data analysis and writing (Boellstorf 2007: 26; Descola 2010: 211). I focus on gender–faith intersections in the Malaysian context, guided by both a holistic and an intersectional enquiry.

I bring methodological holism into a fruitful engagement with intersectionality for two reasons. The first is grounded in empiricism: my open-minded experiences in the field directed me to Muslim women's perspectives and gender as a category and practice. '*Umrah* & *ziarah* Dubai' was sought after mainly by *Muslim* Malay Malaysian *women* for the purpose of, amongst other things, constituting their modern Muslim selves. Bringing gender and faith to the heart of this study therefore suggested itself, so to speak. Then, it is a matter of deciding which social group to start the research with and working out how these groups interact, with whom and why, and how the individual acts within these groups. In this case, Muslim women were the social group chosen as the starting point.

The second reason for drawing on intersectionality as part of a holistic anthropological inquiry is based on positionality. In fact, gender–faith intersections can only be investigated using a holistic view. This does not require further explanation, as every (mutual) connection can and should be researched through a holistic optic. However, to leave it at that would mean that the positionality and bias that are always inherent in research would remain vague. Gender, religion, gendered religion and religionised gender are inherently political and powerful categories and practices. Gendered and religionised relationships define who belongs or does not belong to a social group and therefore who is (to be) included in and who is (to be) excluded from the group. This inherence of power when dealing with gender and religion and its intersections demands a political framework which incorporates power for analysis (Longman 2002: 243).

This is what the intersectionality framework characterises, amongst other things.

Intersectionality: what's in a name?

Intersectionality examines how categories of difference, such as gender, religion, race, ethnicity, sexuality, culture, nationality, class, education, and other axes of identification and differentiation, not only intersect but also are jointly constitutive and, hence, inform and transform one another (see for example Brah and Phoenix 2004; Crenshaw 1989; hooks 2000, 1981; Phoenix and Pattynama 2006; Shields 2008). Axes of identification and differentiation are culture-specific forms of self-perception and imply a certain understanding and practice of functional differentiation. Such axes certainly always intersect and are mutually constitutive. Thus, this form of thinking is not new for social and cultural anthropologists. In fact, 'in the intersectional approach there is a longing for a holism able to account for all that contributes to the subject' (Graham 2014: 104). Despite remarkable similarities between methodological holism and intersectionality, the gene-alogy of intersectionality makes significant differences clear and reveals the additional benefit of its usage in the discipline of anthropology.

Intersectionality, based in Black feminist struggles in the US and 'Third Wave Feminism', has become one of the main theoretical approaches or 'analytic sensibilit[ies]' (Weber 2015: 26) in feminist theory and gender studies. Grounded in these foundations, intersectionality has two interwoven directions: one is related to identifications; the other focuses on power and (institutional) discrimination. The term 'intersectionality' was coined in 1989 by Kimberlé Crenshaw, a Black US lawyer and social activist, when revealing in a trial a specific form of oppression of Black women working for General Motors. Crenshaw was representing Emma DeGraffenreid, a Black woman who had sued General Motors in 1976 because the company had not hired her. The judge did not see a problem for the plaintiff as he saw that there were both Black people and women working for General Motors. Yet he had not recognised that all the Black people were working on the assembly line and that these People of Colour were men. All the women hired by the company were working as typists and secretaries, and these women were White women. He did not realise that there were therefore no job opportunities for Black women.

Given this situation, Crenshaw argued at trial that Emma DeGraffenreid was discriminated against not as a woman or as a Black person of colour at the company, but precisely as a *Black woman*. Until then, US law had addressed only issues relating to gender *or* race, not both simultaneously. In her argument, Crenshaw used the metaphor of a crossroads: one road represents women, the other Black Americans, and the two roads cross at a certain point. This illustrated the social reality of Black women: they do not suffer as women in a patriarchal society and being Black in a racist environment separately, rather they struggle as Black women – which differs from what their male Black fellows experience and their female White companions encounter.

However, a problem arises when thinking about the metaphor of intersectionality that Crenshaw suggests, especially from a holistic viewpoint. Crenshaw invented the (traffic) intersection as an image for intersectionality. In this sense, the axes of identification and differentiation are depicted as lines or arrows. The intersection of the two forms of identification appears as a mere point of contact on straight lines. Once they cross, the intersection evolves, meaning that the axes cannot be studied separately. As the interactions between the different identifications appear only as intersections, critique by intersectionality scholars evolved based on this visualisation (Bereswill and Neuber 2011; Ken 2008; Lutz *et al.* 2011; Puar 2007). To formulate a critique is especially self-evident when having a holistic background as the intersections, i.e. these points, do not exist in real life. Such a metaphor is too simple to illustrate the complexity of the relationships and interactions between the identifications and power structures.

So, will we do more good than harm if we look for a different metaphor? Assemblage, dimension, salt and pepper, configuration, field, web or net might be alternatives. Yet in the end what counts is not the metaphor but the understanding that categories and practices of identification and the hierarchies they (re-)produce are more connected than separate from one another and to document this in empirical grounding (Thimm 2022). This is an approach distinct to intersectionality. 'Assemblage', for instance, as it is conceptualised by Stephen Collier and Aihwa Ong (2005), likewise denotes heterogeneous, unstable and stable discursive, material and collective elements of power that are interconnected in a global world. Ong (2005) examines their developed concept in an analysis of technologies, modernity, capitalism, science and citizenship in Malaysia and Singapore. What her concept lacks, however, is the dimension of identities – collective, but more so the individual identification of people according to their socio-structural position. Their main level of analysis is national, economic, institutional and global.

The empirical basis for the intersectionality approach had in fact already been formed before Crenshaw wrote her canonical piece: Audre Lorde (1984) drew attention to the interdependency of gender and race in her pioneering work *Sister Outsider*. Avtar Brah and Ann Phoenix (2004) describe how during the era of slavery in the US, Sojourner Truth (1798–1883), an enslaved African woman, raised her voice from her specific perspective which stood in contrast to the life-worlds of her and other females' slave owners on the one hand and male Black slaves on the other. Brah and Phoenix (2004) discuss Truth's view as an intersectional condition. Similarly, Patricia Hill Collins (2008) deals with a speech delivered in 1833 by Maria Stewart (1803–79), a Black enslaved woman who revealed how Black women's impoverishment was dependent on White male practices in their position as slave owners.

With these different narratives and writings since the mid-1980s, the narrative of a 'global sisterhood' has been thwarted and the category of gender unmasked as per se anti-essentialist. Consequently, Women of Colour in the US formulated the critique that White feminists in the US speak on behalf of various groups of women, generalising the conditions and experiences of women all over the world. Due to specific subject positions, Women of Colour have argued, these feminists are only able to raise their voices on behalf of women who share the same or similar intersectionally entangled belongings; they should therefore stop speaking for Black women. Intersectionality thus 'decentr[es] . . . the "normative subject" of feminism' (Brah and Phoenix 2004: 78). Given this, intersectionality has the inherent potential to deconstruct normalising and homogenising categories (Knudsen 2006; Staunæs 2003).

Given the experiences of Truth, Stewart, Lorde, DeGraffenreid, Crenshaw and many other Black women in the US, we see that intersectionality is a tool or a framework – not a theory as it is often misunderstood – for investigating how gender is racialised, how class is gendered, how religion is ethnicised, how gender is sexualised – and, furthermore, how race is classed and sexualised, how religion is ethnicised and classed, etc. Thus, this framework allows me to analyse how a Malay Muslim heterosexual middle-class woman is positioned at an intersection of ethnicity, religion/ faith, sexuality, class and gender and how she navigates the various social dynamics and hierarchies, experiencing one or more of her identifications in different ways according to the temporal and spatial context. Religion and/or gender could be the only lenses applied to analyses of social dynamics, but intersectionality shows that social complexity becomes more palpable when these lenses engage with other axes of identification and differentiation as well, and how this is related to power.

The multiplicity of power structures is understood as following different organising rationales. As touched on above, gender and religion or faith function differently. In a similar vein, Nira Yuval-Davis illustrates vividly that race cannot be treated equally with class and class cannot be equal to gender, as all categories of difference have very specific preconditions and outcomes:

> [C]lass divisions are grounded in relation to the economic processes of production and consumption; gender should be understood not as a 'real' social difference between men and women, but as a mode of discourse that relates to groups of subjects whose social roles are defined by their sexual/biological difference while sexuality is yet another related discourse, relating to constructions of the body, sexual pleasure and sexual intercourse. Ethnic and racial divisions relate to discourses of collectivities constructed around exclusionary/inclusionary boundaries . . . that can be constructed as permeable and mutable to different extents and that divide people into 'us' and 'them' . . . 'Ability' or, rather, 'disability' involves even vaguer and more heterogeneous discourses than those relating to ethnicity, as people can be 'disabled' in so many different ways. However, they involve discourses of 'normality' from which all disabled people are excluded. Age represents the dimension of time and the life cycle. (Yuval-Davis 2006: 201)

While intersectionality has inherently engaged with analysing and opposing power structures since its inception, this political dimension has been blurred in some academic contexts in the course of its popularisation through time, spaces and places. On the one hand, it is regarded as 'political intersectionality', i.e. a tool to bring about social change. This strand has been followed up und transformed by decolonial feminists in Latin

America, for instance. Ochy Curiel Pichardo (2014), a feminist academic and social anthropologist from the Dominican Republic, distances herself in her feminist approach from 'Western feminists' by bringing *raza* ('race') to the fore: on the basis of the colonial experience, their *raza* is the precondition for their gendered, classed identification. Yet Argentinian feminist philosopher María Lugones (2010) focuses on gender as a central category of colonialism in Latin America, arguing that the Spanish introduced the heteronormative distinction between man and woman to their region (see D'Arcangelis 2020). Together with other protagonists from Middle and South America such as Sueli Carneiro (2018), Julieta Paredes (2014), Rita Segato (2015), Yuderkys Espiñosa Miñoso (2014) and many more, their *Feminismo decolonial* criticises worldwide knowledge production in order to decolonise hegemonic feminism and to bring *raza* and gender to the heart of postcolonial thought and social practice.

On the other hand, intersectionality serves, in the form of 'structural intersectionality', as academic or intellectual engagement with identifications and its relationships with inequalities. Given this strand, intersectionality has been first and foremost 'deracialised', meaning that its focus has shifted away from race and racism (Bilge 2014). The first generation of Black feminists, such as Audre Lorde, Kimberlé Crenshaw, Patricia Hill Collins, Trinh Minh-ha, bell hooks and many others, who developed, appropriated and advocated for intersectionality, have emphasised that *race* is – at least since its inception as a category in human existence, as I would argue – centrally woven through institutions, structures and power relations. However, many scholars nowadays focus only on 'identities' rather than additionally considering structural power (especially regarding race) when discussing intersectionality. This is especially true for the regional context of Europe, where this 'whitening [of] intersectionality' (Bilge 2014) has developed through an emphasis on gender only or on class, amongst other things (see e.g. Erel *et al.* 2007: 240; Möser 2013: 53; Knapp 2005; Lewis 2013; Puar 2011, 2007; Weber 2015 for discussion). These invocations have been critiqued as problematic and opposing the intellectual and political labour of Black women. Acknowledging the character of those feminists' original ideas, their hard work and constant struggles, I want to clarify here that this study indeed focuses on gender and religion (and thereby not race). However, religion is inextricably intertwined with ethnicity in Malaysia: all Malays are to be Muslims – but not all Muslims must be Malays. Hence, ethnicity runs parallel to religion with all its powerful inclusions and exclusions that Muslim and non-Muslim Malaysians face.

Intersectionality has not only been 'deracialised' but also 'degender-ised', shifting the focus away from gender. Like its loss of political aware-ness by de-emphasising power structures, especially when it comes to race, the category and practice of gender has been blurred. Against this backdrop, intersectionality should not be mistaken for the latest devel-opment in gender research: diversity, regarded as a positive approach to social inclusion (Bilge 2013). The diversity approach is part of neo-liberal logic, because it refers positively to assumed uncountable possibil-ities that exist and that every individual can achieve so long as they exert themselves sufficiently. In this sense, everyone is assumed to be individu-ally responsible for their life path rather than being embedded in struc-tural power hierarchies. Hence, representatives of the diversity approach anticipate 'numerous possibilities' that women, People of Colour, disa-bled persons and so on would have instead of focusing on oppression, power and domination (Bilge 2014). In this respect, those advocating for diversity as a concept and practice do not necessarily feel discriminated against in their role and position as woman, lesbian, working-class etc but feel that they have equal rights (with men, heterosexuals, middle-class people etc). As a consequence of 'intersectionality as traveling theory' (Salem 2018) – in the sense of travelling into the mainstream – 'intersectionality [has developed from] a moment of resistance to . . . a neoliberal approach that erases inequality' (Salem 2018: 404).

Despite – or perhaps precisely because of – this problematic shift of intersectionality, I stick to this theoretical concept as an approach to study categories and practices of identification and its relatedness to power and hierarchies. Having grasped this, it has such a fruitful outcome that 'it is unimaginable that a women's studies programme would only focus on gender . . . [I]n gender studies, any scholar who neglects differences runs the risk of having her work viewed as theoretically misguided, politically irrelevant, or simply fantastical' (Davis 2008: 68). Following these, albeit harsh, words by Kathy Davis, focusing on only one category of difference with its power structures would mean superficially erasing the complex-ity of people's lives, their identifications and the interwoven social condi-tions in which they interact.

Holistic intersectionality

From a gender perspective, it is necessary to cross disciplinary bounda-ries that run between anthropological holism and a more sociological intersectionality. Holism remains a fruitful and applicable approach to all stages of research, from epistemological inquiry to methodology and text production. Being highly critical and aware of hierarchies that structure gender and other axes of identification, as well as the research process, however, necessitates a valuable approach that deals responsibly with social categorisation, boundary-making, oppression, agency, resistance and self-reflection. This is important because anthropological thought is, like every kind of thought, subject to historical and political conditions that affect every form of knowledge production. Social and cultural anthropologists were collaborators in colonialism, they work for national armies, they produce Marxist research, they are activists in feminist movements . . . This diversity exemplifies that anthropology, with its hallmark of holism, is always dependent upon and embedded in the socio-political context of the academy, and is subject to interpretation and to the socio-structural position of the researcher. From a feminist viewpoint, the researcher constantly needs to reflect upon her own positionality, as knowledge is situated (Haraway 1988). This self-reflexivity can and should be made fruitful for one's own research. For instance, we as researchers tell only one 'truth' – manifold truths and realities exist that all have their justification. This awareness and reflection process is provided by intersectionality per se. As Kathy Davis (2008: 72) points out, intersectionality 'can – by definition – be employed by any (feminist) scholar willing to use her own social location, whatever it may be, as an analytic resource rather than just an identity marker'.

Using an intersectionality approach enables the researcher not only to deal with mutually dependent categories, practices and their contexts, but furthermore to adopt and maintain a critical *focus* on power. This marks a difference from holism in anthropology. In a similar vein, Torjer Olsen (2018: 9) explains:

> The issues of holism raise the question of whether intersectionality, interconnectedness, holism and relationality are the same. The answer is probably that they can be, but not necessarily. There is a need to clarify what kind of relationality one is concerned with. The most relevant seems to be relationality wherein a power-related approach holds its ground . . .

A 'power-related approach' is necessary when studying the life-worlds of women in their relationships to men, as this is an inherently powerful and hierarchal relation in which status, social position and agency are constantly negotiated within socio-cultural and political environments.

However, we need to be aware of 'the risk of reducing people to oppressed subjects whose subjectivity is prefigured in the oppression that forms them at an intersection' (Graham 2014: 105). Deeply interwoven in the intersectional bias is a holistic view that functions as a corrective here. As the reader will see in this ethnography, women do not necessarily belong to marginalised and less privileged groups, as is often believed. Differences exist between the social groups of different genders and within the groups of one gender (here, women) concerning their social status, power, inferiority or superiority, and possibilities for action, amongst other things. These complicated conditions need to be examined on the basis of a curious, holistic and intersectional – that is, power-critical – approach.

Given the power-critical quality of intersectionality that focuses on marginalised groups and/or discrimination, its starting point lies on the margins rather than at the centre of society and culture (Degnen and Tyler 2017: 38; Olsen 2018). These margins become the centre of a reflection that can still be holistic. In comparison, using methodological holism as the starting point, with its principle of relating every category, practice, identification and condition with other categories, practices, identifications and conditions, would hardly have a centre – instead, everything could be identified as the centre of analysis.

As the holistic anthropological view is not concerned with power in local contexts in a similar focused way, it 'risks a depoliticized portrayal of people's lives' (Degnen and Tyler 2002: 42). While intersectionality offers a framework for thinking about the mutual constitution of gender, religion, ethnicity, race or class and its production of social inequalities, methodological holism emphasises interrelated belonging, identifications, place and time in the sense of what Jeanette Edwards and Marilyn Strathern (2000), Cathrine Degnen and Katherine Tyler (2017) and Mark Graham (2014: 92–106) frame as *intersections*. 'Intersection . . . evokes what is socially woven together in order to achieve belonging,' say Degnen and Tyler (2002: 39). Intersections define the connected and entangled conditions that we as social and cultural anthropologists are interested in:

[A]n anthropological approach to intersection is located within and emerges from analysis of cultural forms of knowledge, shared discourses and representations about the world. For an anthropology . . . exploring intersection, the theory has in effect come from the ethnography of local . . . people, places, relationships, sites and milieus. (Degnen and Tyler 2002: 41)

Intersectionality, in turn, is not grounded in ethnographic practice, i.e. in empirical, local research. It is a framework that originates in the socio-political situation of Black women, in the sense of their position as marginalised subjects and the oppression they face. The genealogy of intersectionality shows that it has transformed into a lens that pinpoints identification, difference, unity and inequality that can be applied to any local context and scale of analysis. Against this backdrop, intersectionality scholarship often lacks empirically grounded work, as Bilge (2013: 411) asserts.

The weaknesses of the two approaches (potentially) dissolve by merging the qualities of the two. As ethnographers with a methodological holistic view, we first figure out the various axes of identification and their intersections that operate in and are lived by our respondents in everyday life. As social and cultural anthropologists, we then analyse and discuss these intersections in their wider cultural, socio-political and economic contexts, and constantly integrate individual life-worlds and social structures with one another in order to generate understanding. As anthropologists following an intersectionality approach, we furthermore adopt a lens that helps place and embed these manifold and entangled intersections according to classifications of privilege and marginalisation. However, we still need to be careful that these analytical classifications are grounded in empiricism, which means that we are not interested in utilising our researcher's viewpoint of social status, power, privilege and marginalisation; rather we understand first how these are conceptualised, seen and lived in the social contexts we study. The way we analytically position social actors does not necessarily correlate with their own social positioning or their interpretation of it. In this sense, the intersectionality framework brings the (empirical) intersections analytically to a particular positioned stage of research.

In this regard, intersectionality makes sense of holistic intersections in a specific way that takes hierarchical relationships, and the negotiations and agency therein, into the central account. Reciprocally, intersectionality gains a special meaning via ethnographic data that derives from local forms of understanding that have the inherent potential to question, thwart and rethink Western ways of thinking and knowledge production. Privilege and power can attain new forms of conceptualisation that would not be achieved without an ethnographic, holistic style of research. In this way, holism and intersectionality complement one another and enter a reciprocal, fruitful engagement – an engagement that enables a capture in the sense of a *holistic intersectionality*: an anthropological consciousness that searches for social phenomena with its intersections, but then sharpens this holistic view by placing hierarchical orders, inclusion and exclusion at the centre. Reciprocally, this centre is constantly embedded in and connected to broader dimensions so that 'a view from below' ('micro') and 'a view from above' ('macro') dissolve into this holistic intersectionality approach. This means, then, that the idea of a holistic intersectionality does not follow an understanding of investigating phenomena in which gender and religion, for instance, are first reified and second intersect, but rather of investigating phenomena for which gender and religion are in fact insufficient and are therefore flawed terms, concepts and classifications.

Scaling holistic intersectionality

A holistic intersectionality refines both holistic anthropology and intersectionality regarding its *epistemological* dimensions. Admittedly, besides its epistemological weaknesses intersectionality furthermore faces a *methodological* problem that needs to be solved, as I and other scholars feel. As Vrushali Patil (2013) points out, intersectionally interwoven power systems function differently in diverse socio-cultural and political contexts and have heterogeneous meanings applied to them. However, studies using intersectionality usually (implicitly) limit their frame of reference to one nation-state but do not apply it across borders and boundaries – a scholarly practice that Patil (2013) terms 'domestic intersectionality', or, put more broadly by Wimmer and Glick Schiller (2002), 'methodological nationalism'. These more or less artificial analytical limitations, that are obvious from a holistic viewpoint, do not keep pace with developments in globalisation, transregionalism and transnationalism. Given this, colleagues and I have advocated elsewhere (Mahler *et al.* 2015; Thimm 2022, Thimm *et al.* 2017) for applying intersectionality across multiple socio-geographical scales (for example intimate, family, regional, national, transnational) simultaneously. We argue that 'intersectional analyses need to address more intentionally the multiple, related socio-geographic scales in which people live their lives' (Thimm *et al.* 2017: 3).

As the approach of a holistic intersectionality reminds us, shopping for/using an *abaya* cannot be reduced to the field of economy, let alone the economy of a single nation-state. The idea of socio-geographic scales, instead, leads me to an examination of how shopping for/using an *abaya* may be dependent upon transregional travel and on the subject's class position (*transregional geographic scales*), how far it may be embedded economically (*national* and *institutional scales*), how it touches issues of representation (*social scale*), in what ways it is a gendered process (*intimate* and *family scales*), and whether, and if so, how religiously driven it may be (*spiritual scale*).

Alongside being used as an epistemological tool to capture the different orientations of a single social phenomenon, scaling also allows us to differentiate status and power positions. A single individual's or a group's constellation of identifications varies regarding social status and power when analysed on the institutional scale, for instance, versus the family and/or national scale (see e.g. Chaudhuri 2014; Chaudhuri *et al.* 2014; Mahler *et al.* 2015; Thimm 2022, 2014b; Thimm *et al.* 2017). Thus, people and social groups negotiate multiple intersectional social locations simultaneously across different socio-geographic scales. Intersectional positionality then shifts according to the social scale(s) of analysis applied. Mahler *et al.* (2015) coined this approach '*Scaling Intersectionality*'.

Scaling is an analytical ordering, or 'a way of framing conceptions of reality' as David Delaney and Helga Leitner (1997: 94f) put it. By scaling social processes, I draw, for example, on the fruitful concepts of scales as part of scientific epistemology in geography, which deals with cartographic scales (the relationship between distance on a map and that distance in lived reality), geographic scales (the spatial scope of a study) and operational scales (the social situatedness of social dynamics, leading to levels of analysis) (see Marston 2000 for a discussion). Socio-geographic scales include the principle of a level (of analysis) and of a relationship. Both are effective at the same time. Thus, socio-geographic scales with these two facets can be conflated as *analytical levels of representation*. Following Neil Brenner (2004: 9), the relational character consists of an understanding that space, place and social relationships are part of vertical and horizontal relationships. The vertical hierarchy is connected to horizontal places, spaces and networks where social dynamics, relationships and interdependencies have manifold effects. Taking these scales and their connections into account allows us to produce what Anna Tsing (2005: ix, 1) calls 'an ethnography of global connection': an ethnographic study that is grounded in empiricism, based in a local field-site, but that considers the social, political, transregional and global connectivities, encounters and interactions that materialise on manifold social scales.

Acknowledging these global connections, with the differently positioned subjects and social groups therein, *Scaling Intersectionality* is an attempt to overcome the abovementioned 'domestic intersectionality' (Patil 2013) in particular or 'methodological nationalism' (Wimmer and

Glick Schiller 2002) in general. At this point, its applicability in (holistic) anthropology becomes significant: through the expansion of analysis that goes from a domestic viewpoint to transnational and transregional mobile processes, subjects' and social groups' shifts in standpoint can be recognised in a more all-inclusive manner (Mahler *et al.* 2015: 109). Social positions, identifications, and attributions to Self and Other are dependent upon the context that embraces not only local, regional and national environments but furthermore transnational and global ones. *Scaling Intersectionality* can make this condition more visible – whereby the model does not put people into place but enables an analytic illustration and explanation of it. In this way, *Scaling Intersectionality* also allows for a sensitisation of social dynamics in social and cultural anthropology, since it can contribute to preventing universalism.

I use the framework of *Scaling Intersectionality* (Mahler *et al.* 2015; Thimm 2022; Thimm *et al.* 2017) as a heuristic model for the purpose of investigating mutually constitutive categories, practices and structures of gender and faith/spirituality in Muslim pilgrimage from Malaysia via Dubai to Mecca and Medina from an anthropological perspective. Hence, I *scale* holistic intersectionality. Scaling a holistic intersectionality serves as a tool for organising research findings during analysis and, consequently, for organising the chapters of this book. Following the holistic goal of encompassing analysis, scaling is a strategy to overcome limitations on every level of analysis as far as possible, by integrating various scales into the research. My intellectual endeavour to work with scaling when analysing intersectionality began with my *Gendered Power Hierarchies in Space and Time* framework, which I designed in the course of my dissertation research (Thimm 2014a: 33–45, 2014b).[9] However, that framework was developed to study gender as a structuring and yet processual category in transnational migration and migrants' lives. Intersectionality, in turn, focuses on gender as engaged with additional axes of differentiation, mainly adapted to intranational systems of reference. *Scaling Intersectionality* enhanced intersectionality by deploying it for the transnational lives of migrants, thereby integrating a more holistic angle.

In this work, I conflate these three related determinations (gender, transnationalism, intersectionality) and develop them further on the temporal and transnational scales. I expand *intersectionality* – here in its enhanced form as a *holistic intersectionality* – but still with *gender* as one focal point, to *transnational* realities from migrants' experiences to *pilgrims' life-worlds*. Since pilgrimage from Malaysia via Dubai (UAE) to Mecca and Medina (Saudi Arabia) forms the object of investigation, this study is transnationally oriented. Transnational movement is characterised by mobility and sedentarism in two or more nation-states and includes mid- or long-term processes of adaptation and negotiation of socio-cultural standpoints and practices (for example Bonfanti 2016; Endres *et al.* 2016; Fábos and Isotalo 2014; Glick Schiller and Salazar 2013; Gutekunst *et al.* 2016; Hannam *et al.* 2006; Salazar 2016; Thimm 2018; Uteng and Cresswell 2008). At this point, the advancement of the previous three elements becomes operative. Pilgrimage, by contrast, is, in my research context, a practice of mobility that is of short duration: my respondents travel by plane to Saudi Arabia and/or Dubai and Abu Dhabi for a period of two to six weeks. What marks this short-term mobility in contrast to long-term migration is that the pilgrims primarily transform and negotiate gendered identifications *back home* in Malaysia *based on* their pilgrimage experiences. (Transnational) migrants, however, negotiate identifications and practices *in their host* and *in their home countries* – hence, in at least two places which are transnationally related to each other. The scaling of intersectionality, or in this case of the more sophisticated *holistic intersectionality*, however, works in the case of migration *and* pilgrimage, but the focus on the temporal and transnational scales varies.

Furthermore, as discussed above, intersectional analysis has been lacking religion, faith and the spiritual as focal points. Given my angle of gender–faith intersections from which I investigate socio-cultural processes in transnational space, I complement previous conceptualisations and applications of *Scaling Intersectionality* by adding a *Spiritual Scale* into the framework. This will come into play from chapter 5 onwards.

While the approach of scaling gendered and religionised phenomena permeates the whole book, the intersectional analysis of it, i.e. the examination of how and to what extent these phenomena influence each other so that something new is created, is undertaken specifically in chapters 4–6. The epistemological and methodological approach of scaling the analysis of a holistic intersectionality will serve productively for filling the lacunae on embodied gender-Muslim-faith intersections, on the one hand, and on gender in its relatedness to other axes of identification as organising principles of transnational Muslim pilgrimage, on the other.

Doing ethnography, doing it multi-sited

In my work, I aim for a *contextualised understanding* (see Meyer, S. and Sprenger 2011) of my Muslim respondents' (self-)positioning in relation to their gender and spiritual belief system, on the one hand, and to formal and institutionalised action systems, on the other. Drawing heavily on the work undertaken by the late Saba Mahmood (2005) and additionally inspired by Lila Abu-Lughod (1990), I emphasise the importance of foregrounding women's representations, identity formations and agency in Muslim contexts.

The most adequate way to accomplish this task is by doing ethnography, which is a unique 'way of seeing' (Wolcott 2008) or 'a way of knowing' (McGranahan 2018: 1). An ethnographic approach is oriented to the social (inter-)actions, stories and narratives of the subjects. They form the focus of the anthropological gaze. Furthermore, this approach requires a high degree of sincere openness on the part of the researcher towards the respondents and their stories and actions. This provides the basis for opening up the possibility for an understanding of other people's lives. According to Mahmood (2005: 36f): 'Critique . . . is most powerful when it leaves open the possibility that we might also be remade in the process of engaging another worldview, that we might come to learn things that we did not already know before we undertook this engagement.' Ethnography, therefore, is a reflective, curious and sincerely open way of seeing.

The high art of ethnographic research, however, goes even further: doing ethnographic research means exposing oneself to other, unfamiliar life-worlds. Based on curiosity and openness, time and again the ethnographer will be irritated by social conditions they cannot grasp, handle, classify or understand. In my opinion, to encounter or even provoke these situations of irritation needs time and requires that the researcher truly engages in and delves into the social conditions of the research site. Perplexing and puzzling situations provide the most fruitful moments of ethnography: if not ignored but reflected upon, they enable one to question one's own presuppositions. It is the point at which the ethnographer should stop for a moment, distance themself from the situation in the field, and reflect on why the corresponding situation feels strange and what this tells them about their own thought structures and positions. Consequently, the researcher is able to embed their own presuppositions and thought structures in the wider social context from which they come, and is thus able to unmask and dismantle social categories and structures (see e.g. Mahmood 2005; Mead 1935) – which are often regarded as naturally given, irrevocable or merely 'normal'.

To give one example, this was the case when I learned that 'liberation' is not a universal (leftist) category which can be equally applicable to any social condition in the world.[10] While in the West it means an act of freeing oneself from socio-political constraints and assumes an autonomous subject acquiring agency (notably, 'autonomy', 'subject' and 'agency' are all Western concepts and not easily applicable to other socio-cultural contexts), in my Muslim research contexts it means total submission to God (see chapter 5) – and this has bodily expression through the *niqab*, for example: the face veil. Here, the *niqab* means liberation and freedom.

Thus, what distinguishes ethnography or social and cultural anthropology from other disciplines is not the set of methodologies or the investigation of other cultures as such, but the capacity to reflect on social categorisations, relationships and power structures based on the experience of being puzzled and perplexed. If this is achieved, it becomes possible to question categories of gender and religion, for example, and, furthermore, to think about religion (especially Islam) and gender (especially women) together rather than as contradictory aspects.

The findings of this research are based on 14 months of ethnographic fieldwork in Malaysia (eight months), the UAE (five months) and Oman (one month). The research additionally draws on eight months of ethnographic fieldwork undertaken in Malaysia between 2009 and 2013 for my research on educational migration and gender in the regional context of Malaysia and Singapore (Thimm 2016a, 2016b, 2014a, 2014b, 2014c, 2014d; Thimm *et al.* 2017; Chaudhuri *et al.* 2019, 2014).

While female pilgrims lie at the heart of this research, many kinds of social actors will tell their stories in order to help us understand the complexity of identity formation, power hierarchies, transregional mobility and (partly spiritual) economies: males (for example husbands, fathers) on individual and family levels, and travel agencies, *abaya* designers and representatives of *halal* certification bodies on institutional levels. By presenting the entangled approaches of the different groups of social actors, I flesh out the various reconfigurations of spirituality, femininity/masculinity and commercialisation processes, embedded in mobility and notions of modernity. Moreover, profound social transformation processes currently occurring in and between the Arabian Peninsula (as a so-called 'Islamic centre') and Malaysia (as part of the 'Islamic periphery' but, simultaneously, a 'centre of Islamic modernity') will be showcased.

I want to briefly introduce the main characters of this study. My central respondents were the members of my 'Malay family': my 'sister' Masjaliza (36 years old), her husband Ramli (36), their two children (7-year-old boy Aaqil and baby daughter Norani, born in 2017), her parents (mother Kartini 65, father Fuaad 66) and sister Noorhaliza (38) with her husband Haytham. The younger generation live in the state of Selangor near KL; the parents live in a village (*kampung*) in Kelantan.

Other significant roles are played by Irsyad (39) and his wife Suriawati (37), together with their sons Hadees (11) and Haissam (6) who come from a small town in Perak. Irsyad's colleague Farrah (49) and her slightly older husband Ubaidah, from KL, will provide deep insights into their life-worlds too. Sixty-four-year-old Mawar and her family (her 30-year-old daughter Annisa and her husband Muzakir who is the same age; her son Raahim with his wife Nur Sofia, both 42, and their daughter Siti Sabrina, 15; and Mawar's eldest daughter Dewi, 38) likewise feature among my main respondents. This entire family lives in KL, all in nearby neighbourhoods. Female Sufi believer Rabwah (50) from KL and Latipa (52) from Selangor's capital Shah Alam complete the group of central respondents.

The subjects of this study thus come from all over mainland Malaysia (from villages, towns and cities) and they cover different generations (from small kids to wage workers and retired persons). What they have in common is their pilgrimage experience (mostly including a Dubai stopover), their socio-structural position as middle class and formally educated, and their strict or even orthodox following of their belief. Taken as a whole, my respondents depict the Islamicised, economised and feminised situation in Malaysia rather than representing dissenting voices or alternative narratives. This situation was not my intention but is an outcome of an open ethnographic mind that has studied pilgrims' life-worlds and has found deeply devoted subjects.

In total, 277 qualitative interviews, discussions and conversations of various forms and lengths with 217 people were conducted between 2013 and 2018. These interviews were primarily open and narrative, and all of them were transcribed. Some of these interviews were recorded, some were not. In the latter cases, I took verbatim notes of my respondents' statements. Additionally, personal notes were written in a field diary at the end of each day or whenever the situation permitted. Data sources also include photographs, brochures and leaflets recorded and collected during participant observation. The principle of the research design followed here was Grounded Theory – that is, that data collection and analysis typically occur interchangeably and inform each other throughout the course of the research. The interview transcriptions, field notes and all other data material have been analysed using coding methods in MAXQDA – software designed for qualitative data analysis such as Grounded Theory.

Once the pilgrims returned home from Dubai and I returned home from the field sites, contact was maintained and further informal conversations were conducted via email, Skype and messenger platforms.

I conducted the research part with the pilgrimage groups in the UAE and in the Malaysian *kampung* (rural areas) in *Bahasa Melayu*, and I spoke to most of my respondents in the Malaysian cities in a mixture of English and *Bahasa Melayu* (*Manglish*[11]), as is normal there. The English language is so prevalent in everyday urban life that some of my Malay respondents speak only English at home, regarding it as their mother tongue and raising their children accordingly. The specific linguistic and grammatical style of *Manglish* will be obvious in the interview transcripts used in this book, although they have been slightly smoothed for better readability.

Undertaking ethnographic fieldwork in Southeast Asia (Malaysia) and the Arabian Peninsula (UAE and Oman) means following a *multi-sited* approach to fieldwork, data collection and analysis (Coleman and von Hellermann 2011; Falzon 2009; Marcus 2011, 1995). This multi-sited approach, conceptually articulated by George Marcus, implies doing fieldwork in diverse but connected places and is based on the premise that local places are embedded in a global network of goods, knowledge, ideologies and social relationships. Ethnographic objects of study are, therefore, mobile and need to be situated in myriad ways (Marcus 1995: 102). Based on this understanding of manifold connections between the local and the global, ethnographic fieldwork is undertaken in multiple places. In this dynamic and multi-locational research process, the ethnographer's or anthropologist's challenge is to identify the various connections between global and local phenomena (Marcus 1995: 105).

The practical realisation implies, according to Marcus, *Follow the People; Follow the Thing; Follow the Metaphor; Follow the Plot, Story or Allegory; Follow the Life or Biography and Follow the Conflict* (1995: 106–10). Thus, the methodological imperative of 'being there' when doing fieldwork is broadened by pursuing, for example, travellers, material objects and non-material stories. For my research context, however, it made sense to adapt Marcus's suggestions of following to pursue different directions: whereas I indeed followed the people, I also followed the (his)story, the logics of touristic principles, the religious rituals, and the (statistical) material.

Following the people

Based on the multi-sited approach, two groups of Muslim pilgrims from Malaysia on *umrah* & *ziarah* were initially followed in Dubai during ethnographic fieldwork in April 2014 and, subsequently, back in Malaysia on fieldwork between May and October 2017. These two groups formed the two first points of departure and some of those pilgrims enabled me to approach other pilgrims in Malaysia via snowball sampling. Later, I accompanied eight more *umrah* & *ziarah* groups in Dubai and Abu Dhabi as a participant observer during five months of ethnographic fieldwork between December 2017 and April 2018. I followed the 10 groups over periods from half a day to four full days, which was the maximum length of their stopovers before travelling onwards to Jeddah or Medina. These 10 Malaysian groups comprised a total of 264 people, each group between 10 and 31 pilgrims, aged between 8 and around 70 years. Prior to joining these 10 groups, I sought permission to accompany them from the travel agencies in Malaysia and Dubai that organised their tours, and from the tour guides in Dubai and Abu Dhabi, and as soon as I met the groups, I asked the group members themselves whether I could join and interact with them. All of them agreed to do so.

I accompanied the Malaysian pilgrims in their touring coach to the sightseeing stops (see figure 1.3), talking to them while sitting in the bus, listening to the explanations given by the tour guide on the sightseeing tour, and observing the travellers' reactions and practices throughout. We ate our meals together and I slept in the same hotel when I followed the group from Dubai to Abu Dhabi. Along with the local tour guide and bus driver, I saw them off at Abu Dhabi airport, where they caught the flight to Medina. I tended to develop a closer relationship with around six to ten members of each group during each stopover, and I joined these people for their shopping tours or for lunch, for example. I usually felt part of the group after three days, which became evident when I addressed the *mutawif*,[12] the 'religious tour guide', who is part of the group from departure to the return to KL, as '*ustaz*' as everyone else did and not by his given name. '*Ustaz*' is the form of address for a religious teacher in Muslim Malaysia – which I used even though I am not myself Muslim.

I must admit that access to the field of *umrah* & *ziarah* travellers in Dubai and Abu Dhabi was quite difficult to achieve. It was a long slog before I succeeded: it took me the first six weeks of fieldwork in the UAE in 2017/18. Even though I had obtained permission from all the travel agencies in Malaysia that offer an *umrah* & *ziarah* Dubai package (in total not more than a handful) to follow their groups once I arrived in the UAE, it was not possible to find their local counterparts who oversaw the stopover in Dubai and Abu Dhabi – although I had received contact details from the Malaysian agencies beforehand. The fluctuation in cooperation between the two countries was too great. In order to find the correct Emirati travel agency amongst hundreds of them, like a needle in a haystack, so to speak, I spent hours and days waiting in vain at Dubai and Abu

Figure 1.3　The Malaysian *mutawif* (religious tour guide) in the touring coach taking a picture from *Burj al-Arab*, Dubai, United Arab Emirates, 2018.

Dhabi airports according to the flight schedules given by the Malaysian agencies, hoping to welcome a Malaysian pilgrimage group and to get to know the local tour operator. I also looked for information on so-called 'DIY (do it yourself) *umrah*' travellers from Malaysia at car rental stations, and tour operator and carrier desks at Dubai International Airport. While I did this, my Malaysian research assistant Masjaliza met the main

Malaysian *umrah* & *ziarah* package organiser again in KL on my behalf, to ask for the local Emirati counterpart. I mobilised every tourism-related contact I had. All of this was futile. Eventually, one random tour guide gave me a decisive pointer when I was waiting for yet another possible group at Dubai International Airport. After receiving official permission (again) from the general manager of Malaysia's main travel agency and from her Malaysian cooperation partner, as well as from their Emirati counterpart, I got the chance to dig into the field of *umrah* & *ziarah* travel groups in Dubai from January 2018 onwards.

By contrast, access to the field in Malaysia was easy, since I could follow up various known situations and existing social relationships. First of all, I accompanied the *umrah* & *ziarah* pilgrims mentioned above whom I first met in Dubai in 2014 again during fieldwork in Malaysia in 2017 on several occasions, investigating their (and others') pilgrimage experiences and personal transformation processes and their perspectives on the broader social, religious and economic dynamics going on in Malaysia. Moreover, I interviewed Muslim Malaysians who explicitly did *not* travel to Dubai for an *umrah* stopover as a contrast group. This data is supplemented by, amongst other things, interviews conducted in Malaysia with owners or managers of *abaya* shops, and with owners and employees of travel agencies who offer *umrah* & *ziarah* Dubai trips. I met some of my respondents in Malaysia only once. I have maintained a long-standing relationship with others, such as my close friend, 'sister' and research assistant Masjaliza and her husband Ramli, their two children and her parents and sister, whom I have known since 2009. In Malaysia, I lived with my respondents in their houses or apartments, we attended *Qur'an* classes together in the mosques, I fasted with them during Ramadhan, joined Sufi *zikir*[13] sessions, went shopping with them in several malls and morning markets (*pasar pagi*), and tried to visit (*ziarah*) *keramat* graves (tombs of Muslim scholars) with some of them (but failed for various context-bound reasons and, therefore, went without them).

I followed the people from Malaysia to their *ziarah* stopover in Dubai and Abu Dhabi, but I could not follow them further to *umrah* in Mecca and Medina. A study on pilgrimage should ideally include ethnographic fieldwork in the place(s) of pilgrimage. Hence, my research is somewhat incomplete, as it excludes the pilgrimage sites in today's Saudi Arabia. The reason for this is that I am not a Muslim, and non-Muslims have not been allowed to enter Mecca or Medina ever since the birth of Islam. I can enter Saudi Arabia on a business visa or, since April 2018, on a tourism visa,[14] and enter Mecca and Medina just on my own. There is no fence and no gate where religious identity is checked. So in practice, once the country has been entered, anyone can enter the two holy cities. I refuse to do that because it would mean cheating the worldwide Muslim community and especially my Muslim respondents and friends to whom I feel very committed. If I visit Mecca and/or Medina, I would have to pretend to be a Muslim and, thus, cheat those who believe in Islam. I would betray them either indirectly, by the simple act of entering the two cities, or directly, if I obtained an *umrah* or *hajj* visa by fraud – which people with non-Muslim names can only receive after handing in an official letter from a local mosque, confirming that the applicant is a member of the mosque community.

My decision not to enter Mecca and Medina and, therefore, not to extend the research sites accordingly was mainly an ethical question regarding the execution of fieldwork. However, a few of my respondents would not have had any problem in this regard. A 50-year-old *umrah* & *ziarah* Dubai traveller had not known about the ban on non-Muslims visiting Mecca and Medina until I told him about it. This regulation was absolutely incomprehensible to him because, he said, if I got the chance to visit, I would have learnt even more about Islam. He commented: 'If you wear the *hijab* [veil], nobody will know that you are not a Muslim, so why don't you just try?' Whereas I struggle with questions of ethical research, he struggles with, from his point of view, the Islamic approach that values Muslim integrity more than non-Muslims' learning processes.

Following the (his)story

The ethnographic fieldwork phases in Malaysia and the UAE were supplemented by four weeks of fieldwork in Oman, the UAE's neighbouring state. In that country – and extensively in the UAE as well – I followed one theme of my research in particular: *ziarah* in the sense of pilgrimage to the graves of saints and prophets and other historical Islamic sites. Since nation-state borders did not exist in the Islamic past until colonial control, I extended this part of research from the UAE to Oman for the following reason: one recurrent comment when sharing my interest in historical Islamic sites in the UAE with residents in that country was that I would find these places not in the UAE but in Oman instead.

As I am interested in the motivations and meaning-making processes of Malaysian pilgrims when it comes to *ziarah* stopovers on the way to Mecca and Medina, I visited, in addition to many corresponding places in the UAE, seven historical sites across Oman. These sites fulfil my respondents' criterion of being places to '*ziarah*' (i.e. religious visits, but not explicitly pilgrimage visits) but, notably, they are not part of any travel itinerary of the Malaysian travel agencies or Emirati agencies that serve Malaysian *umrah* & *ziarah* pilgrims. Tracing the history of the region, I visited the archaeological excavation site of Wubar, for example, which is believed by some to be the historical location of Iram, inhabited by the 'Ad, who were punished by Allah according to the *Qur'an* (e.g. 89 and 41: 15, 16)'. In the southern city of Salalah, I went to a site believed to be home to the historical footprints of the prophet Saleh's camel, also described in the *Qur'an* (e.g. 7: 73). I also visited several places across the country believed to hold the tombs of prophets (e.g. the prophet Umran in Muscat; the prophet Saleh near Hadbeen; and the prophets Hud and Ayub, both located near Salalah), relevant Islamic scholars, descendants of the Prophet Mohamad (for example the tomb of Bin Ali in Mirbat), and significant rulers of Islamic eras (for example the tomb of Bibi Maryam near Qalhat). By travelling all over the Arabian Peninsula, I developed a feeling for the Peninsula as a whole as the so-called 'Islamic centre', as various graves of prophets and stories mentioned in the *Qur'an* are spread all over the region and as the history of Islam, such as the *Ridda Wars* (wars of apostasy), is visible all over through excavation sites and ancient graveyards.

Following the logics of touristic principles and religious rituals

Malaysians choosing Dubai as a *ziarah* stopover seem to be a relatively small, connected and specific group of people. I realised this on various occasions during fieldwork in Dubai when following the groups. At the end of January 2018, I followed a group of 31 pilgrims throughout their stay in Dubai. At the first sightseeing stop at Dubai Marina, one of the pilgrims asked me whether I had been on TV recently. I said that I hadn't. He said my face looked so familiar to him. At the next stop, Atlantis Hotel on Palm Island, he came back happily and said that he had seen my face on Facebook in a picture taken at a resort run by *Orang Asli* near KL. I had indeed spent some nights there a couple of months previously. In early April 2018, I was sitting with 61-year-old Husna in the hotel lobby in Abu Dhabi, waiting for the tour bus that would take the pilgrim group to the Heritage Village. Her son took a photograph of the two of us, which she immediately sent to her family back home in Malaysia via WhatsApp. She also sent a picture of my business card, explaining to the WhatsApp group that a researcher from Germany was following the pilgrim group, as she was interested in *umrah*. Soon after, one of Husna's nieces replied, mentioning that my face looked familiar to her – and she then sent a picture of me with Suriawati, Irsyad and their two kids, one of the families I accompanied in 2014 on their *umrah* & *ziarah* Dubai trip and whom I met several times after that in Malaysia in 2017, in KL and in their hometown, a *kampung* in the state of Perak. Husna's niece is a friend and colleague of Suriawati. These incidents illustrate that I had become part of a network of Malaysian *umrah* & *ziarah* Dubai travellers, stretching between Malaysia and Dubai/Abu Dhabi on physical, material and virtual levels.

While the research themes, people involved and infrastructures are located in faraway but very connected places, the methodological realisations of the research phases in Malaysia and the UAE were quite different. In Malaysia I accompanied my respondents over a period of several months, stayed with some of them, and spent a lot of day-to-day life with several of them. I met many of my respondents in Malaysia often, developing an intense and intimate relationship which, by and by, led to deep insights into their lives, thoughts and practices. Over the course of several months and even years, we have established mutual trust and confidence. In contrast, my relationships with my respondents in the UAE were the other way round: I was the stationary one, in a fixed location, and the research subjects were passing by – on a flying visit, so to speak. I, as the ethnographer, was the spatial constant and the research subjects were only temporarily present. I did speak to many of them repeatedly, over the course of a single day or over two, three or four days – but the relationships could never grow as substantially as on stationary fieldwork in which both the researcher and the researched are permanently present. This suggests that when it comes to research on tourism and touristic/travel activities in general, information value and gained knowledge operate within limits on the level of pilgrims' trips. Notably, the limits of short-term travel research does not pertain to all levels of analysis. At the the level of travel agencies, for example, I could accompany, query and interview the staff (administrative staff, operational staff, tour guides etc) across the whole timespan of my research.

While the character of specific travel packages and transnational tourism journeys informed the process of research, formal Islamic frameworks also had an impact on the methodology. The temporal framework and chronological sequence of my fieldwork was closely bound to the Islamic *hijri* calendar.[15] The main reason for this is that the timeframe of a pilgrimage depends on this calendar: *hajj* pilgrimage always takes place between 8th and 12th Zulhijja, which is the 12th and last month of the Islamic calendar. During *hajj* season, Saudi Arabia issues visas for the purpose of performing *hajj*, but not for *umrah*. The possibility of obtaining *umrah* visas ends from the month of Ramadhan and restarts in the month of Safar. According to the Gregorian calendar, therefore, it was only possible to undertake *umrah* trips between October 2017 and May 2018. So, in order to follow *umrah* & *ziarah* pilgrims on their stopover in Dubai, I had to conduct my research in that place and within that timeframe.

This timing, furthermore, influenced my research in Malaysia. My respondents who went on *hajj* during my research in Malaysia were not available to me for around two months, since the *hajj* visa lasts about 40 days. Other activities were affected too: in order to prepare themselves for *umrah*, most of my respondents attended *umrah* preparation courses (*kursus umrah*), which were offered by the travel agencies with whom they booked their journey. As an ethnographer, I attended some of these courses as well. As they are not available during *hajj* season, I only had the chance to be part of these courses from the end of August 2017 onwards.

The other main effect of the *hijri* calendar with its Islamic rituals was the month of Ramadhan and the obligatory fasting during that timeframe. Within this month, which was equivalent to the end of May until the end of June 2017 according to Gregorian calendar, it was relatively difficult for me to conduct interviews. Muslims who fast get up around 4:30am in Malaysia, since *sahur*, the morning meal during Ramadhan, is taken until the time of *imsyak*. This is a certain time before sunrise, and was at that time in Malaysia around 5:30am. When I spent time in the home of Suriawati, Irsyad and their 6- and 11-year-old boys during Ramadhan, we had *sahur* comprised of *kurma* (dates), maccharoni or *mee goreng* (stir fried egg noodles), *cucur ikan bilis* (deep fried dough balls with small dried fish) and *teh tarik* (sweet milk tea) at around 5am. We all felt physically and mentally fit during the morning, but from around 10am we became tired and had to take naps. My hunger was so overwhelming from around 3pm that I could hardly concentrate. Similarly, during Ramadhan, some of my respondents asked me to conduct interviews with them in the morning since it was too tiring for them in the afternoon.

Following the material

One form of primary data has been impossible to obtain in Malaysia and the UAE alike: statistics relating to my research issues. Statistical data on Muslim pilgrimage (*hajj*, *umrah* and *ziarah*) are not available for various reasons. Regarding data on *umrah*, there was no established central office or department in Malaysia to collect such information. Data on *umrah* packages are scattered around the individual travel agencies but have not been gathered systematically. However, in 2014 the *Umrah* Monitoring

Council was established, which is supposed to gather and collate such information. At the time of my research and as I write, these data are not yet available. Concerning *hajj*, Tabung Haji (TH: the Malaysian government's pilgrim fund institution) records data. My request for a personal meeting was refused, and I received a message in October 2017, after months of effort, stating that most of their data are confidential and thus not available to me. Alongside these concrete frustrations, the conducting of research is highly regulated and controlled – and the conditions in Malaysia are much stricter than in the UAE (see also Lafaye de Micheaux 2017: 15ff for the Malaysian case). A researcher must obtain both research permission for the visa and an official research pass in order to be allowed to undertake research in Malaysia. These are applied for via the Prime Minister's Department, Economic Planning Unit (EPU). The researcher must be attached to a local university (in my case it was Monash University in Malaysia) and must also disclose where and with whom they wish to conduct research. Even more important is obtaining approval for the research content, as some themes are prohibited from investigation, such as religion and ethnicity, as these are classed as 'sensitive issues'. After completion of the research, we, as researchers, are obliged to send our findings to the EPU in the form of publications – otherwise it is not possible to apply for a research pass again in the future. While I succeeded with my application for a research visa and research pass, I was still not able to gain the statistical data required – even though the EPU officer was willing to assist me in this regard.

Following this challenge to my second research site, I tried to access statistical data on Malaysian tourists and/or pilgrims in Dubai instead. Interestingly, this was equally unsuccessful. When I consulted the Government of Dubai, Department of Tourism and Commerce Marketing in February 2018 in person to ask for statistical data on Malaysian travellers in Dubai, I was told, 'I think there are sections which don't want you to get these info, but I will check with my supervisor.' After checking, the officer informed me that I should write an email and added: 'Inshallah [if God will] they will respond.' 'They' did, stating that 'the requested data is not available for sharing'. My attachment to a local university was not helpful here either, similar to my situation in Malaysia. When someone wants to undertake research in the UAE that exceeds the timeframe of the tourist visa (90 days for EU citizens), the researcher can apply through a local university to stay in the country for an additional 30 or 90 days – which in my case was done through Zayed University. When someone conducts research within 90 days, no attachment to a university or even a research visa is required. So even though the regulations governing research in the country are less harsh than they are in Malaysia, the institutional conditions I faced and the challenges they implied regarding gaining statistical data could not be overcome through the principle of personal following. I tried to follow the existence of certain material (statistics) but only encountered its absence. The intention of following became a mere quest for following.

These many different experiences, conversations and interviews in heterogeneous, sometimes fragmented places made up in its entirety – as a puzzle put together, so to speak – are the key to understanding the complex research issues. A multi-sited ethnography is characterised not only by its multi-locality but equally by its multi-perspectivity. The different localities with their different socio-cultural environments also influenced my social relationships with local people, my own appearance and my bodily sentiments.

Embodied fieldwork

A feminist study drawing on the intersectionality framework is required not only to investigate interwoven identifications of the research subjects but also to reflect on the identifications embodied by the researcher. Following Elg and Qvotrup Jensen (2012), I consider an awareness of my (intersectional) embodied position as a researcher as fruitful for the process of knowledge production. In fact, I could not ignore the categories of difference that affected my relationships with the people I met and spent time with during fieldwork. As these categories of difference are, furthermore, embodied, I was continually obliged to reflect on my own corporeality and, moreover, on fieldwork as a bodily process (see Ortbals and Rincker 2009; Spatz 2017). This process affects social interactions, data collection and knowledge production, or, as Laura Ellingson puts it: '[K]nowledge is produced not by the disembodied voices that speak in official accounts of research in professional journals and books but by researchers, whose bodies unavoidably influence all aspects of the research process' (Ellingson 2006: 298).

Gender, age and religion/faith were the three most obvious embodied axes of differentiation that played a role during fieldwork. Over the course of my various phases of research in Malaysia since 2009, I have recognised developments in how my respondents perceive me. When I conducted field research in Malaysia in 2009, I was 26/27 years old. Leaving my male partner Harry in Germany, I tackled the research phase alone. That I was abroad alone was relatively unproblematic for my Muslim Malay respondents, since I was still young and unmarried. For my research in 2017, Harry accompanied me for the duration. I was 36 years old and had been with my partner for 14 years. Most of the time I met with my respondents alone, i.e. without Harry. Very often I heard, in typical *Manglish* slang: 'How can you come here alone? You have to follow your husband!' Moreover, the fact that we have been together for such a long time but do not have any children was often met with incomprehension. My attributed role as a female shifted from an autonomous young woman towards an obedient female partner or wife who is supposed to have kids in light of my advancing age.

Another example concerning gender relates to social interaction between myself and Malay men, especially when it comes to gender-segregated spaces. In rural areas, I felt this segregation particularly keenly during fieldwork in 2017, but not in 2009, although I was with the same people in both phases. The main difference was, again, that my partner was with me. When I spent time in the *kampung* (rural areas) alone in 2009, everyone, including all males, behaved warmly and cordially towards me. Most of the men I interacted with happily gave me all sorts of explanations on their own initiative and effort. I was often with males as well as females, even as part of their male spaces. In contrast, when on fieldwork with Harry in 2017, I automatically retreated from male spaces because the conditions expected and created by my respondents included that he was supposed to be with them and I should be with the females. Therefore, I was cut off from men's perspective and tried to make these situations as productive as possible for my research. Soon, I realised that the Malay men were speaking to my male partner about much broader themes than I had ever been privy to. I would never have gained information, for example, about sexuality or prostitution, which they mentioned to him.

Being a woman in public space in Dubai was rather different to my previous experiences in Malaysia. Harry and I lived for a period in Deira, the old town of Dubai. My gender, origin and class status dictated my feelings towards my position in that area. Our neighbourhood was comprised of around 95 per cent men, generally labourers from South Asia, but also from various African countries. Within these male-dominated surroundings, I experienced how I attracted attention as I had not felt it before – as a European woman amongst South Asian and African men. Embodied identity on fieldwork was present for me. I was constantly aware of how my body was moving through the alleys and how it looked different from the other bodies around me. I clearly felt the looks directed at me by many men, expressing scepticism, surprise, uncertainty and interest. These looks were never intrusive and never turned into stares.

I did not experience pejorative, invasive or even hostile attitudes. The atmosphere between them and me was rather characterised by distance and coolness, not by the warmth and friendliness I had experienced in Malaysia. Given this, I never felt uncomfortable amongst the men. On the contrary, I felt especially well and comfortable in Dubai and the whole of the UAE and Oman as a European woman, because of the overall reticence of men towards women in general.

Intersecting with my gender identity, (absence of) religious belief was another striking element which influenced the process of research. I am not a Muslim, a fact that I freely communicated to my respondents when asked. From time to time, in Malaysia as well as in Dubai, Malay respondents proposed that I should wear a *tudung*, the Malay headscarf – particularly men of around 50–60 years of age. One respondent said that I would look more 'beautiful' (*cantik*) then. One of the pilgrims in Dubai was of the opinion that I would only look *kemas* (best translated as a mixture of proper, good, neat and decent) when wearing a *tudung*. While stating this, a woman with brown shoulder-length hair, wearing a simple short black dress, passed by. Pointing to her, he said to me: 'Freehair[16] is not *kemas*, this is not *kemas*.' I replied: 'But I'm not a Muslim.' He said: 'That doesn't matter! Christians also want to do something good!'

Alongside the seeming contradiction between men being (sexually) attracted by a veil, which, according to certain interpretations, is not supposed to attract any male attention, and the shaping of the relationship between an older Muslim Malay man and a much younger Western European woman, attempts of Muslims to convince me of Islamic belief were present. My overall experience with my Malay Malaysian respondents was that they wanted to transmit a positive image of Islam. For many, this was a reason why they were so willing to speak to and interact with me. My research subjects were not passive objects; many of them had their own motivations for participating in my research. Sharing their overwhelming, unique pilgrimage experiences and conveying an image of a peaceful Islam were two of the most important ones. At best, I should – according to many of my respondents – convert to Islam soon, or at least appropriate the positive attributed characteristics, such as the veil.

Outline of the book

Chapter 2 *Malaysia – Islam, gender, economy* deals with historical and contemporary developments in Malaysia regarding Islam and gender in the context of the economy, and analyses these processes and their entanglements. National discourses, economic developments and socio-historical dynamics are thus the focus of the chapter. Pilgrimage in Malaysia has developed from an individual practice in the fourteenth century to a highly controlled, regulated and marketised state affair in the twenty-first. State Islamisation[12] processes have led to a deepening of Islamic belief since the 1970s, intermingled with economic development strategies that make these dynamics especially present among the Malay middle class. Products with an Islamic connotation, such as clothing or travel packages, have been developed as an important segment of the capitalist market in Malaysia and are desired targets of Malay middle-class, especially female, consumers. These manifold contemporary and historical interlinkages form the basis for enabling Malay Malaysians to go on '*umrah* & *ziarah* Dubai' or on sole *umrah* or *hajj*. Thus, the entangled dynamics discussed in this chapter will serve as context and background to the personal stories in subsequent chapters.

The first ethnographic chapter, chapter 3 *Marketisation of pilgrimage*, deals with the marketisation of Islam and spirituality mainly from the perspective of travellers and the travel industry. This specific economic sphere is investigated in its transnational conditions between Malaysia and the UAE, especially Dubai. The chapter examines the extent to which Islamic and spiritual values and practices are transformed through absorption into local and global markets. In the context of pilgrimage, '*ziarah*' was formally understood as a visit to certain tombs in Mecca and Medina. Following growth in infrastructure in the travel industry since the 1980s, it now additionally implies travel to other countries, even without any religious or spiritual element. Based on these developments, the chapter furthermore examines strategies, perspectives and practices of the travel agencies in Malaysia and the tour operators and tour guides in Dubai and Abu Dhabi regarding connected pilgrimage and tourism packages. It demonstrates that and how Islamic obligations are turned into commercialised goods. It will be shown that a contradistinction evolves between the commercial requirements of the economic actors and the spiritual needs of their religious customers and consumers. While the former offer 'normal' tourism tours in Dubai to Malaysian *umrah* & *ziarah* pilgrims, the latter aim for spiritual moments. In a broader sense, this chapter demonstrates how tourism, commerce and shopping were introduced into the spiritual journey, and thus sets the foundations for discussions of gendered shopping in subsequent chapters. The chapter is embedded in scholarly discussions on the nexus between economy and religion.

From chapter 4 I begin to analyse intersectional embodiment and embodied intersectionality. While chapter 3 demonstrates the commercial and spiritual characteristics of the *umrah* & *ziarah* journey, chapter 4 *Bodies in place, space and time* focuses on gendered and consumerist motivations for spending the *ziarah* part of the pilgrimage journey in the UAE. This is embedded in a specific 'placial' (Gielis 2009) ordering of and in the Muslim world. Mecca, Medina and the Arab region as a whole are, in Malaysia and on the Arabian Peninsula alike, considered to be at the heart of the Islamic world, mainly because of Islamic history. In accordance with this understanding, Southeast Asia is perceived as being located at the Islamic periphery. This spiritual place-making of certain physical locations has deep repercussions for gendered forms of shopping and of meaning-making of objects that are purchased and used. Many female Malay Malaysian pilgrims aim at a stopover in Dubai to shop for the *abaya* – the long, traditionally black coat or dress worn by Arab women from the Gulf. However, shopping in the 'Holy Land' of Mecca and Medina is done by women *and* men, based on the place- and meaning-making of that placial area and the goods on offer. Men's shopping worlds comprise the *abaya*'s male counterpart: the *kandora*, the traditional male Arab dress. The gendered and spiritual clothing items are connected to notions of modernity and tradition as well as to Islamic history. While the female *abaya* is perceived as a fashionable and modernised yet modest female garment, the male *kandora* is regarded as a mere religious and rather traditional item of clothing.

Whereas chapter 3 and the first part of chapter 4 deal with issues located on the Arabian Peninsula, the regional focus shifts in the second part of chapter 4 to Malaysia, to examine gendered and spiritual consequences of the journey for *umrah* & *ziarah* Dubai pilgrims. The garments purchased on the trip are turned into meaningful items. By bringing the religiously connoted *abaya* into everyday life in Malaysia, i.e. into both private and public spaces, females render visible their deepened spirituality based on pilgrimage and thereby mark their active part in religious negotiation processes. While traditionally male religiosity is present in public spaces in Malaysia through the culture of mosques, female religiosity is not. Thus, by traversing spatial orders on the level of embodiment, women intervene in spatial orders. So, having dealt with notions of time and place in the first section of chapter 4, this is complemented with space, creating a space-place-time nexus that is inherent to this study. Discussions are framed by theories of place, space and modernity (touching on consumption and class).

Chapter 5 *Gendered devotion* examines the gendered embodiment of sacredness in Malaysia. Based on pilgrimage experiences, women and men feel a sense of deeper religiosity and spirituality towards God. However, the two genders express this differently: women embody and practise their transformed relationship to God; men do so only on the level of social actions. Many wives, for example, transform their relationships with their husbands in parallel to their deepened relationship with Allah. This is an ambivalent threefold relationship: women stabilise and consolidate their bonds to their husbands, and they simultaneously liberate themselves and become independent from their husbands: total submission to God means becoming free. On the level of inner disposition, it is a process of liberation from dependencies on social relationships, doubts and sorrows, as God alone will guide the way from that very moment onwards. This simultaneous submission to the husband and to God finds expression in transformed clothing habits: upon returning from pilgrimage, many Malay Malaysian women start wearing an *abaya*, socks, gloves, veil and/or face veil (*niqab*). Men similarly enhance their spiritual dedication to God through the pilgrimage experience. But they do this by enhancing their role as fathers, modifying their relationships towards their children – girls and boys alike – through more responsible parenting. The discussions in chapter 5 are framed by regional Islamic gender ideologies and Islamic forms of thought that cover ideas about Allah and further understandings of gendered Islamic spiritual principles.

Chapters 2 to 5 analyse, *inter alia*, gendered and spiritual meaning-making processes relating to the goods consumed on the pilgrimage journey. In chapters 4 and 5 the issues of consumption, purchase and provision are considered through the object (mainly the *abaya*). In the last empirical chapter, chapter 6 *Spiritual shopping*, these issues are investigated from the perspective of the wider exchange system. This chapter focuses on the act of consumption itself by analysing the gendered culture of spiritual shopping and gift-giving. Ever since the birth of capitalism, consumer culture in the form of buying souvenirs on overseas trips has been understood as 'shopping', aka capitalist consumption. In contrast, in Malay contexts in Malaysia it is the norm to bring home gifts from journeys (*buah tangan*), but buying, consuming or purchasing a useful gift is considered a fulfilment of a religious obligation (*ibadah*) when the intention is to give it to someone who needs it – and is thus a sacred act. So, while the activity as such is not a new phenomenon, its classification and the process of meaning-making attached to it is new.

In addition to the *spiritual* character of (capitalist) commerce and consumption, contemporary shopping on a journey is revealed in chapter 6 as a *feminised* phenomenon. While the culture of gift-giving has long been practised in Malaysia by males and females alike, in contemporary capitalist contexts women are associated with shopping due to the strong influences of the fashion industry and *Muslimah*[17] products as part of the *halal* industry which has arisen in Malaysia. Thus, the practice of gift-giving has transformed from a rather gender-equal to a more gendered (female) phenomenon. Understanding shopping as spiritual and gendered contributes to debates on the sacred-profane divide and thus complements theoretical conceptualisations of tourism and pilgrimage.

The *Conclusion* summarises the research findings, but also reflects on doing research on Muslim women's (and men's) life-worlds. This section situates the research within discourses on and practices of Islam and gender – Orientalist at one pole and feminist at the other – that influence its conception, realisation and outcome. This materialises in, *inter alia,* the relationship between the feminist Western European privileged researcher and the Muslim female (and male) research subject. This framing is understood as a basis for wider reflections in future research.

Notes

1. All vernacular terms and translations are given in Malay (*Bahasa Melayu*), not in Arabic transcription, although it is worth mentioning that the vocabulary in Malay related to Islam is usually based on Arabic.
2. All names are pseudonyms.
3. All ages given in this study relate to the time of research between 2017 and 2018.
4. Muslims refer to Allah in capital letters as it is the proper name of their God. Accordingly, all other terms and pronouns designating Allah are spelled with a capital letter. In this study, I also use capital letters for these terms, even though I am not a Muslim, for two reasons. First, the example this footnote refers to showcases that 'Him' is meant here from the perspective of the Muslim social actors in this research. If they transcribe the same interview, they will write 'He' with a capital letter here. In this and other cases, I follow this approach out of respect for my respondents. Second, I am hesitant to write 'he' with lower case letters when referring to my respondents' God since, from my non-Muslim perspective, this would appear as if I intend to allocate a determined, male pronoun to Allah. However, as will be discussed in chapter 5, gendered or nongendered meanings assigned to Allah are subject to ideological, theological, social, cultural and spiritual debates and are therefore context-dependent. Hence, in these cases I also write 'He' or 'Him' with upper case letters, even though I write from my own scholarly and not from my respondents' perspective, in order to distance myself from Muslim and non-Muslim discussions about Allah having a gender or not.
5. 'Muslim' as an adjective and 'Islamic' are used differently in this study. While the former relates to how people interpret and live their religious and spiritual faith in everyday life, the latter is connected to institutional, formal and/or normative orders and practices.

6. I use 'female(s)' when I refer to female persons in general, in contrast to male subjects. This includes girls and women. In contrast, 'girl' or 'woman' implies a socio-structural position which is age or generation and thereby specifies 'female'. Thus, 'girl' and 'woman' are only applicable in specific contexts, i.e. when only that particular social group is being referred to.

7. In *Bahasa Indonesia*, the Indonesian form of the Malay language which differs from *Bahasa Melayu* only slightly in the sense of a regional dialect, *'ziarah'* is understood differently than in Malaysia: it has a stronger sense of pilgrimage than in Malaysia. Whereas in Malaysia it can also mean to visit people, it does not have this primary meaning in Indonesia. In KKBI (*Kamus Besar Bahasa Indonesia*, Grand Dictionary of Indonesian) on the internet we can see that *'ziarah'* has the first meaning of 'going to a *keramat*' (visiting a tomb or shrine of a local saint) in Indonesia. Only the second meaning is related to 'visit' (*melawat*). According to the Dewan Bahasa website (prpm.dbp.gov.my), in Malaysian Malay, however, the first meaning of *'ziarah'* is 'visiting people'.

8. *Ziarah* can be used both as a verb (to visit) and as a noun (a or the visit).

9. By merging Sarah J. Mahler and Patricia R. Pessar's (2006, 2001) modal *Gendered Geographies of Power* (GGP) and Anthony Giddens' (1984) theory of structuration, my previous framework *Gendered Power Hierarchies in Space and Time* consists of five dimensions, whereas the first four are borrowed from GGP and the fifth is added based on Giddens' theoretical conceptualisation: (1) *Gender* functions as the central category of analysis, investigated on bodily, family, social, state and global levels. (2) *Space* is part of subjective actions and gendered scales which have effects on transnational realities. (3) *Time* is another dimension since spatiality can only be thought of in a temporal manner and, furthermore, refers to the progressive character of negotiation processes. (4) *Social positionality* of subjects which limits or enables *agency*. (5) *Power hierarchies* are structural practices and systems of differentiation. Hence, agency and social practices are to be understood as interdependent with institutionalised practices which only produce (structural) inclusion and exclusion based on social positionality.

10. See Lévi-Strauss (2018 [1955]: 144ff) for a discussion, based on his ethnographic fieldwork in India and Brazil, on people's 'freedom' as dependent upon socio-political conditions and natural resources.

11. *Manglish* is the widely spoken mixture of English and Malay in Malaysia, following distinct grammatical structure and tone, for example.

12. The professional background of a *mutawif* is usually a degree in Islamic Studies, *Fiqh wal-usul* (*Fiqh* and methodological approaches to its sources) or something similar. In order to be eligible to work as a *mutawif* with Malaysia's largest travel agency, *Ibn Ziyad*, for example, the person needs to pass a training course with a final exam on an annual basis. The exam is about the principles and rules of *umrah* which the *mutawif* needs to know in case a pilgrim asks him specific questions, such as 'What happens if I cut my hair [*tahlul*] before I finished all *umrah* rites?', as one *mutawif* told me. He said that he needs to be able to explain to the pilgrim what kind of punishment Allah envisages for certain infringements of rules. In addition to the professional background and the annual exam, the *mutawif* must speak Arabic. Around 300 *mutawif* for *umrah* work at *Ibn Ziyad*. If one wants to become *hajj mutawif*, one needs to enrol on a course (*muzarakah Tabung Haji*) for 1,700 RM after being selected by *Ibn Ziyad* for it. The travel agency then proposes the person to TH, which needs to approve him and issue a *Sijil Pengurusan Ibadah Haji*, the licence for *hajj mutawif*. In 2017 a course on *hajj* and *umrah* management was created at the Institute of Management in KL; this is the most recent pathway for working as a *mutawif*. Ramli's youngest brother was enrolled in this programme during my fieldwork.

13. *Zikir* is the remembrance of God. It can be undertaken individually or in congregation; quietly or together by means of singing. The Naqshbandi Sufi group I joined a couple of times during fieldwork chanted the 99 names of Allah together.

14. Although the tourism visa was officially declared to have been launched, it has never been realised in practice.

15. The *hijri* calendar is a lunar calendar. It comprises 12 months that are based on the motion of the moon. Thus, one year is 354.36 days long. This calendar is based on the *Qur'an* (Sura 9, 36–37) and is named after the central event of *hijrah* in Islamic history: in AD 622, the Prophet Mohamad migrated with his followers from his hometown of Mecca to Yathrib (which he later renamed Medina, 'city of the prophet'), fleeing persecution in Mecca. This event marks year 1 of the *hijri* calendar. Ever since, it has been the central reference point in Muslim contexts to determine religious occasions and rituals, such as *hajj* pilgrimage in the month of *Zulhijja* and

fasting in the month of *Ramadhan*. However, the Gregorian calendar is used for civil occasions in Muslim majority countries. In the West, dates indicating the year(s) according to the *hijri* calendar are usually denoted by AH (Latin: Anno Hegirae, 'in the year of the *hijra*'), similar to the Christian (AD) and Jewish eras (AM). The years prior to the *hijra* are denoted BH ('before *hijrah*'). In Muslim countries, the *hijra* calendar is, in some cases, denoted as H. The Gregorian year of 2018 was the year 1439 according to the *hijra* calendar. During my fieldwork, it was 1438 AH, becoming 1439 AH on 22 September 2017.

16. 'Free-hair' is the expression used in Malaysia for women who do not cover their hair – implying that covered hair is the norm and uncovered is the exception (see Izharuddin 2018).

17. 'Muslimah' is used in Malaysia when emphasis is put on the feminine.

2
Malaysia – Islam, gender, economy

My 36-year-old Malay Malaysian respondent Haneefah was born and raised in Saudi Arabia and performed *hajj* three times during her youth. She left the Gulf state for Malaysia in 2000 when she was 19 years old. Why did she grow up in Saudi Arabia? Her paternal grandmother had set out from Malaysia to Mecca in 1962 at the age of 15, shortly after her marriage to her cousin, who was 15 years older. Her deep desire was to perform *hajj* during her remaining years. Her son and his wife, Haneefah's parents, accompanied her. They took the ship to Jeddah, the port city in the Hejaz. As the journey and the performance of *hajj* were so exhausting and tiring for Haneefah's grandmother, she did not return to Malaysia but remained in Saudi Arabia until she died. Her son and daughter-in-law, Haneefah's parents, also decided to stay, even after the mother(-in-law)'s death. Haneefah's father started a business, and her mother was a housewife. After her husband's death, Haneefah's mother married again and has been living in Mecca ever since.

Haneefah remembers that, ever since she was young, her mother has performed *umrah* every year whenever her health has allowed it. Haneefah herself never understood this regular, laborious performance – until she moved to Malaysia. Only there did she realise the meaning of a '*hajj* quota', implying the requirement to wait for decades for one's turn to go on *hajj*. The possibility of performing pilgrimage thus comes when one is already old and in doubtful health. 'And it's expensive!', Haneefah says:

> Malaysians have to pay 10,000 Ringgit! *Hajj* is a once in a lifetime experience. People would never want to waste it. Tabung Haji brings you to Mecca for 40 days; they organise the plane ticket, accommodation and food. The private travel agencies, which pilgrims can also go with, don't take you for 40 days, but only 20 days. You can go with them once every three years maybe, but that costs you 20,000 to 25,000 Ringgit, I guess. And that only for half the time

of the journey! All the other state governments, they don't give you 40 days, Malaysia is especially long with 40 days. (29 August 2017)

This sketch of Haneefah's cross-generational reflections touches on three issues: (1) the personal and spiritual meaning of pilgrimage; (2) women's roles and agency in the process of pilgrimage and (3) the development of financial and transport infrastructure, as well as the evolution of the 'management' of pilgrimage over time and Malaysia's contemporary particularity in that context. This chapter deals with historical and contemporary developments in Malaysia regarding Islam and gender in the context of the economy, and will analyse these processes and their entanglements.

National discourses, economic developments and socio-historical dynamics are the focus of this chapter, understood as possibilities for appropriation and distinction by my respondents. My work on these national and social scales of analysis is guided by the following question: what are the socio-political and historical backgrounds of Malay Malaysians with strong purchasing power who undertake *umrah* & *ziarah* trips today? My interest is in revealing contemporary and historical interlinkages as common ground, forming the basis for my respondents going on '*umrah* & *ziarah* Dubai' or on solo *umrah* or *hajj*. As part of my analytical framework *Scaling Holistic Intersectionality*, I work on the level of social and national dynamics that have been developing throughout history and continue to do so today. While the history of Malaysia is worth exploring in its entirety, I will limit my exploration of social and national processes in relation to my research focus, i.e. pilgrimage, Islam, gender and consumption/economy. I will trace these dynamics in their interdependence with ethnicity and notions of modernity. Religion and ethnicity in contemporary Malaysia are central elements of identity politics and political negotiation processes. Islamising initiatives and the economic and modernising trends of the past four to five decades form the broader context in which Muslim Malay Malaysians identify themselves and negotiate their social positions and inner dispositions.

Pilgrimage – from individual venture to economised business

Infrastructure, transportation and socio-political makeup have changed over time, and so has pilgrimage. *Umrah* and *umrah* & *ziarah* packages in Malaysia only developed in the 1980s and 1990s, as we shall see in chapter 3. *Hajj*, however, has been performed from the Malay Archipelago since Islam was introduced to the region in the fourteenth century (Yeoh 2016: 75). *Hajj* is a highly structured activity, requiring financial and spiritual preparation, performance of various rituals in Mecca and the return to one's community with the title of *hajah* (for women) or *haji* (for men) (Timothy and Iverson 2006). It can only be performed between the 8th and 12th of Zulhijjah, the last month in the Islamic calendar. Before commencing the rituals (*manasik*) in and outside Mecca, pilgrims formulate their intention (*niat*) to perform pilgrimage and remove their everyday clothes to enter the state of *ihram* – a state of consecration. The rituals in Mecca commence with *tawaf*: circumambulating the *kaabah* seven times. The *kaabah* is the black cube in the centre of the al-Haram mosque (*Masjidil-Haram*) in Mecca, the most sacred site in Islam. It is believed that Ibrahim and his son Ismail erected the *kaabah* as a holy shrine following the instructions of the angel Gabriel. After fulfilling *tawaf*, pilgrims walk or run back and forth seven times between the two hills of al-Safa and al-Marwah (*sa'ir*),[13] where Ibrahim left his concubine Hagar and his son alone. Hagar went in search of water between al-Safa and al-Marwah, and pilgrims drink from the Well of *zamzam* to commemorate this occasion. Pilgrims then head to the hill of Arafah, which is located 25 kilometres outside Mecca. They pray and meditate from noon until sunset. From Arafah, pilgrims go to the plain of Muzdalifa, where they collect 21 (3 x 7) small stones. These stones are thrown at the three pillars of Aqaba in Mina, which symbolises the stoning of *syeitan* (Satan). At the end of the *hajj*, thousands of sacrificial animals, such as sheep, goats and camels, are slaughtered in Mina. Once this is completed, the pilgrims return to Mecca and do the *tawaf* (*tawaf wida*; 'farewell *tawaf* or 'departure *tawaf*') and *sa'ir* again. Pilgrims are not allowed to shave, use perfume, cut their nails or hair or have sexual intercourse during the *hajj*. These rituals have remained the same over centuries.

Within the Malay region, the first *hajj* journeys set off from Singapore. Pilgrims were accompanied by the *syeikh haji*, usually a male figure from the Arab region who was the spiritual and religious guide and additionally responsible for practical matters, such as purchasing the ship tickets, and organising accommodation and official permits. The *syeikh haji* travelled through the Malay Archipelago, recruiting people for pilgrimage and organising journeys from the port city of Singapore in the middle of the Archipelago. A *hajj* trip usually came about as a result of recruitment through his campaigns or through friends' recommendations regarding the *syeikh haji*. Hence, pilgrimage was an individual endeavour organised by members of the community – *syeikh haji*, friends, potential pilgrims.

A turning point in terms of these arrangements and the number of pilgrims undertaking *hajj* came about in the nineteenth century,
during colonial rule. In addition to setting off from Singapore, ships
would also set out from Penang (located on the west coast of today's
mainland Malaysia); large numbers started their pilgrimage from there
in the 1860s and, later, also from Aceh (the northernmost part of the
island of Sumatra in today's Indonesia) (Aiza 2014: 81ff). Nevertheless,
Singapore remained the 'pilgrim hub' (Bunnell 2016: 31) within the
Malay Archipelago in those days, serving pilgrims from Johor, Kelantan,
Sabah, Sarawak and Indonesia.

The British, as colonial rulers in Malaya – the landmass that is now
divided into Malaysia and Singapore – did not show much interest in the
hajj activities of Malays in the early phase of colonialism (Yeoh 2016: 75).
Things were different in Dutch East India (now Indonesia), where the
Dutch colonisers exerted firm control over the Muslim population in
order to suppress (potential) uprisings. The British position changed
when they started to blame *hajj* travellers for outbreaks of epidemics;[14] as
a consequence, they transformed the individual act of pilgrimage into an
institutionalised activity. This laid the foundations for the deeply institutionalised and professionalised pilgrimage that my respondents encounter today.

The colonising power started to record and control *hajj* activities in
what was then Malaya in 1884. That year, 2,806 pilgrims left the region
for Saudi Arabia. The next decisive moment in the colonisers' handling
of the *hajj* came about during the First World War. Muslim pilgrimage
was still going on and, as previously, travellers brought back not only personal spiritual experiences but also political ideas. The British regarded
this as a threat during those politically unstable years. In particular,
they perceived the reformist movement in Islam (*Islah*), which developed at the turn of the twentieth century, as suspicious and dangerous.
Consequently, they started to regulate the *hajj* and intermittently controlled *hajj* activities in Malaya through the Malayan Political Bureau
(the intelligence service), which at the time was based in Singapore (Aiza
2014: 80f). The Bureau monitored pilgrims by issuing passes, which pilgrims had to purchase for 0.50 dollar according to The Pilgrim Pass Rule,
introduced in 1926. Furthermore, the *syeikh haji* had to be registered
with this office and he could only obtain a licence to perform his role following approval from the director of the Political Investigation Bureau.
The *syeikh haji* was required to submit regular reports on pilgrims and
their activities (Aiza 2014: 84). Control of *hajis* and their activities intensified during the Second World War, when the rulers' biggest fear turned

out to be pilgrims bringing home ideas of Pan-Islamism and socialism as practised in the Soviet Union. The British perceived Mecca to be a nodal point for anti-European and, therefore, anti-colonial propaganda, since Muslim pilgrims from all over the world gathered there.

Within this context, pilgrimage became a state affair for the ruling forces. Consequently, *hajj* was controlled and monitored thoroughly both in the Malay Archipelago and in the Hejaz (Aiza 2014: 85; Yeoh 2016: 75). Pilgrimage monitoring is ongoing today in Malaysia, as will be shown in chapter 3 when discussing the consequences of monitoring for contemporary *hajj* and *umrah*.

Alongside pilgrimage monitoring, developments in transportation also affected the characteristics of the journey. From the very beginnings of the *hajj* until the 1960s, Malay pilgrims went on *hajj* by sailing vessel, as Haneefah told me regarding her grandmother's and parents' *hajj* journey, and later by steamship. The journey from the Malay Archipelago to Jeddah took around 30 days. My respondent Adi Puteri, a 60-year-old Malay woman from Bukit Mertajam, recalled (4 September 2017) that she and her grandfather went on *hajj* by ship in 1973 when she was 16. The journey lasted three months in total: a one-month trip to Mecca, a month of religious performance in Mecca and Medina, and a one-month journey back to Malaysia. Back then, she recalls, five ships usually departed on the same day during the *hajj* season, transporting pilgrims from Penang to Jeddah. Developments in transportation transformed the possibilities for contemporary pilgrims and changing concepts of pilgrimage. The effects will be discussed, along with my respondents' views, in chapter 3.

The steamship companies, including the Straits Steamship Company, the Straits Hejaz Company, the Blue Funnel Line and the Ocean Navigation Company of Hong Kong, were trading ships and made additional profit from pilgrimage, resulting in a 'pilgrim trade', as Tim Bunnell (2016: 32) puts it. Trading ships came from various ports located in the Indian Ocean, transporting both goods and pilgrims. Between 1870 and 1872, seven out of 29 British ships which set out from Singapore to Jeddah were overloaded. The pilgrims were forced to stay on deck, while the lower decks were filled with goods (for example rice, sugar, timber) to be sold in Jeddah (Aiza 2014: 89). On the return journey, coffee and other local products from the Arabian region were brought back to the Malay Archipelago. Given good weather and trading conditions, merchants could make a gross profit of 50 per cent on their goods in Mecca. But it was not only the shipping companies that profited from *hajj*: pilgrims did too. Many of them traded in carpets, spices or jewellery on the Arabian

Peninsula (Tagliacozzo 2013: 71f, 207). Religious and commercial profit complemented each other. The *hajj* was thus an engine for trade on different levels. How profiting from the *hajj* from the institutional or even governmental side has played an important role until today, and how this affects my respondents' and other Malaysian pilgrims' possibilities for undertaking their religious obligation, will be demonstrated below.

Hajj pilgrims needed to trade and make money to finance their own trips: alongside the British regulations, economic conditions within the Muslim Malay community influenced the possibilities for *hajj* activities in Malaya as well. Between 1875 and 1895, a return ticket – including the stay in the Hejaz – cost a Malay pilgrim approximately 300 dollars. In those days, many Malays made their way to Singapore but were not able to proceed to Mecca because they had failed to earn enough money on the island for the passage. They became '*haji Singapura*' instead (Bunnell 2016: 31).

Between 1923 and 1941 the ticket price increased from 500 to 680 dollars, and in 1929 it soared as high as 900 dollars. The rise in price reflected the economic situation. It also affected the number of pilgrims: during the rubber boom in British Malaysia between 1909 and 1912, 11,707 pilgrims left in 1911 to fulfil their religious obligations. After rubber prices began to fall in 1913, the number of *hajj* pilgrims fell to 8,344 in 1914 (Aiza 2014: 82).

In addition to personal income, institutional community support existed to finance people's journeys. Historian Eric Tagliacozzo (2013: 72) notes that during British colonialism, *waqaf*, Islamic endowments, played an important role in this regard. *Waqaf* were founded in various locations within the region but mainly in Singapore, where the majority of ships set sail. The crucial actors in these institutions were Arabic families with bonds to their home regions. The endowments lent money to pilgrims to help them purchase their ship tickets. *Waqaf* acted according to Islamic banking principles, in contrast to capitalist institutions in the Malay Archipelago which profited from the *hajj*. Despite this institutional support, pilgrims had to borrow money, sell their lands and spend all their savings in order to be financially able to perform the pilgrimage. Tagliacozzo (2013: 63) puts it in a nutshell: 'Taking an everyday, utilitarian point of view, . . . the pilgrimage was possible not in people's minds or hearts, but rather through their bank accounts.' The relationship between the material and class-based status of pilgrims, on the one hand, and institutional subsidies for pilgrimage, on the other, still plays a crucial role for my respondents in contemporary times and will be discussed below.

Ships were superseded by air travel in the 1970s. This technological development shortened the *hajj* journey from 30 days by ship, as Haneefah's grandmother and parents and Adi Puteri experienced it, to nine hours by plane (Tagliacozzo 2013: 210). The transformation from sea to air travel was partly promoted and organised by a Malaysian governmental organisation: today's *Tabung Haji* (Bianchi 2004: 118), whose role and activities will be discussed in detail in the next section.

Developments in technology, the socio-political and economic conditions of Muslim pilgrims over the past 200 years, and more recent processes of Islamisation and economic development have influenced the socio-structural characteristics of pilgrims. McDonnell (1990: 115) notes that around the year 1900, *hajj* pilgrims from Malaya comprised primarily the traditional male and elderly elite, mostly from the southern parts of mainland Malaya (Tagliacozzo 2013: 72). In the 1920s, students and other members of the then emerging 'old' middle class and peasants began to join the *hajj* pilgrimage. Before the 1920s, there were no references to women going on pilgrimage. In the 1930s, these rural elites started to bring their families to Mecca. From then on, the number of women pilgrims increased. Over the next three decades, women, young students and people from urban centres were becoming part of the Malayan *hajj* pilgrimage.

Since the 1960s, the *hajj* has been performed equally by rural and urban pilgrims, but the majority are middle-aged and from the 'new' middle class (McDonnell 1990: 115). Since the 1970s, the majority of pilgrims from Malaysia have been women. Between 1968 and 1975, the proportion of female *hajj* pilgrims from all over the world was only 35 per cent. Within this timeframe, however, the female proportion of *hajj* pilgrims from Malaya was already above 53 per cent. Since 1979, Malaysian women have consistently constituted approximately 55 per cent of pilgrims. The majority of these women, precisely 35 per cent of all Malaysian (female and male) pilgrims, are housewives. At least 20 per cent of all Malaysian pilgrims are women undertaking wage labour outside their homes (Bianchi 2004: 120, 134). Bianchi (2016: 134) suggests two reasons why the number of women in Malaysia undertaking *hajj* trips has continuously exceeded men since the 1970s. (1) The ratio of female *hajj* pilgrims is particularly high in those regions where *Qur'an* classes and Islamic schools for girls and women have been established, with the result that females are well-educated in Islamic principles and practices. Especially in orthodox communities, husbands and fathers bring their wives and daughters to *Qur'an* schools in the hope of enabling them to achieve social and physical mobility and, eventually, a *hajj* journey. I will show below, however, that women themselves get involved in Islamic education, with a special focus on pilgrimage, and are not dependent on men's will, as Bianchi argues. (2) Local politicians ensure that these Islamic schools for females and their pilgrimage journeys receive subsidies from the national government. As Bianchi neglects the complexities of contemporary socio-political dynamics regarding a female's (religious) status in Malaysia with this argument, I will discuss below different contemporary national policies which aim at a female's (religious) education and the role that Islamic organisations play therein.

No matter whether female or male, the number of *hajj* pilgrims from Malaysia has risen significantly since the 1970s – when air travel was introduced. For example, the total number of pilgrims worldwide between the late 1950s and early 1970s (a total of 4,000–6,000 pilgrims per year) comprised 80–120 Malays annually (Tagliacozzo 2013: 20). Around 2 million pilgrims currently perform the *hajj* each year – in 2013, 22,320 of them were Malaysians and in 2017, 27,900 (The Malay Online, 27 January 2017); in 2018 and 2019 the number rose to 30,200; the envisaged number in 2020 was a high as 31,600 (*New Straits Times*, 22 January 2020). However, due to the Covid-19 pandemic, Malaysians, like all other international guests, were not allowed to go on *hajj* – at least if they would have needed to enter Saudi Arabia via border crossing. Only 1,000 pilgrims were allowed, in an attempt to curb the pandemic. The only foreigners allowed to perform their obligation were those who resided in Saudi Arabia. In fact, they formed the majority of pilgrims: about 30 per cent of worshippers in 2020 were Saudi citizens (BBC, 29 July 2020; CNN, 29 July 2020). The story in 2021 was similar, due to the pandemic. Because of Covid-19, the quota was further reduced in 2022 as well: 14,306 places were offered to Malaysian pilgrims in that year, or 45 per cent of the normal quota given by Saudi Arabia. Malaysia applied for an additional 5,000 places for the *hajj* season in 2022; approval depended on the Saudi Arabian government and had not been decided on at the time of writing (Free Malaysia Today, 16 May 2022).

Pilgrimage in the context of economic development: *hajj* management and business

When I was talking with Irsyad in his house in Perak about his pilgrimage experiences, I could see a piggy bank in the unmistakeable curved shape of *Tabung Haji*'s (TH) KL headquarters in the background

Figure 2.1   A piggy bank (left) in the characteristic shape of *Tabung Haji*'s headquarters in Kuala Lumpur, Malaysia, 2017.

(see figures 2.1 and 2.2): TH gave it to his two sons Hadees and Haissam, 11 and 6 years old respectively, when he and his wife Suriawati registered the children for *hajj* at TH. Some coins were inside. 'Tabung Haji gave *tabung* [funding] for the kids!', he explained.

   Tabung Haji is the government organisation that monitors, organises, controls and subsidises *hajj* for Malaysians who plan to perform their pilgrimage from Malaysia. It was founded as *Lembaga Urusan dan Tabung Haji* (The Pilgrimage Management and Savings Corporation) in 1963. Every pilgrim performing *hajj* with TH pays the same price. In 2017, the year of my fieldwork in Malaysia, the amount was 9,980 RM. This was a lot of money for many of my respondents. The average annual income in 2017 of a medical officer, for example, was 9,000 RM, of an engineer 33,000 RM, and of an executive 40,000 RM. In 2017, the total cost of one regular *hajj* journey was 19,550 RM per person including flights, transportation, accommodation in Mecca, Medina and Jeddah, meals, payment to the Government of Saudi Arabia, as well as notebooks, reference books, medical services, a name tag and a card for the personal TH bank account.

   The amount rose to 25,540 RM per person in 2022 because of tax increases and the *hajj* payment rate in 2022 rose as high as 10,980 RM

Figure 2.2 *Tabung Haji*'s headquarters in Kuala Lumpur, Malaysia, 2014.

per person. *Tabung Haji* subsidises every pilgrim for approximately half the total amount – which was 9,570 RM in 2017 and 12,560 RM in 2022 – when they perform pilgrimage for the first time. The symbolic coins in Hadees and Haissam's piggy bank still need to mount up, but this will happen in the course of their lives through further deposits, progressing from piggy bank to bank accounts. With its subsidy, TH follows the tradition of the abovementioned *waqaf*: lending money to enable people to go on pilgrimage. Pilgrims who go for a second or subsequent time must still register with TH but they need to pay the whole amount themselves.

Tabung Haji paid out 267,950,430 RM in subsidies to pilgrims in 2017 and allocated between 300,000,000 RM and 400,000,000 RM per year for *hajj* subsidies from 2022 onwards. It is able to do this thanks to the business the institution undertakes. Masjaliza told me incredulously that TH, which is supposed to have moral integrity because of its focus on the hajj, is involved in the hotel industry and that they have palm oil plantations in Indonesia. This business model (*modal perniagaan*) is structured on the deposits that pilgrims pay upon registration, as I will show below. *Tabung Haji* invests this initial capital into its businesses (in addition to plantations it also has real estate in Malaysia and Saudi Arabia, contracts with airlines, etc) based on Islamic banking principles in order to raise revenue to support the depositors financially in return (Tagliacozzo 2013: 213).

The strength of TH only evolved over time. Amriah, a retired teacher in her 60s from Kelantan, performed *hajj* in 1986 and 2007 and performed *umrah* five times between the 1980s and 2017. She had to pay 5,000 RM for her first *hajj* in 1986 and received 1,000 RM from TH as a subsidy. She had to cook her own food in Mecca and Medina, bringing along all the ingredients from Malaysia: 'We cooked the *sambal udang*, the *sambal ikan bilis*, the *sambal belachan* [red chilli paste with prawns, red chilli paste with small dried fish and red chilli paste with shrimps, respectively].' She and the other Malaysian pilgrims had to procure all the crockery and cooking utensils themselves as such things were not provided for by TH at the time.

Over the past three decades, the organisation and management of the *hajj* has not only been professionalised by TH, but the ideas about and principles behind the pilgrimage have also been regulated, stand-ardised and canonised. This is because TH ministers to, among other things, potential pilgrims' education. When a Malaysian goes on *hajj*, they can participate in the *kursus perdana*, the grand course, including 14 sessions held at the National Stadium where the full cohort of a year's pilgrims can take part. Bianchi (2004: 136) states that TH additionally supplies brochures dealing with the encompassing questions of wisdom (*hikmah*), mysteries (*rahasiya*) and philosophy (*falsafah*) of pilgrimage. Furthermore, TV programmes are broadcast in which a representative of TH and a religious scholar (*ustaz*) discuss certain questions, such as: What happens if a woman shows her arm to a non-*mahram* (a man the woman is eligible to be married to)? What happens if the seven pebbles thrown against the pillars (*jamarat*) symbolising the devil are not thrown consecutively but simultaneously? My long-time friend and respondent Ramli, Masjaliza's husband, comments on this educational effort by TH:

> Nowadays, the good thing about Tabung Haji is that they educate the people not to mix the terms up. They have the same syllabus for the whole country. So, they educate all people throughout Malaysia how to differentiate *hajj* and *umrah*, for example. This is different to Indonesia, where the people are not so educated in terms of pilgrimage. They don't know what belongs to *hajj* and what to *umrah* because they don't have these programmes. (9 July 2017)

Tabung Haji teaches Malaysians from a very young age and thereby inculcates viewpoints on the principles of pilgrimage in a manner that does not allow discussions of different interpretations of practices. On 23 July 2017, 4,000 six-year-old children from Selangor were chosen to participate in a one-day *hajj* preparation course (*kursus hajji*). Proudly, Masjaliza told me that her son had been selected by the teachers at his Islamic kindergarten, 'Little *Ustaz*', because he was already performing the obligatory prayer (*solat*), which is something rather special. This annual course organised by TH and the kindergartens teaches children how to wear *kain ihram* (the two pieces of white cloth) and how to circumambulate the *kaabah* (*tawaf*) during *hajj* (see also *The Daily Mail*, 24 July 2017). All these activities and efforts undertaken by TH and, thus, by the Malaysian government have led to both a high degree of awareness about Islamic principles and the stabilisation and ordering of pilgrimage.

The institution of TH and the concomitant professionalisation and economisation of the *hajj* in Malaysia is unique. The way it caters for (potential) pilgrims is appreciated greatly by its target group – Malay Muslims in Malaysia. As Ramli put it: 'Tabung Haji is the best *hajj* organiser in the world. Every year. This is also what Saudi Arabia says. There is some kind of ranking and Tabung Haji always ranked best' (20 May 2017). The reason Saudi Arabia comes into play here is that TH not only deals with Malaysian pilgrims inside Malaysia but takes care of them throughout their pilgrimage. Farish, a Malay Malaysian in his late 50s, enthuses: 'TH provides buses, organises the transportation of the people, they provide comfort. Tabung Haji protects the pilgrimage. They even provide tents at Arafah for the Malaysians. Pilgrims from other countries don't even have a proper tent there' (6 July 2017). Alongside having these practical issues dealt with, every Malaysian pilgrim group is accompanied by a *mutawif*, a male religious scholar,[1] who, among other things, gives advice on religious and spiritual matters and guides the pilgrims in their open religion-related questions and their religious practices. Furthermore, the *mutawif* is responsible for all organisational matters on the journey. This figure is comparable to the *syeikh haji* of colonial times.

The personal perspectives of Irsyad, Ramli and Farish on TH touch on three major areas: registration, financial matters and the realisation of the pilgrimage from the beginning of the trip in Malaysia to the return home.

Registering and queuing for *hajj*

Officially, registration for *hajj* is heavily regulated. To register, (1) one needs to deposit a minimum of 1,300 RM into one's personal TH account; (2) one must not have any active record of previous *hajj* registration; and (3) a depositor is not allowed to re-register if she or he has performed the *hajj* in the previous five years (*Tabung Haji*, n.d.). Once a person is registered, they need to wait their turn, based on a period that aligns with the corresponding quota. In 2017, the year of my fieldwork in Malaysia, the waiting period for one's turn to go on *hajj* was shortened from 89 to 50 years due to a rise in *hajj* visas, as we shall see. Thus, Irsyad and Suriawati's 6- and 11-year-old sons will probably perform *hajj* when they are between about 55 and 60 years old. Ubaidah, Farrah's husband, who went to Mecca six times for *hajj* (once) and *umrah* (five times) between 2002 and 2019, talked to me about the exponential increase in Malaysians aiming for *hajj*, which leads to a constant extension of the queue and, thus, to a decreased likelihood of receiving the offer to go. Yet, this should not hamper a sincere Muslim from registering, as even this practical step has a spiritual element:

> Nowadays, if you delay one month for your registration, then you will have to wait a number of years more. The longer you wait to register, the longer your waiting time will be. The queue hasn't always been that long. The first time I registered for *hajj* was in 1998 and I was offered a chance to go after 4 years. I registered for *hajj* again in 2008 and I'm supposed to go in 2022, so I only have to wait for 14 years, which is not that long. The waiting period has become so long because there are more people who want to go nowadays. If you don't register, that means that you don't have any intention [*niat*] to go. Then you die without even going for *hajj*. So better if you just put your name on to the list at Tabung Haji, so at least you have to show this effort that you want to go. Most probably you

won't be able to go because of the quota system, but at least you take the step to register so that you have a reason you can put forward to God that 'I have registered, but somehow I didn't live long enough, then I died without going for *hajj*.' (8 September 2017)

These long queues have only developed since 2008, when the quota system for *hajj* was established. Before then, registration was necessary, but only for administrative reasons. Amriah remembers that when she first went on pilgrimage in 1986, she could start her journey one month after registering, which was the normal administration period. 'Anyone could go at any time!' Nowadays, there are criteria setting out when one is eligible to appeal to be bumped up the queue. This is the case, for example, when a male person functions as a *mahram*, i.e. a close relative who accompanies a female, when a young person accompanies elder people, or when a Muslim is already elderly.

Data on the distribution of *hajj* seats or on variations of the quota are not possible to obtain in Malaysia, which I realised after putting a lot of effort into trying to get them during fieldwork in 2017. The official calculation of the *hajj* quota is based on 0.1 per cent of every country's Muslim population. This formula was decided by the Organization of Islamic Cooperation in 1987. The number of *hajj* places for the year is subject to the quota allotted by the Kingdom of Saudi Arabia for the particular year. Interestingly, the case of Malaysia differs. In 2016, 30,949,962 people lived in Malaysia, of whom 61.3 per cent were Muslims. This equated to 18,971,737 Muslims living in the country. If the quota was in accordance with the rule that 0.1 per cent of a state's Muslim population will get a seat, then 18,972 *hajj* visas should have been distributed for Malaysians in 2016. However, 22,230 visas were distributed. After researching the statics, presenting myself at TH's headquarters, writing emails and making phone calls, TH finally provided information in October 2017 on *hajj* numbers, although brief and only via email. I asked them about the contradiction regarding the numbers I had calculated. They explained that Malaysia is considered an Islamic state by the Organization of Islamic Cooperation, so that the total population counts for the calculation. I also discovered that Malaysia's special status can be enhanced under certain conditions and at certain times. For example, in 2017, the Saudi Arabian government allowed Malaysia to issue more visas than in the previous year, namely 27,999, even though the population did not grow accordingly within that one year. In my email exchange with TH, they justified this by pointing to Malaysia's endeavour to constantly negotiate with Saudi Arabia regarding the number of visas issued. Pilgrimage is a booming business for official bodies, on the one hand, and inspires a strong desire on the part of pious Muslims, on the other. This explains the loopholes that exist and are made use of.

Hajj business

The United Malays National Organisation (UMNO), the party that ruled the country either alone or as part of a coalition between 1957 and 2018, circumvented the quota given by Saudi Arabia to a certain extent and made use of the desire of most Malay Malaysians to perform their *hajj* at least once in their lifetime.[2] At least three options existed for potential pilgrims to perform *hajj* without queuing, based on policies and businesses connected with the *hajj*: first, through preferential treatment provided by a special Prime Minister's programme; secondly, through personal relationships with members of parliament; and thirdly, through the unofficial purchase of *hajj* seats. A fourth possibility is connected not to relationships to the ruling party but to individual efforts to go on *hajj*, namely beginning the trip outside Malaysia.

In mid-July 2017, during the campaign for the 14th general election (GE14), one Malaysian newspaper's headline read: 'P[rime] M[inister]: 1 MDB has done its fair share of good' (*The Star*, 12 July 2017: 2). According to the newspaper, 1 MDB is a special programme[3] that distributes, among other things, 1,100 *hajj* seats to *imams*, 'village heads' and 'community leaders'. When I asked TH whether these seats are part of the official quota or are additional existing seats, my email correspondent mentioned that – as part of the official quota – 4,611 *imams*, *muazzins* (prayer callers), community leaders, village chiefs, Community Development Department officers and Office of the Mufti's representatives benefit from the programme. Because of their roles, these people – mostly males – do not need to wait their turn; they can find themselves on pilgrimage within a very short timeframe.

My 52-year-old respondent Latipa from Shah Alam, who registered for *hajj* in 2016, similarly did not need to wait long. Just one year after registering, it was her turn. The reason? She benefited from a different Prime Minister's programme by taking advantage of a personal relationship to a parliamentarian. She spoke to me just two weeks after her *hajj* experiences:

Viola: How long did you need you wait to go on *hajj*? When did you register?
Latipa: I registered last year.

Viola: How come?!

Latipa: I have somebody to help me.

Viola: At *Tabung Haji*?

Latipa: Yes. My daughter's mother-in-law is an UMNO politician. This mother-in-law applied for the Prime Minister's quota. They have this quota for the old ladies, for those who haven't performed *hajj* yet. She applied for 22 seats and she got 18 eats. One was for me. I got the offer and then went with *Tabung Haji* for *hajj*. Every minister has his own quota, I think so.

Viola: Every minister, like the Minister of Defense, the Minister of Interior Affairs...?

Latipa: Yes, I think so. She applied for the Prime Minister's quota. (27 September 2017)

As well as favouring certain individuals and making special offers regarding *hajj* seats, journeys are also affected by the government's strategy concerning voting. An *umrah* & *ziarah* Dubai/Abu Dhabi traveller from KL told me during our tour through Abu Dhabi in April 2018 that she had originally booked her journey for the period during Ramadhan. Performing *umrah* during the holy month of Ramadhan opens up the possibility of gaining more – in fact double the amount of – *pahala* than during any other month: as much as one can get for *hajj*. *Pahala* are positive rewards Muslims believe they gain for their everyday religious activities and good deeds. Muslims believe that they will be judged on their amount of *pahala* by Allah on judgment day (*qiamat*). The *umrah* & *ziarah*-Dubai/Abu Dhabi booking was already confirmed but after a couple of months the travel agency cancelled the package at short notice because it was scheduled during the general election in Malaysia on 9 May 2018 and the government urged the travel agencies not to undertake any travel so that Malay Malaysians could be present to vote.

Distribution of special *hajj* seats is regarded with great suspicion by most of my respondents and is often debated, in the media and among many Malay Malaysians in this study, in the context of corruption (*rasuah*). *Tabung Haji* and the government try to appease upset Malay Malaysians by clarifying that the organisation of *hajj* is in order. A headline in one of the daily online newspapers read: 'No Favouritism In Selection Of Pilgrims For Haj – TH' (*Malaysian Digest*, 10 June 2016).

Whereas Latipa went on *hajj* with TH, my respondents Kartini and her husband Fuaad from Kelantan, both in their 60s, performed *hajj* in 1994 and again in 2014 with a *private* travel agency. They chose this option as an alternative way to circumvent the queue. I asked Masjaliza, their daughter, about this issue and how her parents could perform *hajj* within 10 years rather than waiting decades for their second turn. She responded:

> That was not official! They went with a private travel agency. They didn't register with Tabung Haji. It goes like this: The private agencies will get maybe 50 seats for *hajj* extra from TH without any specific names. Then the travel agent will ask who wants to go. You need very good relationships and networks for it. My parents went with *Ibn Hawqal*[4] [a travel agency in Kota Bahru, Kelantan] and they have very good relationships to Haji [Ustaz Abdul] Intan [the owner and director of *Ibn Hawqal*]. *Ibn Hawqal* is one of the biggest and oldest travel agencies in Kelantan; that's why Tabung Haji just gave them extra seats for *hajj*. It all depends on your network, your status or your fate. The travel agencies will ask TH: 'Give us 10 or 20 seats more-*lah*!' [The expression -*lah* or -*ah* in Malay and Malaysian English (*Manglish*) is attached to a word which is to be emphasised.] And they will just give them because TH has its own share of seats with the travel agencies. The Tabung Haji officers have only very short waiting periods; they will just go with one of the private agencies for *hajj*. So, these officers can go with the agencies and that's why the agencies just can ask for more unspecified seats. The agencies and Tabung Haji have these dealings, but it's not official. (22 September 2017)

When I interviewed Haji Ustaz Abdul Intan in January 2014 in his spacious two-storey house in Kelantan, with its garden including a koi pond and a luxury car parked out front, he said that the reason why his travel agency *Ibn Hawqal* has gained a licence from TH to serve *hajj* pilgrims is that he has never cheated TH or the Saudi Arabian government. In contrast, Sabooha, a travel agent from KL, complained how difficult it is for a private agency to get a *hajj* licence. *Tabung Haji* needs to recommend the private agency to the Saudi Arabian government first and the latter will approve or dismiss the recommendation on the basis of the relationship between them and TH. A special deposit of 100,000 RM (*duit jaminan*, 'guarantee money') must be paid by Malaysian travel agencies to the Saudi Arabian government, which the latter will use if the corresponding tour operator does not cater well enough for its group. Only five to six private Malaysian travel agencies have such a licence, including TH's own agency *Tabung Haji Travel*.

This unofficial way of accessing *hajj* via a private travel agency is bound not only to a person's networks, as Masjaliza explains, but also to their class status. These informal *hajj* journeys are very expensive, as Haneefah noted in the opening of this chapter. Kuntum, a 67-year-old friend of Kartini from Kelantan who functions as a *upah hajji*, i.e. he performs *hajj* on behalf other people,[5] told me that she had to pay 22,000 RM when she went in 2012 with a private agency. In 2017 she paid 40,000 RM for her *hajj* journey, also through a private travel agency (the cost rose to 50,000 RM in 2022). Considering the 9,980 RM every pilgrim had to pay in that same year when going with TH, we can see that Kuntum had to raise four times the price.

One way to pay less than those who buy their ticket at private travel agencies in Malaysia but still circumvent the queue is to go on *hajj* from outside Malaysia. A furious Ramli told me that rich people go to Thailand or Indonesia to register for *hajj*. Once they have done this, they are under Thailand or Indonesia's quota and no longer under Malaysia's quota. Since most people in Indonesia are not as affluent than the majority of Malaysians, he said, and since the political situation in southern Thailand (where most of the country's Muslims live) is unstable, fewer people perform *hajj* in those countries than in Malaysia. Due to the currency exchange rates, tickets for a *hajj* trip are cheaper than in Malaysia, so Malaysians can benefit from lower prices (when they go via a private travel agency) and/or from a shorter queue (when they register), Ramli stated. In a similar vein, Bianchi (2016: 139) indicates that Indonesia could not exhaust its quota, especially in its early implementation in the late 1980s. The Indonesian state thus distributed 10,000 seats to more affluent countries, such as Malaysia and Singapore, where demand had already exceeded the seats available (see also Tagliacozzo 2013: 212). As Ramli explained, this path to quick and relatively easy access to *hajj* seats still exists today.

The professionalisation and especially the quantitative intensification of the *hajj* is embedded in wider social dynamics: the 1970s and 1980s in Malaysia were characterised by the politicisation of Islam, economic development and modernisation initiated and developed by the ruling elites and institutions. These national and institutional dynamics were highly appropriated and negotiated in Malaysian society, especially in urban areas. Such processes affect not only the development of pilgrimage in Malaysia, but also gender issues which, in turn, relate to class. As I will elaborate below, the politicisation of Islam led to a broadening of Muslim believers – leading, in turn, to an extension of the *hajj* queue – and to the rise of a new Malay middle class (*kelas pertengahan*) which could more easily afford pilgrimage trips – as shown with Kuntum, Kartini and Fuaad. Modernisation of the country, furthermore, implied a rise in women's status (see Frisk 2009). In their entanglement, these socio-political and economic processes are crucial for my respondents as most of them identify as urban, middle-class, pious Muslims, which enables them to perform *umrah* & *ziarah* Dubai or *hajj* trips.

Gender – transformations in the context of Islamic revival and economic development

When I visited the *kursus umrah* (the *umrah* course), which teaches participants the rules and regulations of pilgrimage, at *Ibn Ziyad* travel agency in KL on 27 August 2017, almost all of the 300 seats were taken. The women sat in the front section; the men at the rear (see figure 2.3). I asked the woman next to me why the women sit at the front and not the men. She responded that it was because the women arrive first. 'When it comes to learning about Islam, many women are present. Wherever

Figure 2.3   Women studying at an *umrah* preparation course, Malaysia, 2017.

you look for it. When there is a class in a mosque, then also many women are around. Men are much less present' (*Kalau belajar agama, ada ramai wanita. Mana-mana saja. Kalau ada kelas die masjid, pun ada ramai wanita. Lelaki ada kurang*), she said. This woman, who was in her early 60s, as well as the woman behind me in her 40s, did not have an upcoming *umrah* trip ahead; they participated in the course only for reasons of learning (*belajar*).

One week previously, my 64-year-old respondent Mawar had invited me to one of the fortnightly *Qur'an* classes she organised in a prayer room (*surau*) in her KL neighbourhood. Every second course was for women only. I asked her why. She said: 'Because men often don't understand. They don't really focus. What the teacher tells them goes in one ear and out the other. I myself want to understand.' Later in our conversation she said:

> There are such different people I have to serve when I'm organising the classes at the *surau*. Because some Malays are already well-educated, some are middle, some are not educated in the *Qur'an* at all. I first attended a course for the high class, like for professors, doctors, lecturers, those who are well-educated. But then I changed to the middle-educated ones. (19 August 2017)

The situation at the *umrah* preparation course and Mawar's organisation of her *Qur'an* course indicate females' strong desire to learn about Islam (see Sullins 2006). Mawar, furthermore, pinpoints the high proportion of educated, middle- or upper-class Muslim women who actively engage in their belief. Gender (being female), Islam (being a pious Muslim), class, economic abilities (being middle- or upper-class) and ethnicity (being Malay) need to be understood in their intersectional relatedness and mutual interdependencies in order to comprehend contemporary pilgrimage undertaken by Malay Malaysian women (and men). These entanglements, in turn, need to be addressed in the context of the multicultural and multireligious orientation of Malaysian state policies, as these inform the intersectionally related identifications and structures.

Islamic revival, Malay supremacy and the 'new Malay middle class'

Multiculturalism in Malaysia is created by segregating society into *Bumiputera* (Malays and so-called native people such as *Orang Asli*,

Orang Ulu, Anak Negeri), Chinese, Indians and Others. The theoretical concept of multiculturalism implies the opportunity for cultural recognition of certain ethnic or cultural groups (in this case Malays), but simultaneously excludes other cultural actors (so-called native people, Chinese, Indians, Others). Although native people are classified as *Bumiputera*, they do not enjoy the same privileges as Malays because this classification exists only on a formal, strategic level, not on a practical level. The classification of Malaysian society into *Bumiputera*, Chinese, Indians and Others is done in an essentialist way and prevents intercultural exchange (Goh and Holden 2009: 3). Hence, multiculturalism in Malaysia forms the basis for ethnic segregation.

'Ethnicity' as a theoretical concept of social and cultural anthropology does not describe certain characteristics of groups of people, but a fluid and often powerful relationship (see Goh *et al.* 2009; Holst 2012). Ethnicity is the relationship between two or more groups who believe that they differentiate themselves culturally from others (Gingrich 2008: 102). 'Culture' is used here to constitute ethnic identification through corresponding processes of differentiation.

Despite Malaysia's cultural diversity, its government has legitimised a cultural Malay supremacy in Malaysia (*ketuanan Melayu*) since independence. This supremacy is also linked to religion, as Sunni Islam has been established by the constitution (*ketuanan Islam*) as the compulsory religion for Malay Malaysians (Hefner 2001: 29). This supremacy of Muslim Malays has been linked to class, as the government under the leadership of UMNO induced positive economic transformations of the Malay Malaysian population. In the 1970s, the government introduced the *Dasar Ekonomi Baru*, or New Economic Policy (NEP), between 1971 and 1991 after so-called 'racial riots' between Malay and Chinese Malaysians in 1969 (Kua 2007; Thimm 2014a: 83ff). These programmes were followed by the National Development Policy (1991 until 2001) and the National Vision Policy (Chong 2005: 50). By means of the NEP, the government aimed at broadening access to education and the labour market for Malay Malaysians (Norani 1998: 173), whereby this population was meant to experience direct social and economic strengthening.

The corresponding economic development was interlinked with governmental strategies of local modernisation. The 1980s in Malaysia under Prime Minister Mahathir Mohamad were shaped by economic growth and the constant development of new, 'modern' economic projects which were connected to 'Malay culture' and Islam. Islamic banking was established in 1983 through the foundation of Malaysia's first Islamic bank *Bank Islam* as a means to integrate Muslim Malays into the modern economy (Rudnyckyj 2017a: 274). Through this kind of 'new Malay capitalism' (Hefner 2001: 30), or rather 'new Muslim Malay capitalism', the ideology of Malay and Muslim supremacy (*ketuanan Melayu* and *ketuanan Islam* respectively) was institutionally enshrined and gained political credibility. The policies of the developmentalist state were realised successfully. Malaysia has been developed from a state characterised by agriculture to an industrialised, 'modern' state with a strong middle class within the last four decades: whereas 54 per cent of the total labour force was involved in agriculture in 1970, in 1990, 28 per cent and in 1998, only 16.8 per cent of the total labour force was working in agriculture. Simultaneously, the labour force in the production sector increased from 8.7 per cent in 1970 to 19.5 per cent in 1990 and to 27 per cent in 1998 (Abdul Rahman 2001: 83; see Saravanamuttu 2001: 106f). The number of executives and managers in the Malay population rose from 5,000 in 1970 to 54,000 in 1990. The number of Malay academics and professionals rose from 34,000 in 1980 (comprising 9.1 per cent of the working population in KL) to 59,000 in 1990 (comprising 12.4 per cent of the working population in KL) (Chong 2005: 50). Mawar is part of this developed middle class.

Malay Malaysian women in particular have benefited from these policies of 'neoliberal multiculturalism' (Goh and Holden 2009: 10). The newly created access to formal education and the labour market was now available as much to women as to men (Norani 1998: 173). The reasons behind women beginning to benefit from NEP were wide-ranging. In the course of the transformed economic policies, the salaries of wives and daughters were regarded as necessary for a higher standard of living on the level of social actors (Ting 2007: 82). On the national level, the state needed to activate every possible labour force in order to achieve economic upturn. Being regarded as a 'cheap labour force', women were more sought-after than men (Ong 2003: 272). In addition, the NEP was embedded in state policies of modernisation that considered it democratic to allow broadened scopes of action for women. The social mobility of women has become a matter supported by state politicians, by which they can present Malaysia as a 'modern state' in both domestic and foreign policy. Moreover, the 1950s had witnessed women's struggles as part of anti-colonial movements. In the course of these struggles and debates, women had sought to enhance their social status in society through, for example, formal education (Ng *et al.* 2007: 34). Upon Malaysia's independence from Britain in 1957, institutionalised education took on an increasingly important role for social mobility, and the period also marked greater opportunities for women.

At the level of implementing the NEP, women were first engaged in factory work. By the end of the 1970s, 80,000 women between 16 and 25 years of age from rural areas were employed in urban factories (Frisk 2009: 53). Many Malay Malaysian women from rural areas migrated to the cities in order to take advantage of the new possibilities. Between 1970 and 1980, factory jobs for women rose by 209 per cent and by 79.5 per cent for men (Chitose 1998: 103). Women who participated in the labour market for the first time also benefited from the newly introduced and expanded education establishments. The opportunity to find employment and receive an education resulted in greater social and financial independence. This changed the social status of women and so became a criterion for a 'modern Islam' (Frisk 2009: 53).

Economic growth in the urban centres of Malaysia during the last four decades has led to an enormous increase in female social mobility. More women than men now access tertiary education (Department of Statistics, Malaysia 2007: 130–4) and many women have obtained high-level positions in their jobs. This also enables them to choose between personal career and family (Stivens 2007). However, these developments are mainly applicable to women of the Malay population in Muslim Malay-dominated Malaysia, and less for women of so-called native, Chinese or Indian descent in Malaysia (Thimm 2014a). In the course of these processes, a new Malay Malaysian middle class with male and female subjects has evolved.

What has given meaning and identity to this new local middle class since the 1970s, embodied in the *Melayu Baru*, or New Malay coined by Mahathir (see Chong 2005; Norani 1998; Kahn 1996; Kessler 2001; Saravanamuttu 2001; Sharifa 2001), is a deep belief in Islam, which developed in the context of a revivalist movement (*dakwah*, literally 'salvation' or 'invitation'). Various social forces were negotiating state Islamisation and politicisation of Islam, which had grown in strength through the revolution in Iran in 1979, for example (Ufen 2008: 120). The feminised middle class has left its gendered mark on the ever-widening group of pious Muslims and this, in turn, finds its expression in the *umrah* preparation course and Mawar's *Qur'an* classes, which women use to educate themselves in their belief.

The Islamic self-confidence in Malaysia emerged due to internal and external politics. In the context of this evolving national consciousness, urban middle-class Malay Malaysians, especially university students, founded various groups and movements. Some of them were highly orthodox, such as the Islamic Party of Malaysia (*Parti Islam Se-Malaysia*, PAS) (see Müller 2014), which has been very influential in the northern states of the country; some of these groups and movements aim for an Islamic state and partly want to implement religious-orthodox principles, such as *hudud*, i.e. punishments which are mandated under Islamic law (*syariah*). The PAS's identity politics were directed against expanding consumer markets in the context of globalisation (see Fischer, J. 2008) and are opposed to materialism and consumption, which have gained great importance for the Malay middle class, as we will see in chapters 3 and 4 when it comes to the consumption of *umrah* & *ziarah* travel packages and female clothing on pilgrimage trips.

Islamisation and economic development have led to a direct connection between class position and piety. Involvement in Islamic belief has developed into a matter of prosperity. Malaysian writer Dina Zaman describes incredulously in her book *I am Muslim* (2007) how her religious courses, attended mainly by relatively rich women, resembled a 'Tupperware party with girlfriends' (Dina 2007: 211). One of the participants proclaimed to Dina:

> . . . the rich get more plus points with God [*pahala;* positive rewards Muslims believe they gain for their everyday religious activities and good deeds] than the poor . . . The rich have more time and resources to spend in their pursuit of goodness. The poor, even if they pray five times a day, have no time to sit and *berzikir* (recite supplications) as they have too many worries. The rich are able to spread their wealth in the name of charity and Islam. (Dina 2007: 211)

Dina is upset about this attitude and comments in her book: 'I just think religion sure doesn't come cheap these days. You gotta be a freakin' millionaire to go to heaven . . . It's great to know that you [Malaysian fellows] take religious education seriously, but does it have to come with a price-tag?' (Dina 2007: 213). This connection between class status and religiosity will be discussed in chapters 3–6, when being affluent enough to afford an *umrah* journey, including expensive souvenirs, and to become, in turn, more devout because of pilgrimage, plays a role for my respondents.

Female bodies in the context of Islamic revival

Rivalry between different Islamisation projects has led to an ideological transformation of gender concepts (Stivens 2013: 148). These developments have affected practices of clothing and embodiment by Muslim

Malay Malaysian women. With reference to Islam, the Islamic movements and the government demand that all women be demure and modest. The *aurat* has become an important focus. These are the body parts one should not expose to the opposite gender if one could potentially enter into marriage. This is based on the concept of *mahram*, which defines the relationship between two genders who are eligible or not eligible to marry according to Islamic concepts of kinship. My respondent Farish explained the relationship between bodies and social relationships in detail:

> You need to close the *aurat* when it comes to certain relationships. My *mahram* is my wife, my daughter, my son. My blood sister is *mahram* to my son, so they can touch each other. My blood brother can touch hands with my daughter. I can touch hands with the sons and daughters of my blood brother and blood sister. But my son and my daughter, they cannot touch hands with them! Because they are cousins. They can get married. They are not *mahrams* to each other. Those who are married into the family, they are also *mahrams*. My wife and my father, they can also touch. (6 July 2017)

The female's *aurat* includes more parts of the body, such as hair, arms, legs and neck, than the male's *aurat*, which is only from navel to knees. As a common practice resulting from this, women are supposed to wear, among other things, a veil (*tudung*) when they interact with males whom they are eligible to marry. According to certain orthodox interpretations of Islamic principles, Muslim women must cover the *aurat* due to male sexual desire. When I asked my respondent Siti, who identifies with the norms of the *dakwah* organisation *Angkatan Belia Islam Malaysia* (Muslim Youth Movement of Malaysia), why Muslim women should cover their hair and skin, she answered that men will be sexually attracted if women show too much skin. 'A woman covers her hair and skin in order to protect herself against men and their sexual desire. It is necessary that women wear a headscarf and long clothes,' she said, 'because every woman is naturally pretty and attractive – no matter whether she looks like a model or whether she is fat' (29 April 2009).

Since the early 1980s, devout female Muslims in Malaysia have extensively worn the *tudung*, a headscarf that covers the hair and neck, or the *hijab*, which comes down to the waist and obscures the silhouette of the female body. Women often wear the headscarf together with the traditional Malay *baju kurung*, which consists of a long, wide coloured skirt and a blouse. Many women additionally wear socks, some even gloves or a veil covering the face (*purdah* or *niqab*[6]). This kind of clothing was unknown to Malay Malaysians until the rise of political Islamisation in the 1970s and 1980s (Ong 2003: 279). By wearing the *tudung* or *hijab* and additional garments, such as socks, in male connoted public space, distinct parts of women, namely their bodies, are in the end located in the domestic sphere (Stivens 2006: 357). How these embodied practices play a particularly important role for my respondents following their pilgrimage experiences will be discussed in detail in chapters 4 and 5.

The practice of wearing clothing which covers the female body can be regarded as restrictive at first sight. In fact, these developments have been highly ambivalent: the *dakwah* movement in Malaysia in particular regulates the spaces of action of female Malay Malaysian university students. Even if Malaysian women are encouraged by the state to educate themselves, they do not achieve complete autonomy within this area. Women must be protected from 'Western' influences and male sexual desire in public spaces. The various university campuses in Malaysia were centres of the most intensive *dakwah* campaigns to cover women's bodies. Many male and female students turned to (orthodox) Islam in the 1970s and 1980s. One reason for this was a ban on active political association since 1971: the Universities and University College Act bans participation in party political structures and, furthermore, any kind of party membership. In this situation, Islam offered an alternative for social engagement, so that the *dakwah* movement took root especially amongst university students (Frisk 2009: 46f). The *dakwah* movement's demands regarding clothing became a symbol for the 'educated woman' (Ong 2003: 281). These devout, modestly dressed, educated women are those women Mawar was referring to when talking about her women-only *Qur'an* classes.

Since educated and professionally active women are a characteristic of 'modern' societies, the clothing of Malay Malaysian university students, however, became a symbol for a unique modernity. 'The veiled middleclass woman in particular is a symbol of a specifically Malay modernity that has deep ethnic and class repercussions,' notes cultural anthropologist Maila Stivens (1998: 117). Additionally, 'modern', educated Malay Malaysian middle-class women gained the opportunity to negotiate social relationships in urban space by wearing this type of clothing. Furthermore: '[W]omen become important religious and political agents through the emergence of the veil as a symbol of politicised Islam within modernity' (Stivens 2006: 358).

We can see that the development and intensification of Islamic dressing in Malaysia for females since the 1970s evolved when a so-called 'modern Islam' was appearing. From an institutional and governmental perspective, being a state dedicated to a 'modern Islam' means, among other things, equalising women with men in terms of status, economic and educational possibilities, as we have seen above. According to Islamic understanding, God does not differentiate between men and women: when it comes to His judgment of Muslims on judgment day (*hari qiamat*), the criteria are piety, morality and the performance of good or bad deeds and not gender identity. However, on the level of everyday life, men and women are expected to differentiate from one another according to their gender. Whereas Islam pursues equity of gender on a formal level, Muslims produce and reproduce gender differentiation on a practical level and negotiate this regarding unequal power structures. Against this backdrop, orthodox Muslim clothing for females was introduced, broadened and emphasised in Malaysia during the Islamic revival, when women's status was equalised on a social level based on education and involvement in the labour market. One crucial reason for emphasising orthodox Islamic clothing for females, therefore, was – I argue – to maintain and clarify visibly the ideological assumption that females are still different to males. This is pertinent not only to everyday clothing but also to the garments worn on pilgrimage. As I have argued elsewhere (Thimm 2021), all Muslim men worldwide – the entire male *ummah* – wear two pieces of white cloth (*kain ihram*) during *hajj*. Women, however, just wear their normal clothing according to their cultural backgrounds and individual preferences. My 15-year-old respondent Siti Sabrina linked this condition to the ideological approach to gender roles:

Siti Sabrina: I like the idea of *hajj*. They wear *kain ihram* then and this symbolises that all are equal. Nobody is wearing Gucci or something like that, no one is better than anyone else. There are no rich and no poor, everyone is the same. It's also not allowed to wear perfume; it follows the same idea. It's only between you and God and nobody is supposed to show off. Nobody is supposed to wear something glittering.

Viola: But women don't wear *kain ihram*, so what's the idea then for the women?

Siti Sabrina: Ya, I think they don't wear it because they cannot wear the same as the males. Women and men are different. So, they cannot wear the same because otherwise it would mean that they are all the same gender. (24 September 2017)

The development of conservative Islamic clothing for females in 1970s Malaysia was a consequence of the wider social, political and economic opportunities for girls and women in that country. The latest development regarding female Muslim clothing in Malaysia came about only recently: since about 2012/13, the trend has emerged of wearing the *abaya* – the female garment from the Arab Gulf that is central to this study. The development of and meaning assigned to the *abaya* will be discussed in depth in chapter 4.

'The family': Islamic and 'modern' concepts

Islamisation and modernisation strategies affected not only women's bodies and representations, as demonstrated above, but also their roles within the family. 'The family', which in Malaysia is constructed as the 'Asian family' by official and social actors, is a politicised field. Representations of the Asian family are embedded in discourses on Asian values which are enforced by the state and certain Muslim and Islamic institutions. These values have been conceptualised not as religious but as regional (Asian), since the discourse is embedded in similar dynamics in Chinese-dominated Singapore, which is explicitly not Muslim in its majority and institutional and state strategies and objectives. Malaysia orients itself towards the discourses in its neighbour state. Core elements of the Asian family are respect towards elders and strong bonds within the extended family. In this way, the family is conceptualised as a 'secure space', in contrast to unwelcome elements of 'Western modernisation'. By juxtaposing 'Asian values' and 'Western values', the government suggests an alternative 'Asian' or rather Malaysian way of modernisation based on emphasising the Asian family model (Stivens 2000: 25). Women's roles within this family discourse are a field of political debate:

> Women, and by extension the family . . . become the site of the struggle between state power and revivalist Islam over the changing nature of Malaysian society. Anxieties associated with the process of modernisation are channeled into women. (Frith 2002: 3)

Constructions of femininity, masculinity and family were transformed in the 1970s on both ideological and practical levels. The tension between *dakwah* initiatives and *adat*, which are the local Malay traditions and customs, are of relevance for the transformative process. *Adat* rules, regulations and customs are basically bilateral and cognatic

(Hirschman 2016: 36; see Wazir Jahan 1995). Local conditions and historical reciprocal effects of *adat* and Islam have shaped Malay perceptions and practices of kinship, residency and property (Wazir Jahan 1995: 44, 1992: xiii). Based on *adat* values, Malay women were neither bound to the household nor economically dependent on men, even though the latter had been enjoying privileges relating to religion and property before the 1970s (Zainah 2001: 232). The Malay Malaysian *adat* exists contemporaneously with and is entangled with Islamic values and concepts. Hierarchical gender differences, which are emphasised by elements of the government, the *dakwah* movement and many *Qur'an* schools, are constrained by the bilaterality of the *adat*. However, the growing Islam in Malaysia in the 1970s and 1980s weakened the bilateral principles of *adat*. The local *adat* practice, for example, of providing daughters and sons with the same amount of land, yielded to the Sunni Shafi'i law to give only a half-share to daughters (Ong 2003: 265). Men's control over domestic resources has generally been strengthened since the 1970s and 1980s based on such changes (Ong 2003: 265; see Wazir Jahan 1995, 1992). The entanglements between *adat* and Islam concerning family ideologies and practices will be relevant in chapter 5.

Above all, the *dakwah* movement had a stake in the patrilineal influence on the Malay Malaysian family concept (see Sharifa 2001; Ufen 2008; Warnk 2008). The empowerment of Malay Malaysian women provoked this movement. When, in the 1970s and 1980s, tens of thousands of young Malay Malaysian women migrated autonomously into the cities for reasons of work, the *dakwah* movement felt threatened, as Ong (2003: 281) notes: many male *dakwah* supporters feared that they must restrict their authority in the social public realm on the basis of the strong presence of Malay Malaysian women in the modern economy.

Ever since, various *dakwah* groups and institutions have focused on women's role in the Malay Malaysian family. They emphasise that wives are, first and foremost, obligated to their husbands and that they should obey their husbands in the same way as Muslims should submit to Allah. This emphasis on obedient wives has been perceived as an appropriate ideology by urban Malay Malaysian middle-class women. Ong (2003: 281) assumes that women comply with this role through a fear of losing their new economic and social status. In chapter 5, however, I will discuss how the women involved in the present study do not understand this complex as a contradiction; rather they submit to the husband in alignment with submission to God on the basis of pilgrimage experiences.

The hierarchical ideology of the Muslim family that the *dakwah* movement introduced into social debate was subsequently embraced by state policies. In this way, it was connected to bourgeois concepts of the family. In the *Fifth Malaysia Plan 1986–1990*, the government under PM Mahathir Mohamad propagated the ideal Malay Malaysian woman solely as a mother based on Islamic assumptions. This gender ideology is held up as a central function from the governmental side because it should create political stability:

> [T]he role of women in family development will continue to remain important in helping to build a united, just, stable, and progressive society through the inculcation of good and lasting values in their children. (Malaysian Government 1986: 28, quoted in Frith 2002: 8)

Gender roles were codified on the state level in family legislation in the 1980s/1990s. At that time, the government highlighted the concept of *keluarga*: a bourgeois nuclear family, with the man as head and breadwinner, the woman as housewife, and, ideally, two dependant children (Ong 2003: 269). This was not in accordance with Malay Malaysian norms of having up to six children, especially in rural areas, and living together in one household with several nuclear families. The concept of *keluarga*, with the corresponding Muslim connoted gender roles, has been increasingly achieved by the state side, but not fully. The proportion of nuclear families rose within all ethnic populations from 60 to 65 per cent between 1991 and 2000. The percentage of male heads of households has risen steadily too. In 1991, 81.5 per cent of all Malaysian heads of household were male, and in 2000 the number rose to 86.1 per cent (Department of Statistics, Malaysia 2005: 129). *Bumiputeras* form the largest households with an average of 4.8 people, while the households of Indian Malays comprise 4.6 persons on average and those of Chinese Malaysians, 4.2 persons on average (Department of Statistics, Malaysia 2005: xlvii). Amongst the *bumiputeras,* six or more people live in 34 per cent of their households, whereas only 26 per cent of Indian Malaysian families live in households with more than six people (Department of Statistics, Malaysia 2005: 125).

The government intermingles the political stability that should be created based on family and gender ideologies and practices predominantly with Islamic stipulations. A patrilinear family model, with the father as head and protector of the family and the mother playing a warm and supportive role, has been transmitted in state campaigns on 'the happy family' ever since (Stivens 2007, 2000: 25f; Zainah 2001: 227f). In chapter 5, however, it will be shown that the female social actors in this study certainly perform roles as mothers, but they are simultaneously agents in their families with their own income, rather than being solely 'warm and supportive'.

The embeddedness of the family model in diverse discourses on religious values – Muslim (as they are lived) and Islamic (as they are normatively formulated) – is crucial for an understanding of Malaysian – and thereby Malay – nationalism (Stivens 2006: 355). According to the discourse on Asian values and through the location of women in the family and their motherly duties, women are especially responsible for the reproduction of the population and, therefore, of the workforce in the capitalist system. Women are perceived as being essential for a harmonious family, which, in turn, is crucial for the well-being of the nation: '[In Malaysia], [f]amily values [operate] as a unified and unifying national metaphor' (Stivens 2006: 364). The *dakwah* movement and the ruling elites are of the opinion that women carry the moral duty to create and to nourish the 'modern' Malay Malaysian community. Malay Malaysian women become bearers of cultural values, traditions and Muslim Malaysian symbols based on their ideological role as mothers, which they (should) transmit to their children (Norani 1998: 176). In chapter 5, however, it will be shown that recently fathers have appropriated the role of bearer of values, at least of specifically Muslim and Islamic values, as a consequence of their pilgrimage experience. Nevertheless, Malay Malaysian women are the ones who are stylised as a symbol of cultural values and nationalism (Ng *et al.* 2007: 140f).

Women are not only assigned the role of (nationally responsible) mothers but also wives. In 1990, the government introduced the 'Muslim marriage and family preparation course' (*kursus bimbingan perkahwinan dan keluarga Islam*), which offers teachings on the expectations of women and men (Norani 1998: 185; Roziah 2003: 128). This course is compulsory for all Malay Malaysians who get married for the first time. The course works as follows: every couple needs to pay 200 RM, or rather, every individual has to pay 100 RM for the course. The couple can attend the course in different locations if it is not possible for them to participate in the same location. It is crucial that they can show the corresponding certificate upon registering for marriage. This certificate is valid for one's lifetime; thus, the course only needs to be attended once in a lifetime, even if a person remarries. During the course, the responsibility and authority of the husband is stressed, while the wife should orientate herself towards the husband. My married respondent Fauzana praised the course as useful and was pleased about the content she was taught. Concerning the couple's responsibilities she stated:

> The contents of the pre-marriage course are mostly about the responsibility as a husband and as a wife. The husband should provide all the needs, like paying for house instalments, car, groceries and children. If the wife ever wants to work to contribute to the family income, that is up to her . . . They also taught in the course that the wife should always pay respect to her husband. (Email from Fauzana, 4 December 2009)

The tension between the economic reality of Malay Malaysian women and the patrilineal ideology is solved, as taught in the marriage and family preparation course, by perceiving the wife's income as 'additional' or 'supportive'. Consequently, contradictions between women who want to gain autonomy and economic independence, on the one hand, and the risk of matrimonial conflicts, on the other, can be resolved (Raj, Ri. *et al.* 2001: 122).

A wife can be a second, third or fourth wife, as polygyny is allowed in the Malay Malaysian population according to *syariah* law[7] under certain conditions, including the agreement of the existing wife/wives and the equal financial protection of all wives by the husband (Maznah 2009: 103f; Stivens 2000: 26f). Independent women of the Malay Malaysian middle class especially perceive this option as a threat to their quality of life, as some respondents told me sorrowfully. Adilah, for example, feared neglect by the husband as a potential second wife: according to her experiences, husbands with more than one wife usually prefer the first wife, especially when it comes to public occasions. Thus, being a good husband and, in this sense, performing 'good virility' is measured by his financial well-being and by his authority over the women in the household – which implies, among other things, control over the sexual expression of the wife or wives (Ong 2003: 267). This aspect will be discussed further in chapter 5, when concepts and practices of sexuality, gender roles, corporeality and the role that clothing plays therein will be examined.

These manifold developments regarding gender ideologies and roles, embodiment and middle class had an impact on the habits of the new middle class as well – especially the consumer culture that developed. This will be discussed below as it forms the backdrop to an understanding of contemporary consumption practices of pilgrimage packages and Muslim clothing, such as the *abaya*.

Islam – religion as an engine for economy:
Malaysia as *halal* hub

In an interview with 34-year-old Marid in a subcultural café in TTDI (Taman Tun Dr Ismail, a neighbourhood in Petaling Jaya near KL), he started the conversation by saying that he could not mention publicly that he is a non-practising Muslim who eats pork and drinks beer. He calls himself a 'liberal', but, being embedded in pious Sufi family structures, he can reflect on Islamic issues in Malaysia from both outsider and insider perspectives simultaneously. He said:

> What I noticed when I drive down from Petaling Jaya towards Bangi, you have to take the North-South-Expressway, there are so many billboards along the highway. My friend informed me that a lot of these billboards are illegal. But the content of the surprising majority of these billboards are *Muslimah* products and very like aggressively marketed. I even have no idea what the products are. But from what I can see is that these products are either targeted at women and they are beauty products.
>
> There will most often be a sex sell in that, there will be a beautiful woman wearing a *tudung*, like very well made up, endorsing a product like diamond face cream, or collagen, and then there is this other brand of product called '*Mesra Wuduk*', with the woman with the full mask [*niqab*], prerogatively we call it 'Ninja-*lah*'! [laughs]. This woman is very sexualised; we can only see her eyes and wonder what she looks like. I have no idea what the product is about. But I'm assuming it's for some very personal feminine product. But my question is also 'Why?' When you see all these kinds of images, all this commodified Islam on these billboards, you can see 'Is there this dominant kind of market? Is there this growing market for Islamic products?' (9 October 2017)

Six weeks before this interview, in August 2017, I visited 'Halfest' in Serdang. Halfest is the largest consumer fair and exhibition in Malaysia, organised by HDC (the Halal Industry Development Corporation). At Halfest, I was introduced to the product '*Mesra Wuduk*' [intimate ritual washing] that Marid had mentioned (see figure 2.4): a soap which is particularly suitable for washing away cosmetics when a woman does her *wuduk*, the ritual washing before formal prayer (*solat*), so that she is free from the remains of makeup during prayer. Marid's words, the *halal* fair and the involvement of HDC refer to an entangled complexity of

Figure 2.4   The '*Mesra Wuduk*' (intimate ritual washing) booth at Halfest, Serdang, Malaysia, 2017.

marketing *halal* ('allowed' according to *syariah*) products, a high degree of feminine and sexualised products in this segment, and an institutionalised approach to the marketisation of Islam in Malaysia.

While '*halal*' and its counterpart '*haram*' ('forbidden' according to *syariah*) originally applied to food products (for example it is *haram* – forbidden – to eat pork and to drink alcohol), this classification has been broadened to clothing (*Muslimah* wear) and cosmetics (*Mesra Wuduk*), and also to the travel industry within the past decade. Unlike Bianchi (2016: 139), I argue that Malaysia is at the heart of this process through the professionalisation and industrialisation of the so-called *halal* industry by being at the forefront of standardising *halal* certification.

Commodification of Islam finds its expression in the *halal* industry, which encompasses the fashion, travel and food industries, the pharmaceutical sector, Islamic insurance (*takaful*) and the Islamic finance system. The latter is of particular importance in Malaysia. This economy, or 'Islamic capitalism', developed in Malaysia under PM Mahathir

Mohamad with the aim of opposing Western modernity projects, and was embedded in the wider discourse of Asian values. Islamic capitalism seeks the identification of Islamically 'authentic' concepts based in the *Qur'an* which stress support for and protection of individual rights to private property, commercial honesty and competition tempered by concern for the disadvantaged. Islamic banks are a highly developed example of Islamic capitalism: they seek to centralise investment and power, while sharing risk and profit and avoiding interest payments at fixed rates (Kuran 2005; Rudnyckyj 2019, 2017a, 2017b, 2013; Tripp 2006: 46–76). This segment, which coexists with conventional capitalist banking in Malaysia inherited from the British, is of huge importance for the Malaysian state, which aims at making 'Kuala Lumpur the "New York of the Muslim World"' (Rudnyckyj 2013: 832).

In 2006, the Malaysian government under PM Abdullah Ahmad Badawi decided to develop Malaysia, as a 'modern, progressive and politically stable Muslim country' (HDC, n.d., a), as the worldwide *halal* hub (Fischer, J. 2018, 2016; Rudnyckyj 2013). Islam, as part of the economy, has been part of the picture in Malaysia in the form of 'halalisation' (Fischer, J. 2008) – and therefore religionisation (see Weller 2011: 16) – of the market since the 2000s. This followed the period of economic development and Islamic revival in the first era of PM Mahathir Mohamad in the 1980s, as discussed above. Imagining 'that Malaysia should lead the change in the global *halal* industry' (HDC, n.d., b: 5) brings the previously somewhat unconnected areas of Islamisation and economic development together as one, or rather as *the* 'new source of economic growth' (HDC, n.d., b: 5).

A first milestone that placed Malaysia at the centre of the worldwide *halal* industry was the release of the first *halal* standards in 2000, when Malaysia became the first country in the world to have a documented and systematic *halal* assurance system. According to this system, *halal* food and goods are defined, among other things, as follows: (1) they do not contain any part of a forbidden animal, such as pork, and they have been slaughtered according to *syariah*; (2) they do not contain any part of a human being or its yield; and (3) they are not poisonous or hazardous to health (Aiedah 2018: 201). In 2005, the swift progress of *halal* certification in Malaysia prompted the Jabatan Kemajuan Islam Malaysia (JAKIM; Department of Islamic Development Malaysia), the agency responsible for Islamic affairs, including *halal* certification, to extend its *halal* section to form a larger organisation: JAKIM's *Halal* Hub. This was the second milestone. JAKIM was the world's first *halal* certification body, responsible for monitoring *halal* food products and pharmaceuticals by introducing and controlling the Malaysian *halal* logo and its related processes. A product certified with a *halal* logo issued by JAKIM always means that it is simultaneously *halal* and *toyyib* (clean) and, thus, indicates the quality and safety of the food and its production process. In 2015, JAKIM issued 744 *halal* certifications to Malaysian hotels and resorts, of which 80 per cent were issued to non-Muslim companies. The Malaysian *halal* logo is considered to be 'the most sought-after, globally-recognised hallmark that serves as an emblem for the country's reputation as the world's leading *halal* hub' (ITC, n.d.), as evidenced by the use of the Malaysian *halal* standards by international companies such as Nestlé and Unilever. This dynamic process was a means to boost the nation-state's reputation, especially in Asia and the Muslim world beyond, and thus became a powerful advertising instrument.

Building on this, the government founded HDC, the corporation that organised Halfest mentioned above, in 2006 as a subsequent milestone, under the Ministry of International Trade and Industry, to realise the strategy of becoming a *halal* hub. Malaysian *halal* standards led the United Nations to cite Malaysia as 'the best example of *halal* labelling' (HDC, n.d., b: 5). The relevance of Malaysia's position as a *halal* hub, with an annual export value of 39.3 billion RM for *halal* products in 2016, becomes obvious when considering that Gulf states, which are generally perceived to be the so-called 'centre of Islam' and, therefore, the benchmark for Islamic principles, began to follow Malaysia's example. I visited HDC four times between July and September 2017 and spoke to various representatives who pinpointed, amongst other things, the relationship between the two regions:

Farish: In Middle Eastern countries, they don't have any certification, because we rely on the government over there.

Haneefah: People will even feel offended when you ask them 'Is it *halal*?' They will say something like 'Of course it's *halal*! It's *halal* by nature! We are in Saudi [Arabia]!' Because being in Saudi, everything will be *halal*. They don't sell pork and they don't sell alcohol, so we are fine over there. We don't even think about it there. But just recently, it was last year, the Emirates [UAE] applied for a certification. And it was like 'Oh, there is the first Arab country which announces that they are *halal*.' That's so weird, because in every Arab country all the food is *halal*, there is no issue about it. So then nine countries like the Emirates, Saudi, Bahrain, Egypt, Morocco, Jordan . . .

nine countries without war applied for the certification and introduced it just last year.

Viola: Why did they do it?

Farish: Because of the market in Southeast Asia. They noticed that we [Malaysia] are the hub for *halal* products and they realised that they need to follow. Because they see the potential of this industry. If they want to export their products to Southeast Asia, it's better for them to have a certificate. (13 July 2017)

The UAE's orientation towards Malaysia in terms of its *halal* standards is relevant not only for food products but also for *halal* tourism ('Islamic tourism' in Malaysia) and clothing as two sections of the *halal* industry. Below, I will zoom into the travel and fashion industries, as these form the broader socio-political and economic context for the consumption dynamics of the (fashionable and sexy) *abaya*, on the one hand, and of pilgrimage packages, on the other.

'Islamic tourism' and 'modest fashion'

A cornerstone of the development of the tourism industry as a *halal*-related segment was the foundation of the Islamic Tourism Centre (ITC) in 2009 under the Ministry of Tourism. Muzakir, one of the ITC's directors, explained to me the concept of Islamic tourism in Malaysia:

> We were set up to promote Malaysia as an Islamic Tourism destination. The Ministry [of Tourism] noticed the trend of Arab Tourists or basically Muslim tourists coming into Malaysia after the 9/11 incident. So, our goal is to facilitate these tourists coming to Malaysia . . . The services we are trying to offer are, for example, meant to help Muslim travellers to find a mosque or *surau* (prayer room). So that they can go to the park and find a place to stop by and pray. And also, to help them to find clean toilets, *halal* restaurants and *halal* hotels which must have at least one *halal*-certified kitchen. We already have our standards for *halal* food and now we are trying to extend it further to services: to accommodation, restaurants, package-tours and tour guides. So, we would like to basically come out with some kind of guidelines but with strong authority, basically to benchmark. (13 December 2013)

The strategy of establishing and intensifying so-called 'Islamic tourism' has helped to create an industrial sector that combines and sometimes even interweaves the religious and spiritual with tourism – on both practical and conceptual levels. The meaning and role of '*ziarah*' as a blurred form of leisure and religious travel is of interest here as it is at the heart of this study. Fatimah, a representative of the ITC whom I met three times in 2013 and 2017, talked about the entanglement of *ziarah* and Islamic tourism:

> *Ziarah* and Islamic tourism are about the same. Some packages for *umrah* include *ziarah* in the package. Islamic tourism is usually similar to conventional tourism but with an added Islamic value . . . For example, you could go for golf. But in the meantime, as a Muslim, you still have to stop for prayers and have *halal* food. When you use 'Islamic tourism', it refers to a *ziarah* with an Islamic element. Because *ziarah* can just be anything, like normal tourism. So, using '*ziarah*' when relating to Islamic tourism means to bring it back to visits being done in an Islamic nature. (25 May 2017)

Fatimah noted that *ziarah* packages which are part of *umrah* are conceptually aligned with the strategies and practices of Islamic tourism, and are thus part of the same move to 'religionise' the (travel) economy. 'Malaysia, I would say, was the first of all countries in the world establishing this centre [ITC] to focus on a Muslim traveller's needs,' Fatimah stated during our conversation. The travel industry aligns its products with the government's strategy to embrace religious elements in its economy. *Ibn Ziyad*, the biggest travel agency in Malaysia with 32 branches in 2017,[8] sells a *Pakej Pelancongan Muslim* (Muslim package holiday), for example. Mohamad Any, a representative of the company, explained to me that

> *Pakej Pelancongan Muslim* is Islamic tourism. It is about the prayer times, and we visit the mosque on the trip as well as the historical areas of Islam. In Germany, for example, we go to Heidelberg, because they have a mosque there. So, for *Pelancongan Muslim*, we go to the mosque and visit the Muslim community there. (21 June 2017)

New packages are constantly being developed. Browsing through *Ibn Ziyad*'s catalogue while talking to Mohamad Any, I could see that the company had launched a religion-embedded cruise tour called *Penyucian Jiwa – Fun Islamik Cruise Untuk Semua* (Cleansing the Soul – Fun Islamic

Cruise for Everybody). Mohamad Any defines it as 'a pure Islamic cruise' with no alcohol or gambling on board. The differences between the terms 'Islamic tourism', '*Pelancongan Muslim*' and '*umrah* & *ziarah* packages' highlight that this segment of the economy is not standardised, compared to the *halal* food industry. JAKIM, which is responsible for *halal* certification in general in Malaysia, does not certify any travel packages or elements of the travel industry, such as hotels, as one JAKIM representative pointed out.

Nevertheless, while *umrah* & *ziarah* packages are not standardised or certified by a state institution, these packages – and thus this form of religious tourism – are still a distinct, standardised form of travel in Malaysia. The travel packages are located at a certain intersection between the state's promotion of religiosity in everyday life and the capitalist market. While the state does not promote *umrah* & *ziarah* directly and has not integrated such travel packages into any particular political or economic strategy, modernisation and Islamisation pervade Malaysian society and have a corresponding impact on the travel industry. The travel industry, then, is the institutional actor that developed and now promotes religious travel tours. The combination of the state's overall influence, the religious market segment and the pious needs of consumers is what makes these travel packages flourish.

These needs are in turn part of Malaysia's state Islamisation strategies. At this point, I would like to bring the political implications of *ziarah* tourism and its cultivation into dialogue with Johan Fischer's (2011) ethnography *The Halal Frontier: Muslim consumers in a globalised market*. Fischer shows how the Malaysian state uses the labelling of products with the *halal* logo to target expatriate Malay Muslims in Europe, specifically in the United Kingdom. By doing so, the Malaysian state regulates their Muslim piety and ensures their submission to the state from their living situation abroad. Similarly, the state also benefits from *umrah* & *ziarah* packages, even though they are not directly under its control or influence.

Fischer states that, 'As halal proliferates, it moves frontiers and contributes to new forms of space making, thus lifting halal out of its base in halal butcher shops into public space, advertisements, and hypermarkets' (Fischer, J. 2011: 5). In a similar vein, Islamic tourism, or *halal* tourism as it is also called, extends spirituality and religion into all areas of the touristic stopover. Thus, the proliferation of this form of tourism challenges and redraws the lines between the religious and the secular, because it is a 'global flow of religious goods' (Fischer, J. 2011: 15) in itself. This suits the Malaysian government very well, as it has faced repeated accusations of secularism since the politicisation of Islam in the 1970s. '[H]alal is promoted as bridging the religious and the secular,' as Fischer (2011: 36) states, and *umrah* & *ziarah* tours are part of this. The purity of a sacred state is ensured and promoted in this form of travel vis-à-vis the impurity of the secular.

Moreover, religious tourism in Malaysia shifts the boundaries between Southeast Asian 'peripheral Islam' and the 'Islamic centre', i.e. the Arabian Peninsula (see chapter 4). Malaysia has become the rising star in Islamic tourism. It not only established benchmarks in the *halal* industry in general but is also at the forefront of industrialising religious travel as a worldwide standard. At the time of writing, the Global Muslim Travel Index (GMTI) by Mastercard-Crescent Rating has ranked Malaysia number 1 for Muslim-friendly tourism worldwide every year since 2010. The evaluation criteria include safety, the availability of *halal* food, and prayer facilities. In 2016 and 2017, the UAE placed second, right after Malaysia (*Arabian Business*, 3 May 2017). Muslim visitors accounted for approximately 10 per cent of the global travel market in 2016, with a total of 117 million journeys undertaken. As stated in one Emirati newspaper, 'Global Islamic travel . . . is expected to keep growing at a compound annual growth rate of 5.5 per cent until 2020 . . . UAE is the fastest-growing *halal* market in the GCC region in terms of attracting or exporting *halal* tourism products. The UAE – and Dubai in particular – stands to benefit from this trend' (*The Khaleej Times*, 23 September 2015). With its stated aim of achieving 20 million visitors by 2020, Dubai strives to become a key player in the global *halal* travel industry, and thus competes directly with Malaysia.

Notably, when it comes to other segments of the *halal* industry, Dubai beats Malaysia: for example in the field of Islamic fashion. According to the State of the Global Islamic Economy Report 2018/19, the UAE ranked first among 73 countries regarding modest fashion, even though Malaysia topped the Global Islamic Economy Indicator for finance (*Arabian Business*, 29 October 2018). In Dubai, so-called 'Modest Fashion' or '*Muslimah* fashion' is generally related to the *abaya*. Arwa Al-Shujairi, a fashion blogger writing under the name *Muslimah Life*, states on the internet:

> *Abaya* fashion is officially on the runway and making a bold statement globally! . . . *Abaya* designs are more beautiful than ever before, from different colours to different cuts, it can be too overwhelming to simply choose one! Dubai has become the *fashion hub* for upcoming *abaya designers*. (*Muslimah Life*, 1 November 2015; emphasis added)

Making Islamic-related garments fashionable and situating them in the global capitalist economy through production, retail and consumption is achieved in Malaysia with a much wider variety of clothing, but male clothing is not part of this, just like in Dubai. Fashionising female Muslim clothing started with the *tudung*, the Malay headscarf, in 2012. While wearing a brown scarf with a gradient from light brown to dark brown, Masjaliza told me:

> The *tudung* has become more fashionable over the past one or two years. We have such a variety of scarves now, with different layers and different colours. The *tudung* became a fashion-thing, it wasn't like this before. Only six years ago, the Ariani headscarf developed, which is the one that is ready-made to wear, you don't need to fold and pin it yourself around your head. You just pull it over and it's ready to wear. This *tudung* now came up with designs for oval, angular and round faces, so the design has developed. The one I'm wearing right now is a very simple one. I don't want to wear the colourful ones and Ramli [her husband] also says 'You shouldn't wear those fashionable ones; you look like a rainbow!' [giggling] (11 January 2014)

Masjaliza then raised the issue of femininity as part of the fashionisation of Muslim female garments:

> I have a colleague who says that wearing a colourful *tudung* makes her prettier. Because she can decorate herself with it. This is true because we as Malays only have black hair, right? Maybe you can dye it with red colour or something like that but apart from this there is nothing much you can do with it. But when you wear a *tudung*, you can make your head very colourful! Ramli says, as a mother, I shouldn't wear these colourful ones. (11 January 2014)

Meanwhile, *Muslimah wear* is widely promoted in Malaysia and encompasses scarves, dresses, skirts, *abayas*, *baju kurung* and other clothing items. Many local designers create their own sought-after brands which make women look 'modest, chic and fashionable', as noted by one Malaysian lifestyle blog (TallyPress, 13 November 2015). Five hundred scarf and Muslim fashion brands were recorded in Malaysia in 2017 in a database created by *Moslema In Style* (*The Malay Mail*, 4 October 2015), a KL-based company that aims at supporting Muslim fashion designers. This number shows how lucrative this industry is.

The *abaya* is sometimes regarded not only as a fashionable, but also as sexy. Masjaliza's colleague wears the *tudung* to look prettier, but also started to wear an *abaya* in 2012 because she feels that it makes her sexier, as Masjaliza incredulously told me. This aspect emphasises the fact that *Muslimah wear* is at the intersection of a simultaneous selling of Islam and of sex(iness), as Marid mentioned at the beginning of this section. Hence, fashionable Islam as a strategy and an economic segment, in this case, is aimed only at women.

This segment is bound not only to gender but also to class. When the Malaysian fashionista Vivy Yusof launched her dUCk scarf 'Al-Hambra', inspired in its design by the carvings of the Alhambra in Granada, Spain, for the Muslim feast of *Hari Raya* in 2017 for a price of 300 RM, it sold out in her store at the luxury Pavilion mall in KL within 30 minutes (*New Straits Times*, 30 May 2017). Earlier that year, an 800 RM scarf by the same brand sold out within five minutes. This market is dependent upon the purchasing power of consumers. The new Malay middle class, with its distinct class position and deep belief in Islam, is therefore crucial for the marketability of 'halalness'. In turn, the *halal* economy is dependent on the demand for and consumption of certain products, such as Muslim fashion and Islamic-related travel packages (for example *umrah* & *ziarah*). *Muslimah wear* and trips abroad are part of an expanding consumer culture, which, in turn, is bound to class status and an affluent society.

On the level of social actors, evolving individualism and materialism formed the background for increasing practices of consumption such as going shopping. Malls have become important domains in the ordinary lives of middle-class families for consuming goods, food and entertainment as well as for meeting friends (Fischer, J. 2008: 160f). The state enables the Malay middle class to live a modern and materially saturated life but, in return, expects from its subjects 'patriotic consumption' and, therefore, 'shopping for the state' (Fischer, J. 2008: 227). The culture of shopping malls is highly contested within the Muslim middle class in Malaysia: some reject them as immoral or *haram* temples of consumption; others reject them as places of loitering, which is neither nationally educative nor patriotic shopping for the state (Fischer, J. 2008: 165); yet others appreciate these sites as shopping opportunities and, therefore, markers of class distinction. This connection between class position and consumption as part of contemporary modern life in urban Malaysia will be discussed in chapter 4.

While 'halal', 'haram' and the notion of modesty are common principles in Islam worldwide, the way in which they are interpreted and negotiated varies depending on the socio-cultural context. As Sandıkcı and Ger (2011) indicate, and as we have seen in this section, morality, consumption and marketing also come into play. Islam and capitalism are not separable spheres in this regard (see e.g. Jafari, A. and Süerdem 2012; Kitiarsa 2011; Moors 2012: 275; Sandıkcı 2018; Sandıkcı and Ger 2011; Sandıkcı and Jafari, A. 2013). Muslim consumers are as interested in international brands as non-Muslim consumers. Muslim entrepreneurs strive to make a profit as much as any other capitalist entrepreneur does. A distinct feature, however, is cautious compliance with Islamic principles, which includes giving a share to the needy (*zakat*) on the practical level, being compassionate and generous on a moral level (Sandıkcı and Ger 2011: 494), and not being wasteful (*israf*) (Jafari, A. and Süerdem 2012: 66). The Islamic side of consumption will be at the heart of chapter 6.

In this chapter I have discussed the socio-political and economic context of this study on the national and social scales. In chapter 3 I will turn to the perceptions of particular social actors in the *halal* market regarding Malaysian *umrah* & *ziarah* Dubai packages: travellers (consumers), travel agents and tour guides (producers). Given this, the scaled analysis will shift from the national and social to the institutional.

Notes

1. *Mutawifa*, the female counterpart, only acts in Medina, namely in the *raudha*, which is a place between the prophet's grave and the *minbar* (pulpit). Due to the restricted size of the *raudha*, it requires some management to let pilgrims flow through this space as it is usually very crowded, especially during *hajj* season. The *mutawifa* regulates the practical time constraints in the women's section and advises female pilgrims when it comes to spiritual Islamic questions.
2. As Malaysia was governed by the *Pakatan Harapan* (Alliance of Hope) only between May 2018 and February 2020 and by the *Perikatan Nasional* (The National Alliance) only since February 2020, at the time of writing, no information about either their politics or policies on pilgrimage are yet available. After a political crisis, the *Yang di-Pertuan Agong* (literally 'He Who is Made Lord', Supreme Head or the King who is the constitutional monarch and head of state of Malaysia), Abdullah of Pahang, appointed the president of the *Parti Pribumi Bersatu Malaysia* (Bersatu; Malaysian United Indigenous Party), Muhyiddin Yassin, as the eighth prime minister on 29 February 2020. Without going through a general election, Muhyiddin then declared his coalition government *Perikatan Nasional* (The National Alliance). The alliance has been in power since March 2020 with a majority of one in the *Dewan Rakyat* (literally 'People's Assembly' which is the 'House of Representatives'); the narrowest majority that any government of Malaysia had up to that point. *Perikatan Nasional* (The National Alliance) was formed by *Barisan Nasional* (BN; National Front), United Malays National Organisation (UMNO), *Parti Pribumi Bersatu Malaysia* (PPBM; Malaysian United Indigenous Party), Malaysian Islamic Party (PAS), *Gabungan Parti Sarawak* (GPS; United Sarawak Party) and *Gabungan Bersatu Sabah* (GBS; United Alliance of Sabah); UMNO left the alliance in July 2020.
3. The *1Malaysia Development Berhad* [company] (1MDB) has turned from a strategic company into a political scandal that has been ongoing since 2015. In that year, Malaysia's then-Prime Minister Najib Razak (UMNO) was accused of channelling over RM 2.67 billion (approximately US$700 million) from 1MDB to his personal bank accounts. On 28 July 2020, he was

found guilty of one count of abuse of power, three counts of criminal breach of trust, and three counts of money laundering: a total of seven charges for the SRC International trial. He was sentenced to 12 years' imprisonment along with a fine of RM 210 million (US$49.5 million) (*The Guardian*, 6 July 2020; *New Straits Times*, 28 July 2020).

4. The names of travel agencies are pseudonyms.

5. One week before Kuntum left for Jeddah, Kartini, my partner Harry and I visited her in order to bid farewell to her and to hand over an envelope containing money. Kuntum explained how it works to be *upah haj*. There are two circumstances in which one can function as *upah haji*: first, for people who have passed away and were not able to perform *hajj* during their lifetime; and secondly, for sick people who are still alive but who cannot go on *hajj* because of the state of their health. One must be *hajjah* or *hajji* in order to fulfil the role as *upah haji*. On an administrative level, there are no differences to going on *hajj* for one's own purposes. When Kuntum registered herself for *hajj* with TH, she had not yet thought about functioning as an *upah haji*, which means that she could personally decide on this issue once she got the offer from TH. As an *upah haji*, one can only perform *hajj* for one other person, not for multiple people at the same time. The amount of *pahala* (positive rewards Muslims believe they gain for their everyday religious activities and good deeds) she gets, she explained, is the same as if she goes on *hajj* for herself. The only difference is the *niat*, i.e. the intention a Muslim indicates towards God when starting to perform pilgrimage. Kuntum performed *hajj* for the mother-in-law of a friend's son. She received 4,000 RM from the mother-in-law to act as *upah haji*.

6. *Purdah* is the Malay term and *niqab* the Arabic one. Both expressions are used in Malaysia, but *niqab* is used much more widely.

7. In Malaysia, *syariah* law is applied to issues regarding family status. Criminal matters are under civil law, for non-Muslims and Muslims alike.

8. Mohamad Any, who worked with the company, mentioned that *Ibn Ziyad*, which was set up in 2003, is the biggest travel agency not only in Malaysia but throughout Asia. Furthermore, it is the third biggest travel agency for *hajj* and *umrah* and in the top 10 for leisure holidays worldwide. When the company was founded, it started by selling *hajj* packages and, additionally, *umrah* packages with Saudi Airlines and Malaysian Airlines. After that, it launched *umrah* & *ziarah* Jordan, Cairo, Palestine and Syria, also in 2003. The *umrah* & *ziarah* Dubai/Abu Dhabi package has been part of its offer since 2010. It then introduced the latest packages – *umrah* & *ziarah* London, Paris, Italy and Switzerland, in 2011 and 2012. At the same time, in 2011, *Ibn Ziyad* set up its leisure department, i.e. the section dealing with tourism-only packages. A staff of 750 people work in its 32 branches and 150 are based in its KL headquarters. The *umrah* preparation course is held in the same building.

3
Marketisation of pilgrimage

Between 14 and 18 February 2018, I accompanied a group of 40 Malay Malaysian *umrah* & *ziarah* Dubai travellers and their *mutawif* throughout their four-day stopover in Dubai and Abu Dhabi: 2.5 days in the former and 1.5 days in the latter. The entire tour – the itinerary, food and accommodation – had been planned and organised by a local Emirati travel agency, including local tour guides, in line with the requirements of the Malaysian travel agency with which the pilgrims had booked their journey. On the first morning the itinerary provided a stop at *Oriental World*, a small, luxury shopping centre in Dubai where travellers can shop for carpets. The group was brought into a room where carpets were hanging on the walls. One of the vendors presented pieces of different designs and sizes. 'Every carpet is hand-made by local Emirati families and each family follows their own design. You can see golden threads and beautiful stones that are knotted into the carpet,' he explained to the group. 'The stones come from Iran or other neighbouring countries and have specific meanings: to finish one carpet, a family needs, depending on the size, between seven months and two years because the women only work on each piece once a week.' Silence amongst the Malaysian pilgrims. I could see many clueless and perplexed faces. The salesman told the group: 'If anybody is interested in the price, I can tell it to you.' Nobody asked for it, but everybody seemed to be curious. 'The small one costs 280 USD [1,090 RM], the bigger one 480 USD; the big one 880 USD and the biggest one 1,500 USD [5840 RM].' Given these astonishingly high prices, the whole thing was over for the group and everybody stood up quickly to leave the room. The vendor hastily encouraged them to go upstairs to have a look at the other things they could buy. On the upper floor were, amongst other items, textiles (shawls and *abayas*) and jewellery. Everything was extraordinarily expensive: the *abayas*, which Malaysian pilgrims usually bought for a price between 80 Dhs and 180 Dhs in the market (*souq*), were on sale for 900 to 1,100 Dhs.

Whilst upstairs I met Esah, an IT specialist from KL in her early 40s who was travelling with her husband. Irritated, she started the conversation as follows:

Esah: This is not my intention!
Viola: What's not your intention?
Esah: We should focus!
Viola: Focus on what?
Esah: Focus on our *umrah*. We have this intention to perform *umrah*. I'm here for my *ibadah* [religious obligation; act of worship], so I want to focus.

We went downstairs and left the building, heading for the tour bus which was parked between *Oriental World* and the adjoining mosque. Esah continued:

Esah: I want to do my *ibadah*, so no shopping like this in *Oriental World*, no luxury. It's distracting. Today, the day is okay, it's sightseeing only. You *can* [she emphasised] go shopping, to get souvenirs for your family and friends, but from the markets. Last time I went for direct *umrah* [without any stopover], this is better for me-*lah*. Maybe tomorrow at least I can see something about the Arab life.
Viola: You are interested in the life of the Arabs?
Esah: Yes, because Islam is out of the Arab world. So, I want to learn and study, to get more knowledge about the *kitab* [Qur'an, literally meaning 'book' in Arabic]. You know, it's not easy to go for *umrah*, you have to have money, knowledge, you have to prepare. This [she points to *Oriental World*] is distracting! This is shopping for luxury only. Maybe tomorrow I can learn about the *souq* [local markets]. They should bring us to a mosque! It's our intention to see such places!

This exchange reveals three issues: (1) there is a strong emphasis on shopping in the *ziarah* stopover itinerary offered by the travel agency; (2) pilgrims have a sincere desire to perform religious obligation on the journey; and consequently (3) there is an inconsistency between the travel agency's offer and travellers' needs. This chapter will deal with the marketisation of pilgrimage predominantly from the perspectives of travellers and the travel industry. This economic sphere will be investigated in its transnational conditions between Malaysia and the UAE or, more specifically, Dubai. The travel agencies in Malaysia and the tour operators and tour guides in Dubai are the main objects of analysis in this chapter, including their influence on and the outcome of their work for the pilgrims (their customers) and their products (pilgrimage packages).

Dealing with the strategies, perspectives and practices of these institutions and social actors requires an analysis of the conditions on an institutional scale and, therefore, on the intermediate social level as part of my framework *Scaling Holistic Intersectionality*. The analysis on this scale focuses on religion and spirituality intersecting with capitalism rather than on any intersection of these categories and practices with gender. Intersectionality is thus central to the analysis, especially in the segment of power systems – but in this case, gender is not the starting point of *Scaling Holistic Intersectionality*. In a broad sense, this chapter demonstrates how tourism, commerce and shopping enter into the spiritual journey, and thus forms the basis for discussions of *gendered shopping* in subsequent chapters. By examining local processes on the institutional scale, I am interested in: (1) what kinds of spiritual and religious practices are to be fulfilled in order to be acknowledged as an appropriate *ziarah* stopover and, more generally, as *ziarah* as such by the travellers; (2) to what extent Islamic and spiritual values and practices are transformed through absorption into local and global markets; (3) how Islamic principles, such as performing pilgrimage, are turned into commercialised goods; and (4) in what ways the relevant business actors navigate their economic requirements and the spiritual needs of their customers and consumers. Particularly in relation to the last three questions, this chapter is framed by theoretical scholarly discussions on the nexus between economy and religion, in this case Islam.

'*Ziarah*' on holiday

The incident with Esah and her group at *Oriental World* has revealed one specific element of the schedule in Dubai. To get the full picture, I want to describe how the pilgrimage package with a stopover in Dubai and Abu Dhabi is characterised. A typical itinerary of a *ziarah* stopover in Dubai and Abu Dhabi goes as follows:

> Day 1: Arrival at Abu Dhabi Airport at around 6am. The local tour guide and bus driver pick up the group, usually ranging between 15 and 40 people, aged between 2 and 80, and the group generally do not know each other. The group is transported to Dubai, which is a two-hour ride in the tour bus. The first stop (15 minutes) in Dubai is at *Dubai Marina*,

a luxury neighbourhood with skyscrapers, bars and cafés, to take pictures. Then they head to *The Palm*, an island in shape of a palm with its luxury hotel *The Palm Atlantis*. There is a 10-minute photo stop in front of the hotel. Back to the mainland and drive to *Souq Madinat Jumeirah*, a touristic shopping mall in the architectural shape of an ancient Emirati *souq*, to have a glimpse at the building. Next, a photo stop for 15 minutes at *Jumeirah Beach* to take pictures of *Burj al-Arab*, the famous opulent hotel in the form of a ship's sail. Possibly a stop at *Oriental World*, as described above. Lunch follows in the form of a South Asian buffet at *Ibrahimi Restaurant*. Then check-in to a 3-star hotel, such as Landmark Grand Hotel in the area of Deira. Following time to relax in the hotel, the tour guide takes the group to *Dubai Mall* in the evening, to show them the waterfall and aquarium inside the mall and the fountain show outside in front of *Burj Khalifa*, the tallest building in the world. Day 1 ends with a dinner buffet in Deira at around 9:30pm.

Day 2 starts with a ride at 9am to, again, *Dubai Mall* in order to go up to the top of *Burj Khalifa*. This is followed by a Western and South Asian lunch buffet. Then souvenir shopping (key chains, fridge magnets, small statues of *Burj Khalifa*, bags) at *Day to Day*, a discount department store in the area of Al Fahidi where all items are priced from Dh1 to Dh10. This is followed by a visit to Dubai Museum, which is located in the old fort of Dubai. From this point onwards, the group is exposed to the so-called 'old part of Dubai': a short ride across Dubai creek by an *abra*, a small wooden boat which holds a maximum of 10 people, brings the group to the market (*souq*) area, where spices, shawls, *abayas*, gold and kitchen utensils can be purchased. Day 2 ends, again, with a dinner buffet.

Day 3 possibly starts with a stop at the Dubai Hard Rock Café in case the pilgrims wish to visit the store and café.[1] The bus driver then takes the whole group to Abu Dhabi, where they visit the famous white *Sheikh Zayed Grand Mosque*, the largest mosque in the country, which is visited by Muslim and non-Muslim tourists alike. Dinner in Abu Dhabi stadium and overnight stay.

Day 4 starts with the Abu Dhabi city tour, including a stop at the corniche and the *Ruler's Palace* to take pictures. Then comes a visit to *Al Hamdan* gallery, which is similar to Dubai's *Oriental World*: luxury, overpriced carpets and other souvenirs. After lunch, the tour ends with a visit to *Yas Mall*, from where the travellers can have a look at *Ferrari World*, a theme park with the fastest roller coaster in the world (but cannot enter it as part of the package because of the steep entrance fee). The group flies off in the late evening to Medina from Abu Dhabi. The journey usually continues with three days in Medina and four days in Mecca, before the group flies back to Malaysia.

Offering tourism to pilgrims

Before I became part of various *umrah* & *ziarah* groups in Dubai and Abu Dhabi myself, I spoke with the various Dubai tour operators that deal with these groups about the conceptualisation of their tours. I was interested in the specifics of the itinerary and content of the tours regarding the travellers being primarily pilgrims, not tourists. I asked the tour operators whether any differences exist between the tours they offer to the *umrah* groups and those on offer to normal tourists. I was given similar information by all the travel agents I spoke to in Dubai. Robert, who managed the travel agency *Desert Winds*, responded:

> The programs are the same. The only differences are no alcohol, no nightclubs and Muslim guides. *Umrah* people don't do the waterpark, because they are conservative; they don't go to the waterpark because of the clothing, the skin gets exposed. But the tours are the same, it's a standardised program. It's not complicated. (20 December 2017)

Arjun, a travel agent from India who had worked in Dubai for almost 20 years, answered the same question as follows:

> There is nothing special about the tours for the *umrah* groups, they are purely tourism. The tours are the same as the normal tours except the safari [which includes a belly dance] and we have to take extra care of the prayer times. (10 December 2017)

These statements show that the Malaysian pilgrims are offered the same holiday or leisure tours as tourists from all over the world but with certain exceptions. Interestingly, these Dubai travel agents are not Muslims themselves. However, similar attitudes and practices regarding the handling of Malaysian pilgrims in Dubai can be observed with Muslim tour guides. I asked Raghib, a Muslim tour guide from Pakistan, whether he includes special religious elements in the tour for the Malaysian *umrah* & *ziarah* pilgrims. He answered:

Raghib: No. It's all the same, all people [I guide, regardless of nationality, religious belief or intention of the journey] are the same and the places we go to are always the same. It's the same tour for everyone.

Viola: And is there anything you explain to them about the local Islam here?

Raghib: No, I don't want to discuss Islam with them.

Viola: Do you tell them about the history of Islam in the UAE?

Raghib: No, I sometimes tell it to Americans. (24 January 2018)

The explanations Raghib usually provides to the travellers are as follows: when travelling on the bus through Dubai, he tells the group via the microphone mainly about Dubai's accomplishments and absurdities. He informs them, for example, about the severe penalties one faces in Dubai concerning road transport (for example for driving too fast or for the illegal crossing of a road as a pedestrian) and how the toll systems of the biggest highway, the Syeikh Zayed Road, works. When passing the showrooms of Lamborghini and Porsche, he comments on the most expensive cars there, and he tells the group about the most expensive cocktail in the world for 27,321 Dhs at *Burj al Arab* when passing that building. He continues with the information that the Dubai metro was launched on 9/9/2009 at 9:09am and that Dubai holds a total of 56 world records.

According to the practice of offering normal tourism tours to Malaysian *umrah* & *ziarah* pilgrims, the Dubai travel agents and tour guides do not have an understanding of the element of *ziarah* in relation to their tours. While the packages are called '*umrah* & *ziarah*' in Malaysia, this expression gets lost in the transnational market sphere between Malaysia and Dubai. I asked Robert about this matter:

Viola: In Malaysia, they call this tour '*umrah* and *ziarah*'. *Ziarah* is, in combination with *umrah*, a religious form of visit and they normally use it for visiting historical, Islamic-related places. What do you call this tour here [in Dubai]?

Robert: Just *umrah*. Not *ziarah*. I don't know that term. The tour is not about visiting mosques, it's not religious-based. And basically, Dubai doesn't have any history, it's a modern world. (20 December 2017)

Arjun was similarly clueless about the term '*ziarah*' as part of what he dealt with:

Arjun: I've never heard '*ziarah*' before; I didn't know they call it '*umrah* and *ziarah*' [in Malaysia]. For me it's always '*umrah* groups'.
Viola: '*Ziarah*' is usually related to visiting graves of prophets or religious scholars . . .
Arjun: I've never heard about this before. There are no graves in Dubai. But you can visit the pre-Islamic side of Islam in Oman. In Dubai, there are some archaeological sites too, in Jumeirah. But people are not interested in going there. I bring them to the Dubai museum instead. They can get some information about the life in the past there. Going to this place in Jumeirah is not part of the packages we offer; we only go there if there is a group which is particularly interested in going there. The people coming over here are not interested in the history of Dubai, in real knowledge about the country; they are only interested in shopping and eating. (10 December 2017)

Aarav, a freelance tour guide from India, likewise answered the same question as follows: 'It's not *ziarah* here. It's just a touristic purpose of the visit here. We never do any kind of religious practices in our tours for the *umrah* travellers. It's purely shopping' (9 January 2018).

So, these tours have a heavy focus on shopping, which Esah, and many other travellers, were fed up with. Many of the travel agents in Dubai – but also in Malaysia – mentioned in my conversations with them, similar to Arjun, that the Malay Malaysian *umrah* & *ziarah* travellers were primarily interested in shopping and that this was their main motivation for visiting Dubai on a stopover.

Arjun mentioned explicitly that the travellers were not interested in the local history of Dubai. On the contrary, from what I experienced with the travellers themselves, there was a unanimous appetite for just this experience. Being pilgrims, most of the travellers were deeply interested in historical Islamic places, i.e. *ziarah* sites, in the UAE, which certainly exist but are not part of the itinerary. For instance, Jumeirah Archaeological Site in Dubai is a big site, 80,000 sq.m., comprising a whole village including the oldest mosque in the country, which used to be visited by pilgrims on their way to Mecca in the past. In Dibba one finds *Masjid Bidiyah* (Bidiyah Mosque), one of the oldest mosques in the country (possibly from 1446) and therefore a symbol of Islamic history. In Ras Al Khaimah the excavated site of Julfar Kush illustrates the importance of maritime trade in today's Ras Al Khaimah during the Sassanid empire in the thirteenth century. Notwithstanding all this, Dubai travel agents and tour guides include almost no information or stops relating to religion and religious history in the itineraries for *umrah* & *ziarah* travellers; they focus on shopping instead.

To *ziarah* Islamic places

The economic dimension of the spiritual packages obviously influences their content, and this, in turn, engenders irritation for the travellers, as we saw with Esah's reaction to *Oriental World*. One can therefore assume that Esah and her fellow travellers had something very different in mind from the social actors of the travel market when thinking about *ziarah*. So, what is the exact understanding of *ziarah* in the Malay Malaysian context and how does this understanding relate to the reality of the journey they experience in the UAE? Firdaus, Marketing Manager at *Sedunia Travel*, a travel agency in Kota Bahru, talked about the historical dimension, i.e. the original idea of *ziarah* in Malaysia:

> In Arabic, *ziarah* only means 'to visit'. But in Malaysia, this term is related to Islam. Because the Arab *ustaz* [religious teachers] used it when they came to Malaysia to bring Islam to the region . . . So, the Arabic term came into the country via the *ustaz*, who are religious people, which means that the term *ziarah* was originally used in Malaysia in a religious context. (17 July 2017)

Amriah and Kartini, who are from Kelantan, similarly considered *ziarah* as having immanent religious elements. Sitting in Kartini's living room wearing their *telekungs* (female prayer clothes), waiting for the *azan* (call) for *maghrib* (evening) prayer, they recalled the meaning of *ziarah* at a time when it was not yet common to book *umrah* & *ziarah* packages:

Viola: Has the meaning of *ziarah* changed throughout the past 10, 20, 30 or 40 years?

Amriah: Back then, *ziarah* was only to Arab countries, to *tanah suci* [the Holy Land, i.e. Mecca and Medina].

Kartini: *Ziarah* and *umrah* were always together at the same places. In the past, *ziarah* meant 'going to Mecca at any time' [compared to *hajj*, which can only be performed between 8th and 12th of Zulhijjah].

Amriah: In Malaysia, *ziarah* means 'visit'. Back then, when we used *ziarah* for Arab countries, then it always meant *umrah* and *ziarah* together.

Kartini: When I talked about *umrah* and *ziarah* back then, the *ibadah* [fulfilment of religious obligation] of *ziarah* was only in Mecca and Medina. For example, we *ziarah*[2] *Masjid al Quba* [Al-Quba Mosque] in Medina, we went there to get *pahala* [rewards to be judged by Allah on judgment day]. (16 July 2017)

Like Esah above, Amriah and Kartini mentioned that *ziarah* is an act of piety (*ibadah*) and, in this sense, it is normally used for spiritual visits to the Holy Land (*haramain*, *tanah haram* or *tanah suci*). On this understanding, *ziarah* is related to physical places and their spiritual and Islamic meanings. This approach still holds for many of my respondents in relation to contemporary *ziarah* stopovers. Annisa noted the degrees of religious meaning that different places had for her when thinking about *ziarah*:

> The [*umrah* & *ziarah*] package which goes to Palestine, this one is the real *ziarah* for me, because it includes a visit to *Masjid Al-Aqsa*. In Islam we have three mosques that we have to visit at least once during our lifetime: *Masjid Al-Aqsa* in Palestine, *Masjid Al-Haram* in Mecca and *Masjid Al-Nabawi* in Medina. So, when you go for *umrah* & *ziarah* Palestine, you have all three mosques on one single journey. So, that's the only real *ziarah* out of the *umrah* & *ziarah* packages for me, it's the only religious package. It will be a very heart-breaking trip-*lah*, because you will see how the Muslims are treated by the Jews and so on . . . There are other offers such as *umrah* & *ziarah* Istanbul . . . In Istanbul you will learn about the Ottoman empire, you will see 'Oh, Muslims once occupied this country'. So, then it is a religious trip. But if they only want to go shopping there, like in Dubai, for example, then it's not a religious trip. (26 August 2017)

In a similar vein, Mohamad Any, manager of *Ibn Ziyad*, classified the different *umrah* & *ziarah* packages his company offered according to the religious degree they implied:

> *Umrah* & *ziarah* London is mostly sightseeing, Buckingham Palace, the London Bridge, this is not full *ziarah*. Full *ziarah* is only in an

Islamic country. We also have *umrah* & *ziarah* Italy and Switzerland now. So, these are mostly tourism, no full *ziarah*. And then we have the *umrah* & *ziarah* Dubai, *umrah* & *ziarah* Oman, *umrah* & *ziarah* Qatar, *umrah* & *ziarah* Morocco; all these are more for leisure. Istanbul, however, is pure *ziarah*, because we visit the historical Islamic sites and learn about the Ottoman Empire. The *umrah* & *ziarah* Spain and *umrah* & *ziarah* Baitulmaqdis [Muslims call the *Al-Aqsa* mosque Baitulmaqdis or the whole area (Jerusalem) as such] are also pure *ziarah* because of the historical Islamic sites. (21 June 2017)

However, Othman, a Malay Malaysian travel agent from Seremban, brought the possibility of tourism-related leisure activities and spiritual travel *together* when he emphasised that *ziarah* is meant neither for the places the travellers visit nor for the activity itself. Instead, it is meant for the inner attitude towards the *ziarah* part of the journey. Within this context, he was aware of his corresponding responsibility as a travel agent towards his customers:

Viola: Is it important for you that *ziarah* is somehow Islamic-related?

Othman: Yes, it must be Islamic-related. Our aim is going to Mecca. But we should take the advantage of transit time and explore other places too.

Viola: Some people say that *ziarah* is just a holiday . . .

Othman: It's a holiday yes, but it all depends on how you manage your holiday . . . in an Islamic way. If you go for *ziarah* as a holiday, then you still want to see how Muslims in other places find their food, how do they mix with Christians, with Jews . . . We do not just go for holidays, but we as the agents, we give our clients Muslim food, we go to Muslim restaurants, we go and see the Muslim community. (15 June 2017)

Irsyad performed *umrah* with a *ziarah* stopover in Dubai in 2014. Similarly, he regarded *ziarah* as a possible combined form of religious, spiritual and touristic travel depending on the inner stance:

Irsyad: When we talk about *ziarah*, this means . . . we go to Medina, we go to Dubai, Abu Dhabi. Normally, *ziarah* is like a social visit. Like a holiday or trip, [to an] interesting place, but normally, when we go on an *umrah* trip, [the *ziarah*] will take us to some places which have a history. Close to Islamic history . . . So, for example, . . . when we perform *umrah*, it means we try to purify, we ask for forgiveness. That's why, after we perform *umrah*, we try to go to some places where there are not too many social or leisure activities. Normally, we visit places of our previous leaders, their graves, and then we visit mosques. Because there is a story of the mosque, right? Like how the mosque was built, who built the mosque, who was our previous leader there. That's why, in my opinion, when we perform *umrah*, we go for *ziarah* to visit places which must be related to Islam . . .

Viola: But at the beginning you mentioned that *ziarah* is also some kind of holiday trip . . .

Irsyad: Ya, it is holiday, but not to enjoy, not [to do] too many activities that are not acceptable in Islam, for example, we are not going to some places like Universal Studios [he is talking about Universal Studios on Sentosa Island, Singapore]. Because if we go, for example, to Universal Studios, there are a lot of happening things there, right?

Viola: But would you go to Universal Studios if you were not on *umrah*? Or would you never go there?

Irsyad: We go there. But not on an *umrah* or *ziarah* trip. (17 May 2017)

Grounded in the original meaning of *ziarah* as exemplified by Firdaus, Amriah and Kartini and contemporary forms of *ziarah* as a tour package, Annisa highlighted that in combination with *umrah*, *ziarah* is always, or rather should always be, related to Islam or Islamic history. Othman and Irsyad added to this understanding that the inner attitude towards the journey is of importance too. Amriah and Kartini, who are in their mid-60s and have performed pilgrimage since the 1980s, perceived *ziarah* as an *ibadah* (religious duty) performed in Mecca and Medina. Irsyad and Othman, who performed their first pilgrimage in the mid-2010s, regarded it as a combination of both: a religiously saturated leisure journey to whichever place. Given these different viewpoints, my respondents' ages and the era in which they perform pilgrimage are crucial for an understanding and definition of *umrah* and/or *ziarah*.

Ziarah as a religious and spiritual act

Othman and Irsyad suggested a combined understanding of *ziarah* that attaches an inherently spiritual meaning to *ziarah* stopovers. This is worth exploring as it challenges the consumption and holiday-focused perspective of travel agents and tour guides, on the one hand, and on the other, it provides insights into the possibilities of widening the ideas and practices of *ziarah* towards a more flexible concept in the context of *umrah* trips. Farrah talked about her approach to *ziarah* as a spiritual activity in a broader sense as follows:

> *Ziarah* can have different purposes, okay? Like one of them will be *kembara ilmu*, knowledge seeking . . . [W]hen you go to Spain and stuff like that, it's just a normal *ziarah*, but definitely everything is in the intention, so, if you want to find *ilmu* [knowledge], there is one saying say 'If I want to die, I want to die when I'm in seeking knowledge'. Because there is a *barakah* [Allah's blessing] in seeking knowledge . . . So, when you travel to Jordan or Istanbul, for example, it can become a *barakah* [Allah's blessing] but it can also be nothing. Because everything is in the intention . . . Searching for knowledge is an act, an *ibadah* [submission/surrender/obedience to Allah] that generates, that invites *barakah* [Allah's blessing] . . . I think that in your *ziarah*, you still can feel the *ibadah*, not only in the *umrah* . . . [B]ecause *ziarah* is an instruction [by God]. So, once you submit, you surrender, you obey [to God], then the *ziarah* is an *ibadah*. (1 June 2017)

As Farrah said, a journey turns into a *ziarah* in a spiritual sense when it is fulfilled as a religious obligation. In this respect, any form of travel can be a fulfilment of a religious duty. Thus, going on *umrah*, on *ziarah* or on any journey whatsoever *can* be considered a spiritual activity. How are the *umrah* & *ziarah* trips framed by this overall spirituality of travel in Islam?

Travelling (*bermusafir*) is meant to reveal new knowledge which brings a Muslim nearer to Allah (see Schimmel 1994). While travelling with Masjaliza by car from KL to Kelantan in December 2013, passing through many villages and landscapes, she explained the connection one can see through travel with the beauty that Allah created, such as nature, animals and cultures. As a traveller (*musafir*), one can experience how beautiful the earth is and that only a supernatural force could have created it. One becomes 'addicted to travel', Masjaliza said, because the more one travels, the more one gains new impressions. I asked Masjaliza what makes an activity 'travel' – whether she considers a journey from Puchong, where she lives, to KL which is a distance of about 30 kilometres and a 45-minute drive, travelling. She explained that travelling starts with a distance of 55 miles, which equals two *markalah* or 90 km. In ancient times, when people still travelled by foot or by camel as in

Arabia, a journey was tiring after around two *markalah*, especially for older people. Beyond this distance, Muslims ought to find a place to pray, but during travel, a prayer room (*surau*) or water for ritual washing (*air sembayang*) were hard to find.

Later on, Masjaliza framed the Islamic and spiritual substance of travel by drawing my attention to Imam Asch-Shafi'i's words on the relevance of going on a journey. Muhammad Ibn Idris Al Shafi'i (150 AH/766 AD – 204 AH/820 AD) was the Imam who established the Shafi'i law school (*mazhab*) of jurisprudence (*fiqh*) which is followed by Malay Malaysians. His poem says: 'There is no rest in residence for a person of culture and intellect, so travel and leave where you're residing! . . . If one travels, he is honoured like gold.'

Many of my respondents regarded the act of travel as a religious obligation as it is mentioned in the *Qur'an*:[3] 'Do they not see how Allah begins the creation, then repeats it? That is easy for Allah (to do). Travel through the Earth and see how he begins the creation. Then, Allah makes the latter creation. Allah is capable of doing everything' (Sura 29 [Al Ankaboot], verses 19–20). There are numerous other verses in the *Qur'an* which advocate travelling. Take Surah Al-Rum (30:42), for example: 'Say: "Travel through the earth and see what was the end of those before (you): most of them worshipped others besides Allah".' Travelling increases the unity of Muslims from different regions of the earth (*ummah*) by coming together, and thus strengthens Muslim brother- and sisterhood (*sillaturrahim*) (Scott and Jafari, J. 2010: 11).

Ziarah as a form of fulfilling a religious duty is not tied exclusively to the act of travel. *Ziarah* can be any form of visit as long as it is practised as an *ibadah*, i.e. as submission to God's demands. Farrah explained: '*Ziarah* can also mean visiting the sick. In Islam there are a few *ziarah* that have got *barakah*. For example, visiting the sick or when you attend a wedding after being invited to it. Another *ziarah* with *barakah* is giving charity' (1 June 2017). Irsyad added visiting the grave of a relative or a recently deceased person as *ziarah*:

Irsyad: If somebody passed away, we are not saying that we 'go to' them but we '*ziarah*' them. Even to the dead person's grave, we call it *ziarah* also . . . Because, as Muslims, if we talk about *ziarah*, we try to make it like an activity which is Muslim-related.

Viola: And when you go to, parents whose child passed away, how is it Muslim-related then?

Irsyad: We go there and pray for them. We see their relatives and then try to calm them down. We also go the mosque for them and pray for them there, we recite the *Qur'an* for them. For example, if you visit your friend if his father passed away, are you going to bring along your radio? No, right? . . . If I *ziarah*, if I visit, my friend whose relative passed away, I do some activities related to that dead person . . . And when I go back to my hometown, I go *ziarah* my Ex-ex-grandfather who already passed away, I go and *ziarah* his cemetery. (17 May 2017)

In this sense, *ziarah* is an activity bound to religious identification and not to the practice itself or the place, as discussed above. Irsyad put it in a nutshell: 'Muslims can also *ziarah* to non-Muslim countries.'

The different spiritual meanings and practices of *ziarah* are as old as Islam itself. Masjaliza and I began reading through historical Malay manuscripts in order to find out whether and how the meaning of this term has changed in Malaysia. I was interested in the transformation of the concept since Islam has been practised and documented in written form in the Malay Archipelago. Malay manuscripts are in part digitised and available online (http://mcp.anu.edu.au/cgi-bin/tapis.pl). Entering the keyword '*ziarah*' brought up a total of 135 listings for all manuscripts on this platform in July 2017. *Ziarah* is used in these documents either in the context of visiting Mecca and Medina, visiting graves of Islamic saints, or visiting family members. In a document from 1931 (Saudara (2Oct37:9 [1931]) it is stated: '. . . *hendak* ziarah *ke tanah yang mulia* [*tanah suci* – the Holy Land – Mecca and Medina] (I want to visit the Holy Land).' The use of *ziarah* implies the fulfilment of the religious duty in Mecca and Medina. In another example (Tuhfat al-Nafis, 304:18 [1866]), *ziarah* is used as an indication to gain *pahala* for the practice undertaken: '*Dan lagi baginda itu suka* ziarah *kepada rumah-rumah sanak saudara*' (And later on the king wants to visit his sibling's house). Masjaliza explained that they as Muslims get rewards when they visit family members, because they come closer to one another. A third example (Surat Farquhar, 47:42) relates to visits to graves that are not bound to figures of Islamic history: a Sultan writes in a letter in 1820: '*Apabila kita sudah* ziarah *kepada makam ayah kita itu* . . .' (When we already visit father's grave . . .). In this case, the use of *ziarah* indicates the religious intention of the visit to the grave, probably implying the recitation of passages of the *Qur'an* for the dead person, 'to make his punishments less', as Masjaliza said, and to recite the *du'a* (individual prayer).

These various practices – visiting historical Islamic places, travelling, visiting sick people or family members, attending a wedding, giving charity, undertaking condolence, visiting graves – only become *ziarah* when there is a sincere *intention* (*niat*) to fulfil the religious obligation demanded by Allah. So, whether a visit to a sick person is a normal visit or a *ziarah* depends on the purpose of the visit. This means that in the Malay language, one can linguistically either say '*Saya* melawat *kawanku sakit*' (I visit my sick friend) or '*Saya* ziarah *kawanku sakit*' (I visit my sick friend). The meaning differs in the sense that *melawat* is a visit without any spiritual intention (*niat*), as Farrah pointed out above. For Muslims, to '*ziarah*' a sick friend will mean that the Muslim visitor follows an Islamic motivated intention and that the visitor as well as the Muslim sick person will get *pahala* (rewards) that connect the earthly life with the afterlife (*akhirat*). Masjaliza said regarding the importance of the intention:

Masjaliza: You [Viola and Harry] will *melawat kubur* Tok Kenali [Tok Kenali's tomb]. Me and Ramli, we will *ziarah kubur* Tok Kenali. I'm sorry to say that, Viola, but will you visit his grave for your afterlife [she asked a bit pejoratively]?

Viola: No.

Masjaliza: You see, we also visit his grave to gain *pahala* [rewards] for our afterlife. So, you only visit his grave for your purpose in your current life, but we also visit the grave for the purpose in afterlife. You will visit the grave for your research. So, the intention is different. It depends on the intention and the purpose after that. We want to recite the *du'a* [individual prayer], we know that he [Tok Kenali] was a *keramat* person [a person granted a 'super-power' by Allah based on their piety. This is a term used by my respondents in English themselves when talking about *keramat*]. Maybe we will learn about the *keramat* which is the highest ranking by Allah. (7 July 2017)

Given this, *melawat* cannot be used to describe a visit to the graves (*kubur*) of prophets, for example, in Mecca and Medina; only *ziarah* is appropriate, as Masjaliza stated in this context:

We *ziarah kubur*. We perform *ziarah* to a grave because of the intention, we visit the graves of the Prophet's friends in Mecca and Medina, of *syahid* and *syuhada* [male and female martyrs, respectively]. We go there and learn about their difficulties to distribute Islam, about what was their profit they gave to our religion, what were their good deeds. You [addressing me] can also *melawat*

Medina or *pergi ke* Medina [go to Medina] if this is what describes the intention. But for us, as believers, we can only *ziarah* Medina; there is no other option. You can just visit the place. But we *ziarah* Medina and we will get more *pahala* [rewards] for it. (7 July 2017)

This approach aligns with Amriah's and Kartini's understanding of *ziarah* above: (in the past), *ziarah* was used for the visit to Mecca and Medina or the broader *tanah suci*, where the Prophet and his companions had acted and had been buried. Given the different approaches to *ziarah* shown above, we can see that some activities understood as *ziarah* are bound to whether or not they are performed by Muslims. Some depend on the place of the visit. Again, other undertakings can turn into *ziarah* when the inner stance and the intention allow it. We therefore find different characterisations of *ziarah*, and this touches on what *ziarah* implies in the present research context when Malay Malaysian Muslims, such as Esah, perform an *umrah* & *ziarah* Dubai/Abu Dhabi journey.

Furthermore, the above approach offers a first explanation for the touristic dimension of the '*umrah* & *ziarah* Dubai' journey. Visiting family and the sick and grave visits may be religious-related, and thus be understood as *ziarah*, but this is not necessarily the case. These three forms of *ziarah* and the ambiguity inherent in the concept open up the possibility of a range of meanings for *ziarah* that become compatible with extra-religious activities. This eventually leads to an expansion of *ziarah* in the direction of tourism in a manner that would not be possible with regard to *umrah* and *hajj* journeys.

This ambiguous understanding, then, means that doing a sightseeing tour through Dubai *can* nowadays be considered as *ziarah*, when, for example, the motivation for visiting the city is to visit a family member who lives there and that family member takes the city tour with the traveller in order to strengthen their relationship. A holiday in Dubai and strolling through *Oriental World* can furthermore be *ziarah* when, for example, the motivation is to understand how a Muslim majority country with ancient roots in Islamic history has come so far economy-wise. Or, as suggested by Esah, a trip to Dubai can be *ziarah* when the pilgrims are taught something about Arab and Muslim culture (about *souqs* and mosques, for example) in the country where the *ziarah* stopover takes place.

Nile Green (2015) notes that in the nineteenth century, *hajj* travellers experienced shocking encounters with non-Muslims on the journey. En route to Jeddah by steamship, *hajj* pilgrims had to make stops at various ports on their way to the Holy Land and came into contact with, for example, prostitution in Alexandria. These stops and the things they encountered were not intentional; they were a necessary part of the long sea journey. Nowadays, pilgrims from Malaysia deliberately include stopovers in locations where Muslims and non-Muslims live together (such as Dubai) or where non-Muslims are the majority (such as Paris or London), even if they will face irritating situations there. In this way, 'holiday' or 'tourism' indirectly takes on a new definition: it is understood as a form of religious tourism which automatically evolves when a sincere Muslim makes a stopover somewhere on the way to pilgrimage, motivated by obeying Allah (*ibadah*), for instance in form of learning about Islam-related issues. In that way, travellers connote the holiday religiously.

A religious market segment

I met Arjun on 1 December 2017 in Dubai Mall, the biggest shopping mall in the city. He had just brought a Malaysian tourist group to the mall, giving them two hours to spend there. During these two hours, he was free to talk to me about his market segment that serves Malaysian *umrah* & *ziarah* pilgrims in Dubai. He explained that he began offering *ziarah* stopovers in Dubai in 2005 and started with Malaysians. 'Malaysia is a backbone,' he said. He also dealt with the Indonesian and Singaporean market, but most of his bookings were from Malaysia – that is, from Malaysian travel agencies that book his packages to cater to Malaysian travellers. I asked him why there were such large numbers of Malaysians. He said: 'Because their [the Malaysian] pocket allows it compared to Indonesians. And the Malaysian agencies have their incentives to boost their sales.'

Arjun pinpointed two factors. First, Malaysians can afford to travel overseas, as economic development beginning in the 1970s has created a large Muslim Malay middle class. Secondly, Islamic products, in this case *umrah* & *ziarah* packages, have been strongly promoted and, thus, commercialised as part of the emerging and promoted *halal* industry since the 1990s and 2000s. Hence, the economic, modernising and Islamising processes in Malaysia described have direct repercussions on the moulding of materialised Islamic goods.

As these developments in commercialisation were going on, Arjun began to develop a business involving Malaysian *umrah* travellers in Dubai in the mid-2000s. Even going on sole *umrah* (without a stopover) from the Malay Archipelago only developed in the 1970s/80s, in contrast to the *hajj* journey, which has been undertaken from that region ever since Islam was introduced there. The main reason for the recent evolution of *umrah* and later *umrah* & *ziarah* trips was the broadened infrastructure in the travel industry which affected such religious journeys directly. Othman, who had been working in the travel industry for nearly 20 years, explained with regard to sole *umrah* to Mecca and Medina:

> *Umrah* flights from Malaysia only started in the 70s. Before that, people had very seldom gone for *umrah*. In the 70s, the first airlines started their flights, such as Emirates, Qatar Air or Etihad. The airlines asked the Malaysian government whether they can approach the country. So, these carriers started to serve Malaysia. (15 June 2017)

The Malaysian government began to professionalise and standardise this new type of travel in the mid-2010s. Since 2014, the Ministry of Tourism and Culture (MOTAC), under the Umrah Monitoring Council (*Majlis Kawal Selia Umrah*), has monitored such packages. In 2016, a quota for *umrah* was implemented in Malaysia. The *umrah* quota does not affect the number of pilgrims directly, unlike the *hajj* quota (see chapter 2); rather it regulates frequency by allowing the performance of *umrah* only once in a *hijrah* year. Furthermore, those travel agencies that want to sell *umrah* packages have been required to obtain a special MOTAC-issued *umrah* licence since October 2017.[4]

Outside the evolution and professionalisation of *umrah*, the next decisive moment in the pilgrimage industry came when Malaysian travel agencies began to offer *umrah* journeys connected with *ziarah* in the 1980s. While travel agencies offer '*umrah* & *ziarah*' packages, there are no comparable '*hajj* & *ziarah*' offers. Owing to the huge number of pilgrims undertaking *hajj*, TH goes for *hajj* direct, without stopovers. Furthermore, pilgrims remain in Mecca for at least 40 days to perform their obligations, which means that the journey is intensive, on the one hand, and they need and want to focus on their rituals, on the other. Including a stopover at any other place on the *hajj* trip to or from Mecca was not an option for my respondents.

Ziarah in connection with *umrah* developed for practical reasons, due to the long transit time of the *umrah* journey. Travel agencies began to create tours in the places where transit took place. Othman continued:

> At the beginning, when only MAS [Malaysia Airlines] and Saudi Air flew back and forth between Malaysia and Saudi Arabia, there were only these direct flights, so there was no option for *ziarah*. Then

when Emirates and others introduced their flight to Malaysia, it implied that people have to transit. Back then, people often needed to wait like two days for the next flight, so transit time was very long. So, what are you going to do during transit? Just stay in the airport? No! So, in the 1980s, [travel] agents created these *ziarah* packages to attract the people. They asked the authorities, 'Can we go out of the airports during transit times?' (15 June 2017)

As Othman mentioned, this form of *ziarah* developed when the travel industry infrastructure grew. Initially, this process did not lead to satisfaction amongst pilgrims. Amriah and Kartini told me:

Amriah: Nowadays, *ziarah* is also used for a stopover [to Mecca and Medina], a holiday. People have become rich and they can now afford such trips . . . People go to Egypt or Dubai for *ziarah* . . . I went to Dubai in 1997 on my way to *umrah*. But I asked for *umrah* only, I didn't want to go there! But my flight was by Emirates, so they stopped in Dubai for one day. I was forced to go. There was shopping there. They organised a bus which took us to the shops. There was only shopping there and nothing else!

Kartini: On my last *umrah* in 2014, I had to transit in Sri Lanka, although I didn't want to! On my first *umrah*, I had to transit in Singapore. (16 July 2017)

Amriah's emotional outburst included the statement '[p]eople have become rich and they can now afford such trips'. Indeed, *umrah* & *ziarah* journeys are expensive: when booking with *Ibn Ziyad*, the company most of my respondents used, the price during my fieldwork in 2017 for an *umrah* & *ziarah* Dubai/Abu Dhabi package ranged from 7,190 RM to 8,790 RM, depending on the time of year (holiday season) and the number of people sharing a hotel room. In contrast, the same company charged between 7,690 RM and 9,290 RM for the *umrah* & *ziarah* Istanbul package and between 5,190 RM and 9,790 RM, for direct *umrah* (without any *ziarah* stopover), depending on the airline, the time of year and the number of people sharing a room.

Umrah & *ziarah* trips have become expensive because, amongst other things, *Ibn Ziyad* has almost completely monopolised this market segment: through my observations, calculations and information gathered from interviews, I realised that Malaysian *umrah* & *ziarah* travellers are on the whole served by just this one Malaysian travel agency, alongside *Ibn Ziyad*'s several subsidiary companies (*anak syarikat*), which in turn commission only one travel agency (*Blue Bridge*) in Dubai.

Just two or three other small Malaysian travel agencies serving only a few travellers and two or three additional travel agencies in Dubai complement the market dominated by *Ibn Ziyad* and *Blue Bridge*. *Blue Bridge* handles 15 to 20 international travel groups each month, of which three or four are Malaysian *umrah* & *ziarah* groups. Arjun deals with three or four Malaysian *umrah* & *ziarah* groups each month, often comprising VIP guests or other privately organised tours booked by families, but no big groups. Another travel agency from Sharjah, one of Dubai's neighbouring emirates, takes on average one Malaysian *umrah* & *ziarah* group every two months. One or two other Dubai travel agencies only serve these kinds of groups during the peak season in November and December (because these are the coolest months on the Arabian Peninsula and coincide with school holidays in Malaysia), but only very few and sporadically. The travel period for *umrah* pilgrims is outside Ramadhan and, to a certain extent, outside the *hajj* season. Within the *umrah* travel season, the average number of *umrah* & *ziarah* travellers in Dubai/Abu Dhabi is seven per month.

This number used to be higher. Arjun recalled that between 2005 and 2008, which was the first time he dealt with stopovers on the way to *umrah* in Dubai, he served between 1,000 and 2,000 Malaysian *umrah* & *ziarah*-travellers – that is, between 30 and 40 groups – in Dubai each month. This changed drastically during the global financial crisis of 2008 and 2009. Until then, the majority of Malaysian pilgrimage groups were brought to Dubai for a stopover by Malaysia's national airline, Malaysia Airlines (MAS), Arjun explained. Following the recession, MAS no longer flew to Dubai but worked with Emirates, the airline of the Emirate of Dubai, which brings MAS customers instead. Arjun's contact at MAS left the airline and his liaison with MAS ended. The stability or instability of the religious-related market segment is directly connected to broader economic processes.

Commercialising *ziarah*

Within the above system of production, purchase and sale (see figure 3.1), fluctuations amongst and within the companies in Dubai is relatively high. While *Blue Bridge* acted as *Ibn Ziyad*'s counterpart in Dubai during my fieldwork in 2018, this did not constitute evidence of a steady relationship. During my ethnographic research between 2013 and 2018, *Ibn*

Figure 3.1   Some travel agencies have their own *hajj* and *umrah* shops, contributing to the commercialisation of pilgrimage. Pilgrims can purchase specific items, such as *tawaf* socks, a spray bottle for *wuduk* (ritual washing) during travel, a nasal filter against the dust in Saudi Arabia, *umrah* guidebooks, or a whole set as in this shop in Kuala Lumpur, Malaysia, 2017.

Ziyad's local tour operator in Dubai changed three times. *Desert Winds* served *Ibn Ziyad* until late 2017. After that, *Blue Bridge* took over. During my fieldwork in 2014, Arjun's company was *Ibn Ziyad*'s local tour operator in Dubai. I learned from my many conversations and interviews with these three Dubai travel agencies and with various staff at *Ibn Ziyad* that the reason for such fluctuation is that *Ibn Ziyad* constantly searches for the cheapest price a local tour agency can offer them. This has repercussions for local tour guides and the products they offer. Aarav and Sai, who toured Malaysian *umrah* & *ziarah* travellers from *Ibn Ziyad* in Dubai as freelancers during my fieldwork in 2014, but were no longer doing so by 2018, described their situation in the market and thereby distanced themselves from these travellers and the travel agencies handling them:

Sai: Aarav and I have done our job as tour guides already for many years. So, we can choose our customers; where do they come from. [He looks around to see whether someone in the café can hear him.] We don't prefer the Malaysians. Because the tip is low,[5] the price is low. Malaysians are served more by tour guides who are new in this area who still need to gain experience. But those who have worked as tour guides already for a longer time, they have their market with higher prices. I toured *Ibn Ziyad*'s Malaysian *umrah* groups for Robert's company [*Desert Winds*] until last year. The company is quite new here in Dubai too, it was only launched 2.5 years ago. I stopped touring their Malaysian groups because of the prestige and reputation. Robert's company doesn't have a good reputation and other agencies who serve the Malaysian *umrah* groups either. Because those agencies are bad employers: Robert always expected us to work more and more. At the end I worked 16 hours per day without getting extra money for it! In fact, at the end of the day, I even had to pay my own taxi to get home!

Aarav: Until two years back, Malaysian companies paid better. Now there is a lot of competition going on in Malaysia and the prices went down. For two months, I haven't toured any Malaysians anymore because we get less and less paid by them. (9 January 2018)

Aarav and Sai mentioned keywords including 'bad reputation', 'low prices' and 'bad employer' according to their perspectives as former employees. *Ibn Ziyad*'s interest in pushing prices down therefore influences the quality travellers experience on their journeys. This leads to the situation where, for instance, travel agents and tour guides contradict their own claim that they take care of Muslim needs. I certainly saw during the multi-day tours I followed that these specific needs and travellers' general needs are regularly ignored. Hotels in which the groups were based often sold alcohol and could thus not be considered 'dry hotels'. Furthermore, not all tour guides are Muslim: some are Christian, such as one of the freelance Indonesian tour guides in Abu Dhabi. From time to time, I heard some of the Malaysian *umrah* & *ziarah* travellers complaining about parts of the stopover in Dubai. Some were not satisfied with the food (they preferred to eat Arab food rather than the Indian and Western food they also have in Malaysia); many of them could not understand the tour guide's explanations as they only spoke Malay, not English; some of them had special requests, such as going to *Souq Naif*, the '*abaya souq*', that were not fulfilled even though the timeframe of the itinerary would have allowed it; Jamil, a tour guide from Pakistan working with *Blue Bridge*, tended not to stick to the schedule; and shopping was the pervasive element the groups had to face.

The goal of generating profit from the spiritual journey is therefore apparent not only on the Malaysian side of the travel market. Returning to the discussion at the beginning of this chapter, it is not only the concrete arrangements of the days spent in Dubai that are influenced by economically driven approaches; the itineraries of the city tours themselves are a direct outcome of the profit motive. Stopping at *Oriental World* is no coincidence. After visiting *Al Hamdan* gallery, Abu Dhabi's equivalent of *Oriental World*, Jamil told me:

> When someone from the group buys a piece [carpets made by Emirati families], we get a share of the price paid. Vietnamese and Chinese people especially buy carpets there; they are crazy about it! Last week I brought a Vietnamese group there and they spend 56,000 Dhs at the gallery. But the Malaysians have never ever bought anything there, but it's still the company's policy to bring them here. There is an agreement between *Blue Bridge* and the *Al Hamdan* gallery stipulating that, in the case of a purchase, *Blue Bridge* as a company gets 5 per cent, *Blue Bridge*'s tour guide gets another 5 per cent, the groups' tour guide [here the *mutawif*] gets an additional 5 per cent and the driver gets 2.5 per cent of the price paid. This is why the prices are so high – because the gallery gives us a total of 17.5 per cent of what they gain! (6 April 2018)

The entire transnational *umrah* & *ziarah* Dubai market between Malaysia and the UAE is subject to economic motives, which leads to travellers experiencing frustration, as we have seen with Esah, Amriah and Kartini. The quality of the journey and of the city tours is entirely dictated by the commercialisation of *umrah* & *ziarah* trips.

Religion and the economy

My Malaysian respondents' different understandings of *umrah* and of *ziarah* are based on their age and, if applicable, the time of their own performance of *hajj*, *umrah* and/or *ziarah*. My respondents' approaches to *umrah* and to *ziarah* furthermore depended on their positions within the travel market. Talking with Othman, the travel agent from Seremban, about his approach to *umrah*, he said:

> For us, *umrah* is business, right? We assist them [the pilgrims] to perform their *umrah*. Every year, we need three groups per

month which goes, one group is 30 persons. We've already planned the *umrah* packages for 2018, we need 3 groups per month, so, at least we need 100 persons per month who perform the trip. (15 May 2017)

If the *umrah* and *umrah* & *ziarah* trips are, from the travel agents' perspective, so economically driven, what role does the *ziarah* part play for the travel industry in Malaysia – where they explicitly emphasise *ziarah* in contrast to the travel agencies and tour guides in the UAE? Firdaus revealed in his interview:

Firdaus: It's not very suitable to use *ziarah* for Dubai. Because Dubai is a totally new world, there are no historical things to see. But we cannot call the package '*umrah* & *shopping*', because you cannot do a good thing [*umrah*] and going shopping right after that. So, in the context of Dubai, *ziarah* is just a term, it means nothing here in this context.

Viola: But if you term it as such and in the end, you only offer shopping, what do the customers actually expect from your package?

Firdaus: They will also think 'We cannot combine *umrah* with *ziarah* as shopping!' So, they are also more comfortable with the term '*umrah* & *ziarah*' in the case of Dubai. (17 July 2017)

Firdaus had underlined a strategy behind the naming of the packages as '*umrah* & *ziarah*'. Travel agent Mohamad Any got to the heart of this matter:

> *Ziarah* is from the Arabic language and just means 'tourism'. But when it comes to *umrah* and *ziarah*, it doesn't sound good if we term it '*umrah* and *tourism*', although it is *umrah* and *tourism*. That doesn't sound good . . . That's why we call it '*umrah* and *ziarah*', because it sounds much better in combination with *umrah*. In *ziarah*, we usually visit the Islamic historical places; *ziarah* is Islamic-related. *Pelancongan Muslim* [Muslim tourism] is more about the shopping, the leisure. That's why we call it '*umrah* and *ziarah*' and not '*umrah* and *tourism*'. (21 June 2017)

In these ways, Firdaus and Mohamad Any explained how *ziarah* is used as a marketing strategy for the Malaysian tourism sector to attract Muslim travellers to choose this kind of package tour. This illustrates how *umrah*

& *ziarah* packages are positioned at the interface between capitalist commercialisation and spiritual satisfaction in a broader sense. Yet, specific forms of moral economy in Malaysia, according to the principles of *syariah*, are not to be misunderstood as fully absorbed into a Western system in the sense of 'mimicry' (Bhabha 1984). Malaysia, given its role as a *halal* hub, including *halal* entrepreneurship, Islamic finance, the *halal* certification system and 'Islamic Tourism', points to the evolution of a new global economic sector which contradicts the perspective of an overall incorporation of any critiques against capitalism into the hegemonic capitalist system (see Boltanski and Chiapello 2003). Malaysia's leading role as a *halal* hub challenges Western economic realms and provides alternative forms of economic activities and markets.

Under neoliberal regimes, economic and religious practices become entangled in 'economies of morality' (Osella and Rudnyckyj 2017: 12) that navigate the products, the form of production and the form of consumption through the – sometimes contradictory, sometimes aligned – requirements of producers and consumers. Capitalism and morality (or Islamic principles) should not be regarded as separate phenomena that require reconciliation or compatibility. This approach would reveal a form of historicisation in the sense of a 'historicist trap' (Chakrabarty 2000). According to this understanding, social conditions in non-Western societies are measured solely by Western concepts of modernity, innovation and progress. Local negotiations of global capitalist circumstances would be misunderstood (see Shamsul 2008). However, forced incorporation of postcolonial economies into the hegemonic capitalist system cannot be ignored either. Filippo Osella and Daromir Rudnyckyj (2017: 10) argue regarding this dynamic process that 'transformation in economic thought and practice has inspired changing forms of religious practice, just as religious moralities have been deployed in new ways in the market'.

One reason why spirituality and Islamic values and practices can be easily absorbed by the economy – leading to a 'pious neoliberalism' (Atia 2012) – is the fact that certain principles are shared in Islam and in business. Both inhere in the idea of 'work-on-the-self' (Osella and Rudnyckyj 2017: 11). Neoliberalism is based on tenets such as meritocracy, individualism, autonomy and market calculation. These tenets do not relate solely to the economic sphere but are incorporated by the subjects and, thereby, shape subjectivity in a broader sense. Similarly, Islam encourages principles such as rationalisation or transparency, which are perceived and lived as moral values that are approaches to life (and afterlife [*akhirat*]) – but not to certain social, cultural, economic or political spheres. This is similar to what Max Weber dubbed, in relation to

Christianity, *The Protestant Ethic* when arguing that modern capitalism in Western Europe and the US was enabled through Protestant, especially Calvinist, principles of asceticism, progress and hard work. Labourers internalised these principles to such an extent that they drew on these doctrines in secular life – i.e. in their life as wage earners – as well. In this regard, capital accumulation was considered a virtue. This entanglement between religion – be it Islam or Protestantism – and capitalism is, therefore, grounded in an overall mobilisation of dispositions that go beyond strict rational logics of market calculations (see Mauss 2016 [1925]; Polanyi 1944).

This condition leads Rudnyckyj (2019, 2010) to the conceptualisation of an inherently entangled web of Islamic and economic elements. In his most recent work, *Beyond Debt* (2019), Rudnyckyj understands neoliberalism as a force that creates and influences selfhood. By investigating Islamic economy in Malaysia – Islamic finance in this case – he shows how this finance system aims at establishing and deepening bonds of the *ummah*. The basis for this process is a reconfiguration of the economic sphere – that is, the sphere of Islamic economy (see Sloane-White 2017). Rudnyckyj illustrates that in the case of an Islamically approached economy, social relationships and personhood are also created, shaped and transformed *through* economic processes.

Rudnyckyj's argument builds on his concept of *Spiritual Economies* that he developed based on an examination of the entanglement of the market and Islam at a steel factory in Java, Indonesia. He conceptualises *Spiritual Economies* as a model that describes economic development as a matter of religious piety. He defines this concept as consisting of three elements:

> 1) [R]econfiguring work as a form of worship and religious duty; 2) objectifying spirituality as a site of management and intervention; and 3) inculcating ethics of individual accountability that are deemed commensurable with norms of transparency, productivity, and rationalization for purposes of profit. (Rudnyckyj 2010: 131f)

Spiritual Economies denotes an Indonesian reformer's understanding of combining asceticism, productivity, transparency and rationalisation, which they believe is inherent to Islam and neoliberalism alike, for personal development. This, in turn, leads to corporate productivity and overall economic development. 'Self-discipline, accountability, and entrepreneurial action are represented as Islamic virtues that should inform conduct both within and beyond the workplace' (Rudnyckyj 2010: 132).

The concept of *Spiritual Economies* thus describes how Islamic principles are mobilised so that workers can cope with and adapt to the challenges of the capitalist and specifically neoliberal economy. Wage work is interpreted as a form of worship and working hard as a means of salvation. Hence, the model of *Spiritual Economies* follows an understanding that regards economy not as a separate social sphere of production, reproduction and consumption but as a technique to shape subjectivity and social practices – and hence, to influence the ethics of self-management and self-government (Rudnyckyj 2010: 138f). In this way, Rudnyckyj shows how Islam in Java, Indonesia is understood and practised not as a counterculture or vehicle of resistance against 'the capitalist West' and globalisation but as a beneficial means of transnational competition.

Ever since their inception, capitalist structures have evolved, and new consuming practices have been developed in order to satisfy consumers' needs in the same way as new marketable products have emerged. Religion, in the case of this study Islam, has been tied directly to the capitalist and neoliberal market. As Osella and Rudnyckyj (2017: 4) note: '[I]t is the global spread of market capitalism and neoliberal techniques that . . . has been turning religiosity into a means of capital accumulation.' Economic markets are mechanisms that promote and serve the (imagined) needs and wishes of religious consumers, as becomes apparent with Islamic forms of consumption such as *halal* products. Furthermore, religious principles and practices, such as pilgrimage, are mobilised in order to allow economic growth according to the logics of the capitalist market. However, it is not just capitalist principles that are effective agents when it comes to the search for new conflations; as shown above, a strong moral self is likewise capable of synthesising capitalism and religion in a fruitful way.

Pilgrimage in the marketplace

Studies in anthropology, geography and tourism & management research (for example Pinto 2007; Reader 2014; Timothy and Olsen, D. 2006; Vukonić 2010) examine how religious groups influence consumption-oriented markets, regarding both European and non-European countries. Most of these studies, however, neglect to examine specific religions and, thus, religious-shaped differences between, for example, Muslim, Christian and Jewish forms of travel (Poria *et al.* 2003).

Some studies based in management research and cultural sciences, however, deal with Islam in connection with travel and consumption, mostly specified by the keywords 'Islamic tourism' (as it is also termed in Malaysia) and '*halal* tourism' (Henderson 2011, 2010, 2009, 2003; Jafari, J. and Scott 2014; Raj Ra. and Morpeth 2007). The tourism industry worldwide is currently growing faster than other industrial sectors (Vukonić 2010: 38). The travelling patterns of Muslims changed drastically after the Islamist attacks against the World Trade Center and the Pentagon on 11 September 2001 ('9/11'). Then US President George W. Bush's self-proclaimed 'War on Terror' stigmatised all Muslims world-wide as dangerous or even terrorist. Before 9/11, many Muslims had holidayed in the US and Europe. Since that moment, most Muslim tour-ists travelled instead to other Muslim regions, as indicated by Muzakir, one of ITC's directors, in chapter 2, because of certain 'regimes of mobil-ity' (Glick Schiller and Salazar 2013): restrictive safety regulations in Western countries make it more difficult for them to enter, even for a short period of time (Henderson 2010: 82). As Muslims, these tourists require particular facilities and conditions, such as prayer rooms, *halal* restaurants and regular breaks in the itinerary for obligatory prayers. Against the backdrop of wider 'Islamic' or '*halal*' tourism, previous stud-ies (Jafari, J. and Scott 2014; Henderson 2010, 2009; Vukonić 2010; Raj, Ra. and Morpeth 2007) dealt with the corresponding relationships between the travel industry and their Muslim travellers.

'Islamic tourism' (*Pelancongan Muslim*) still follows a different concept than *umrah* & *ziarah* packages, as Mohamad Any pointed out above: it is much more committed to leisure only. However, both forms of Muslim trip denote a specific Muslim activity. Yet most previous works that touch on issues of commercialisation processes and commodifica-tion of religious travel (Jafari, A. and Sandıkcı 2016; Moufahim 2013; Rinallo *et al.* 2012) lack any analytical selectivity when it comes to *differ-ent forms* of Muslim pilgrimage or travel. An exploratory study by Mona Moufahim (2013), however, makes a pioneering contribution with her investigation of connections between consumption and *ziyara* in Syria and Iraq. Within the context of a religious journey to tombs and shrines in these two countries, Moufahim shows, through a focus on gift-giving, how objects and images which are relevant during pilgrimage can repre-sent emotions. These emotions are generated in physical and symbolic activities during the religious journey, such as travel, rites and contact with sacred objects. Goods influence religious belief and are important for making the pilgrimage complete and tangible.

As part of a Muslim pilgrimage and Islamic tourism interface, *umrah* & *ziarah* packages are themselves an entangled net of morality and market strategies. Due to their conceptualisation and realisation, they simultaneously encompass elements of religion and economy (see Tripp 2006). In a broader sense, Osella and Rudnyckyj stress that

> capitalism and market economy might constitute a moral *economy*, but not a full-fledged *moral* economy, limiting, then, the possibility of an engagement with and theorization of the working of contemporary economies of morality. (Osella and Rudnyckyj 2017: 9)

While Osella and Rudnyckyj define this clear focus on the economy rather than on morality, in the research at hand religious principles form a part of the overall commercialisation of pilgrimage and spirituality – and vice versa. On the one hand, *ziarah* has become a 'de-religionised' concept and practice, as I would like to put it, and can be understood as an expression of a 'profanation' of the religious. On the other, *ziarah* is not only a marketing strategy but also part of a 'religionalisation' of the economy (see Sprenger 2014). Haji Ustaz Abdul Intan, the owner of *Ibn Hawqal* travel agency, emphasised: 'I'm doing religious but no tours [tourism].' This statement implies the notion of 'I'm doing religious *business*'. He was doing religious business, not just commercialisation of the religious. He created added value on a material level through the religious dimension of the packages he was selling. At the same time, the religious was the added value of his business. The religious dimension of his packages was sold at a relatively high price, otherwise the particularity of this dimension would not be tangible.

However, it remains the case that the transregional economy pulls those elements out of the religious journey that can be transformed into a saleable product. This commercialised condition of the religious *umrah & ziarah* journey leads not only to the fact that, for example, '*ziarah*' as a term and a concept is unknown to the local tour agents and tour guides in the UAE, as shown above, but also to a transformation of the meaning of '*ziarah*' in Malaysia itself since the 1980s. The manifold dimensions that *ziarah* can imply in the Malaysian context furthermore show the flexibility of this concept and practice, which eventually facilitates its commercialisation more easily. This process, then, makes '*ziarah*' compatible with activities that blur the lines between religion and the mundane. This, among other things, again points back to the Malaysian state's intention not only to condone but indirectly to promote these travel packages (see Fischer, J. 2011 and chapter 2). The tourist-associated *umrah & ziarah* packages ultimately religionise the entire environment, including the secular one.

To sum up, religion is mutually constitutive with capitalism on the institutional scale of analysis. Today, *ziarah* implies travel to other countries, so that *ziarah* can be part of *umrah*. This leads to irritation for travellers in the transregional travel market: especially when it comes to a *ziarah* stopover in Dubai, travel agents include the term, but exclude the concept and activities of *ziarah* from the package for strategic reasons. For travel agents, incorporating the ambiguous concept of *ziarah* into *umrah* trips is more or less a ploy to attract consumers of *umrah* & *ziarah* journeys that may even take them to London or Paris. The travel industry's strategy results in an offer of normal tourism packages – including significant amounts of shopping and sightseeing – for pilgrims. As a consequence, on the institutional scale of analysis, i.e. the analytical level of the travel industry, pilgrims' and the travel agencies' needs do not match on all levels of the journey. As a consequence, the capitalist dynamics in the economy contradict Malaysian pilgrims' motivations to increase their knowledge (*kembara ilmu*) of Islam and spirituality on their journeys.

However, the integration of *ziarah* into the market has led not to a full 'de-religionisation' of the spiritual, but rather to a 'religionisation' of the economy. Such 'religionisation' becomes even more obvious when we consider the contested dividing line between *ziarah*-as-tourism and *ziarah*-as-religion. Pilgrims' agency turns this strategic journey (from the travel agents' perspective) into a religious act. The mere naming of the travel package as *ziarah* does not of itself lead to a religious trip but it *invites* social actors to 'religionise' it. This is what the travellers do when connecting *ziarah* with knowledge seeking (*kembara ilmu*), for example. For travellers, *umrah* & *ziarah* Dubai is accordingly a religious rather than a touristic trip since travelling (*bermusafir*) is still a spiritual, Muslim practice with a long, rich tradition in Islamic history that can be appropriated in the form of gaining knowledge about the place they are visiting.

The next chapter shows the gendered dimensions of the journey. In fact, the *umrah* & *ziarah* journey *is* very much about shopping for the Malay Malaysian travellers of this study; especially the female ones. But it is not about luxury shopping, for example at *Oriental World* or *Al Hamdan* gallery, as the travel agencies offer it. It is about a specific form of gendered shopping and about specific gendered objects that are to be shopped for: predominantly the *abaya*. The religious connotation comes into play on the stopover as the women of this study are eager to buy their religiously attributed *abayas* on precisely this trip. Thus, the *ziarah*-stopover becomes religionised, especially by women when purchasing *abayas*.

Notes

1. The visit to the Hard Rock Café Dubai was highly contested amongst the pilgrims. It is not part of the regular itinerary but the tour guide usually asks the group whether they want to go there. In some cases, a traveller himself (I observed only males requesting it) asked for this short stop. Usually, this provoked heated discussions in the tour bus. Many pilgrims considered such a visit to be potentially *haram* because of the music played in the shop and the dancing, alcohol and music in the café. According to the detractors, it will most probably be *haram* because the music, for example, will distract one from thinking of or being connected with Allah. Once, a *mutawif* explained this to me with the short expression: '*Macam* Megadeath!' (It's like Megadeth [a US-American heavy metal band]). Yet the proponents were not convinced of this argumentation; they were very keen on buying souvenirs (mostly T-shirts) there. For example, the group of which Esah was a part spent about 40 minutes in the shop and some individuals also had a look at the café. Of the 40 group members around 20 of them bought between five and eight T-shirts each. Interestingly, Esah, who presented herself as someone who is not interested in shopping at all on her pilgrimage journey, spent the largest amount of money in the Hard Rock Café I ever observed during my fieldwork: 815 Dhs for T-shirts she purchased for her brothers.
2. Using *ziarah* as a verb in Malay is grammatically correctly called *menziarah*. Since prefixes and suffixes such as *men-* are usually only used in written but not in spoken language in the Malay language, Kartini only uses the root '*ziarah*' here.
3. I want to clarify here that I do not cite sequences from the *Qur'an* in order to interpret it from a theological perspective. I rather wish to demonstrate the character of Islam as 'lived religion' and its manifold interpretations in different socio-cultural and historical contexts.
4. To gain the licence, the *umrah* operators must undergo a two-day *umrah* operators enhancement course organised by the ministry. Before an agency can register for the *umrah* licence, it needs an International Air Transport Association licence. For that, they need a 200,000 RM bank guarantee and, after approval, the agency must procure an additional 100,000 RM bank guarantee for the registration for the *umrah* licence. According to travel agent Othman, the application for the licence is only approved after checking how experienced the staff are, who the appointed agents of the local tours are, how many packages they sell and how many pilgrims they can bring.
5. In fact, after the four-day tour through Dubai and Abu Dhabi from 14 to 18 February 2018, tour guide Raghib and driver Hassan received 200 Dhs in the form of banknotes and many, many coins as a tip which the group had collected. After the group entered Abu Dhabi airport to fly off to Medina and we started to head back to Dubai in the bus, Raghib commented on the tip as follows: 'The tip is especially low from the Malaysians. When I have a Vietnamese group with 40 people, then I will get 500 USD. They pay in USD.' When we sent the Malaysian *umrah* & *ziarah* group who had stopped over in Dubai and Abu from 4 to 7 April 2018 to Abu Dhabi airport, Jamil, another tour guide from *Blue Bridge*, was given a tip of just 20 Rial [currency of Saudi Arabia which equals around 18 Dhs]. The group had not collected any tip for the tour guide or driver. One family of six collected their last Dirhams but forgot to hand them over.

4
Bodies in place, space and time

Puspawati, the Managing Director of Malaysian travel agency *Ibn Ziyad*, mentioned in one of our first conversations:

> We get this request [to book '*umrah* & *ziarah* Dubai'] from women, then they too bring the spouse. Because for *umrah* they need *mahram* [a man the woman is eligible to be married to]. We get the feedback from the agents, from our clients, that the women require Dubai . . . Women are most excited about Dubai . . . Because it's modern; the buildings, the shopping places . . . [T]hey buy the *abaya*, like the one I'm wearing right now. They are beautiful there. (7 January 2014)

Four years later, in Dubai, I visited Layla, a self-proclaimed Emirati 'modest designer' who created and produced *abaya*s, at her office and production site. She revealed:

> The impact of our traditional garment, the *abaya*, developed in Malaysia because they follow our influence. In Malaysia, they adopted the concept of *abaya*. For Emirati people the *abaya* is like haute couture. The main concept of *abaya* is already absorbed in Malaysia: a modern kind of modesty. (8 January 2018)

Puspawati observed, without prompting as to questions of gender, that it is primarily Muslim Malay Malaysian *women* who wish to spend part of their *umrah* enjoying consumption and leisure in Dubai. She thereby revealed that women are the protagonists when it comes to the travel route via Dubai and also when it comes to consumption. Dubai and consumption are in their connectedness, according to Puspawati, linked to modernity. *What* the women want to shop for and why are raised by

Layla's keywords: a modern, high-class yet modest and traditional garment from the Gulf.

These two quotes reveal that Dubai is widely understood as a modern shopping haven by *female* Muslim travellers because of the simultaneously modern and modest *abaya*.

Farrah complemented this gendered dimension of shopping activities on pilgrimage by reflecting on Mecca in this respect:

> In Mecca, I think I ended up with 30 *abayas* which I bought for my friends, office mates and one for myself . . . Usually that's the most popular souvenir if you go to Mecca . . . Because it is something that the people in Mecca wear and they wear it to do their religious rituals. When you also wear it, you are part of it, you are the one who presents them here in Malaysia. (1 June 2017)

Similar to the women Puspawati talked about, Farrah was eager to shop for *abayas* on pilgrimage, but specifically those she could get in the Holy Land – not in Dubai. Her reason for this was to bring back home a sense of Arabic and religious feeling and to communicate this to the outside world.

The three quotes above introduce the issues discussed in this chapter: modernity, traditionality, gender, space and place in Muslim contexts. Situated mainly on the transregional and intimate scales of intersectional analysis, the questions that will lead and structure this chapter are: (1) How is the continuum from modern to traditional locally situated in the journey from Malaysia, through Dubai and Abu Dhabi, to Mecca and Medina? (2) How is this meaning-making embedded in the places (Dubai, Mecca and Medina), objects (*abayas*) and activities (shopping and pilgrimage) on the journey? (3) In what way are these conditions intersectionally gendered and spiritualised – or in other words, what objects and activities do Muslim *men* prefer in which physical places and why? (4) How and with what meaning do women and men use the objects purchased on the pilgrimage journey upon returning to Malaysia and what do they embody through them? The discussions in this chapter are theoretically framed by theories of place, space and modernity and, to a certain extent, by consumption and class.

Sacred place and space-making

The '*umrah* & *ziarah* Dubai/Abu Dhabi' trip brings travellers from KL through Dubai and Abu Dhabi to Mecca and Medina. A development of the inner attitude and the outer practices of the pilgrim, which is bound to the geographical places involved, can be observed in the temporal course of this journey. From the moment an individual registers for the journey in one of Malaysia's travel agencies, s/he prepares her-/himself for it gradually – practically, mentally, financially and spiritually – until the final destination is reached.

When still in Malaysia, various concrete preparations are made on a practical level. Going on pilgrimage implies the possibility of not returning home because of severe sickness or, more importantly, death. This narrative draws on conditions in the past, when the journey from Southeast Asia to Mecca lasted several months, pilgrims were usually elderly, and hygiene standards were generally low (see chapter 2). However, high death rates are still a reality during pilgrimage in Mecca today (Bianchi 2017). Many of my respondents therefore prepared themselves and their families accordingly, for example regarding inheritance: some prepared *wasiat* (testament) and *hebah*, i.e. giving one's belongings to someone when one is still alive.

The possibility of encountering difficulties during pilgrimage leads not only to financial and testamentary preparations when still in Malaysia but also to preparations that stabilise the family situation. Several of my respondents who were leaving their children in Malaysia made arrangements as to who would take care of them in case of death on the journey. Another practical preparation when still in Malaysia concerns Islamic rules and rituals. Potential pilgrims usually attend the *umrah* and *hajj* preparation courses (*kursus umrah* and *kursus hajji* or *kursus perdana* ['grand course'], respectively). People learn the rules and regulations of *umrah* or *hajj* on these courses: what to wear as males and females; the correct sequence of pilgrimage rituals; and the moments for reciting certain *du'as*.

The practical preparations made in Malaysia aim at, amongst other things, cleansing (*sucikan*) oneself internally. It was important for many of my respondents that they felt 'ready' to take the next step on the journey – that is, to leave Malaysia for the trip. Preparing mentally for *umrah* or *hajj* by means of certain practices supports the inner stance of being prepared for pilgrimage on a general level. My respondents mentioned many times that people only go on pilgrimage when it is their fate (*takdir*) to do so: when they feel Allah has called them (*Allah dipanggil*) for this obligation. Once a person feels this invitation by God, s/he is ready to submit totally to God on pilgrimage.

The practical and mental preparations for *umrah* or *hajj* in Malaysia are not an end in themselves. One of the main reasons my respondents want to learn about the rules of pilgrimage and why they want to feel that they are fully prepared is that they aim for an acceptance of their pilgrimage performance by Allah (*hajj/umrah maqbula*) and for forgiveness by their God (*hajj/umrah mabrur*). The practical preparations for *hajj* or *umrah* undertaken in Malaysia are therefore spiritually driven: they are located not only on a practical level but also on a cognitive-spiritual level. The cognitive appropriation of intellectual knowledge about pilgrimage touches the spiritual dimension of getting a sense for how one's relationship with God can feel and how far one can come to terms with it.

I observed a clear development in the pilgrims' inner stance on the last day of the *ziarah* stopover – on the day they were due to leave Abu Dhabi to proceed to the Holy Land. Some of the pilgrims changed their clothing habits on that particular day and started to wear traditional Arab clothes (*abaya* for females and *kandora* for males). I asked some of them, 'Why?'. 'Because we are going on *umrah* soon,' one of the pilgrims replied. The next change in clothing habits after Abu Dhabi will come in Medina. When entering the point where the Holy Land begins geographically and spiritually (*miqat*), all pilgrims – no matter where they come from – will formulate their intention (*niat*) to perform pilgrimage and will change their clothes: males will start wearing *kain ihram* and females will wear relatively simple everyday garments (Thimm 2021). The sacred location transforms the pilgrims' bodies. Hence, different forms of preparation are related to different places on the journey from Southeast Asia to the Arabian Peninsula. Inner stances, embodied social practices and the different geographical places correspond with one another (see Rahimi and Eshagi 2019: 28f). This leads to the issue of place-making through imaginations, on the one hand, and social practices, on the other.

This research approaches place as a physical location that is constituted by material territory *and* dynamic social practices performed in and around places which are, in turn, embedded in the meaning-making of the territories. Cultural anthropologist Samuli Schielke and Islamic Scholar Georg Stauth (2008: 14ff) argue that sacred places can evolve through relationships between manifold locations that constitute, in turn, saintly landscapes or territories (see Thijl 2018). In a similar vein, Desplat (2012: 16) discusses the constitutive processes of making Islamic and non-Islamic places by referencing a central Islamic concept: whereas regions with Muslims in power or where Islam is the official religion are regarded as *dar al-Islam* ('house of Islam', but also translated as 'house of peace') – set interestingly against the *placeless ummah* (the Muslim global community) – those areas where Islam does not play any role are termed *dar al-harb* ('house of war') (Ansary 2010: 88f; see Parvin and Sommer 2018).

In contrast to this relational approach, scholarship has applied the category of 'place' broadly to specific locations and geographical sites in the sense of static entities and has thereby dealt with it through an understanding of 'containers' (see e.g. Günzel 2006: 41; Harvey 1969; Löw 2015; Luutz 2007). Desplat (2012: 12) draws attention to the colonial background of this idea of linking 'cultures' with 'territory', especially when it comes to Islam or Muslim majority regions. As a colonial legacy, the world was treated as 'a mosaic of cultures' (Desplat 2012: 12) in social science research, in order to handle complex social, cultural, political and economic dynamics. Recent studies on 'Indonesian Islam' (Millie 2017), 'Moroccan Islam' (Burke 2014) and 'Ethiopian Islam' (Petrone 2015) reproduce the idea that socio-cultural dynamics and identifications are bound to certain locations.

Understanding place as constituted through territories *and* social practices means including space in the analysis: spaces are constituted through social relationships and social actions (see Lefebvre 1991 [1974]; Löw 2001; Massey 2001; Schroer 2006; Werlen 1987). Place and space are usually treated as two opposed categories in studies dealing with Muslim contexts (for example Desplat 2012; Desplat and Schulz 2012; Falah and Nagel 2005; Gale 2007; Metcalf 1996; Mittermaier 2008; Nasser 2003; Schielke and Stauth 2008; Zayed 2008); place is regarded as a materialised objective site, whereas space is composed of relations between subjects and objects. To overcome this dichotomy, Jakob Egholm Feldt and Kirstine Sinclair (2011: 7) rely on an idea of 'Lived Space', which they borrow from geographer Tim Cresswell. Space – or place – can be lived through spiritual practices that, in turn, shape the spirituality of spaces and places. Similarly, historian Barbara Metcalf (1996: 3) argues that Muslim space is not bound to a specific territory or architecture but is based on a social practice. This is shown by geographer Richard Gale (2007: 1017) when he investigates how places acquire spatial meaning for Muslims based on ritual practices. The Islamic construction of space creates the possibility for every Muslim to turn a public or worldly space into a private or sacred space. A mosque, for example, is not consecrated, as a church or a synagogue is. The mosque turns into a Muslim space, he argues, through the ritual of ablution (*wuduk*) which Muslims perform before every formal prayer in the mosque. El Guindi (1999: 78) suggests that an individual sacred space can be constituted by any Muslim by performing the obligatory prayers: during prayer, a Muslim is in a sacred state based on special dressing and ablution and facing Mecca.

Going beyond this understanding, the wearing of objects (*abayas* and *kandoras*) in certain locations (Abu Dhabi and the Holy Land) draws attention to the fact that spaces and places are shaped by territorial, social *and* material dimensions (Sen and Silverman 2014: 4). Hence, 'religious spaces' (Knott 2014) also become tangible through materiality – through things (Meyer, B. and Houtman 2012) such as Arabic dress. This form of 'embodied placemaking' (Sen and Silverman 2014) with its socio-spatial relationships reflects territorially based mechanisms of appropriation and allocations of different discourses (Werlen 2010, 2005) and of material substances alike. Hence, following an analytical topological approach in this study, I understand place as constituted by territorial materiality and space, while the latter is, in turn, a place of entangled social and material order.

Muslim hierarchical landscapes

According to my observations, dynamic place-making based on lived social practices is, in this research context, undertaken by, amongst other things, locating the Arabian Peninsula in general and Mecca and Medina in particular as an Islamic spiritual centre. The reason for understanding the Arabian Peninsula as the Islamic centre (for example Desplat 2012) is its historical background as the 'cradle of Islam'. As part of this imaginary, Mecca is the centre of the Muslim world (Abaza 2011, 2007, 1996). According to Islamic belief, the prophet Abraham, together with his son Ismael, erected the *kaabah*, the black cube, in Mecca, and this has functioned as the mark of the 'middle of the earth' for Muslims ever since. This is the place to which 30 million pilgrims travel annually.

Beyond Mecca and Medina, the Arabian Peninsula as a whole, together with today's Palestine and Jerusalem (*Baitulmaqdis*), is incorporated into the notion of an Islamic centre, since the incidents narrated in the *Qur'an* are located across this entire region. The history of Islam is another crucial element in this regard: the early spread of Islam took place from Medina throughout the region. Until nation-state building began, people moved from place to place on the Peninsula between Oman, Kuwait, Bahrein and Saudi Arabia for formal education, trade and work. This notion of a contiguous region is what my Malay Malaysian respondent Masjaliza had in mind when she told me about a fellow 'working in the Arab region' (*kerja di Arab*) without specifying the location further.

An additional angle to consider when dubbing the Arab Peninsula the centre of Islam is connected to the history of Islamic empires. Julfar, for example, in today's UAE and Zafar in today's Oman were important trade centres and settlements in the heyday of Islamic empires and, therefore, were places visited by (Muslim) traders and pilgrims on their way to Mecca.

Locations in the Arabian Peninsula in general and Mecca and Medina in particular are the desired destinations of my respondents. The historical significance of this geographical area as it relates to Islam is of greater relevance for them than the experiences to be had in Saudi Arabia as a *contemporary* Muslim majority society, as many of my respondents noted. While many of them were interested in elements of current 'Arab' culture, such as food and architecture, their main purpose was to perform pilgrimage at that historical place. Societies in places classified as 'pure Islamic' based on history (Saudi Arabia, Turkey) were regarded by the vast majority of my respondents as not being 'very Islamic' today. Saudis were described as offensive and arrogant, and particularly the men as sexist and as people who are primarily interested in showing off their wealth to the outside world. Sofea, the *abaya* designer, lived in the UAE for a couple of years and put it pointedly: 'Arabs are so rude, they are not civilised. For example, in a restaurant, the waiters or waitress must serve them first even if they come last to the queue.' This overwhelmingly negative perception of contemporary 'Arabs' underscores that the travellers in this study wanted to experience their journey in physical places that have 'authentic Islamic history' rather than in a present-day Muslim society with its Muslim culture. The visit to Mecca and Medina – and also to Dubai, as we will see – is, therefore, depicted as a 'placial' (Gielis 2009) visit rather than a social visit. Given this, the shopping and sightseeing-based itinerary, originally developed for tourists, that my Malay Malaysians experience on their *ziarah* stopover in Dubai partially thwarts the travellers' religious motivations for their stopover in the UAE.

Muslim landscaping, in which world regions are mapped based on grades of Islamic authenticity, is not limited to the Arabian Peninsula. It sprawls far into Muslim Southeast Asia. While Mecca and Medina and the whole of the Gulf region are considered to be the 'Islamic centre', Muslims in Asia are consequently positioned (and position themselves) on the margins or periphery of these sacred landscapes. From what I experienced, such narratives are present in the Gulf and maritime Southeast Asia alike. This leads to social patterns that express a very stringent following of Islamic principles in Malaysia – even more stringent than in the 'the Islamic centre' itself. During a family gathering at Mawar's house to break the fast together, I talked to her granddaughter, Siti Sabrina, who had lived in the UAE for two years, about the differences between her life in Malaysia and her experiences in the Gulf. She reflected:

> In Malaysia people follow Islamic rules more rigorous. For example, it's typically Malay to reject dogs. I find them very cute. In Dubai, many of my [Muslim] friends had dogs as pets, so they don't have any issue with it. But here in Malaysia, people say they are *haram*. (29 May 2017)

Another dimension is the practice of young girls wearing headscarves: in Malaysia, girls start wearing a scarf from around the age of five; this has developed only since 2012, according to my observations – and the same goes for the introduction of the *abaya*. In the UAE and in Oman, however, only female adults wear the headscarf – not young girls.

A rather different ordering of the Muslim periphery has evolved over the past 15 years, locating Malaysia at the heart of Islamic *modernity* due to its becoming a worldwide *halal* hub. With these modernising developments, Malaysia has placed itself at the centre of a *commercialising* Islam. In this way, I argue, this state has complemented the 'spiritual centre of Islam' – Mecca, Medina and the whole region of the Arabian Peninsula – with an economic Islamic centre.

Hence, the *umrah* & *ziarah* Dubai journey starts in a place which represents 'modern Islam' (Malaysia), goes on to a 'modern but spiritual' place (Dubai/Abu Dhabi) and ends up in the 'Islamic spiritual heart' (Mecca and Medina). This meaning-making of places has deep repercussions for the gendered embodiment of sacredness in the temporal course of the trip, related gendered shopping practices, and the intersectionally interwoven usage of the goods purchased upon return.

The 'modern Dubai *abaya*': fashionising a religious garment

Clothing, as part of the many inner and outer preparations for pilgrimage, as noted above, is not just an expression of geographical and spiritual place- and meaning-making. Material clothing items are also a means to create and reproduce these places spatially, as we shall see. Most female Malaysian pilgrims in this study do not just start wearing an *abaya* when they come closer to the Holy Land; they are eager to purchase this particular garment in exactly that 'placial' area where they prepare themselves further for pilgrimage: in Dubai.

However, in that location, they want to purchase 'the *abaya*' not in a general sense but very specifically: the 'Dubai *abaya*', as my Malay Malaysian respondents often call it. The *abaya* evolved in the Arab Gulf states long before any of my Arabic respondents could remember. Yet, Arab women have only worn the *abaya* since the 1990s as a general, cover-all garment in public space. In Malaysia, the *abaya* only developed around 2012 according to my observations. Why do Malay Malaysian women aim for this traditional public Arabic garment? What does it mean to them, and how does their meaning-making process relate to the development, significance and connotations of the *abaya* on the Arabian Peninsula itself?

When I visited the Dubai's Women's Museum *Bait al Banat* (Daughters' house or Girls' house) in December 2017, the founder explained to me: 'The *abaya* is not part of our religion but of our culture. It has existed in the region ever since clothing has been worn.' There is no scholarly agreement as to where the *abaya* developed. Al-Qasimi (2010: 46) finds its origin in the eastern region of Saudi Arabia, while El Guindi (2005: 73–85) states that the garment was developed by pious Muslim women in the context of religious movements in Egypt in the 1970s. Alongside these vague estimates, my respondents in the UAE, coming from the UAE, Saudi Arabia, Qatar, Egypt and Algeria, depicted very differentiated ideas of the varied developments, meanings and styles of the *abaya* throughout the region.

Most of them often emphasised that the *abaya* in the UAE (see figure 4.1) evolved not just in the course of religious dynamics but also as a status symbol. The importance of this meaning for my Malay Malaysian respondents will be examined further below. Huda, an Emirati research officer in her mid-30s, explained the development of this connection:

> Here in UAE, women wearing *abaya* meant that they are of high status. That was in the 1960s, 1950s. Back then, people started trading with India. The traders and businessmen went to India and got the fabrics there. Upon return, they gave gold and fabrics to their wives. So, these women wearing *abaya* were of the high class of society. The traders and businessmen who went to India were of higher status than the Bedouins. Their wives wanted to identify with high class and disassociate from low classes. (11 January 2018)

Figure 4.1 Arab women wearing *abayas* in Dubai, UAE, 2014.

Similarly, Lindholm (2014: 47) explains that covering the body (and the hair and/or face) in the Arab region has been related to economy and class: increasing oil extraction practices in the 1950s led to an enormous surge in wealth among these populations. This, in turn, led to higher social status of the majority society, which was symbolically represented, at first, by Western clothing. This was the case for both females and males (Khalaf 2005: 252f). However, this phase of bodily representation ended in the Gulf in the 1990s with a return to traditional cultural values and practices, such as wearing Arabic clothes, in order to differentiate the affluent and cultured in society from others.

While the *abaya* had long been worn culturally in the Gulf area and as a status symbol since the 1950s, the meaning of the garment changed once again in the 1970s. It is now perceived as a religious garment in the Arab region, especially since the Iranian revolution became effective there (Khalaf 2005). This went along with the practice of veiling: millions of women in the Arab world adopted the headscarf in the 1970s and 1980s. This 're-veiling phenomenon' (Patel 2012: 302) correlates with a transformed meaning assigned to the *abaya*: as a symbol of religiosity, it now represents the modesty of women – a significant meaning mentioned in the introduction to this chapter by *abaya* designer Layla.

This connotation will be of relevance for the Malay Malaysian pilgrims, as we will see further below.

It is important to note that covering up is not only done for religious purposes; it is also a tradition for females and males alike on the Arabian Peninsula, for example, to protect the face and eyes against the desert sand. Based on this motivation, Emirati women have long been wearing the *burqa*, a face mask covering the nose, mouth and cheeks that protects the skin but also, simultaneously, symbolises modesty and their status as married women (see Bristol-Rhys 2010; Wikan 1982).

Modesty, especially performed by females, is considered an inherent Islamic principle according to the *Qur'an* (predominantly sura 24, verse 31). It is stated there that women should cover their beauty in general and their breasts in particular. In order to cover their décolletage, they should wear a long headscarf:

> And say to the believing women that they should lower their gaze and guard their modesty; that they should not display their beauty and ornaments except what (must ordinarily) appear thereof; that they should draw their veils over their bosoms and not display their beauty except to their husbands, their fathers, their husband's fathers, their sons, their husband's sons, their brothers or their brother's sons, or their sister's sons . . . [A]nd they [the women] should not strike their feet in order to draw attention to their hidden ornaments.

Conforming to specific orthodox interpretations, modesty is a means of reducing social interaction between women and men in general and of keeping 'shame' or so-called 'dishonourable behaviour' away from women's families in particular. The *abaya* has achieved this by being made of plain black fabric – no colour, decoration or transparency. Until the 1990s, the *abaya* was a square piece of cloth without sleeves made of wide, soft fabric. It was worn as a cloak over the usually colourful dresses, as recalled by 49-year-old Emirati Tabaan, who started wearing the *abaya* in 1981 at the age of 12. The aim of the *abaya* was to avoid being attractive to men and more generally to ensure that females were not gazed at. In this sense, the *abaya* was meant to represent Muslim identity and morality (El Guindi 2005: 76).

The design and attributes of the religious *abaya* underwent a profound transformation in the 1990s. The modest rectangular cloth was replaced with a long robe with defined sleeves and was tailored to fit women's sizes rather than being used as a cloak. A decade later, decorated *abayas* evolved on the Arabian Peninsula. These *abayas* are embroidered, decorated with (colourful) sequins or additions such as metal rivets. While the cloth is still usually black, other colours, such as brown, beige, blue and wine-red, can be found. Today's *abaya* is not only worn shorter but also has a modified fit – no longer loose, it can also be figure-accentuating, like the 'waisted' *abaya* (*al-abaya al-mukhassara*) (Al-Qasimi 2010: 59). This type of *abaya* comes close to what the Malay Malaysian pilgrims in this study consider the 'Dubai *abaya*'. In addition to the *abaya*, women usually wear the *sheyla*, the Arab headscarf, in a matching design to the *abaya*, and many women nowadays also highlight their eyes and eyebrows with makeup and wear stilettos.

Since the 2010s, the *abaya* has increasingly been integrated into the international fashion industry. Female designers create spring and autumn collections which are introduced at fashion shows, primarily in the UAE. This country – and especially Dubai, with its 'Dubai Design District' – has become the hotspot for the latest *abaya* trends: something the Malay Malaysian travellers were well aware of. Layla noted:

> UAE is number 1 [for *abaya* fashion]. Then comes Saudi Arabia. They started three to four years back. Then Bahrain, they are also famous for *abaya*. Those are the three main ones. Kuwait also has *abaya*, it's famous for modest clothing in general, but not for *abaya* in particular. (7 January 2018)

Long before the *abaya* was integrated into the international fashion scene, women of the local elites in Saudi Arabia, the UAE and Kuwait had been wearing expensive designer fashion from Paris, Milan and London. However, they had been wearing it *under* their *abayas*, and the latter were still rather simple in terms of design and style. The ordinary *abaya* had thus served as a 'cloak of invisibility' (Sobh *et al.* 2014: 393) – a means of hiding expensive, luxurious clothing and beauty from those responsible for moral guardianship. In the last few years, however, European and Arabian designers have reimagined the *abaya* as luxury clothing in its own right, which can be as glamorous as the clothing underneath.

The integration of the *Muslim* fashion piece *abaya* into the international fashion scene is remarkable when one considers the gendered aspects this implies. As Woodhead (2013: xviii) argues, 'the fashion world is seen to be dominated by women – not just as producers, but as consumers'. By contrast, the religious sphere is usually perceived as a male one (see Carstens 2005: 102–21): men are the main religious figures and they lead prayers as they lead rituals. Yet, in the last few decades, women have increasingly been appropriating religiously related practices and have thus been challenging the gendered imbalances of religious ideologies, doctrines, spaces and places. Given this, religious fashion life-worlds are highly gendered: they are feminine worlds that provoke male religiosity.

Fashionising female garments such as the *abaya* is, furthermore, embedded in social conditions of the body, its gendered notions and its connection to fashion and dress. The socio-cultural sphere of being and living is that of dressed bodies – being naked is, in most situations, regarded as inappropriate. Hence, to dress oneself means to think about how to encounter upcoming (social) situations, how to (re-)present oneself, how to produce respect, acceptance and/or desire – or rejection and evasion – in other people.

> [F]ashion [is] a structuring determinant on dress . . . [T]he body
> [is] the link between [fashion and dress]: fashion articulates the
> body, producing discourses on the body which are translated into
> dress through the bodily practices of dressing on the part of individuals. In other words, in everyday life, fashion becomes embodied.
> (Entwistle 2015: 4)

Through the body, one experiences the world and acts in the world. In this sense, women navigate social (hierarchical) conditions based on gender through, among other things, representations of their bodies. The Malay Malaysian women of this study are more conscious about their outer appearance than the men – about styling and fashioning the body, about how they dress – which, in part, explains their eagerness to purchase the fashionable *abaya*. Thanem and Knights (2012: 12) draw attention to the fact that females' awareness of their bodies, at least in contemporary 'Western' contexts, is based on the condition that they are considered to be objects gazed upon by males, specifically gazed upon in the sense of a body moving around in social space rather than a subject. Hence, women have to be beautiful, as they are constantly eyeballed; and this can be shown by fashion – here by fashionable *abayas*.

The '*abaya*-as-fashion' (Al-Qasimi 2010) depicts a transformative process of this garment, with changed meanings allocated to it on the Arabian Peninsula: those who consider this transformation process a positive one regard the *abaya* as a modern article of clothing. The *abaya* developed on a continuum from merely modest to modern, as Layla touched on at the beginning of this chapter. However, this religious-connoted garment still embraces the religious requirements of female attire. As Layla put it:

> The *abaya* is part of our religion and of our culture and tradition as well. It represents our faith, culture and tradition. It's part of our everyday life because it's about modesty. As a country we have developed and modernised but the garment still holds the meaning. We just modernised it. It's reflecting the modern Arab woman. (7 January 2018)

Classing the 'Dubai *abaya*'

The notion of symbolising both modernity and modesty is especially appropriate for the *abaya* from Dubai. Tabaan's 27-year-old daughter Arwa, from Dubai's neighbouring emirate Sharjah, emphasised that she wears 'the UAE modern style', thereby defining the characteristics of the *abaya* in and from the UAE as inherently modern. From her perspective, the modern elements of her own *abayas* are the cut, the fabric and the specific details which make them different from regular ones. Wearing an *abaya* with big, decorative golden buttons, she explained that regular *abayas* do not have any buttons, the fabric of the latter is softer, and they are usually cut straight. For my Malay Malaysian respondents, the 'Dubai *abaya*', which they classify as 'fashionable' and/or 'modern' and sometimes even 'sexy', i.e. as revealing a woman's shape and potentially provoking the male gaze, is usually adorned with decorations and/or glittering stones ('*bling bling*').

A modern *abaya* from Dubai is an *abaya* desired by most of my Malay Malaysian respondents – for pilgrims and *abaya* designers alike. Sofea and other designers in KL with whom I spoke orientate their business primarily towards Dubai: Sofea visited Dubai twice a year to find inspiration, to see the latest trends and to buy the resources needed to design her collections there. One particular fabric for *abayas* (*nida emirates*) is available only in Dubai, and Sofea and other *abaya* designers I interviewed obtained it there. Since this fabric is so special, it is not retailed in bulk – it is sold only to personal acquaintances who are going to produce the *abaya* in Dubai. The *abaya* in and from Dubai is a unique and famous *one*.

The exclusive 'Dubai *abaya*' is a luxury item which primarily meets the requirements of local Emiratis. What the Malay Malaysian *umrah* & *ziarah* travellers in this study imagine as the Dubai *abaya* is not in fact what Arabian women or Malaysian *abaya* designers consider it to be. The Malaysian traveller's 'Dubai *abaya*' is a much cheaper fashion item, with different designs (for example, more colourful and opulent) from the Emirati ones, which *they* especially like and wear (see figure 4.2).

This becomes tangible when one considers where local Emiratis and Malay Malaysian travellers shop for their *abayas*. *Souq Naif* is of great importance for the latter. *Souq Naif*, located in Deira near the famous Baniyas Square in the old part of Dubai, is a market where people can buy predominantly ready-made *abayas*, alongside cloth, incense, make-up, hair accessories and saffron. It is a busy place, where the majority of the customers are women and all vendors are men from South Asia. The customers are generally tourists: local Emiratis do not buy their *abayas* there; they prefer places where they can purchase tailored pieces, such as

Figure 4.2 Malaysian *umrah* & *ziarah* group interested in buying *abayas* (hanging above) in Dubai according to their taste, UAE, 2018.

Dubai Mall in Uptown Mirdif. Most tourists in *Souq Naif* are from Saudi Arabia, with others from Egypt, Bahrain, Qatar, Sudan – and Malaysia.

When talking to the salesmen, it became obvious that every customer group has their own sense of taste. Ahmad from Afghanistan, who has worked at *Souq Naif* as a vendor since 2011, showed me the different designs: the simple black *abayas* made of black fabric with subtle black decorations are mainly bought by Arab women. The *abayas* with colourful elements which are 'shiny' are the most sought-after *abayas* for Malay Malaysians, Malay Singaporeans and Indonesians. Malaysians furthermore like one type of *abaya* which Dubai is famous for: the 'Princess Style' or 'Butterfly Style'. This *abaya* is tailored with a wide skirt. The *abayas* in *Souq Naif* cost between 50 and 160 Dhs, approximating to 50–160 Malaysian Ringgit in 2017 [around 12–38 USD]. Malaysians usually pay around 130 Dhs, as Rahmad explained – and this corresponded with my observations. In contrast, ready-made *abayas* in '*Abaya* Mall' for Emiratis cost between 300 and 600 Dhs [80–160 USD] or between 600 Dhs and 800 Dhs [160–220 USD] for tailored pieces. The fabric used in those *abayas* is very different from those found in *Souq Naif* and of better quality: velvet, coarse cotton, linen, raw silk; some *abayas* even had feathers.

It is clear, then, that different product groups and customer groups exist, differentiated by design, price range and the customer's region of origin. This led me to the observation that a unique Malaysian style of *abaya* exists. This style is not produced 'top down' by designers but has evolved on the basis of the demand of the customer group. The Emirati designers I interviewed, like Layla, adapt their production lines according to the customer's needs and desires – and thereby transform the original Arab style of the *abaya*.

While the Malay Malaysian travellers of this study followed their own taste in Arabian *abayas*, they still aspired to own a 'Dubai *abaya*' and not a 'Malaysian *abaya*'. The reason they crave the so-called Dubai *abaya* is that these Malaysians are striving to create a connection to Dubai. This is realised through the garment, because they want to appropriate a fashion element with which they can mark difference. The connection to the original Dubai *abaya* and the distinction it signifies was expressed by my Malay Malaysian respondent Basharat, who possessed such an *abaya*:

I have an *abaya* from Dubai . . . but that one is too fashionable for me. If I wear [this *abaya*], it feels like 'too much', it does not suit my personality. It's a different class-*lah*! A different class of *abaya* compared to the Malaysian or Saudi *abaya*. When I wear the *abaya* from

Dubai, people will ask me: 'This *abaya* is so nice! Where did you get it from? Oh, from Dubai?!' I have experienced this already several times. And I don't like it, I don't feel comfortable then because I know that many people don't have the chance to get it [because] it is so expensive. (4 August 2017)

Sofea and other designers' orientation towards Dubai when it comes to the fashionable, luxurious *abaya*, along with Basharat's impression of the Dubai *abaya* as 'too much [class]', are linked to the high-status position that Emiratis enjoy in their country. Huda explained further above how class position is connected with the *abaya* by referring to former trade. Many Emirati women still assign this idea of a status symbol to 'their' *abayas*. In fact, Arwa wanted to retain the *abaya* as a symbol of her Emirati class position by differentiating herself from the lower classes:

[I] always have the fear that our *abaya* might be misused by some of the non-local women. Like [in] the case of beggars . . . I know [that] foreigners would not be able to differentiate between locals and non-locals. And in the case of beggars, if a lady is wearing *abaya* and she is begging, foreigners would shape a misconception about local [Emirati] women. In the case of beggars, I feel that there is an insult to our part of tradition since *abaya* is part of it. (18 January 2018)

By indirectly suggesting that Emiratis do not beg, she revealed her understanding of the *abaya* as a symbol of Emirati identity in the sense of class position; she indicated, therefore, that Emiratis belong to a high class. This is generally true, based on the country's wealth due to oil and gas resources and the distribution of this wealth to all Emirati nationals (see e.g. Mohammed Al-Fahim 2013). Sofea put this relationship between being Emirati, being of a high-class position and wearing traditional clothes in a nutshell: 'If Emiratis want to claim privileges, they need to show up in black and white robes [*abayas* and *kandoras*] . . . They are not as used to working as we are; they are born privileged; they are born rich.'

The Dubai *abaya* is a symbol of a high class position, which in turn refers back to modernity since being modern means having the ability to navigate through the material world with ease due to strong purchasing power. This garment has been transformed into a very fashionable garment in one of the most modern and opulent places in the world. Against this backdrop, my Malay Malaysian respondents aim for a garment that stands for, amongst other things, a distinct class position. The modern element of the clothing in terms of style and design is complemented by this social position. This modern religious garment is specific to the rich city of Dubai. Considering this entanglement, the Malay Malaysian subjects of this study desire the perceived high status and modernity of the Arab city of Dubai through the *abaya*. Contemplating the Muslim world order, in which Dubai is perceived as simultaneously modern and religious, the original object and place are aligned in its attached meanings. Purchasing an *abaya* on an *umrah* & *ziarah* Dubai journey, therefore, means acquiring the unique, religiously saturated modern garment that is available only there.

Consumption, shopping, class

The spiritual and partially modern objects and their places are connected by the activity of shopping. Shopping, as part of the everyday lives of my urban Malay Malaysian respondents, is not only practised as a mere form of consumption or capitalist lifestyle but needs to be practised within the context of a Muslim, pious life. Ordering sacred landscapes through consumption in this case does not mean shopping in the sense of purchasing luxury, or necessary items, which the term 'shopping' often implies. On the contrary, shopping here is understood as consuming objects that fulfil the needs of spirituality. In this sense, the *abaya* is an item that is both desired *and* needed in everyday life, as we shall see.

I follow Don Slater (2010: 280) in my understanding of consumption: he states that consumption 'embraces all the ways in which people use material and symbolic objects in their life practices, as well as things that are stabilised in object-like form (for example services, leisure activities)'. A key function of consumption is to create meaning (see Hahn 2008), as Mary Douglas and Baron Isherwood (1980) revealed in their pathbreaking study *The World of Goods*, which discussed consumption in relation to socio-cultural practices for the first time. In a similar vein, Slater asserts,

> [C]onsumption . . . is a space in which people formulate and perform fundamental questions concerning their most substantial values and ends, their sense of who they are and who they should be, what 'the good' is for themselves, their family, friends and community, and what the good life is. (Slater 2010: 282)

Following this approach, consumption can be understood as a form of communication and touches on questions of identity and identifications.

People shape their identifications around consumption; consumption is about what gives meaning to people, how they value things and for what reasons. '[W]e "discover" [identity] by exposing ourselves to a wide variety of products and services, and hence it is by monitoring our reaction to them, noting what it is that we like and dislike, that we come to "discover" who we "really are",' argues Colin Campbell (2004: 32) from a US perspective. It is not the product or item itself that shapes identifications, and identifications are not created from products. Instead, people's behaviour and attitudes towards and reactions to products and goods are what relate to their identifications. Consumption in the form of shopping is, in this regard, a search for one's inner self – be it a spiritual or a spiritual, modern self; it is an attempt to create this self.

In this sense, consumption is part of a social process around culture, cognition and motivation. Eva Illouz (2009: 382) claims that emotions are key to understanding consumption within this entangled web. The *abayas* of the Arabian Peninsula function as objects of desire (see Campbell 2004) – not as objects of need, in terms of satisfying daily needs. To desire something (or someone) means to follow an inner wish to be recognised and acknowledged by others – be it by a human being or by a spiritual being. This dimension relating to the individual references back to the economic market, which encourages people to think about how one's body, food, movement or dress will be recognised and valued by others. This, in turn, influences decision-making around the products we purchase.

The aspect of shaping identification and differentiation within the realm of the economy is especially significant for the middle class. As a sign of distinction, this class integrates itself, according to Dick (1990), into the consumer society with its 'culture of consumerism and lifestyle' (Ansori 2009: 88). When conceptualising class in Malaysia, I follow the theoretical approach of anthropologist Johan Fischer (2008: 53–73).[1] While determined class distinctions or, generally speaking, conceptualisations of class do not exist in Islam, Muslim Malays in Johan Fischer's study refer to the middle class (*kelas pertengahan*) when talking about their own and others' social position (Fischer, J. 2008: 60). This is the case for the vast majority of the present study too. As Fischer notes, an important factor of being middle-class in Malaysia is consumption.

Monetary income is turned into consuming various commodities. This is crucial for the performance of middle-classness. Purely economic consuming practices are complemented, however, by a form of regulation for middle-class Malay Malaysians: 'Ideally, *balanced* consumption signifies modes of Malay consumption that convey social mobility and status *without being excessive*' (Fischer, J. 2008: 64, emphasis added). According to Johan Fischer (2008), the Malay Malaysian middle class wants to distinguish itself from the upper class through its form of 'proper Islamic consumption'. This means consuming in a restricted, not extreme, manner. The latter, by contrast, is assigned to the upper classes, who are regarded as immoral according to Islamic principles based on improper use of the consecrated and the material alike. Proper Islamic consumption follows Islamic ethics of being modest and moderate and of consciously creating a happy and balanced life for oneself.

Consuming a travel offer to Dubai, Mecca and Medina and shopping for certain items in those places is embedded in interpreting practices of what is perceived as moral behaviour – or, more precisely, moral consumption in an Islamic sense. Carla Jones (2010) describes this entanglement as 'pious consumption' in her work on lifestyle magazines targeting urban middle-class Indonesian women. The interface between capitalist consumption and having a devout relationship with God as a Muslim 'embraces both the promise of piety and the thrill of being attractive, expressed through purchasing power' (Jones 2010: 96) – as we have seen with the 'Dubai *abaya*'.

This interface is subject to a constant struggle against *riak* (arrogance) and explains in part the specific Malaysian style of *abayas* that evolved and can be purchased in *Souq Naif*. Being attractive is part of a spiritual stance that is embedded in an Islamic understanding of beauty. In this sense, feeling or being beautiful is not only located at the bodily surface; it is inherently spiritual. Being spiritually beautiful means being a devout and pious person, leading to a framing of one's own body that reproduces and expresses piety at the same time. The outer appearance can be, according to this Islamic understanding, a manifestation and even multiplication of this inner state of beauty (Jones 2010: 105). Furthermore, God encourages and values beauty as He himself is beautiful. This is revealed in Sahih Muslim, the Hadith collection followed in Malaysia. Hadith 6902 Al-Mu'jam al-Awsatt says 'Allah is beautiful and loves beauty' when a man asks about wearing nice clothes and shoes. The beauty referred to in this Hadith therefore explicitly includes garments. Sura 7, verse 26 of the *Qur'an* additionally indicates that garments are meant both to preserve modesty and to adorn at the same time: 'O you Children of Adam! We have bestowed raiment upon you to cover your shame, as well as to be an adornment to you. But the raiment of righteousness – that is best.' The spiritual significance becomes clear when one considers that, according to the *Qur'an*, Allah created mankind 'bare and alone' (sura 6, verse 94), i.e. with a naked, pure, beautiful body and soul. The pure, beautiful body has no guilt and if the ornaments of the body are good in terms of intention and motivations, they symbolise purity and beauty.

This condition of being spiritually beautiful is, then, not to be undermined by extravagant consumption. Consuming a beautiful, fashionable *abaya* from Dubai is potentially too excessive an act of consumption. Being beautiful without being modest leads to the state of potentially practising *riak* (being arrogant). Dressing the body with an *abaya* considered to be beautiful or fashionable, such as the 'real Dubai *abaya*' (i.e. made and bought by Emiratis), invites this possibility. This was indicated by my respondent Basharat above: she distanced herself from the 'Dubai *abaya*' because 'it feels like "too much", . . . [i]t's a different class-*lah*'. The 'real' *abaya* from Dubai is of high quality and of high material value and represents not just a class-related status position; simultaneously, purchasing it would mean performing extravagant and superfluous consumption. Thus, inner and outer beauty need to be persistently balanced in order to not lose the connection to God – for example, by buying and wearing relatively cheap *abayas* from *Souq Naif* that are especially tailored to the tastes and requirements of pious Malay Malaysians.

Being a pious Muslim is therefore a crucial constitutive element for my respondents' identification as middle class (see Frisk 2009; Sharifa 2001). As we have seen with the beauty of the woman and her fashionable *abaya*, piety here develops not only through proper forms of consumption but also with the act of appropriation and use afterwards, i.e. with the style of the consumed good and the inner stance of how to wear it and what to express with it, namely without performing *riak* (arrogance). Obviously, capitalist developments relating to consumption need to be understood here in the context of their linkages to religious devotion, virtues and practices of Islam in everyday life (Jafari, A. and Süerdem 2012; Sandıkcı and Jafari, A. 2013).

Consumption (adequate before God), piety (submission to God) and the place of consumption (Dubai) are constitutive for the notion of being Muslim Malay Malaysian middle class in this study. Buying an *abaya* from Dubai means, for my respondents, imagining and/or actually shopping for a modern, religious female garment that is not 'too much' but proper in terms of material value and religious requirements. Thus, not only can the places and objects be simultaneously modern and spiritual, so can the activity (shopping).

Abayas in sacred landscapes

After shopping for *abayas* in Dubai, the pilgrims go on to Mecca and Medina. Considering the development of the *abaya* as the most widely used garment in the *whole* Gulf region, and Farrah's statement at the beginning of this chapter about buying *abayas* in the Holy Land, the relationship between the garments and the various places of purchase is of further interest. Indeed, besides the *abaya* from Dubai, most of the Malay Malaysian women of this study shop for a second type of *abaya* on their religious journey: a type they call 'simple *abaya*', which they buy, like Farrah, in the perceived centre of Islam. In terms of design, these *abayas* are still decorated (for example with floral patterns or black pearls) but do not usually have any *glittering* elements ('*bling bling*') on them, in contrast to the fashionable or modern *abaya* from Dubai. In terms of the meaning attached to this *abaya*, this garment is embedded in the attribution of meaning that the 'placial' area of *haramain* (literally: the two holy areas/places) is considered 'a land full of blessings', as my respondent Ubaidah put it. Ubaidah exemplified this in its connectedness to material objects from that area:

> [W]hatever is from there [the 'land full of blessings'] has sort of more meaning to it. So, people will value it more, if you have the same item, you buy one from China and one from Mecca, people will value the one that comes from Mecca more because it's from Mecca. Is has certain, not blessings, but certain value [*harga*²] because it comes from Mecca . . . We cannot measure that, but we will appreciate it more if it comes from Mecca. (8 September 2017)

Items from the spiritual land are, according to Ubaidah, connected directly to the holiness of the territory. Annisa specified this aspect of the *abaya* as follows:

> If you buy an *abaya* there [in Mecca and Medina] you feel something. You feel you can perform your religious obligations in the *abaya*. There is something there compared to the *abaya* from Malaysia.³ Our intention how we see the *abaya* is different. If we see the *abaya* from Mecca and Medina, we can recall how we were in Mecca and Medina . . . It feels like 'something' . . . it has something because of the mosques. Because those *abayas* are always from a trip which was for *umrah*. So *abayas* have different memories and it's different how we see it. (26 August 2017)

According to Annisa, an *abaya* from Mecca or Medina is associated with the religious journey because the only reason one would travel to these sacred territories is to undertake pilgrimage. Obviously, when something is bought in the Holy Land, *haramain*, it still has this 'special something'. In this sense, the place becomes more important than the item itself: most of the *abayas* sold in Mecca and Medina are not produced there, which my respondents were well aware of, as these goods have become part of the global market. *Abayas* are designed by local designers in the Gulf, produced in China or Pakistan, shipped back to the Gulf states and retailed there (see Appadurai 1986: 41). My respondents still valued the *abayas* more if they were brought back from this particularly sacred territory, no matter where they were produced. The product has this 'special something' for them because it is sold and bought in an authentic environment. An *abaya* from Mecca or Medina becomes religious because of the holiness of the place from which it was purchased; an *abaya* from Dubai becomes religious and modern due to the spiritual and glamorous place in which it was bought.

Things, objects and goods are not religious or secular as such. Whether or not and how a good is transformed into a religious good depends on the production process, circulation, consumption and the intention with which it is treated (Moors 2012: 276). *Abayas* purchased on the Arabian Peninsula are believed to have intrinsic value, depending on what people make out of them within market exchange *and* within sacred landscaping. The value assigned to *abayas* from Dubai is not only a spiritual value but also an economic value (in contrast to those from Mecca and/or Medina), and therefore touches on the concept of commodity fetishism developed by Karl Marx (see Jones 2007). Marx (1968 [1844]) created this term by borrowing the notion of the fetish from anthropology, where it refers to a sacred or symbolic object that, according to its worshippers, has supernatural power. According to Marx, commodity fetishism is the perception of the social relations involved in production, not as relations between people, but as economic relations between money and commodities. As such, commodity fetishism transforms the abstract aspects of economic value into objective, real things that people believe have intrinsic value. Ignoring the labour involved in the production process of an object, a commodity is treated as though its value is intrinsic because of its economic price and, thus, because of its abstract relationship with money and product within the exchange system. Thus, commodity fetishism denotes the erroneous view that the value of a commodity is intrinsic; it is not, but rather depends on what people make of it within the market. Things are fetishes in this sense, because through the power of people's belief in them they create an obscure value order that places a diamond above fresh water, for example – even if a diamond in itself does not have more value (on the contrary, it is in fact completely useless). In the Marxian sense, the religious or spiritual part of commodity fetishism is only a metaphor to indicate that market exchange, the production of economic value, etc are based on people's belief in it.

Fashionable *abayas* from Dubai are imagined as expensive, luxury items because of their classed character. Consuming the object within a Muslim world order makes its value spiritually driven too, as discussed above. The sole aspect of spiritual value is, however, what turns *abayas* from Mecca and Medina into fetishes: Muslim pilgrims attach meaning to them based on their origin in sacred territories. This valorisation as a fetish is, for my respondents, embedded less in market exchange (even though the production process is concealed here too from an analytical perspective) than in Muslim place-making. 'Since the signature item of Saudi is the *abaya*, so many people get the *abaya* . . . Especially [because] Malaysian women can wear it for religious purposes, they can wear it to the mosque, they can wear it for anything that requests modesty in their dressing,' is how Farrah put it (8 July 2017). The spirituality inherent in these garments from that particular territory is, in turn, embodied by means of using it: 'We are close to Allah when we are modest, that's how it influences the relationship to God when I'm wearing *abaya*. I remember Him when I remember not to wear something shiny. It must be loose and modest,' as Sofea said in the introduction to this book. The *abaya* from the cradle of Islam has intrinsic religious – not material – value due to the place it comes from and the characteristics of the garment this automatically implies. The value of an *abaya* from the land of the *haramain* is predominantly spiritual, whereas the value of one from Dubai is spiritual and economic. However, both types of *abayas* are outward expressions of moral principles which are part of place-making and habitual shaping of identifications within sacred coordinates.

Gendering spaces in Malaysia by materiality

The intrinsic value of an *abaya* from the Arabian Peninsula has ramifications for whoever buys and wears which *abaya* and on what occasions back home in Malaysia. From what I observed, 'fashionable *abayas*' are generally worn by women who describe themselves as 'moderate' (a term used in English), 'liberal' (*Muslim liberal*) or 'modern' (*moden*).[4] They wear 'simple *abayas*' too, but these are also worn by very pious or devout Muslim Malaysian women. This latter type of woman, however, does not wear the 'modern' *abaya*. Hence, two different types of Malaysian women purchase two different types of *abaya* in the two different physical locations.

Those Malay Malaysian women who call themselves 'modern' or 'moderate' Muslims wear their fashionable *abayas* from Dubai on 'special occasions', such as evening outings, weddings (*kenduri kahwin*) or graduation ceremonies (*konvokesyen*), in order to inwardly strengthen and outwardly express spirituality at lavish events. The occasions on which a 'simple *abaya*' from Mecca or Medina is chosen are, however, slightly different. Amriah called herself a 'simple, not modern' woman. She commented that the two *abayas* she purchased in Mecca are the garments she wears for *Hari Raya Haji*, the ceremony at the end of the *hajj* season which is celebrated by Muslims all over the world. The reason for this? Because she feels connected to the pilgrims and the atmosphere ('I feel the same as the pilgrims' [*merasai sama dengan orang hajji*]) and wants to create a bridge between herself and those who are performing *hajj* pilgrimage at that very moment through her *abaya* from Mecca. Many other Malay Malaysian women in this study wore their *abayas* on Fridays, i.e. at the 'head of the week' (*sayyidul ayyam*). Others wore them for Muslim occasions, such as fast-breaking or a religious lecture at the workplace during Ramadhan.

Sulayman Khalaf (2005: 265) argues on a general level that '[d]ress does not only transform the human body into a cultural form, but also transforms it into a walking script, a social language. When clothes are framed by particular dress items, the body becomes a moving constellation of symbols and signs that speak out to the social world.' Amriah and many other of my respondents use the *abaya* as a symbol to experience and to speak out about religiosity in Malaysia. Considering Ubaidah's words quoted above – 'whatever is from . . . [the 'land full of blessings'] has sort of more meaning to it' – however, leads to the question why *this object* in particular is chosen as the symbol to express religiosity rather than any other material or non-material manifestation brought back from sacred landscapes. Why do my female respondents consider this garment especially suitable as the material interface between their inner spirituality and its external visibility in social spaces?

Marking the feminine public

The ways in which my Malay Malaysian respondents experience Arabian women and their clothing during their stay in Mecca and Medina is of relevance here. Being on pilgrimage and not on a social visit, the pilgrims mingle with Arab women, who usually wear the *abaya* on a daily basis, solely within the context of mosques, restaurants or streets where other pilgrims are predominantly present too. These spaces are thus religiously connoted public spaces. This means that Malay Malaysian pilgrims encounter local Arab women in their *abayas* in public spaces – explicitly not in private – because the encounters take place only in wholly religious contexts.

Malay Malaysian pilgrims are therefore not exposed to women not wearing the *abaya*. At home, in private spaces, older women in Saudi Arabia and other parts of the Arabian Peninsula wear colourful dresses (*kandora* or *jallabiyah*) and young women wear Western clothes (see Maneval 2019: 170–215). Due to the rigid social ordering of gendered public and private spaces, colourful/Western Arab dress is therefore not seen by Malay Malaysian pilgrims. For Saudi Arabian women, the *abaya* is a garment of and for public space, and therefore illustrates only this public element of their clothing realities. Thus, beyond the 'placial' reasons explained above, Malay Malaysian pilgrims furthermore assign a religious and spiritual meaning to the *abaya* because they know it only from public life on pilgrimage – a meaning that does not exist for Arab women relating to their garment. Hence, Malaysian pilgrims connect the holy places of Mecca and Medina and their inherent spirituality to an object of public space. It is this feeling of the public, religious space during *umrah* that they want to bring home to Malaysia via the *abaya*, as Farrah illustrated above with her words '[The *abaya*] is something, that the people in Mecca wear . . . to do their religious rituals. When you also wear it, you are part of it.'

The background to the implementation and development of the wearing of *abayas* on the Arabian Peninsula was to obscure the outer appearance and visibility of women in the public realm and to explicitly avoid drawing attention to the female subject, as shown above. In Malaysia, on the other hand, the wearing of *abayas* is still such a recent phenomenon that wearing it is a particularity – the black *abaya* is conspicuous and makes those who wear it 'visibly Muslim' (Tarlo 2010). This condition of making something or someone visible through garments in Malaysia becomes even more evident in case of the *niqab*, the face-veil. The *niqab*'s function is, amongst other things, to explicitly avoid provoking a gaze on the female who wears it. My respondent Annisa told me that after her first *umrah* trip, she actually wanted to start wearing a *niqab* back home in Malaysia. Her motivation was to keep at bay any distracting elements between herself and Allah – thus expressing her connection with God via the *niqab*. However, she said, since the *niqab* is worn so infrequently in Malaysia – it is much rarer than the *abaya* – she would become visible precisely through the *niqab* and thereby gain attention. Everyone would stare at her. This is what discouraged her from wearing a *niqab*: the original purpose would be thwarted.

While the *niqab*'s visibility derives from the garment itself, the *abaya*'s visibility evolves by means of colour. Against the backdrop of traditionally very colourful clothing styles for both females and males in Malaysia, the black *abaya* immediately attracts attention in Malay Malaysian social spaces. Modes of expression in Malay culture are generally very colourful; this is true not only of clothing but also of architecture, for example. In the *kampungs*, residential houses are painted green, pink, yellow, purple – usually in different colours simultaneously (see figure 4.3). Colour is thus highly visible in the public and private spaces of the Malay Malaysian population. Colourful Malay clothing – green *baju kurung* with blue and yellow floral designs, purple *jubah* (one-piece dresses) for women with orange geometric patterns, pink, blue or green *Baju Melayus* for men – forms the backdrop against which pious female Muslims have developed transformative clothing practices – most visibly with the black *abaya*, no matter whether it has decorations, '*bling bling*' or is simple in style.

Figure 4.3 Purple painted house in Melaka. The tapestry shows the *kaabah* in the holy mosque in Mecca. Malaysia, 2017.

Black as a colour is traditionally used to neutralise the female person who wears the *abaya*. This was expressed by a Malay batik artist and craftsman while he was showing me his colourful handmade dyed and printed cloths in his workshop:

> Black is to neutralise. It's not a colour. Like white. Black and white are only for the contrast . . . So, the Arab women [who are] wearing the *abaya*, they just neutralise themselves. Not to show any emotions or energy. They have all their beautiful clothes underneath; they have their expression and energy underneath. When they don the *abaya*, they neutralise it. (11 July 2017)

The appropriation of the *abaya* means, therefore, that more and more Malay Malaysian women neutralise their colourful clothing (see figure 4.4) by means of the black colour. This neutralisation process relates to both the materially visible level and the emotional level, as stated by the batik artist. Hence, Malay Malaysian women who have travelled to the Arabian Peninsula only really become visible in Malaysia by means of neutralising their visual appearance.

Figure 4.4   Colourful Malay clothing for women on sale in a market in Tanah Merah, Malaysia, 2017.

It is important to note that most Malaysian women are not used to dressing themselves differently inside and outside the home, or rather in private and public space, in contrast to Arab women. What a woman wears in Malaysia is what she wears as normal clothing throughout the day, in any social space. Hence, the Malay Malaysian women in this study do not reflect upon the public aspects of the *abaya* in the Arabian context and do not disconnect this garment from spiritual or religious activities in public spaces, such as mosques. The *abaya* is a noticeable expression of a spiritual disposition which has developed further or deepened on the pilgrimage journey and is communicated to the outside world. The female Malay Malaysian pilgrims of this study take the *abaya* as a particular part of Arabic public space through transregional space into private and public spaces in Malaysia by wearing the *abaya* within these spaces. Thus, the object makes changing, intersected gender–faith processes visible in social spaces.

Men's clothing worlds

Shopping for female garments on the *umrah* & *ziarah* Dubai journey in order to wear them back home in Malaysia is a practice undertaken by women. The objects, social practices and social actors are therefore gendered. What role do men play in this regard? Do they also shop for anything on the *umrah* & *ziarah* Dubai journey? If so, where do they buy their things and what meanings are assigned to them? How do they make sense of them in Malaysia?

I observed that male travellers do not shop for anything special in Dubai. However, they do purchase certain goods on the pilgrimage trip. Interestingly, they also shop for a particular garment and they shop for it predominantly in Mecca and/or Medina: the male counterpart of the *abaya*, which is the male Arab dress (*kandora* in the UAE). So, they do not purchase clothing in the modern, spiritual place where women shop for their fashionable, modern garments. Irsyad, who brought back a *jubah* (as the *kandora* is called in Malaysia) from Mecca for himself, said: 'Actually in Malaysia you can also get it [the male Arab dress] [laughing]. But it's so special when you are going to Mecca, because then this clothing is right from Mecca.' The intrinsic religious value my female respondents assign to the female garment described above has meaning for male dress too.

Men wear the traditional long, white garment on a daily basis all over the Arabian Peninsula. The name for it differs from region to region – *kandora* in UAE, *dishdasha* in Oman, *thawb* in Saudi Arabia, *kamees* in Yemen – but design-wise, it is basically the same throughout the area: a long, ankle-length and wrist-length garment which is generally loose but a bit tighter at the waist. 'The *kandora* has remained the same. It works with the lifestyle, it symbolises the Arab countries,' as Layla, the Emirati *abaya* designer, put it. However, as I have learned from my observations and from male and female tailors and retailers of Arab clothing in various shops and markets in Dubai and in Oman, even if the garment is basically the same everywhere, it gets its unique regional expression through subtle details, especially on the collar or buttons.

The unique Emirati design has five small, round buttons down the chest and a long strip (*furakha*) with a pompom (*tarbusha*) attached to a low-cut collar (see Khalaf 2005: 245) and a V-weld at the neck. The Omani *dishdasha* has a short *tarbusha*. While the latter is made of a soft, coloured material (for example pigeon blue), the former is made using a harder material (cotton or polyester), or cashmere during winter, and is white. Emirati men now wear coloured *kandoras* during the summer, but this only began in 2012. The Qatari design comes with a Western collar and shirt sleeves with cufflinks; the Kuwaiti design has a pocket on the chest and hidden buttons at the front. The Saudi *thawb* usually has a Chinese-style collar and two buttons.

Many different designs have been introduced over the last few years, especially when it comes to colour, but this has not been widely appropriated in social practice. Individual or group styles are expressed more by means of transforming the headgear. In addition to the *kandora*, men in the Arab region traditionally wear a square scarf over their head, held by a black rope. The scarf is completely white in the UAE (*guthra*), whereas it can be red and white or black and white in other parts of the region. The robe (*agal*) represents the robe with which camels' front feet were bound together at night by the Bedouins so that their treasured cattle were not able to run away, as one Emirati explained to me. Recently, young men, especially teenagers, have developed an Emirati style of headgear: without an *agal*, they bind the *guthra* up, which is then called *asama*.

The *kandora* in the UAE remains a long white garment. My Emirati respondent Huda once commented, amused by her husband: 'You have 10 *kandoras* with the same style, they are all white!' One male *kandora* tailor put it in a nutshell: 'For the *kandora*, there is no fashion.' *Abaya* designer Aliya noted: 'The *kandora* is not as revolutionising as the *abaya* is.' Aliya suggested why the style of Arab male dress has remained the same for so long: 'The *kandora* has been the same for a very long time, there is no need to change it. It makes a man looks amazing. Back in the days, it derives from the Bedouin. It's a pure representation of the Arab man' (7 January 2018). The representation of cultural customs via the male garment is what it seems to be meant for.

This culturalised meaning of the *kandora* marks an interesting differentiation to the *abaya*. The earlier reference to the Bedouins as the inhabitants of the desert on the Arabian Peninsula is a very different point of reference from Emiratis' notion of the *abaya* as preserving the modesty of females. Layla went on:

> They [men] always wear *kandora*. But men don't need modest clothing. The *kandora* is only a tradition, it's not religious. The *abaya* is a tradition and it is religious clothing. Women, when they are out of the UAE, they need something else for their modesty [when they don't wear *abaya*]. But when men travel, they can wear whatever they want, like jeans or whatever. This is the only difference between *abaya* and *kandora*: the *abaya* is also religious. (8 January 2018)

The key word regarding the *kandora* is 'tradition'. This is the central idea regarding the male Arab garment on the Arabian Peninsula itself. In order to understand gendered and intersectionally interwoven shopping and meaning-making processes on the *umrah* & *ziarah* Dubai trip, it is valuable to gain an insight into how, in turn, Malay Malaysians pilgrims use and understand this garment back home in Malaysia.

Embodying male religious status

On 4 June 2017 I joined Muslims in KL during Ramadhan for their fast-breaking at the public event Iftar@Dataran_Merdeka (Fast-breaking at the central Independent Square). Over 1,000 people gathered, most of them Malays. Mats were rolled out with food on them. Some of the seats were taken by around 200 students from *pondok* (Islamic) schools. Most of them were male but around 30 female students were present too. All the male students were wearing the simple white *jubah*. All other male attendees at the event were dressed in Western trousers and shirt.

A month later, Noorhaliza and Haytham, Masjaliza's sister and brother-in-law, organised a barbecue dinner at their house near KL for friends and neighbours. Around 10pm, one of the neighbours arrived wearing a light-grey *jubah*. He was the only person out of the 50 guests dressed in this Arabic garment; all the others were wearing Western clothes (both males and females) or Malay clothes (some of the females). I asked him why he was wearing the *jubah*. He responded:

> Because I've just come from my prayers which I performed at home. I have always worn *jubah* during prayers since I came back from Mecca. I went for *hajj* in 2012 and for *umrah* in 2010. I bought the *jubah* in Mecca in 2010. Since then, I have been wearing it back home in Malaysia during prayers. Before, I wore *Baju Melayu* [traditional Malay suit] during prayers. (8 July 2017)

Haytham was standing next to us and I asked him whether he also wears the *jubah* when he prays. He laughed and said that he never does this; he just prays in the clothes he is wearing at the time, such as jeans and a polo shirt.

While the *abaya* is shopped for and worn by the vast majority of my respondents, no matter which region they come from or how they are socially positioned, the *jubah* is apparently used by very few people. The variety of male attire I witnessed at the fast-breaking and barbecue events (students from Islamic schools, a *haji* and all others) therefore leads to the question: who is considered eligible to wear the *jubah* in Malaysia, on what occasions, and what meaning-making processes are embedded in these conditions? Farish, the HDC representative, noted that the *jubah*'s meaning becomes significant when related to certain occasions:

Farish: I wear *jubah* only for *Eid al-Adha* [same with *Hari Raya Hajji* or *Hari Raya Korban*] . . . *Eid al-Adha* is actually for people who go to Mecca and for slaughtering [*korban*] . . . I brought it with me from Saudi, but apart from *Eid al-Adha* I don't wear it.

Viola: Why not?

Farish: Because it's not suitable to wear it in Malaysia! (21 September 2017)

While Farish wears his *jubah* only once a year, for the special occasion of *Hari Raya Hajji*, other Malay Malaysian males wear this garment more frequently. When Irsyad, Suriawati and I were looking through some of their personal photographs at their house in Perak, I noticed that in one picture their six-year-old son Haissam and his kindergarten classmates were all dressed in *jubahs*. Suriawati commented that all male students wear this Arabic dress every Friday. This connection between the special Islamic day and a meaningful garment also applies to adults. Friday is the day when the important Friday prayer (*solat jumaat*) takes place.

The *jubah* is related to this Islamic practice – and to others too. I interviewed 60-year-old Qawi at his office on a Friday after *solat jumaat*. He was not wearing a *jubah* but Western clothes. When talking about men's clothing habits in Malaysia, he stated:

> You can mostly see men wearing the *jubah* on certain days of the week like Fridays, when they go to perform their Friday prayer or in the months of Ramadhan when they go and do the special prayer at night. But other than that, to wear it on a daily basis, to work or whatsoever, we hardly ever see. (3 June 2017)

As Qawi pointed out, Malay Malaysian men do in fact wear *jubah*, but only for the purpose of prayer. From what I observed, they change their clothes for prayer but, in contrast to the *haji* cited above, do not usually remain in this garment after fulfilling their religious obligation. Farrah told me about her son and her friends often playing soccer in their leisure time. Once the call for prayer (*azan*) sounds and they want to go to a mosque to perform one of their five daily prayers, 'they say they don't want to go like that [in their sports kit], so in their car they always have a *jubah*. And suddenly they are dressed properly related to the places they visit.'

Raheem, Annisa's elder brother, likewise changed his clothes from jeans and a shirt to a grey *jubah* when he visited his mother's house to break the fasting together (*buka puasa*) during Ramadhan. While we enjoyed our festive meal together in the living room with the whole family – parents, children and grandchildren – I asked him whether he wears a *jubah* in everyday life as well. 'No,' he said, 'because of the world, the culture. Because we follow the Western attire here. And those who wear *jubah* in everyday life are the *ustaz* [religious scholars]' (29 May 2017).

Raheem's comments are backed up by Muzakir, who told me about the problems for a Malay Malaysian man who does not feel eligible to wear the *jubah*:

> If we wear something that is close to the Prophet, like *kopiah* [Muslim male's cap] or *jubah*, I feel that I must have a lot of knowledge about Islam. But I don't have it! I'm afraid people will ask me about *fiqh* [Islamic jurisprudence] and *tawhid* [Oneness and Uniqueness of God] when I wear *kopiah* or *jubah*, that's why I don't wear it all the time, people will interpret me as an *imam*. The responsibility comes with the attire. There is a heavy responsibility based on what you wear. (7 October 2017)

Thus, the Malay Malaysian men and boys of this study who wear the Arabic *jubah* in Malaysia use it only for Islamic events and dates. Notably, this is only true of ordinary males who do not have any particular religious function or position, such as *ustaz* or *imam* – or the *pondok* students at the public fast-breaking. Only those men with a religious function wear the Arabic and, simultaneously, religiously attributed *jubah* in Malaysia in everyday life. Not all of my respondents wear a *jubah* – in fact, very few do – but it is more likely to be the case where men have already performed their pilgrimage, as we saw with Haytham's neighbour. For these men, wearing a *jubah* represents, among other things, religious status.

Layla noted above that the *kandora/jubah* is generally considered a traditional garment on the Arabian Peninsula. In contrast, in Malaysia it is perceived as a religious garment due to its holy place of origin. The cultural and religious meanings of the garment shift within *transregional* sacred landscaping. Interestingly, within *regional* landscaping, the meaning does not differ regarding culture or religion but does differ regarding gender. Purpose and implication are strikingly different for the male and female garments. The *kandora* is understood on the Arabian Peninsula as an item of cultural clothing that nods to Bedouin tradition, whereas the *abaya* is a cultural and, simultaneously, religious item of clothing that aims at preserving a female's modesty. While Mecca, Medina and the *kandora* are connoted as traditional and religious, Dubai, the fashionable *abaya* and shopping are connoted as modern and religious at the same time. While the former relates to males, the latter relates to females. Objects (*abaya* and *kandora/jubah*), places (Mecca, Medina, Dubai) and activities (shopping) are, therefore, highly gendered in their intersection with spiritual meaning.

Gendered cityscapes

As we have seen, Malay Malaysian women become 'visibly Muslim' in Malaysia when they wear the *abaya* throughout their day. Ordinary men, however, do not wear their religious garment in private and public spaces throughout the day – only, if at all, on the specific occasion it is meant for. When public spaces in Malaysia can be marked by women as religious and feminine through the *abaya*, how does this social space relate to males and masculinity?

Following pilgrimage, many of my male respondents changed their religious practices back home in Malaysia. Othman, for example, told me: 'After *umrah* . . . I [started to] perform my prayers five times a day now; I often go to the mosque' (15 May 2017). Ubaidah expressed in a similar vein:

> [B]efore you go for *hajj*, you don't go frequently to the mosque . . . We, as Muslims, are encouraged to do two days of fasting every week, Monday and Thursday; and going to the mosque for Islamic classes to increase your knowledge about Islam. After you have done your *hajj* . . . you go more frequently to the mosque. (8 September 2017)

Othman and Ubaidah focus on performing their Islamic obligations more frequently, or more strictly, after having performed pilgrimage. Consequently, they go more often to the mosque to pray or, as many of my other male respondents told me, to attend *Qur'an* classes. These classes are usually held in a mosque after *maghrib* (evening) prayer. Thus, these men become more present – and visible – in mosques after pilgrimage. They join spaces that are public religious spaces with more frequency.

Strikingly, in Malaysia and on the Arabian Peninsula alike, mosques are generally strongly associated with males. Whenever I accompanied Muslims to a mosque, these places and spaces were most often visited by males. The important Friday prayers in particular are meant for and attended only by males. Furthermore, every time I was with my respondents in mixed gender groups (as *umrah* & *ziarah* travellers, as couples or as families), whether travelling to a faraway place or in the city, sooner or later the question arose as to where the upcoming prayer would be performed. In the case of a couple, it was always the husband who took care of searching for a mosque or *surau* (prayer room) where they could go to pray. Every time the call to prayer was approaching, the wife would ask her husband whether he had decided about the place they would stop to pray. While the wife then performed her prayers in the mosque as well, the responsibility lay in the husband's hands and it was always up to him to look for a place where *he* felt comfortable.

One reason for the strong relationship between mosques and males is entrenched in the condition that males are generally encouraged to pray in a mosque whereas women should do so at home. When I gathered with Masjaliza, Noorhaliza, Kartini and Ramli at Noorhaliza's house for a '*nasi kerabu* family dinner' (flavoured rice with herbs, salad and *keropok* [prawn chips]), only Ramli, the sole man present, prayed in a room on the ground floor. All the women prayed upstairs where the bedrooms are.

After he had finished his obligation, I asked him about the reason for this spatial separation. He answered:

Ramli: They [Masjaliza, Noorhaliza and Kartini] perform their prayers upstairs in the bedrooms in order not to be seen by men. Men are encouraged to pray in the mosque, but women are not, they should rather pray at home. Because in Islam we take care of the women. Sometimes we need to go quite far to the mosque, we walk or we go by bike. So, they should rather stay at home because it can be dangerous for them.

Viola: But you could go together to the mosque . . .

Ramli: Yes, but not everyone is married. There are single women who would need to go there alone. So, it's better for them to stay at home. So, you see, women are used to not being seen during prayer. (7 July 2017)

Ramli emphasised that women need to be taken care of by men, explaining the spatially gender segregated prayers through an assumed weakness of women. Anwar, however, focused not on the attributes of females but on males when making a similar argument: 'For men it's recommended to pray in the mosque. For women it's better to pray at home. Because to become a man, you need to struggle, so you better go outside the house' (12 December 2017). Irsyad extended Anwar's explanations about roaming and gathering in public (and) religious spaces as a basis for becoming a man with further normative male roles:

> The Prophet recommended all men to go to the mosque for the Friday prayer because men should pray together and get close, that's why they should gather in the mosque. When it's *jumaat* [Friday] prayer, there is also the *khutbah* [speech by the *imam*]. The *khutbah* is provided by the government because they want to avoid politics from opponents in the mosque. (17 June 2017)

As Irsyad pointed out, men are (supposed to be) involved in religious policies. The internalised reasons, based on gender ideologies as formulated by Ramli and Anwar, for spatial segregation between men and women during prayer, especially when it comes to the Friday prayer as the most important prayer of the week, are complemented by political reasons. Besides weekly involvement in these policies, the mosque is generally simultaneously a place for prayer *and* for social gatherings for males, as many of them take the opportunity to chat before or after prayer, exchange information, build networks and thereby 'get close' to each other, as Irsyad mentioned. The ideological gender assumptions about females and males lead to the practical consequence that Kartini, Noorhaliza and Masjaliza not only pray in a 'general' home but specifically in the bedrooms and, therefore, in private, familiar, safe spaces. The men, however, pray in public spaces, gathering with others who are not closely connected to each other. Hence, a male's religiosity is traditionally present in public space in Malaysia through the culture of mosques, whereas a woman's is not. Based on pilgrimage, these spaces become even more dominated by males, as noted by Othman and Ubaidah.

This interlinkage between space, place, exteriority and interiority has important repercussions for the conceptualisation of female and male subjectivity. Elizabeth Grosz (1995: 103–10) discusses architectural space-making in relation to corporeality. Cityscapes and architecture on a broad level and houses on a concrete level are perceived as physical places associated with males. The space in between, however, is considered to be something female. While the solid, formal place of a mosque is, in Muslim contexts, a male place and social space, the roads in between, the metro, buses and cars, and the gardens of houses are appropriated and used by men *and* women.

These gendered conceptualisations of space are challenged in the context of Malaysia. The male public spaces and places of mosques are inherently religiously connoted and materialised in architecture. According to Grosz, the public space in which females are present is a general space with no particular gendered or religious meaning which is outside material and solid buildings and, therefore, fluid and indefinite. The women of this study, however, mark the public space following pilgrimage not through Islamic practices and bodily visibility in religious institutions, as the men do, but via embodied practices – by wearing the *abaya*. Hence, while Grosz states that a '[w]oman is/provides space for man, but occupies none herself' (1995: 99), I argue that Muslim Malay Malaysian women become visible subjects in gendered public spaces based on the gendered embodiment of sacredness they produce therein. However, Muslim women become more present in both solid *and* fluid public spaces – in buildings and streets, on public transport, etc – but men do so specifically in solid ones (mosques). Whereas the former reclaim *new* spaces for themselves via their visibility, the latter deepen and broaden their visibility in their long-lasting traditional spaces and places. These dynamics evolving around feminising public spaces and places via the *abaya* furthermore touch the private realm, especially within families. While Ramli stated above that females should perform their prayers in protected private spaces, precisely these social actors undermine this order when marking the public as feminine.

Muslim modernity is female

As shown above, my ordinary male Malay Malaysian respondents, who do not serve as religious figures, wear the religiously saturated *jubah* back home only on certain occasions. The circumstances in which women wear their *abayas* in Malaysia were mentioned above when comparing and contrasting the occasions on which fashionable or simple *abayas* are worn. Subsequently, the issue of *who* wears which intersectional garment *when* will be revisited in a comparison between the *jubah* and the *abaya*, as this will lead to further gendered conditions of traditionality and modernity.

During her *ziarah* tour through Dubai, the *umrah* & *ziarah* traveller Citra, a teacher in her late 30s from the town of Kuantan in the state of Pahang, told me about her *abaya*:

> In Malaysia, I wear the *abaya* on Fridays. Because on Fridays, the Prophet was always eating special fruits, he made special *wuduk* [ritual ablutions before prayer] . . . This way [through wearing the *abaya* on Fridays], we remember the Prophet's life. (22 April 2014)

Masjaliza expressed similar feelings regarding the relation between her body, her clothing and her Islamic spiritual stance: '[With] the *abaya*, I want to sustain the Islamic culture and history, it is a recommendation, at least I want to wear it to the mosque, to follow the Prophet's way of life' (16 July 2017). Both Citra and Masjaliza integrate the *abaya* into their pious life in Malaysia and use it as a means to connect themselves to the Islamic past.

This bond to the Islamic past through the wearing of the Arabic religious garment is true of my male respondents too. Zulkifli and his 20-year-old daughter Dinihari wore *jubah* and *abaya*, respectively, on *umrah* & *ziarah* in Abu Dhabi in January 2018. Zulkifli said: 'We wear it [*jubah* and *abaya*] to follow *Sunnah*.' *Sunnah* are the *Hadith*, the sayings and deeds of the Prophet Mohamad that form the most important reference point for Muslims alongside the *Qur'an*. Citra, Masjaliza, Zulkifli and Dinihari relate Arabic life directly to the Prophet Mohamad's life and history – what they want to feel and express through their religiously saturated garments.

This connection of the Arabic garment(s) to Islamic tradition has further gender-specific implications. Annisa and her 30-year-old husband Muzakir invited me to dinner at their apartment in a condominium ('condo') in KL. After we had eaten, Muzakir left the table to perform *maghrib* prayer in a neighbouring room. He changed from jeans into *kain pelikat* for this purpose. This is the Malay male *sarung* men usually wear at home in rural areas or for prayer throughout Malaysia. After he had prayed, I asked him:

Viola: Does it feel different praying in *jubah*, *kain pelikat* or trousers?
Muzakir: Yes, it does. Because when we wear *jubah*, we apply *Sunnah* which means that we follow the Prophet. So, we get more rewards [*pahala*] then. We have to follow *Sunnah* because of *nikmat. Nikmat* is a gift from Allah related to what we enjoy. We can breathe and *nikmat* is the oxygen we can breathe, it's the eyes that can see, it's the mouth that can taste. *Nikmat* is the facilities that Allah gave us to run our lives. So, we have to follow *Sunnah*. The Prophet was wearing *jubah*, so, we also must wear it. And also the turban, the *serban*, because he was wearing it. If we wear it, the *jubah* and the *serban*, then we follow the *Sunnah* . . .
Viola: And why does it feel different when you pray in *jubah*?
Muzakir: Because of our *roh* [spirit], like the *rohani* [soul]. *Roh* is the inner feeling. In *jubah* we feel more peaceful. When we wear *kopiah* [which is considered to be a transformed *serban*] we also feel more peaceful. For example, if we want to scold somebody, it doesn't feel right to do so when wearing *jubah* or *kopiah*. Because it's a spiritual thing. If I wear it, I feel that I want to do good deeds . . . Wearing *jubah* [during prayer] means going back to *Sunnah* but the *telekung* [the female prayer garment] is not *Sunnah*. The Prophet was a man. So, the women cannot follow the male Prophet in the same way! . . . The feeling how men perform their prayers is different because the Prophet was a man and he can only be followed by men, what he did can only be followed by other men. (7 October 2017)

Muzakir differentiated males from females in terms of spirituality by referring to the prayer attire. The *telekung* and the *jubah* have two different functions: the *telekung* is a means of covering the female's *aurat* during prayer; the *jubah*, however, is a means of following *Sunnah*. This is directly linked to the person's gender: the prayer garments are different for women and men, as is the embodiment of spirituality, i.e. the connection to the Prophet, that is expressed through this attire. As Muzakir said, females are perceived as never being able to follow the

Sunnah completely. Since *Sunnah* is one of the two fundamental elements (besides the *Qur'an*) on which all Muslims base their belief, Islam is generally male connoted, as only males can be fully devoted to it. The intersection between gender and faith/spirituality marks inequality for women here.

This unequal intersectional relationship, however, reaches a common cause with both genders concerning the will or intention to connect oneself to the Islamic past by wearing traditional Arab garments. As these garments symbolise a connection to the Islamic past, the Malay Malaysian social actors in this study transcend time by wearing them. The use of contemporary clothing for a relationship with the Islamic past – and thus with tradition – and especially the classification of the 'Dubai *abaya*' as 'modern' leads to more theoretical debates on modernity.

What modernity means is highly contested and negotiated inside and outside academia. Modernity is an important point of reference for dealing with one's own social position. Understood as an analytical concept, modernity is not to be equated with perspectives of social actors on what it means 'to be modern'. This approach implies a conception that 'traditional cultures' have not been marginalised by 'modern' influences. Local actors within modernising socio-cultural, political and economic processes rather adapt to dynamics perceived as modern based on their backgrounds, wishes and requirements, and thereby actively create their own ways of 'being modern' (Kahn 2001: 657–9). Thus, a homogenous Southeast Asian or Western Asian modernity does not exist, as different groups of social actors have created their own strategies of development. In this sense, an understanding of 'multiple modernities' (Eisenstadt 2000) is more appropriate when examining the ideas and practices of 'Malay', 'Malaysian', 'Arab', 'Emirati' or 'Muslim' modernities, with their specific processes of industrialisation, urbanisation and bureaucratisation (see Kahn 2001: 659). Thus, a twofold differentiation is needed between, first, analytic and emic concepts of modernity, and secondly, between a monolithic understanding of modernity by modernisation theorists and a flexible understanding of multiple modernities on an analytic level.

However, as Bunnell (2004: 20) points out, the notion of multiple modernities should not be conceived of as a global Western condition that is localised differently in manifold places outside the West. 'Rather, to recognize the modernity of other(s') places is to acknowledge the non-West as a source of self-theorization and truth-claims – the non-West as producer, as well as mediator, of knowledge, which is extra-local, even global in scope' (Bunnell 2004: 20). Popular discourses on modernity in Malaysia or the UAE are, in fact, shaped as an opposition between modernity and tradition (see Houben and Schrempf 2008: 11). In search of a balance between the two poles, social actors formulate modernising processes in Asia specifically by means of redefining local cultural elements in relation to 'Western modernity' (Muhammad Khalid 2010; Ong 2005: 37–38). In this sense, modernity and tradition are to be understood in the sense of 'context-bound articulations' (Hermann 2011: 1). However, modernity and traditionality are codes deriving from Western classification systems that have globalised and thereby reached regions such as Southeast and Western Asia.

A shared notion of the concept of modernity – not only in anthropology – is a break with the past, i.e. what came before. This past is commonly understood as the traditional or premodern and refers to a chronology of certain eras (periods before enlightenment or capitalism) or temporal developments (conditions before industrialisation). In this sense, and drawing on Hegel and Habermas, Daniel Miller (1994) understands modernity as a rupture of socio-cultural, political and economic processes. Antonio Rappa (2002) situates modernity in the era of modernisation based on capitalist production processes. He argues that capitalism and neoliberalism in its recent form have enabled processes of consumption and the development of middle and high classes involved in consumerism. Subjects constitute identities as 'modern' by being affluent and through consumption. This corresponds with my respondents' ideas regarding the *abaya* as a simultaneously middle-class and modern garment.

In *Modernity at Large*, Arjun Appadurai (1996) claims that modernisation theorists too often take the opposition between tradition and modernity for granted rather than differentiating the various notions they imply. The theoretical opposition between the two concepts

> has steadily reinforced the sense of some single moment – call it the modern moment – that by its appearance creates a dramatic and unprecedented break between past and present. Reincarnated as the break between tradition and modernity and typologized as the difference between ostensibly traditional and modern societies, this view has been shown repeatedly to distort the meanings of change and the politics of pastness. Yet the world in which we now live – in which modernity is decisively at large, irregularly self-conscious, and unevenly experienced surely does involve a general break with all sorts of pasts. (Appadurai 1996: 3)

Even though Appadurai questions the category of tradition, he preserves the idea of modernity as a force of rupture. Harri Englund and James Leach (2000) understand modernity conceptualised in current anthropology as organising assumptions – or even metanarratives – about the past rather than being chronologically measurable and, thus, a condition that can be theorised explicitly. Modernity is more a depiction of how we understand ruptures and discontinuities – here caused by modernity – or, as Bruno Latour puts it in *We Have Never Been Modern* (1993: 10): 'The adjective "modern" designates a new regime, an acceleration, a rupture, a revolution in time . . . "Modern" . . . designates a break in the regular passage of time.' Following this, modernity is not the opposite of tradition but humans' understanding about how we relate to the past.

Against this backdrop, theorising modernity requires an analysis of how people relate to, reflect on and engage with places, chronological sequences and other people, while constituting themselves as modern. I understand modernity as a theoretical-analytical concept that targets social dynamics which refer to modernisation, for example, to the introduction of technology and industry (Hopwood 1998: 2). The basis for what I refer to as 'modernisation' was the evolution of capitalism in the modern era. Many scholars term this historical development and the processes therein 'modernity' (see e.g. Rappa 2002; Lee and Ackerman 1997). By contrast, I understand modernity as a depiction of appropriation and differentiation of certain transformed ways of living and thinking. These transformations aim at articulations of norms and values that have emerged based on rational thinking during the modern era (Waardenburg 1996: 318). Given this, I do not perceive modernity as a distinct historical period but as a concept and a perspective, i.e. a way of framing situations, conditions and transformations (see Mee and Kahn 2012). This concept or perspective is not neutral and unbiased but a powerful and hierarchical way of creating truth. It functions as 'an objectifying story', as Wendy Mee and Joel Kahn (2012: 7) put it, 'that narrate[s] a history of progress and emancipation'. This narrative is predominantly produced and circulated by subjects who position themselves in the 'modern West' and who simultaneously disparage all others they exclude as non-modern or traditional.

Based on this exemplified understanding of modernity as a theoretical concept, I take the previous conceptualisations by Rappa, Miller, Appadurai, Englund & Leach and Latour beyond their frameworks by extending them based on the *abaya* as a certain material good and the possibility and ability to purchase this good (resources, class status). Through the *abaya*, Malaysian pilgrims retain their bonds with the

Islamic past; they consider it to be a religious garment related to the holy places in the Arab world. This is equally true of the male *kandora/jubah*. Both garments are, therefore, an expression of temporal transcendence. Time is deconstructed by this object – an object that becomes coeval with ancestral subjects and, thus, a tangible trace of their presence in present times. The constructed time acquires chronological depth but with a tangible starting point (the era of the Prophet Mohamad) instead of being considered a limitless sequence of past and future events. Time is understood as linear, as 'before' vs 'after', by my Muslim respondents, not cyclical or anything else (see Gell 1992). Since this is an Islamic understanding of time, the longer the time, the more subjects (Muslims who form the *ummah*) it embraces. However, the Arabic garments have become physical objects that symbolise a palpable reference only to the Prophet and his companions – not to the whole *ummah* ever since.

Women simultaneously embody their idea of being modern through the 'modern and fashionable' *abaya* from Dubai. Here, at the level of class status, which is expressed by the involvement of female pilgrims in the glamorous fashion world and consumer culture in Dubai, the pilgrims break temporally with their ordinary life in Malaysia. At this point, modernity can be understood as a situation of rupture at first glance. However, at the point of purchasing and wearing the fashionable *abaya*, pilgrims do not encounter a clash with the past; rather they frame a world in which modernity is 'unevenly experienced', as Appadurai puts it in the passage cited above. This unevenness is embedded in the condition of religion representing timeless truth and thereby being detached from oppositions of modernity and tradition. However, the active reference to modernity through gendered clothes by my Malay Malaysian respondents is still operative. Modernity, in this context, refers not to distancing oneself from the past but to actively and explicitly searching for a connection with the history of one's religion. Modernity means being aware of one's own history, and preserving, appreciating and appropriating it. The female pilgrims overcome the experience of rupture by consuming and wearing the Dubai *abaya*. The male pilgrims overcome the experience of rupture too, but since their garment is not connoted as modern at all but as solely traditional, it is not embedded in the context of how to experience modernity.

Given this, I come to the conclusion that modernity is not the force of rupture, but the ability and possibility to bridge the past with the present via things and/or activities that are perceived as 'modern', which means intersecting at exactly this point of transcendence. This kind of modernity is intersectional: it is Muslim female. Being modern in this sense is a Muslim female condition: the women constitute themselves as modern based on the place (Dubai), the object (fashionable *abaya*) and classed shopping. Consumption, i.e. the social practice of transferring goods – which symbolises the connection between past and present – into one's own possession, is an ambivalent expression of transcending the past and the present and of being modern, and thus constitutes a particular under-standing of Muslim female modernity. This Muslim female modernity is furthermore constituted by the embodied practice of dress which means that, conversely, men can be religious as we have seen, but not religious and modern in an intertwined manner in their forms of dress.

Thus, being a modern and religious person depends on one's gen-dered subject position within a Muslim hierarchical world order. The une-qual intersectional condition of males being able to connect themselves to the Islamic past on the basis of 'following *Sunnah*', unlike females, as Muzakir noted above, is reversed when the modern dimension comes into play: the intersection between gender and faith/spirituality marks an enhancement of subject positions here that is not accessible to men.

To summarise, by wearing the *abaya*, women are in an active rela-tionship with the body in space and time and navigate the different status positions they want to emphasise regarding religion, femininity and class. By bringing the religiously connoted *abaya* into everyday life in Malaysia and, therefore, into private *and* public space when wearing it at home, in the streets, on trains, on buses or at work, females make their spirituality visible and thus mark their active part in religiosity – as men have always done. These women transcend spatial orders when they wear the *abaya* in private and public spaces in Malaysia: they appropriate the public space, which has been a predominantly male space, just by being visible. Paradoxically, my respondents claim this space by wearing a dress that was originally designed on the Arabian Peninsula to de-emphasise the female presence in public space. Thus, based on the transregional trans-formative process of the garment, the Muslim Malay Malaysian women in my study intervene on the transregional level with their bodies in spa-tial orders as they make females' spirituality, their appropriation of and involvement in Islamic principles and history, their ability to travel and to gain knowledge, and to actively challenge the male presence of religi-osity in public space visible, tangible and, presumably in the long run, negotiable.

Modernity in this context is intersectionally female and religious, and opens up a broader variety of status positions for women within a male Muslim environment on the socio-geographic scale of analysis. This environment declassifies females, in turn, on the intimate scale when it comes to the embodiment of attachment to Islamic history. Having dealt with intersectioned gendered and spiritual characteristics of the *umrah* & *ziarah* trip and its outcomes on the intimate, transregional and temporal levels of analysis in Malaysia, the following chapter will turn to its consequences on the family scale and on a newly introduced spiritual scale.

Notes

1. See Ahmad Fauzi (1999) for a purely Marxist approach to class in Malaysia. He adapts theoretical elements of the relationships between the state and class formation to postcolonial states in general and to Malaysia in particular. He argues that when Karl Marx developed his theoretical framework, two distinct classes evolved in industrialising Western Europe: the capitalist bourgeoisie and the proletariat, the latter oppressed and exploited by the former. However, he argues, the class situation in postcolonial states was rather different. In emerging capitalist societies, the bourgeoisie used the structure of the state for the sole function of maintaining and expanding capitalism. In postcolonial societies, however, no local ruling or possessing class existed and local elites were weak due to colonialism. Class structure was, therefore, more differentiated than in the twofold class structure in industrialising Western European states. In Malaysia, the local 'old' middle class, comprising Chinese traders, rural landowners and the postcolonial powers, existed as three competing elite classes. Due to the relative weakness of the local elite classes, the state in the postcolonial phase was still shaped and controlled by the former colonial power and, therefore, did not function as a means for the local ruling classes to ensure capitalism – on the contrary, in Malaysia, the state only developed and shaped the local 'new' Malay middle class in the course of the postcolonial phase.
2. In *Bahasa Melayu*, a gift from a place such as Mecca or Medina, i.e. a gift that a person values (*menghargai*, from the root '*harga*' which means 'price') in a particular way, is termed '*dihargai*' ('valued' or 'appreciated') or '*penghargaan*' (literally 'appreciated; in this context best translated as 'valuable gift').
3. Nowadays the *abaya* is also produced in Malaysia.
4. These terms are normally used interchangeably, as synonyms.

5
Gendered devotion

Shortly after returning from her *umrah* trip, my Malay Malaysian respondent Basharat told me about her experiences and thoughts:

> I feel more attached to God and the Prophet through *umrah*. But how to measure spirituality? Spirituality is not only about the rituals but also about morality. It's about how you behave. In Islam we have the rituals, the actions, like praying five times a day and the spirituality which nobody can see and know. And when we think about the males, they don't even change at all when you look at the outside! They still dress the same, they don't change their clothing style at all, unlike women. (9 October 2017)

Basharat reflected that through *umrah*, she and other pilgrims created or maintained a sense of spirituality and morality. This, in turn, is connected with a transformation of the outer appearance. By saying that this process does *not* pertain to males, she indirectly reveals that this is something specifically female.

Change of scene: Sofea, the Malay Malaysian *abaya* designer from KL, performed her pilgrimage in 2016. She said:

> *Umrah* and *hajj* are journeys to train people to be modest. And the *abaya* is a way for a woman to cover herself completely after she comes back from *hajj* or *umrah* . . . When we are wearing *abaya*, it protects us from men choosing you because of your appearance. (16 August 2017).

Complementing Basharat's position, Sofea explicitly indicated that the *abaya* is an adequate means for women to deal with changed inner dispositions achieved through *umrah* or *hajj*. This gendered garment can, furthermore, guard against the male gaze on the female body. Pilgrimage seems to encourage females to direct their attention inwards and toward God but not to men. Sofea thus highlighted the specific elements relating to Basharat's comments on changes in female attire after pilgrimage with reference to the *abaya* and its capacity to help women stay focused.

These two quotes reflect four factors: (1) Pilgrims undergo a process of spiritual transformation through *umrah* or *hajj*. (2) This transformed spirituality happens within a pilgrim's personal, inner world and is communicated to the outer world via rituals. These first two factors form the prerequisites for the next two central features in this chapter: (3) Female pilgrims materialise both these inner and outer transformation processes by altering their outer appearance. While these three factors can also be traced in chapter 4, the fourth issue points to a further direction: (4) Women want to use the *abaya* to protect themselves from being approached by men. As men do not seem to change their clothing practices at all following pilgrimage, the process of communicating transformed spirituality after pilgrimage is gendered.

This gives rise to three further questions. First, do Malay women alter their clothing style after pilgrimage only by donning an *abaya* or do they appropriate, renounce or transform any other elements of their outer appearance as well? Second, how are changed spirituality after pilgrimage and gendered changes in clothing habits connected to one another? Third, do males translate altered spirituality into changed social practices beyond attending mosques more regularly?

Whereas the previous chapter dealt with the question of how women and men become visible in public spaces as pious believers following their pilgrimage, i.e. how the bodily surface transmits spiritual enhancements to *outer* surroundings, the focus in this chapter is on the other side of the coin. It relates to the subject's *inner* disposition on the one hand and, on the other, to the *inner*, private world of the family, with its distinct gender relations in contrast to those between men and women (and their bodies) in non-related relationships in social environments.

This chapter will show that both females and males undergo processes of spiritual development as a result of undertaking pilgrimage and, as a consequence, that their religious practices take stricter forms. This is, as I will show in this chapter, especially true for women and men who have started their own families, i.e. women and men who have roles as wives and mothers and husbands and fathers. Given these conditions, the two genders overlap in their practices. However, females and males differ in the outcome of transformed spirituality. My argument goes as follows: first, female pilgrims maintain deeper spirituality following their pilgrimage by communicating with God by wearing the *abaya*. This results from the belief that Malay women need to treat their bodies in a special way in contrast to males – what marks disregard for females here from an intersectionality standpoint – in order to be able to create a communicative space with Allah, and the *abaya* is especially suitable for this purpose. Second, women not only transform their bodily practices in their relationship to God but, in their position as wives, they furthermore modify their bodies in their relationship to their husbands. This is achieved not with the *abaya* but with clothing items that conceal the *aurat* in addition to those that cover the torso, arms and legs. This is embedded in communication processes with non-*mahrams*, i.e. men they are eligible to marry, in which they signal that they cannot be approached and are only available for their husbands. Third, since Allah is generally perceived as male in this research context, these women submit to *male characters*, i.e. to Allah and to the husband, as an outcome of their pilgrimage journey. This process is to be understood as ambiguous for these Malay Malaysian women as submission here means, to a certain extent, freedom. Women's subordination and liberation are directly related here, occurring on different levels that are organised in a hierarchical way, but still enmeshed. Fourth, men reconfigure their roles as fathers upon pilgrimage. Consequently, whereas transformed inner dispositions as a result of pilgrimage are embodied practices when it comes to females, they are instead related to social action and social relationships when it comes to males.

In the following sections, the reciprocal influences between pilgrimage, spirituality, religiosity, gender, body and family are investigated on a general level. On a concrete level, the evolution of a spiritual realm between the believer and God through the female body and its attire is analysed. Furthermore, Muslim Malay family norms and practices concerning roles as wife and husband are examined. This will be complemented by a discussion of enhancements in gendered parental roles – as Muslim Malay mother and as Muslim Malay father. Given this, the analysis in this chapter is situated on the family scale of the framework *Scaling Holistic Intersectionality*. It is furthermore located on a scale that I will introduce in the course of this chapter in addition to those scales that have previously been dealt with in the literature on scaling in general and on Scaling Intersectionality in particular (see my detailed discussion in chapter 1): a spiritual scale. Religion and faith have not been integral parts of intersectional analysis, not to mention analysis that follows the approach of scaling for heuristic reasons. This explains the previous lack of such a scale. As this chapter (and the subsequent one) will show, the incorporation of a spiritual realm, space or scale, that grows between a believer and God, into intersectional research that centres on religion, faith and/or spirituality is a requirement for a comprehensive understanding of corresponding local complexities.

The overarching questions that will guide the analysis are: (1) In what ways are religious practices after pilgrimage intersectionally connected to concepts of the gendered Muslim Malay body and its complement, the mind? (2) How are Malaysian conceptualisations and practices of Muslim and Malay families connected to gender, embodiment and faith, and how is the social institution of the family affected in turn by broadened pilgrimage experiences in Malaysia? (3) In what ways are the ideas of Allah intersectionally related to gender, body and family concepts and practices in Malay Malaysian contexts? Given these questions, this chapter is embedded in discussions of regional Islamic gender ideologies and in orthodoxy that covers ideas about Allah and further understandings of gendered Islamic spiritual principles.

Pilgrimage engenders religiosity and spirituality

Sharifah from Shah Alam, whom I accompanied on a *ziarah* stopover in Dubai in 2014, met me for a drink three years later in Subang Parade, her favourite shopping mall in her Malaysian hometown. I asked her whether the pilgrimage had changed or affected her life. She responded: 'Yes, it changed my life. After coming back from *umrah*, I became more religious, I got nearer to my Creator . . . I changed because I had the opportunity to perform *umrah*, I'm so grateful for it, so I didn't want to be the same as before, I wanted to increase my *iman* [belief]' (20 August 2017). Rabwah, a Sufi believer from KL, went on *umrah* six times because when her husband was working in New York they stopped in Mecca to perform *umrah* whenever they travelled. She additionally went twice for *hajj*, in 1992 and in 1995. She reflected: '*Hajj* and *umrah* are journeys to come closer to the Creator and the Prophet . . . When I was young there was no satisfaction in what I was doing. It was empty. After meeting a Sufi *syeikh* [spiritual master], I went on the *hajj* and I realised: it's about loving God!' (25 September 2017). Spiritual enhancement was described not only by my female respondents, but also by my male interlocutors. For example, Ubaidah revealed:

> So obviously, after *hajj* or *umrah*, you feel like you have lifted your spirituality after the trip, if you are really sincere and really committed. At least that is how we feel because it's not easy to describe

to others. You have a certain different mood compared to before you went because you really put your mind into it and in the end of it you feel some spiritual uplifting. (8 September 2017)

Apparently, my respondents became more involved in their beliefs as a result of their pilgrimage experiences. This was true for the majority of the pilgrims in this study – only a handful declared no alteration in any regard as a consequence of their pilgrimage. The emotional involvement and closeness to Allah that most of my respondents developed in Mecca are feelings that they wanted to maintain in Malaysia, as Farrah expressed:

> Once I went on *umrah*, I feel I was in constant communication with God. In Malaysia I sort of hadn't felt it. But during *umrah* you always talk to your Lord, you go to the mosque, it's always constant communication; you feel the presence of your God most of the time. After I came back, I still have these feelings. Even when I'm alone and I don't have any ideas, I ask God: 'Please inspire me.' When I do my writing, for example, I always ask God for His help. Last time it had been all about *me*, and like 'Oh, *I'm* so good!' [she emphasised], I got As for this and for that. And the feeling when I got an A last time, during my Masters, I was of the attitude like 'If it's not because of you, I wouldn't imagine I got that idea.' You know? But now I know it's inspiration from God . . . So this continuous connection to God only evolved during *umrah* and when I go to the university or to work, I want to have this constant connection. So that's why I do a lot of monologue [speaking loudly with God], I continue to do this in Malaysia. (1 June 2017)

Farrah and other Malay Malaysian pilgrims in this study aimed to preserve their deeper relation to God back home in Malaysia. An obvious and measurable means of doing this is to transform their usual habits, religious practices or lifestyles. While Farrah talks to God in the form of a verbal monologue ('[God, [p]lease inspire me') and started to restrain her ego ('Last time it had been all about *me*, and like '"Oh, *I'm* so good!"'), Othman, for example, described a wider change in social practices after pilgrimage: 'I changed my lifestyle after *umrah*. It's difficult to explain. It's like "from bad to good". Before *umrah*, you hang around . . . but as a Muslim, there is no clubbing. After *umrah* you should not go clubbing, "don't do anything wrong!"' (15 May 2017). Many other Malay pilgrims in this study started to read the holy book after *umrah*. Sharifah said: 'I want to get myself nearer to my Creator by reading the *Qur'an*. Before going on *umrah*, I seldom read the *Qur'an*, but since I came back I read it every day. I go to classes now to read the *Qur'an* properly' (20 August 2017). Likewise, Suriawati started to read the *Qur'an* more often following pilgrimage, but she also increased her communication with Allah by means of additional prayers. Three to four times a week, she gets up at around 4am in order to pray *tahajud*, one of three prayers additional to the five compulsory prayers (*solat*) that are recommended (*sunnat*). Similarly, Masjaliza began to perform additional prayers. She said:

> After my second *umrah* [in 2012], I started performing the *duha* prayer.[1] . . . I had already started this type of prayer during my first pregnancy in 2011. But after my second *umrah*, I started to do it more consistently. Because my second *umrah* was sponsored by my father, I felt so blessed, so *duha* prayer is related to *rezeki* [luck coming from God], I have so many gifts and blessings from Allah: my husband, my son, my family . . . During the *duha* prayer, I have other feelings as compared to the other five compulsory prayers, it's very calm, it's perfect. I'm in love with the *duha* prayer. The intention, the love towards this extra prayer is different than the other prayers because it's an option, it's not compulsory. (26 October 2017)

Likewise, Irsyad performed prayers more after *umrah* but he focused on the five obligatory prayers (*solat*) rather than the recommended prayers. In a similar vein to Masjaliza, he explained the reasons for his increased prayer with reference to luck and blessings from God:

Irsyad: I changed after *umrah*. Before *umrah*, I sometimes skipped my prayers, for example. But now I make sure that I don't skip *solat*.
Viola: What was it that made you change?
Irsyad: Because sometimes, people go for *umrah*, but they get sick there, so they cannot do anything there and at the end they come back without having performed *umrah*. But I feel blessed by God, I performed my *umrah* together with my wife and son, so we feel Allah loves us. So that's why we need to perform our obligation well now we are back, we cannot skip our prayers. (1 October 2017)

Masjaliza's and Irsyad's gratitude at having performed *umrah* was manifested through practical outcomes of pilgrimage in worldly life; Ubaidah, however, brings in an additional, spiritual element:

When people go on *hajj*, they aim for '*Hajji mabrur*', which is '*Hajji* acceptable in the eyes of God'. Why I relate to *Hajji mabrur* is that those who attain this *Hajji mabrur* will be accepted by God into paradise [*jennah*]. This is really the highest level of *hajj* . . . But how do you know that you get this *Hajji mabrur*? Once you attain this *Hajji mabrur*, you will [automatically] change for the better . . . For some [it] is a tough thing to go almost every day there [to a mosque], five times a day. You have to be in the mosque before sunrise for *fajar* [morning] prayer which now [during this time of the year] is about ten minutes to 6am . . . After you . . . attain the level of upliftment [through *hajj*], you go more frequently to the mosque, for example . . . Even in the *Qur'an* it says the *solat* [compulsory prayer] is a burden for mankind except for those who have *kussyuk*. These people's hearts are only with God. All these difficult things become easier once your heart is with God. So after the *hajj*, you become a better Muslim because it helped me to be more committed to Islam. Because once your heart is close to God, you would do anything to get closer to God, to be in touch with God. So things that God commands you to do become easier for you to do. (8 September 2017)

Ubaidah specified that fulfilling religious obligations more frequently after pilgrimage inevitably derived from a deep spiritual connection to God that developed on the pilgrimage. This was not something he needed to work on or had great difficulty with; it simply arose automatically due to his emotional closeness to God. Like my other respondents, he furthermore articulated that he realised this transformed inner disposition through social practices and rituals such as additional prayer, fasting or attending Islam classes.

Both the female and male Malay Malaysian subjects of this study increased their focus on performing Islamic obligations (*solat*, avoidance of clubbing) and or/recommendations (*tahajud* and *duha* prayers, additional fasting, Islam classes) in order to follow their deeper religiosity and spirituality following their pilgrimage. Admittedly, whereas most men and women feel a spiritual transformation though *umrah* or *hajj* and adjust their social practices accordingly in similar or identical ways, in other areas their corresponding expressions differ profoundly. As Basharat revealed in the introduction to this chapter, females change their clothing as a consequence of spiritual enhancement – and not solely to make their pilgrimage experiences more visible in public spaces, as discussed in chapter 4.

The *abaya* is devotion to Allah

We have seen that the women and men in this study feel a deeper connection with God through pilgrimage and, as indicated by Sofea, that women start wearing an *abaya* upon returning home in order to preserve a modesty that only evolved during the religious journey. Thus the question arises: in what way is the *abaya* related to a personal connection to Allah and its resulting transformed inner stances?

As noted above, some of my female respondents sustained their spiritual bond with God through the practical performance of prayer (obligatory and recommended prayers alike), because the bond is especially intense during prayer. Is the *abaya*, then, particularly linked to praying? What role do garments in general play in this regard?

Praying bodies

Typically, when it comes to the performance of prayers, no matter when they are performed, Malay women pray in *telekung*, which they wear over their everyday garments. Interestingly, sometimes they wear an *abaya* instead of a *telekung* during this ritual. Sofea stated that the *abaya* is most convenient for prayer, especially during work time:

Viola: Do you also wear the *abaya* for prayer?
Sofea: Yes, we can wear it for prayer. When you wear the *abaya* in the office, then you can go for prayer directly, you don't need the *telekung*. I also do that. But when I pray at home, I wear *telekung*. I only wear *abaya* for prayer in the office, so I don't need to change clothes. (16 August 2017)

That Sofea does not 'need to change clothes' when using an *abaya* for prayer highlights that when a woman wears her *abaya* instead of a *telekung* during public or semi-public prayer, she usually does not follow the common habit of wearing the garment over clothing worn only during prayer. Instead she uses the *abaya* for the duration of that specific public occasion (in this case office work). At the public event Iftar@ Dataran Merdeka, I observed a similar practice, which I wrote about in my field journal:

> I spent my time together with Zamira and Fatimah who work together in the Islamic tourism industry and who promoted their institution in a booth [at Iftar@Dataran Merdeka] there. At 7:22pm, the call for

prayer (*azan*) started to call believing Muslims for *maghrib* prayer. Most people around us with whom we broke fast together immediately set into motion toward a big yellow mat the organisers of the event had placed beside the eating area for a congregational prayer. Zamira and Fatimah, however, did not join the group but individually built a temporary 'wall' out of two of their promotional panels right behind their booth. Two small flyers from their work institution served as their prayer mat. Fatimah used a small drinking bottle with water for her *wuduk* [ablution]. Both Fatimah and Zamira started praying on the flyers without changing or replacing their garments. During the whole event both were dressed in *abaya* with adornments but no '*bling bling*'. (Personal fieldnotes 4 June 2017)

Zamira and Fatimah were dressed in their 'simple *abayas*' for their formal prayer at the public event. What motivated Sofea, Zamira and Fatimah to wear *abayas* instead of the usual *telekung*? How are female garments characterised as prayer garments and thereby as garments worn while communicating with God? A couple of days after observing Iftar@ Dataran Merdeka, Zamira explained the various gendered regulations for women during prayer in an email:

There are certain requirements when it comes to performing prayers for Muslim women:

1. The clothing that is prescribed for women to pray in is any clothing that covers her entire body apart from the face and hands; it should be loose and opaque, so that it does not show the shape of any part of her body. If it is a blouse or shirt, then it should be long enough to cover the behind.
2. The garment should not be a thin or see-through garment, rather it should be a concealing garment which will cover the woman completely. The garment must not be thin and show what is beneath it i.e. like the colour of the skin. This is then regarded as not covering.
3. Based on this, it is not permissible for a woman when praying to wear tight clothes that show her *aurat*, or show the limbs and the shape of a woman's body. Examples are jeans, tight pants or trousers, body hugging blouses or shirts. Hence they need to use a *telekung*.
4. It is also obligatory to cover the feet.
5. Attire must be clean.

Zamira ended her email with: 'In this case, an *abaya* suits me fine as it meets all of the above criteria just like the *telekung* does' (7 June 2017). This was underpinned by Suriawati when she explained how she needed to dress for formal prayer (*solat*), what she wore and why:

> We have to close the *aurat*. For this purpose, we wear socks and clothes must be like this [she pulled her sleeves down to her wrist and pulled them tight so that there was no space between the cloth and her skin]. For *solat* [obligatory prayer] I wear *abaya* or *telekung*. I put on a *telekung* when I'm not dressed in an *abaya*, so I think the *telekung* makes me comfortable. I usually don't wear *baju kurung* [two-piece traditional Malay clothing] because some *baju kurung* might be fitting to the body, so some of them are not suitable for prayer. *Abayas* are always suitable because they're already loose. (17 June 2017)

As Zamira and Suriawati indicated, there are certain characteristics that their clothing needs to have during the intense communication with God in order to cover their *aurat*. Suriawati explained the reason for this requirement: 'We need to cover our *aurat* during prayer [*solat*] because it's an Islamic regulation. It's part of the mandatory requirements for *solat* [*syarat sah solat*]. It also says that we have to do the ablution [*wuduk*] prior to *solat* and that we must pray in a clean condition. Otherwise our *solat* is not *sah* [valid]' (17 June 2017). Some garments, such as shirts, blouses and jeans, have to be hidden under a *telekung* for prayer. The *abaya*, however, also fulfils these requirements. *Abaya* and *telekung* function as garments that cover the *aurat* during prayer, hiding the bodily silhouette and reducing the visibility of skin during prayer.

These requirements for covering the female body during prayer give rise to the question of requirements for men. A couple of months later, when I visited Suriawati, Irsyad and their sons over a weekend, I observed the prayers they performed at home. I asked Irsyad afterwards how men need to attire themselves when it comes to formal prayer. He said:

> The men wear whatever they wear as long as we confirm that our clothes are clean. I just wear whatever I wear during prayer, I even often go for Friday prayer in my office clothes. If our *aurat* is exposed during prayer, *solat* is not *sah* [valid]. We can have this problem when we are wearing a shirt that is too short. During *sujud*, which is when we kneel down and place our foreheads on the floor,[2] our *aurat* could be exposed at the back if our shirt is too short, and then our *solat* is not *sah*. That's why we have to wear a

long shirt or we tuck it in, so we are not worried about showing our *aurat*. (30 September 2017)

As Irsyad noted, the only bodily and clothing element he needs to take care of as a praying man is to cover the lower back, which can easily be achieved by wearing a long shirt. As long as the males wear clean clothes when fulfilling *syarat sah solat*, no additional requirements need to be met as the male *aurat* contains fewer body parts than the female *aurat* and these are usually covered anyway. The abovementioned demands on female bodies and their clothing, such as wearing opaque and loose garments during prayer, are not applicable to males. The distinct clothing requirements my female and male respondents elaborated on and practised accordingly lead to the question of why the bodily condition of cleanliness and covering the *aurat* is required. Irsyad elucidated in this regard:

> If you want to meet someone special, you also need to meet him in a proper way, right? You cannot meet him with a smelly body. So we also want to meet Allah in a good condition. Even though we cannot see Him, He can see us. So we prepare ourselves in a nice condition, same as if I meet special friends. (30 September 2017)

Irsyad was referring to the interaction with God that evolves once a Muslim starts to pray. Whereas the preparation of the body for prayer differs for women and men, the meaning of prayer in terms of facing God applies to both genders. Similar to Irsyad, Zamira stated:

> In Islam, when you meet God, you have to be properly dressed and attired. You have to be at your best. Don't put on old clothes or dirty clothes. You want to look good when you want to face God. As long as your clothing is clean, you are clean, you are at your best based on your own ability. (3 June 2017)

Suriawati and Irsyad explained above that meeting God during prayer in a proper way is bound by structural guidelines (*syarat sah solat*). Rabwah brought up a further aspect when I attended a *zikir* session with her at her Sufi order (*tariqat*) in KL. We talked about the meaning of covering the *aurat* when facing God just before she and her female Sufi fellows prepared for *maghrib* (evening) prayer. She said:

> It's *adab* ['We follow "the good manners of Islam"'] to cover *aurat* during prayer because we are facing the Creator when we pray.

Adab is the way, the culture, the right or proper way when we face the Creator. It's like when you meet the king or prime minister, you cannot just go like this, in whatever you're wearing. You need to dress properly. It's the same with the Creator. You cannot just talk to Him when looking the same as at any other time. Because you praise the Prophet first [*salawat*] and then you face the Creator. (25 September 2017)

Adab are good manners in Muslim thought towards Allah, the Prophet and fellow human beings. Following *adab* during prayer by attiring one-self in a manner that is considered to be proper implies a spiritual element and thereby complements the structural requirements noted by Suriawati and Irsyad. Muslims need to dress appropriately according to religious and spiritual understanding in order to involve themselves appropriately in a spiritual relationship with Allah. At this point, the *abaya* comes back into play.

Spiritual body treatment

The *abaya* is perceived as a garment that is *syariah*-compliant. Furthermore, wearing an *abaya* specifically affects one's spiritual connection with God, as Basharat stated: 'If people want to become better in terms of religiosity, become closer to God, they will change their clothing to *abaya* because this way, they dress more modest' (1 August 2017). The relationship between the *abaya* and a connection with God was similarly expressed by Hidaya, the founder and fashion designer at Malaysian company Hidaya International. When describing her latest *abaya* collection in 2017 in three words, she said: '"Obey in style" as when one covers up their curves, they are obeying God' (*The Star*, 27 August 2014).

Obviously, the *abaya* functions especially well when creating and fostering a connection with God. This complements Zamira's comments regarding structure and form, when she talks about the *abaya* as a garment that follows the prayer regulations concerning the female body. Since praying opens up a communicative space with God, the *abaya* becomes particularly relevant when it comes to prayer situations. Rabwah chose a comparison between Allah and worldly powerful men (king and prime minister) for her explanations about female bodily behaviour during prayer. However, to cover the female *aurat* – or to wear *abaya* – during prayer relates, in this particular situation, to the relationship with God and not with other men. Covering the *aurat* during formal prayer thus has a different meaning from covering the *aurat* as a woman in everyday life in terms of gender relationships. Masjaliza and I discussed this issue:

Viola: Why do women have to cover their *aurat* during prayer? I mean when you pray in the mosque, you are only amongst females. And when you pray at home, you are alone or maybe together with your husband. So there are no non-*mahrams* around, why do you have to cover then?

Masjaliza: When we cover our *aurat* during prayer, it's not about other males. It's different, it's because of the prayer itself. It's like a uniform then. It's not particularly *what* we wear but *that* [she emphasised] we cover our *aurat*, that's the most important thing during prayer. Because we interact with God.

Viola: But why do you need to wear certain clothing when you pray, I mean God can even look *through* [Viola emphasised] your clothes, right? He can even look into your heart, so He can also see behind your clothing . . .

Masjaliza: *Solat* is formal communication with God. We can pray anywhere at any time, but *solat* is the formal communication and the uniform makes it formal. (20 September 2017)

This discussion of behaving according to good Islamic manners (*adab*) and creating a formal situation through distinct clothing, as Rabwah and Masjaliza intimated, raises the further question of why males are not required to produce formality and to act appropriately when facing God since they can perform their formal prayer in whatever they are wearing – they do not need to change clothes or put on additional clothes. A week after Masjaliza gave me her explanation, I met her and her family at her sister's house for another family dinner. Before we sat down on the floor mat for our meal I took the chance to ask Ramli about this issue. He said:

> Men don't need this formal situation for prayer, they just need to cover their *aurat* and then they can just go for prayer. Islam says 'Better to pray wearing something formal or something special, but if you don't have something like this, then you can just wear anything.' I don't wear anything special for prayer. What special clothes should look like is not defined, this is up to you. Specialty or formality during prayer is not as standardised for men as for women with their *telekung*. At home, I wear *kain pelikat* [a coloured piece of chequered cloth folded around the hip]. Sometimes I take *kain*

pelikat with me for prayer, I have it in my car then. But not really to wear something special but only because I'm worried about cleanliness. So when I go to the construction site, I always wear it, because it's dirty there and I've been wearing my trousers since the morning; I sit on different chairs, maybe there is bird's pee or lizard's pee somewhere. (28 September 2017)

Both Muslim women and men create a space of communication and interaction between themselves and God during formal prayer. However, males create this space once they start praying whereas females additionally need to embody their inner disposition towards God on the basis of their attire. These gendered dimensions of covering *aurat* and the constitution of a spiritual space between the believer and Allah can be traced by the linguistic senses of the word 'veiling', as Fadwa El Guindi explains. She argues that the English word 'veiling' implies different notions. It covers four dimensions: material, spatial, communicative and religious. The material dimension is that of clothing and decoration. The spatial dimension refers to a veil in the sense of a curtain or a hanging that separates different spaces from one another. The communicative dimension refers to veiling as making oneself invisible and concealing oneself. The religious dimension denotes veiling as a form of separating oneself from worldly life and from sexuality (El Guindi 1999: 6).

Yet 'veiling' has no direct expression in Arabic – the most similar term is '*hijab*', derived from the root *h-j-b*. 'Hijab' refers to a curtain, screen, separation or, most commonly, a veil as a form of dress for the hair and neck. It additionally relates to protection: a *hijab* is a veil but also an amulet for a child's protection (El Guindi 1999: 157; Kokoschka 2019: 271f). On the personal level of a Muslim woman, El Guindi argues, veiling in the sense of donning a *hijab* in the Arabic sense of the term is an expression as well as a constitutive process of gender identity, sanctity and protection. Once a woman dons a veil, she creates a sacred (private) space, which she can do in any public and secular place in the world. In this way, she argues, women who veil express privacy and publicity at the same time in the sense of public intimacy. The veil signifies both in one by emphasising the public/private divide: '[V]eiling is mobile, carrying women's privacy to public spaces. A woman carries "her" privacy and sanctity with her' (1999: 95).

Hence, according to El Guindi, a *hijab* defines, creates and depicts the sanctity of the female body. Veiling is a constitutive process of a personal or individual sacred space. So when Muslim women in Malaysia cover their *aurat* for the purpose of prayer, they seem to prepare their bodies for this sacred, i.e. cleansed and desexualised, condition in order to enter into conversation with God. In the context of deepened spirituality through pilgrimage, more communication with God upon return (especially via praying) and starting to wear an *abaya* in Malaysia after pilgrimage, the question remains as to why the female body needs this particular processing and treatment through the *abaya*, *telekung* and/or veil in contrast to the male body.

Approximating a sacred female body

Suriawati, Irsyad, Zamira and Ramli mentioned above that their attire and their condition in general must be clean during prayer. In fact, when Muslims want to enter into communication with God by means of prayer, they are not only required to be dressed in clean clothes but additionally have to *bersucikan* – from the root '*suci*', to cleanse and purify – their bodies first. The Malay term '*suci*' has a worldly, tangible and concrete meaning of 'clean' (similar to '*bersih*') on the one hand. On the other, it has a spiritual, abstract meaning. In addition to 'clean', it can be translated as 'chaste', 'virgin', 'holy' (as in *tanah suci* which denotes the Holy Land of Mecca and Medina) or 'consecrated'. In this sense, *bersucikan* means to attain the required bodily state for prayer. This is done by believing, practising Muslims all over the world via ablutions (*wuduk*), for example. Through this form of cleansing, chastity as an inner disposition can be achieved and communication with Allah can evolve.

While the creation of this bodily circumstance is a precondition for all Muslims, females need to attend to their bodies more than men in preparation for prayer, as we have seen. They are specifically required to produce the essential state of chastity, unlike men, and need to put more effort into it. The reason for this is that in Islam the ideological assumption exists that the female body is inherently less chaste (*suci*) than the male body. This is justified, for example, with reference to women menstruating. This attribution of females being less chaste is applicable not only to the body when it becomes part of prayer situations but is a general assumption, as indicated by Masjaliza: 'Sometimes women are not *suci*, not only without *wuduk* [ritual ablution] but also when they have their period. Women can cause *fitna* [discord]. We *wuduk* the body [wash the body ritually] and [thereby] make it *suci*' (17 July 2017). When a woman is menstruating, her body is considered to be impure. El Guindi (1999: 113) explains that this does not mean that women are regarded as impure in general. Rather, the state of purity or impurity is something fluid and temporary for every individual, depending on the conditions.

This attribution to the female body does not apply equally to the male body, although a male body is not considered to be chaste when there are faeces on it, for example. Yet women's bodies are perceived as especially and more often impure on the basis of menstruation. In any case, as Masjaliza mentioned, the temporal state of impurity can be ended through ritual washing, which is a requirement for attaining a sacred state, for example for the performance of prayer.[3]

The two meanings of *suci* (worldly and spiritual) and Masjaliza's explanation that women in general can cause disharmony or chaos (*fitna*), no matter what physical condition their bodies are in, reveal a worldview that portrays women as physically dirty under certain conditions (for example when they have their period), but also as morally, psychologically and emotionally impure, making them weak and unstable. This Islamic understanding of women leads to the second argument as to why women are required to take care of their bodies to a greater degree than men when it comes to prayer. In the Muslim Malay worldview, the inner characteristics of women and men are attributed differently based on the Islamic conception of reason, intellect and rationality (*akal*), and sexual lust and passion (*nafsu*) (Frisk 2015; Peletz 1995). *Nafs* and *'Aql* are Arabic terms occurring in the *Qur'an* and are thus applicable to Muslim contexts in general. In Muslim Malay gender ideology, women are associated with the latter characteristic and men with the former. The ideological conception of *akal* and *nafsu* is especially relevant in rural areas where Malay culture is most strongly practised. In essence, the normative Islamic conception of *akal* and *nafsu* implies the belief that Allah granted *nafsu* to all living beings – humans, animals and spirits alike. It refers to the requirement to satisfy basic needs such as eating and drinking, breathing and sexual activity. *Akal*, however, is believed to be granted solely to human beings and therefore differentiates humans from animals and spirits (Frisk 2009: 167). Adults are perceived as having more *akal* than youngsters or children, as it evolves over time.

Within the category of adults, men are normatively believed to have more *akal* than women. This perception is entangled with Islamic theory of female and male sexuality, deriving from the *Qur'an*. As Mir-Hosseini (2009: 35) explains, it is believed that Allah granted greater sexuality to women compared to men, and this is regulated by men's sexual honour on the one hand and by women's modesty on the other. As a consequence, this includes the assumption that the unrestrained desire and sexuality of women (*nafsu*) must be disciplined by men on the basis of their rationality and ability to self-regulate (*akal*) (Frith 2002: 13; Peletz 1995: 88–93; see Peletz 1996). Hence men have a responsibility to control the chastity of their sisters, daughters and wives (Ong 2003: 266), which means that virility here is conceptualised in relation to women's sexuality. According to the understanding of *akal* and *nafsu*, men generally feel responsible for the moral condition of women. If women's sexuality is not controlled by men, then social order will collapse into chaos (*fitna*) – a state that can be reinforced when women are considered to be impure, as mentioned by Masjaliza.

Yet in Muslim Malaysia these normative ideological assumptions are not followed in their fullness. On the contrary, due to local customs and traditions (*adat*), a partly reversed understanding and practice of the relationship between *akal*–men and *nafsu*–women exists (Peletz 1995; Frisk 2009: 168). As Peletz shows on the basis of his research in Negeri Sembilan, men are regarded and represent themselves as less rational and, as a consequence, less responsible when it comes to monetary issues, for example. This is entangled with a Malay view that considers men to be less reliable concerning their social obligations towards their wives and children due to gambling – which, in turn, indicates their desirous and thus *nafsu*-driven character in this regard. Hence, women are in charge of managing structural and financial issues and are responsible for the corresponding decision-making in their families, as they are understood to be able to control their *nafsu* better than men (Frisk 2009: 168).

Nonetheless, Islamic gender ideology is still effective and operative and also touches on approaches to the gendered body. On the basis of the moral Malay Islamic ordering of *akal* and *nafsu*, Muslim women need to take care of their overall bodily self-representation, i.e. how they dress, in order to work on the condition of purity/non-purity and equally to control their desire. Especially when it comes to formal prayers (*solat*), Muslims should be attired as well, cleanly and formally as possible in order to face God in an appropriate way. The method of covering the body is the main mediator between the visible and the non-visible, between the material and the non-material – between God and believer. This 'in-between-ness' – or, analytically speaking, this spiritual scale – is constituted by the interface of formal prayer and gendered attire. It only evolves when the inner stance is embodied accordingly. In any case, women need to be properly attired during prayer, no matter how exactly a *telekung* or *abaya* is designed or characterised. I argue here that since women intrinsically cannot fully reach the state of a generally chaste body, they change their clothes for prayer (i.e. they either put on the additional *telekung* or they decide beforehand to wear an *abaya* in order to be properly attired for the upcoming prayer[s]). This shows, intersectionally speaking, a form of declassification of females on the spiritual scale, in contrast to male privilege here.

As discussed above, El Guindi states that a believing woman creates an individual sacred space in, on, and around her body by donning the veil. The Malaysian context furthermore shows that this sanctity of a female individual produced by garments that comply with Islamic rules such as the *hijab*, *telekung* or *abaya* is a precondition for the creation of a sacred, spiritual space between the female believer and God. Women are required to communicate with God in garments regarded as somehow sacred in order to produce the notion of a sacred body and a controlled emotional inner world. The *abaya* as a means to control an assumed condition of impurity, emotionality and sexuality is a means to handle spirituality and Muslim Malay normative orders and perceptions.

Both the *abaya* and the *telekung* not only express an inner relationship with God but even constitute or transform the relationship with God. These garments constitute the feeling and perception of one's own body during prayer. In case of the *telekung*, it is this particular costume and not the everyday clothes worn underneath. This is different to men and their attire: no matter whether they perform prayer wearing everyday clothes, *jubah* or a Malay skirt (*kain pelikat*), the garment touches men's bodies and is simultaneously visible to the outside world. When praying in a *telekung*, women wear more than one layer of clothing and the outwardly apparent layer does not touch their body. The *abaya* is the only garment that can replace the *telekung* during prayer (see figure 5.1). In this case, their prayer garment is, similar to male prayer attire, the interface between body and outer world.

Interestingly, some women wear fashionable *abayas*, which are often referred to as 'sexy', during prayer. Against the backdrop of the differentiation between *akal* and *nafsu*, and the allocation of the former concept to males and the latter to females, there are negative connotations to a Muslim Malay woman perceiving her *abaya* as sexy. Because of *nafsu*, which is regarded as inherently present within females, they should repress surges of emotion instead of showcasing or provoking them. A woman wearing an *abaya* perceived as sexy contravenes the expectation and demand of constraining her *nafsu*. On the contrary, she showcases and encourages her *nafsu*. Hence, when wearing an *abaya* considered sexy during prayer, the idea of communicating with God in a state of chastity is thwarted to a certain extent. I asked Rabwah whether, in her view, it is possible to pray wearing a fashionable, or sexy, *abaya*. She answered:

Figure 5.1   Malaysian *umrah* & *ziarah* pilgrims praying in the Sheikh Zayed Grand Mosque, Abu Dhabi. Most of the standing women wear *abayas*, UAE, 2018.

Yes, you can pray wearing the fashionable or sexy *abaya* but you will lose points [*pahala*; 'points' for good practices], you will get *dosa* [points for sins; opposite of *pahala*], when people complain about it, for example because of the beautiful embroidery. This happened to my friend. She was wearing a fashionable *abaya* with beautiful embroidery in the mosque. Then a lady from the back row tapped on her shoulder and said 'It's not nice, you are showing off, I cannot concentrate!' If this happens, then you will get *dosa*. But basically you can pray in fashionable *abaya*. If you say 'I want to wear the best for Allah, I want to present the best for Allah' and this means for you to wear the fashionable *abaya*, then it's totally fine, then you will get full *pahala*. But if somebody else doesn't like it, then it creates *fitna* [discord], meaning it creates evil eyes, and you will get *dosa*. *Syeitan* [Satan] will put words into their hearts [the heart of those who dislike it] and they cannot concentrate on their prayers. If you go to an ordinary place and you wear the extraordinary and others cannot concentrate on their prayer, you will get *dosa*. But I seldom hear about that. You must look at your crowd, be with others. (25 September 2017)

According to Rabwah's understanding, wearing a fashionable or even sexy *abaya* when connected with God is not physically provocative but is presenting oneself in 'the best' way one can imagine while facing God. However, praying is not only an inner, spiritual practice but also a social exercise. Rabwah shows that Muslims, and particularly Muslim women, simultaneously have a responsibility to Allah regarding their outer and inner stance and to their fellow Muslims when communicating with God. They need to cope with the requirements relating to both the spiritual and the earthly public space.

In contrast, men do not need to take as much care of their inner self, of their bodies or of their fellows during prayer. This is shown by the fact that they usually do not change their clothes in order to perform their ritual. They can pray in their everyday (profane) clothing as their bodies are conceptualised as intrinsically sacred and their *nafsu* is regarded as being controlled by their *akal*. Despite these and the above-mentioned concrete gendered differences in the relationships between subjects' bodies and their material coverage, both genders have to fulfil the gendered requirements of Muslim bodies. Only then can the spiritual space between the subject and God evolve, even though the sanctity of the female body remains approximate.

Rabwah made a connection between wearing an *abaya* and the effect it can have on a female's relations with other humans. This leads us to further female attire that women in this study started to wear when on pilgrimage. While the *abaya* displays the transformation of the pilgrim's inner disposition, these other clothing elements are less correlated solely with God. They are additionally connected to the husband.

Devoted wives, devoted fathers

Back home in Malaysia, many of the Malay Malaysian women in this study not only started to wear *abayas* upon returning from pilgrimage; strikingly, several also began wearing veils, cuffs or long gauntlets and socks. When I stayed with Suriawati for a weekend, I observed that she put on additional cuffs and socks when we left the house, which she promptly removed once she got home. When I asked her about this practice, she said: 'Before we came back to Malaysia [from *umrah* & *ziarah* Dubai], I did not wear my socks or cuffs when I went outside. As Muslim women we need to wear socks and cuffs when we go outside. So, after I came back from *umrah*, I started to wear them' (17 June 2017).

Other respondents concentrated on body parts other than feet and hands/wrists in the course of the pilgrimage journey. For example, Rabwah did not cover her hair, neck or ears with a veil before she performed her first pilgrimage, but she began to do so afterwards. Furthermore, she stopped wearing makeup to a certain extent. She recalled:

> I went on *hajj* in 1988 . . . I was not covered back then [but] I wanted to cover after that [the *hajj*]. A few months before *hajj*, I became allergic to my makeup.[4] I always used makeup back then. So I stopped using makeup and I already started covering. My boss, I'm an accountant, wanted to transfer me to another department because I started to cover up. I said to him: 'It's about loving God!' Then I stayed with my department! (25 September 2017)

Other examples show that many women who already wore the veil before *umrah* or *hajj* altered their *form* of covering after their journey. For instance, they chose a different type of veil. Sofea explained in this regard:

> After *umrah* I started to wear my scarf longer, it now also covers my boobs. And my blouse now always covers my bum and my sleeves cover my arms completely up to the hands. Because *syeitan* [Satan] hangs at the boobs and at the bum and asks men to look there! Before *umrah*, I wore three-quarter sleeves, my blouses didn't cover my bum and my scarves only covered my hair and neck but not my boobs . . . I get more *barakah* [God's blessing] if I cover fully. I feel *bershukur* [grateful], which means that I feel good in my heart, that I have enough. When I follow *Al-Qur'an* in terms of what a woman shall wear, I feel full, I feel happy . . . *Umrah* and *hajj* are . . . journeys to prepare yourself to change after *umrah* . . . Before *umrah*, I didn't follow religion fully, that's why I didn't cover fully. (16 August 2017)

Sofea's explanation that '*syeitan* [Satan] hangs at the boobs and at the bum and asks men to look there' points to a social condition that goes beyond the correlation between 'following religion fully' and 'covering fully', i.e. devotion to God: namely social relationships with men in earthly life.

This interlinkage between putting on female garments, religious and spiritual experience, and relationships to men was underscored by

45-year-old Nur Fazura, a mother of four whom I accompanied on an *umrah* & *ziarah* Dubai trip that she undertook with her husband:

> After he [my husband] came back [from *hajj*], a lot of things changed. Ever since, he has been better than me; better belief [*iman*], better attitude. I wear my scarf [*tudung*] properly since then. Before that I had also worn *tudung*, but a smaller one and not a *tudung* which covers the neck to the chin . . . So I changed because he told me how to wear it. He also asked me to wear socks, so I started to wear socks. My daughters also wear them since he came back because he taught us how to wear them properly. Since he came back, we have been closer together and together we are closer to Allah. (25 April 2018)

Whereas Sofea reflected upon 'men' in general, Nur Fazura focused specifically on her spouse. She recalled the changes in her marriage after her husband returned from his *hajj* a couple of years earlier. She was grateful for her husband's advice regarding her gendered clothing habits because, for her, it formed the basis for a shared journey to God.

Nur Fazura is no exception in terms of the socio-structural position of the women who started to wear veils or cuffs/long gauntlets in order to cover themselves after pilgrimage. All of them were already married, aged between 35 and 50, and had children. Their changing clothing habits are an expression of changed gendered relationships, as touched upon by Nur Fazura. As wives they transform their bonds with their husbands due to their changed relationship with God through pilgrimage. Interestingly, the deepened submissive role towards the husband was not required by the husbands, nor was it an issue that I observed in other situations (media or 'gossip talk' amongst females, for example). It was only obvious in this circumstance of family life in the course of pilgrimage.

As we saw above, Sofea explained that she covers her silhouette in order to protect her body from the male gaze. This gendered motivation for dressing the body is applicable to my other respondents as well. In their specific phase of life (middle-aged, married, with children), these and other women justified their new clothing items by saying that their bodies must only be approached by their husbands, and not by any other men who are provoked by *syeitan* to stare at them. Sofea elaborated on this issue when commenting on the *abayas* she produced as a designer: 'My *abayas* are straight; A-cut. That means that they are small at the breasts and bigger at the hips . . . Because we are not supposed to show our body. The body is only for the husband, not for the boyfriend or anyone else' (16 August 2017). In a similar vein, Suriawati stated: 'I cannot wear something fitting to the body. In Islam women cannot show their bodies to people, this is forbidden [*haram*], [we can show it] only to our husbands' (19 June 2017). The reason for this was given by Latipa: 'Boys and men are always attracted to women, they always like to see pretty women. So women avoid boys and men who do bad things. That's why we [as women] cover up and we can only show our hair to our husbands' (27 September 2017). On this understanding, women themselves are responsible for social actions and occurrences – in the sense of maintaining the high moral standards that prevent men from following their lust (Norani 1998: 183f). This not only relieves men of responsibility for their own sexualised thoughts and actions, but also thwarts the inner logic of the Islamic concepts *akal* and *nafsu*. However, Latipa indicated in her statement that the female body is uniquely meant for pleasing husbands in order to create and maintain a harmonious, religiously saturated marriage. This means that the women in this study who began to dress differently after pilgrimage draw boundaries against any other men they are eligible to marry (non-*mahrams*) by wearing additional garments that cover their *aurat*.

At this point I want to highlight the Malay expressions '*buka*' ([to] open) and '*tutup*' ([to] close) which are used for showing *aurat* ('*buka aurat*') or hiding *aurat* ('*tutup aurat*'). In English one uses the linguistic expression 'to cover' *aurat*. Yet in *Bahasa Melayu* the term for 'to cover' is not used in this context, so covering is not the main emphasis Malays want to put on the treatment of *aurat*. If the Malay meaning highlighted the 'covering' of *aurat*, it would be expressed as '*tudung aurat*', for example. '*Tudung*' is the term for 'to cover', 'cover' and a 'lid'. However, in Malay the terms '*tutup*' (to close) and '*buka*' (to open) are used to express the practice of concealing or showing *aurat*. Hence '*tutup*' and '*buka*' *aurat* mean to close and to open the *aurat*. This is how my respondents usually translate this social practice. Yet in the Malay language the terms '*tutup*' and '*buka*' are also used in the sense of 'to switch something off' or 'to switch something on' (as in *buka aircon*, 'to switch on the aircon'; *buka kipas*, 'to switch on the fan'; *buka lampu*, 'to switch on the light'). In these cases, '*buka*' rather means 'to activate'. Thus, in the Malay language, the common expression '*buka aurat*' implies the notion of 'activating the *aurat*', which means that it becomes active, it radiates, it communicates to the outside world, to other people – and this is exactly what should be avoided by wearing the corresponding attire. Once a woman shows part of her skin that, according to Islamic thought, she is not supposed to show to certain people (i.e. males she is eligible to marry), she activates her *aurat*, which means that she activates her sexiness and sexuality. Hence I suggest translating *buka* in the context of *aurat* as 'activating' rather than 'opening' or 'showing' as it is usually translated in the Malaysian context.

By means of wearing additional clothes such as a long, loose veil, socks and/or long gauntlets, the wives and mothers Suriawati, Rabwah, Sofea, Nur Fazura and others communicate to other men that they do not intend to activate their *aurat* for them, and hence that they are not 'available' to them. They devote themselves more to their husbands, which they ultimately express to other men through their clothes. Thus, through the *tudung* and long, loose garments, communication towards non-*mahrams* is switched off, and the female body does not give off signals or subtexts.

A sense of belonging to the husband arises especially from the effect a pilgrimage journey has on marriage: many women described, similar to Nur Fazura above, how their matrimonial relationship developed towards a more harmonious life between the two of them. This was expressed, for instance, by 60-year-old Noora, who performed *umrah* with her husband: 'A lot of things changed after *umrah* between us. We became closer. We love each other more. Because during *umrah* . . . I learned about my role as a wife from a Muslim perspective. I learned about the sacrifice as a wife' (30 January 2018). Putri framed this relationship during her *umrah* & *ziarah* Dubai trip in February 2018 in a more reciprocal way: 'Before *umrah* and *hajj*, we [my husband and I] made each other angry. After *umrah*, not anymore.' 'Sacrifice as a wife', as Noora put it, had led to a satisfied married religious and spiritual life that was grounded in (shared) pilgrimage experiences.

This correlation between being married and being a devout Muslim wife provokes the question of how the Malay Malaysian men in this study reflect upon their pilgrimage experiences with regard to their family role. In fact, some of my male respondents not only intensified their ritual practices, such as going to Islam classes or performing additional prayers; they also transformed their behaviour in family life. However, whereas women altered their matrimonial roles as wives, the men in this study made changes to a different status position within the family: not that of husbands, but of fathers. I talked with Ramli about alterations to his life after his performance of *umrah*. He explained:

Ramli: I'm trying to teach [my son] Aaqil the five pillars of Islam more [since my return from *umrah*]. I realised that when you are doing your best, you will get the best. If your kids don't pray and you don't ask them to do so as a father, you will get punished [by Allah].

Viola: Is this only related to the father or is it the same responsibility for the mother?

Ramli: This is 100 per cent for the father, it's not related to the mother. That's what I totally realised during *umrah*. But normally the mother will help her husband to take care of the child . . . As a father and as a husband, I need to establish my wife's and my children's comfort zones first. (20 September 2017)

Ramli mentioned that after reflecting on *umrah* he had taken more responsibility towards his son regarding the transmission of Islamic regulations and stressed that this was his responsibility in his role as father. According to Ramli, the mother plays only a supportive role in this regard. Ramli's reflections were based on the various Islamic teachings that Malay Malaysian pilgrims experience in the course of the journey. Islamic scholars instruct the pilgrims first in the *umrah* preparation courses and then throughout the journey in their roles as *mutawif* ('religious tour guide'). Additionally, Ramli, and other pilgrims, heard speeches and sermons by *imams* and scholars in and from Mecca and Medina. Such interactions with religious authorities and formal religious teaching led to Ramli's inner development.

The gendered difference in parenting that Ramli described was practised by Irsyad and Suriawati as well. During one of my weekend stays with them during the holy month of Ramadhan, they acted differently when it came to the sphere of Islamic rules and regulations, and their roles as father and mother of their children concerning this issue. For example, before I arrived at their place, Irsyad had emphasised that I needed to fast with them if I wanted to stay with them. He justified this with reference to his two sons Hadees and Haissam who would not understand why I, as an adult, would be able to eat or drink when with them. In contrast, when Suriawati picked me up from the train station with their kids, she promptly asked me whether I wanted anything to eat or drink before we went to her home. She kept asking this question during the car journey and stressed that it would not be a problem for their children as the youngest son Haissam (6 years old) had not yet started to fast anyway.

Fasting is the fourth of the five pillars of Sunni Islam, which Irsyad, as the father, was carefully teaching his children, ensuring that there were no distractions. He reflected on his attitude towards his role as

Muslim father when I asked about changes in his life after his *umrah* & *ziarah* Dubai journey:

> [Since we came back from *umrah* & *ziarah* Dubai], we cannot skip our prayers [anymore]. I cannot become an *imam* or *ustaz* [religious teacher] or change drastically, or immediately, but at least I can remind my kids to do their prayers, to show them what to do and how to behave. I have been wearing *jubah* more often since I came back from *umrah*, I wear it now for *hari raya* prayer [during the festivity of *hari raya*] and for *jumaat* [Friday] prayer, I don't know why I've been wearing it more often since then, but at least to show to my kids, to perform our religious obligations well. Deep in my heart I have changed, but not so much from outside. (1 October 2017)

Irsyad indicated that he was not only taking greater care in his prayers after pilgrimage, but he was transmitting this attitude to his children. Irsyad emphasised that he had 'not so much' altered his outward appearance, underscoring Basharat's statement at the beginning of this chapter that women change their clothing styles following pilgrimage but men do not. In their position as fathers, Ramli and Irsyad modified their relationships with their children as a consequence of their *umrah* journeys. The experience of pilgrimage and the increased social status it engenders influences men's attitudes and practices regarding their responsibility for the transmission of Islamic knowledge to their children. These men, and in fact others in this research too, took an active part in parenting that they had not thought of before their pilgrimage journey. They consider themselves to be role models for others, especially for their children, after performing pilgrimage. From this position, some of my respondents, such as Ramli and Irsyad, urged their children to fulfil their religious obligations (for example praying obligatory prayers [*solat*] or fasting during Ramadhan), which they had not been so keen to do before pilgrimage. Both altered roles as wives and as fathers are embedded in Islamic family ideologies in Malaysia.

Muslim Malay family ideologies

Islamic family ideology concerning (married) couples and its result, corresponding Muslim family laws, are situated between what is believed to be divinely intended and created, and what is theologically constructed by humans within socio-political and cultural contexts.[5] Approaching family matters and ideologies as a Muslim is therefore a balancing act that depends not just on belief but equally on interpretations of the holy sources. As Zainah Anwar (2009: 1), a Malay Malaysian advocate for women's rights, notes, many Muslim women who want to alter laws that discriminate against women 'are told "This is God's law" and therefore not open to negotiation and change'.

Considering family concepts and practices engenders a confrontation with gender arrangements as these organise roles as wife, husband, mother, father, grandmother, sister, uncle, daughter, etc. As Gatens (1998: 2) argues:

> The family is the single most important institution which constructs and shapes the behaviour of both sexes. The family produces sexed individuals with particular sorts of sex-appropriate preferences and tastes which are carried over into other institutional settings . . . where these preferences are reinforced and, in case of deviance from social norms, 'corrected'.

Amina Wadud (2008: 139), an African-American Muslim women's rights campaigner who studied and acted in Malaysia between 1989 and 1992 and co-founded the Malaysian Muslim feminist NGO *Sisters in Islam* (SIS), makes a similar point: '[F]amily is a construction of gender relations.' According to Islamic family law, the relationship between husband and wife grows on the basis of the marriage contract (*akad nikah*, literally 'contract of coitus' or 'contract of sexual intercourse'). This contract is an agreement of exchange, especially in order to legitimise sexual relationships between a man and a woman. Hence sexual activity is allowed only when a woman and a man are married (Raj, Ri. *et al.* 2003: 174; Zainah 2001: 235). In particular, the contract stipulates that the woman must be sexually available to the man (Mir-Hosseini 2009: 28). Ideally, it consists of three areas: offer by the woman (*ijab*) or her male guardian (*wali*) who 'is required to protect the woman's interests [and] to safeguard her moral integrity' (Hammudah 2008: 71f) (usually the female's father or any other nearest male relative), acceptance by the man (*qabul*), and payment of dowry (*mas kahwin*).[6] Once a marriage is concluded, the husband has to give sustenance (*bagi nafkah*) to his wife, not only in the form of dowry (*mas kahwin*) but more generally in terms of living expenses (*nafkah*), food, clothing and accommodation (Hammudah 2008: 148f). This means that he is materially and morally responsible for his wife, and equally for his children. This was most recently shown during the Covid-19 crisis in 2020 and 2021. Several government orders included prohibitions against anyone leaving the house – except one male family member to buy groceries, as he represents the head of the family. As Masjaliza explained, single mothers and single women were equally allowed to go out to buy foodstuffs.

The financial obligations of the husband towards the wife are directly linked to the normative Malay Malaysian wife's duties as, according to Amira (2009: 196), in return she needs to be submissive (*ketaatan*). More concretely this means serving the husband sexually, obeying him, giving birth to offspring and respecting him. If the wife is disobedient (*nushuz*), the husband is no longer obliged to provide for her (Azizah and Badruddin 2010: 108).

The normative Islamic and Muslim orders concerning sexuality are evident (not only) in Suriawati's, Nur Fazura's, Sofea's and Rabwah's concrete social actions in terms of granting exclusive access to their bodies to the husband. In the Malay Malaysian context, this sole availability for the spouse is based in entangled socio-cultural dynamics in which Islamic gender ideology, again, intersects with Malay *adat* (customs and traditions). According to *adat* rules, women use their knowledge for, amongst other things, the intensification of sexual pleasure between oneself and one's husband (Ong 2003: 267). Based in social values, an important medium for arousing sexual interest in the partner is the way a wife wears her clothes, such as draping a shawl (*selendang*) loosely over her hair and shoulders (Ong 2003: 267). Pleasing the husband sexually as a wife complies with the normative Islamic assumption that it is the husband's right and the wife's obligation to grant him sexuality, i.e. to make herself available for and attractive to him (Hammudah 2008: 170).

An ideal Muslim man, in his role as a father, is not only materially and morally responsible for his wife and children, but he furthermore has greater rights regarding his offspring than the mother does. For example, the mother is, according to formal Islamic thought, only allowed to have custody over her child if the child is below the age of discernment (*mumaiyyiz*), i.e. until the child is seven years old if male and nine years old if female. After that, custody is automatically awarded to the father. While the mother can lose her right to custody on the basis of either remarriage (Nik Noriani 2003: 62) or 'immorality', for instance, this is not applicable to the father at all (Yusuf *et al.* 2016: 1758f).

Even if the mother has custody over her children, the father, as the lawful guardian (*wali*), is still required when it comes to general maintenance for the children or to certain regulations such as schooling or medical treatment (Hammudah 2008: 34, 149), ownership of the children's property (Banks 1976: 577) and the inheritance of one's own property by one's offspring. These legal rules and regulations, as part of Malaysian Islamic family law, show the strengthening of Islam in Malaysia in the 1970s and 1980s, which has generally weakened the bilateral principles of *adat*. For example, due to *adat* regulations, women in Malay Malaysian society have been able to hold property and are granted the right to pass it on to their children (Zainah 2001: 232). However, based on the Islamic legal regulations that are operative in Malaysia, the local bilateral *adat* practice of giving daughters and sons the same amount of land has given way to Islamic Sunni Shafi'i law, which grants daughters only half a share (Ong 2003: 265).

In this entanglement, the two operative systems in Malay Malaysian society, i.e. *adat* and Shafi'i law, imply that mother and father are granted equal emotional attachment to their children – no matter whether girl or boy. Furthermore, according to Masjaliza, both parental sides have to take care of educating their girl(s) and boy(s) in terms of general knowledge as well as Islamic knowledge. Emphasising equal responsibility for the children as mother and father, she moreover stated, 'In Islam it is a duty for parents, for both father and mother, that makes no difference, to prepare the house for the child in a comfortable way, especially in order to perform *ibadah* [worshipping God]' (30 January 2020). When Ramli and Irsyad took more responsibility for educating their children in terms of Islamic thoughts and practices, they mitigated this bilateral value and strengthened the idea that this matter should be in the father's hands.

Ramli and Irsyad appropriated the transmission of Islamic traditions to the children on the basis of pilgrimage and its consequence, namely deeper submission to God. As exemplified above, there is, according to the Malaysian Family Law Acts or to *Qur'an* and *Sunnah*, no particular requirement, regulation or rule that requires a father to be especially responsible for Islamic education or transmission of Islamic knowledge to his children. On the contrary, this is attributed to both father and mother. Thus, men transform part of their role as fathers as a consequence of pilgrimage and deeper devotion to Allah.

Given this, in their role as fathers, they consequently adopt attributions as bearers of family and tradition, even though in the Malay Malaysian context it is usually women who are regarded as the bearers of family and of tradition. This female attribution is, again, based in *adat*. The abovementioned Islamic rules and regulations that require the husband and father to be responsible for providing food for his own family (wife and children) are, as Masjaliza noted, thwarted by *adat*. The Malay customs influence this male role insofar as it is the mother who is normatively and practically regarded as the caretaker of the household. She is thus expected to fulfil a 'second shift' at home after her (full-time) work (Hirschman 2016: 39). Hence, grounded in *adat*, child-raising and parenting are contemporarily attributed to women, and this is embedded in the wider picture of Malaysian women as the bearers of family and of tradition. Yet as a consequence of men's pilgrimage experiences, at least in the sense of *Islamic* traditions, this attribution becomes more applicable to fathers than to mothers, as shown by Ramli and Irsyad. Given this, the male pilgrims in this study transformed gender roles in the broader socio-cultural context based on their strengthened belief. This intersectional situation shows the active role that males play here in the family that potentially strengthens their position as Muslim men in parenting and childcare, and therefore relieves the mother of her double duties.

We have seen that while women transform their role as wives on the level of social action and embodiment by treating body parts (*aurat*) accordingly, men develop their role as fathers and this development, resulting from pilgrimage experiences, takes place at the level of social action only. However, both gendered transformations align, in that they take place within family constellations. The Islamic family norms and rules discussed so far are situated on socio-cultural and formal levels. However, they are not only formally regulated but moreover spiritually operative. At this point, and following on from the deeper devotion to Allah after pilgrimage as described above, the female perspective on social transformations in family and spiritual life-worlds comes back into play.

Submission to male figures

When a woman is a grateful servant to her husband, she will gain positive rewards from Allah (*pahala*). In contrast, if a woman does not follow this principle, she will get the opposite of *pahala* – sin points (*dosa*), as Mawar explained: 'If we do not obey our husbands, we sin [*berdosa*] and will go to hell [*neraka*] . . . If we commit a sin [*berdosa*], satan [*syeitan*] will get into our heart' (29 July 2017).

In this regard, social anthropologist Patricia Sloane-White (2017: 31f) states in relation to the Malaysian context: '[A] good wife does her marital duty with a smile, because she knows this duty is *wajib* [obligatory] in Allah's eyes, and to serve the husband is to serve Allah.' This connection indicates that my female respondents' enhanced spirituality and more intense submission to God as a result of pilgrimage was a process they also underwent in relation to their husbands.

On an unconscious, symbolic level, a wife's submission to God is expressed through a deeper dedication and devotion to her husband, as shown by wearing additional clothing items after returning from pilgrimage. This devotion, I will argue below, is incorporated into gendered concepts of hierarchical relationships in the earthly and Muslim spiritual worlds alike. This issue of hierarchy and equality in Islamic principles and Muslim practices is controversial in (transnational) Muslim contexts. Mir-Hosseini (2009: 24) states: '[T]here is neither a unitary nor a coherent concept of gender rights in Islamic . . . thought, but rather a variety of conflicting concepts, each resting on different theological, juristic, social and sexual assumptions and theories.'

Wadud (2009, 2008: 24–32), for example, posits that hierarchies between humans are not inherent to Islam. She states that positioning men as superior to women in worldly life is a form of *syirik*, i.e. polytheism or, in this case, the association of humans with God. This argument is grounded in the Islamic principle of *tawhid*, which denotes that Allah is One and Unique and, as a consequence, always the highest hierarchical point in any social order (see Barlas 2015: 95–99). According to this understanding, authority and power are applicable only to God, not to any human being (Ali 2014: 30).

Moreover, the *Qur'an* teaches principles of justice, equality, equity and dignity (Zainah 2009: 15), which form the main orientations for good Muslim behaviour, but which are contradicted in hierarchical relationships. In particular, in the *Qur'an* men and women are conceptualised as ontologically equal before God since they are created from one single soul (sura 4, verse 1). According to this particular sura, man and woman are created for mutual benefit, but not for the purpose of the other gender, and therefore one is not regarded as superior to the other. Furthermore, the *Qur'an* states that on the day of judgment (*qiamat*) Allah judges individuals not according to their gender but solely according to their piety (*taqwah*) (sura 33, verse 35; sura 49, verse 13); measured in *pahala* and *dosa*, for example.

Yet in the socio-cultural context of this research, the practised obedience (*ketaatan*) of wives to husbands and simultaneously to God is, according to my observations, a highly hierarchical circumstance in social praxis even though this is not formally or theologically acknowledged. To understand the parallel devotion to Allah and to the husband in more detail, I want to focus first on the wider issue of the concept of God. According to Islamic orthodoxy, Allah is body-, space- and timeless (Barlas 2015: 99–101). For example, Wadud (2008: 31) argues:

Allah is [not] a physical thing, an object, let alone a person. She or He is not separate from the creation, especially from the human creature. St. Augustin's articulation to consider God as a circle, the centre of which is everywhere and the circumference of which is nowhere, reflects the metaphysical reality of the universe, which I agree with, provided it is considered at the level of the three-dimensional sphere.

In their booklet *Are Women and Men Equal before Allah?* the Malaysian organisation *Sisters in Islam* (SIS)[7] (1991) concretises this approach by stating that 'Allah does not have a gender'. However, gendered relations between Allah and human beings do certainly exist in the *Qur'an*. Four *Qur'anic* verses exist that declare men's authority over women (sura 2, verses 222, 228 and sura 4, verses 2, 34), which is even acknowledged by Muslim feminist institutions such as SIS and the transnational network *Musawah* ('Equality' in Arabic), also founded in Malaysia. Apart from concrete guidelines for men that are revealed in these four verses, the overall conceptualisation of the holy book as well as the revelation process as such are and were gendered too: Allah 'speaks' to prophets and messengers (*risalah*) who are solely male (Barlas 2015: 99–101; Şeker 2020: 180–96, 2019). Even SIS points out that the *Qur'anic* verses 21:7, 8 explicitly state that messengers are men. Since the content Allah transmits to the prophets in these four verses is about their position as men, when revealing their duties as husbands, both Allah and the prophets are constituted as subjects.

Yet female characters do exist in the *Qur'an* and Wadud examines their positions in her work *Qur'an and Woman: Rereading the sacred text from a woman's perspective* (1999). She comes to the conclusion that in the holy book women are

> [mostly] wives and the *Qur'an* [and thereby Allah according to Muslim understanding, V.T.] refers to them by means of a possessive construction (the *idafah*) containing one of the Arabic words for wife: *imra'ah* (woman), *nisa'* (women), or *zawj* (spouse, or mate) pl. *azwaj*, and the name of a particular male; for example, the *imra'ah* of Imran, or the *zawj* of Adam. (1999: 32f)

Only one female is referred to by her own name rather than by her relationship to a male relative: Maryam, the mother of Isyak (Jesus in Christianity). This sole exception is made because according to the *Qur'an*, Isyak does not have a father and usually Islamic names are constructed by adding the father's name to the given name. As this is not possible in this case, Isyak is called 'son of Maryam' (Wadud 1999: 39).

This is due to the belief that Maryam did not get pregnant as a result of sexual intercourse but because of Allah's will. While God determines and ensures that she gets pregnant and therefore accesses her body, she is passive.

While females are present in the *Qur'an*, most of them are conceptualised as characterless, as they are only mentioned in stories about male prophets and do not speak or perform any actions by themselves, as Wadud (1999: 106f) points out. An active role is only applicable to six women, according to Wadud's examination: Hawa, wife of Adam; Mary, mother of Isyak; Hannah, wife of Imran and mother of Maryam; Asiyah, wife of Pharao; Umm, mother of Moses; and Bilqis, *imra'ah* (woman) and Queen of Sheba (see Lamrabet 2016: 21–70). Addressing only men, referring to women (with one exception) only in relationship to men and conceptualising most of the women as passive means that females are perceived as objects.[8] Wadud summarises the male-centeredness of the *Qur'an* and its revelation as follows:

> With the exception of *Hadith* transmission and *Qur'anic hifz* (commitment to memory), women did not participate in the formation of Islam's paradigmatic foundations. Put another way, not only did men and men's experiences of the world – including their experiences with women – determine how Islam is defined for themselves, they also defined Islam for women. In other words, men have proposed what it means to be Muslim on the very presumption that the male experience is normative, essential and universal. (Wadud 2003: 92)

Overall, in what Allah revealed to the Prophet Mohamad, according to how Muslims understand and transmit it in the form of the *Qur'an*, there is a male omnipresence which is constituted by the relation between Allah and male figures. This male or gendered conceptualisation and its hierarchical gender orders, in turn, are operative in the social context of this research. In order to explain my argument, I furthermore have to unfold the following intersectionally hierarchical relationships: certain male social positions exist in Muslim Malaysia that are directly intertwined with religiosity. Islamic scholars are attributed a high level of religiousness. While Allah is not represented on earth by Islamic scholars such as *imam*, *ustaz* or *guru*, I regularly heard people saying that 'Islamic scholars are closer to Allah than ordinary people' on the basis of their wealth of knowledge (*ilmu*) about Islam. Thus this group of people can be ranked on a hierarchical level beneath Allah in terms of religious authority.

Second, and more applicable to the argument in this section, the male head of the household, i.e. the husband or father, can be understood as a symbolic figure for a higher male divine power. Every male head of the household, i.e. every married man, can be situated one level below Islamic scholars concerning the representation of religion. The reason for this ordering is that a husband or father serves as *imam* when the family prays at home. Only the man will lead the prayer, never the wife or mother. When I talked with Haneefah about gendered praying habits, she stated: 'When a family prays at home, the *imam* must be a man, then the other men come behind him, and only then the women and the children' (26 June 2018). She explained this in an email: '[T]here are some *Hadith* [records of the sayings and deeds of the Prophet Mohamad] that have been circulated saying that "A man's prayer is not correct/valid if a woman and/or a dog is in front of him"' (29 April 2018). Indeed, when I stood with Suriawati, Irsyad and their two sons in their house, I observed that Irsyad alone led the prayer. The two boys positioned themselves behind him, and Suriawati, in turn, behind her sons. I asked Irsyad about this and our conversation went as follows:

Irsyad: I serve as the *imam* when we pray together.
Viola: Is it always you or can Suriawati also lead the prayer?
Irsyad: No, a woman cannot be *imam*. You know Adam and Hawa [Eve in Christianity]? She was made out of Adam's left rib. And the man is the leader.
Viola: Is it necessary that you are always in the front?
Irsyad: Of course, if you follow a leader in a war, he also cannot be behind, right? Then nobody will hear him. So the man is the leader he must be in front . . . If the woman were in front for prayer, then she would also need to lead the prayer, and that's not possible! (17 June 2017)

This connection between a husband and an *imam* and the gendered hierarchical order it creates was put in a nutshell by Malaysian student Amina: 'In Islam, we have to follow the husband; like an *imam*.'

Other examples relate to the father as head of the household instead of husband. This is embedded in the Shafi'i condition that a female's father is her 'compelling guardian' (*wali mujbir*) (Mohd Asri 2013: 157). Some of the Malay Malaysian women in this study consulted their fathers regarding important questions about earthly life while they asked Allah for guidance on the same questions in spiritual life. For instance, Suriawati shared her story of marrying Irsyad:

At *Hari Raya* [a festive event at the end of Ramadhan], he [Irsyad] came to my house, to my parent's house – alone! He asked to be friends with me . . . I then prayed to Allah and asked God to have a close relationship to Irsyad – if not, God should keep Irsyad away from me. Three months after we met, he asked me be engaged with him [*bertunang*]. I asked my father about it and he agreed. That was in August 2005. Then in December we got married. (18 June 2017)

These different practices illustrate a connection between Allah and the male heads of households, i.e. fathers and husbands. Against this backdrop, when Malay Malaysian wives embody transformed relations with their husbands following pilgrimage via additional garments such as cuffs, socks or veils, they transform their deepened relationship with Allah based on *umrah* (or *hajj*) in parallel to their husband. In their role as wives, they show their intensified relationship via a consolidated marriage that arises from the pilgrimage experience and, hence, out of deeper submission to Allah. This intensified relationship is expressed in, amongst other things, a consciousness of being only (sexually) available to the husband, belonging to him and obeying him, as discussed above. That form of greater obedience is parallel to greater obedience to Allah following pilgrimage. This intersectional condition on the family and spiritual scales alike arises out of the wider hierarchical gendered ordering of Allah first, *imams* or other Islamic scholars second, and husbands (or fathers) third – who females follow or even submit to. Thus, the corresponding women in this study simultaneously show devotion to male figures or rather figures perceived as male (Allah and husbands) that cannot be understood separately, but in a mutually constitutive manner.

Liberation through submission

This intersectional condition seems to disempower Muslim women. Yet the entangled and parallel submission to God and to their husband needs to be considered as an ambiguous twofold relationship. While women stabilise and consolidate their bonds to their husbands, they simultaneously liberate themselves and become independent due to their preconditioned devotion to God: total submission to God means becoming free. This is an overarching understanding and is not just applicable to gendered family relations. As Ubaidah said: '[If] you submit yourself to God, you are under the care of God. No matter how disadvantaged you are. When . . . you submit everything to God's will, you are free.' He continued:

> You know that God will take care of you. Even in difficulties, even in hardship. There is always a way out. That's why the *Qur'an* is important . . . For example, in one of the sura it says that if you have *taqwah* [godliness], meaning that you put your trust in God, then God will give you a way out of your problems . . . So that's what I'm trying to say to you, if you have a connection with the *Qur'an* and you believe the *Qur'an* is the word of God, then Allah never breaks His promises . . . So Allah will be sufficient for you. (8 September 2017).

The liberating character of total submission is, furthermore, evident in the principle of '*redha*', which Masjaliza translated as 'freedom' and Annisa as a feeling of 'just letting it go'. Annisa described *redha* as an attitude that 'anything annoying or negative goes in one ear and out the other' as 'Allah will make it for you. *Redha* means to place 100 per cent faith in Allah' (19 August 2017).

To *redha* means to wholeheartedly accept what has been decreed by Allah. It defines absolute contentment with God's will. Muslims who *redha* accept their fate (*qadar*), which they believe to be prescribed by Allah. To believe in this fate is the sixth pillar of faith (*rukun imam*). Accepting one's fate implies choosing to live with positive thought and emotion. This, then, means trying to improve all opportunities in life that enable a better condition for oneself and others. Thus, my respondents considered the option to *redha*, or to 'submit everything to God's will', as Ubaidah put it, as a freedom to choose options for positive situations and steps in life, i.e. to choose a life one wants to live and to be grateful (*syukur*) for what one has. *Redha* is the freedom to select existing alternatives for the better. This implies taking responsibility for the choices one makes.

This form of responsible submission (*redha*) is markedly different to mere surrender (*pasrah*). The latter means accepting conditions as they are and surrendering to one's situation or to what has happened. It is a rather passive form of handling life as it lacks effort on the part of the subject to actively deal with it or to improve it. If a Muslim chooses *pasrah*, she/he/they loses the freedom to shape and develop a desired way of life. To 'place 100 per cent faith in Allah', to use Annisa's words – to submit perfectly under Allah's decree – is what Wadud (2008: 15–17) describes as 'engaged surrender'. This approach suggests that a believing Muslim is a moral agent (*khalifah*) and a servant before Allah (*abd*) simultaneously. Moral agency (*khilafah*) grows when a Muslim is in, according to Ubaidah, constant 'connection with the *Qur'an*', which requires *taqwa*, a moral consciousness (Parray 2011; Shaikh 2003: 107f; Wadud 2008: 31) or a 'trust in God' in Ubaidah's words. Given this understanding, only *taqwa* makes an agent a moral agent. Since a believer has the moral responsibility to master their life and to harmonise situations and social relationships, the moral agent is also an active agent because they face numerous options that lead to possibilities for actions.

This form of agency (*khilafah*) is in a state of tension with Allah's will. His decree is set and all-embracing. However, Muslims realise their agency within the frame of God's will, so that being a moral agent and being a servant become one (Wadud 2008: 24). This is embodied in the trustee or viceregent (*khalifah*) of Allah.

Given the principle of *redha*, on the level of inner disposition, sincere submission is a process of liberation from dependencies on social relationships, doubts and inner sorrows, as from that moment onwards God alone will guide the way. A way that a believing Muslim needs to shape within the frame Allah has created. At the same time, sincere submission is an increase in responsibility – not to passively surrender to social situations but to actively form life according to Allah's will. On the level of gendered family relationships, this condition means that when the wives of this study submit to Allah and to their husband simultaneously, they become liberated *khalifas*, saturated with agency (*khilafah*). This form of submission, then, is the positive opposite of agency rather than just the absence of agency. My respondents feel safe and secure so that they can rest assured in every single situation. Hence, on the basis of engaged surrender, gaining agency (*khilafah*) and equanimity in the sense of 'just letting it go' (*redha*) dissolve into one another.

I have shown that Malaysian pilgrims – both women and men – experience transformations in their gendered as well as spiritual inner dispositions as a result of their pilgrimage journeys. The experience of *umrah* or *hajj* leads to a deeper spiritual feeling towards God for the majority of my female and male respondents. They described how they profoundly submitted to God after pilgrimage because of their closer connection to Him.

The women in this study expressed this deeper spirituality by changing their clothing habits. On the one hand, many of them started to wear the *abaya* upon returning in order to create a spiritual space (or scale) that is not bound to physical location but constituted through the relationship between the Muslim subject and God. This relationship is based on the female subject's relation to her body. Using an *abaya* as the proper attire for communicating with God during prayer is an embodied spiritual connection to God. This is embedded in Islamic perceptions of gendered bodily conditions and of Malay customary views on gendered inner dispositions that denote women as impure and radiating sexuality. Wearing an *abaya* is a means to control this condition in order to be properly prepared for the connection with Allah. Through an intersectional lens, this shows how women are in an inferior position to men on the spiritual scale when it comes to embodied spirituality, since they have to put more effort and energy into their daily religious routines.

Furthermore, the women in this study expressed their deepened and enhanced spirituality following pilgrimage by starting to wear additional (gendered) clothing items such as veils, long gauntlets and socks in order to cover their *aurat*. In this case, newly adopted clothing elements are not directly related to God but rather to their roles as wives. As middle-aged women, they consolidate their roles as wives to their husbands following *umrah* or *hajj* and embody this consolidation by covering their gendered bodies. These women draw boundaries against other men by covering their *aurat* more fully in order to signal to their husbands that they are dedicated only to them.

These two processes relating to females are not separate developments but are directly intertwined. These wives transform their relationships to their husbands in parallel to their deeper relationship with Allah following their pilgrimage experiences. As this process is expressed through transformed clothing habits, it becomes an embodied practice. Hence the women in this study transform their spiritual stance and their familial gender roles on the intimate level of the body following pilgrimage. The intersectional, submissive role as a Muslim wife on the family scale is complemented by a simultaneously elevated and exalted role on the spiritual scale. Devotion to the husband is embedded in a situation in which the wife is liberated from any sorrows and gains (moral) agency (*khilafah*) – and therewith, eventually, freedom (*redha*) – through total submission to God.

Conversely, men deepen their spiritual connection to Allah by concentrating on the formal character of their religion, such as performing more prayers throughout the day. Additionally, some of them develop their gender role and thereby alter their family situation upon returning from pilgrimage. Yet in contrast to their wives, they do not focus on their role as spouse but develop their gender relations as fathers in the form of strengthening their parental role. This reinforcement happens in particular in the sphere of transmitting and teaching religious rules, regulations and knowledge to children. Given this, the fathers in this study transform gender roles on the basis of spiritual experiences on the family scale in the form of action and not in relation to their bodies, as the wives do.

Notes

1. *Duha* prayer is to be performed after sunrise, between 8am and 12 noon.
2. Formal prayer consists of particular movements and other practices and inner forms of communication. According to Shafi'i *madhab* (law school), the pillars of *solat* (formal prayer) including the movements, etc are the following: (1) *niat* (formulating the intention to pray); (2) *takbir* (standing: the individual raises his or her hands to the level of her or his ears); (3) *qayyam* (standing: lowering of the hands to the waist; (4) reciting Sura al-Fatihah (first sura in the Qur'an); (5) *ruku'* (bowing forward with hands on knees and the back held straight, repeating 'Glory be to God, the greatest' three times); (6) *qayyam*: returning to a standing position; (7), *sujud* twice (kneeling down and putting one's forehead to the ground, repeating 'Glory be to God, the highest' three times); (8) *tashahhud* (sitting, taking a moment to pause and reflect on one's prayer); (9) wishing peace upon the Prophet; (10) uttering the first *salam* (greeting) to the angels on one's shoulders and to other people around oneself. One complete circle of this praxis is called *rakaat*.
3. When a woman has her period, it affects the pilgrimage in Mecca (see Thimm 2021). For example, the circumambulation of the *kaabah* (*tawaf*), is an act of praying to God. Since the female body is not considered to be clean and chaste during menstruation, a woman cannot perform this required ritual. Several rituals (*manasik*) need to be altered and compensated for in case a woman is menstruating. This requires certain knowledge and some precise accomplishments.
4. At a later point in the interview Rabwah mentioned that this allergy was a sign from Allah.
5. This distinction is obvious regarding gender-related matters in the difference between *syariah*, which is believed to be (literally) 'the way' or 'the path' revealed by God and *fiqh*, Islamic jurisprudence made by humans. *Syariah* is, according to Muslim thinking, the set of values and principles that were revealed to the Prophet Mohamad that should lead to a just and harmonious life. *Fiqh* (literally 'understanding') are the human interpretations of the Qur'an and Sunnah that have been used to form legal rules. While *syariah* is rather ethical in its content, *fiqh* is more a set of juridical rules. Often, *fiqh* rules are declared to be *syariah* by Islamic authorities in order to pacify discussions, debates or struggles (Ali 2014: 65; Mir–Hosseini 2009: 25).
6. In that case of Masjaliza's and Ramli's marriage, for instance, the dowry paid was 8,000 RM (during the time of her marriage in June 2009 approx. 2,290 USD).
7. SIS struggles for women's rights in Muslim Malaysia and beyond. Some of the activists call themselves 'Feminists', others do not. The NGO as a whole is hesitant to call itself feminist too. This is due to the fact that, as an activist explained to me, this would exclude too many interested women from the outset as 'Feminism' is very much associated with 'the West' and therefore something to be rejected.
8. According to the *Qur'an* interpretation (*tafsir*) by Tabari and Ibn Kathir, the fact that the *Qur'an* only addresses men and not women was acknowledged by women during the Prophet Mohamad's time and influenced the process of revelation: Umm Salama (literally 'mother of Salama'), one of Mohamad's wives, asked the latter about this issue and demanded Allah's words be equally addressed to women as to men (Lamrabet 2016: 93; Şeker 2020: 147–179). As a consequence, two verses (3: 195; 33: 35) were revealed that acknowledge women as equally capable as men regarding their piety (Ali 2014: 17, 31). However, the gendered subject-object relations in the content were not transformed in the course of the revelation.

6
Spiritual shopping

I was sitting with Farrah in her office, where she was showing me the prayer mat (*sajada*) and *Qur'an* she had brought back for herself from one of her *umrah* journeys. Full of happiness and longing, she told me:

> [W]hen anybody goes for *umrah*, . . . then I usually give money for her to spend in Mecca or Medina . . . So, the Malaysian custom is that to those who leave for Mecca, they will usually give them money to spend. I also have money to spend [received from others in advance of the journey]. Usually, for those who gave me money, I buy something directly for them. I can use the money [for anything], but usually I bring gifts [for them, bought from the money]. Especially things like *abaya*. And some of it, they want me to use [the money], so usually . . . [I] went shopping [in Mecca and Medina]. Some of their extra money, I used for the cleaner in the mosque and I give them 5 Rial, 10 Rial, 5 Rial. And I came back and told some of my friends 'Your money, I used it like you wanted, for the *barakah* [God's blessing]. So, the *barakah* is for you and, at the same time, the *sedekah* [voluntary charity] is for the poor, those who clean the mosque.' [My friends then said] 'Oh thank you, thank you!' So, it's their charity, I gave it and they feel they are also giving charity indirectly. (8 July 2017)

In the same interview she said: 'Shopping is a *ziarah* [a visit that can potentially invite God's blessing] and can be an *ibadah* [submission and obedience to Allah], because once you shop in order to give charity, that is also an *ibadah*, something that you obey. You buy things and then you give charity with the things that you buy.'

This sequence reveals that shopping during the pilgrimage journey implies manifold social and spiritual dimensions for Malay Malaysians.

First, shopping is integrated into a system of give-and-take between private givers and takers and, partially, the needy. Secondly, givers acquire material objects from *umrah* in the form of gifts from the takers, especially *abayas*. Thirdly, this implies that shopping has a gendered notion, since *abayas* are purchased and meant only for females. Fourth, the give-and-take is understood as a specifically Malay custom. Fifth, once the needy are included in this system, then a spiritual sense becomes part of this relationship through the possibility of God's blessing (*barakah*) for the giver. This leads to the sixth and last condition: against this backdrop, shopping can transform into a spiritual act.

Given this, the activity of shopping and utilising the goods consumed is more diverse than previously assumed in this study. Shopping on the journey in the Holy Land is undertaken not only for oneself but also for others. This chapter will discuss the difference it makes when a system and network of give-and-take and barter evolves in the context of pilgrimage. Once the additional dimension of shopping *for others* is incorporated into the relationship of giving and receiving, not only does a further part of my respondents' spiritual world develop; the valuation of the practices, objects and goods related to the act of shopping also begins to shift: through the spiritual part, shopping becomes *providing*.

The culture of giving, taking and returning is a long-lasting tradition in the Malay Malaysian context, and echoes of it can be found in shopping on an *umrah* trip. Against this backdrop, I argue in the course of this chapter that the act of obtaining something with money on pilgrimage only becomes understood as shopping when viewed from the perspective of capitalist consumption and, thus, from a pilgrimage-(capitalist) *tourism* nexus. Furthermore, I argue that this capitalist framing of contemporary pilgrimage influences the gendered sense of exchange. While the Malay tradition of exchange has been more or less gender neutral, i.e. women and men have been equally involved as gifter and giftee and in the type of gifts given, the sense of shopping is connoted as female and, in fact, is mainly practised by the Malay Malaysian women of this study. Yet, the *spiritual* implications of the exchange relationships remain stable, no matter whether they are understood as 'culturally Malay' or as contemporary consumption. Thus, gender intersects differently with religion and spirituality according to the socio-cultural context in which the exchange activities are framed.

In chapter 4 I discussed the relationship between the buyer (Malay Malaysian pilgrim) and the good (predominantly *abaya,* and, to a lesser extent, *kandora/jubah*) and in chapter 5 I discussed the relationship between the user (Malay Malaysian traveller back home) and the good(s) and object(s) (*abaya* and other female garments, such as socks and long gauntlets). In this chapter I will analyse the relationship between giver, taker, buyer, object, returner and taker (in the sense of someone who takes something back from the returner, not from the giver). Once spirituality becomes part of this relationship, it transforms into the following: giver and taker remain, buyer transforms into provider or arranger, the intention becomes part of the situation, the object persists as before, and returner and taker enter the relationship. In chapters 4 and 5 the issues of consumption, purchase and motivation were approached from the angle of (1) the object (mainly *abaya*) and (2) the user, who was tantamount to the pilgrim. Subsequently, these issues will be approached from the perspective of the wider exchange system – this implies, among other things, users who are not the pilgrims themselves and other people (indirectly) involved in a person's pilgrimage journey. Since this system is framed by spirituality, the analysis will mainly be situated here on *Scaling Holistic Intersectionality's* spiritual scale.

The main research questions that will be addressed in this chapter are: (1) What do my respondents purchase on the journey besides the *abaya* and for whom? (2) How do my respondents classify and assign meaning to souvenirs? (3) Is shopping for souvenirs embedded in broader socio-cultural backgrounds of gift-giving in Malay Malaysia and, if so, how? (4) In what ways do barter and exchange systems in this research context relate to spirituality? And finally: (5) In what sense are shopping and gift-giving interwoven spiritually and gender-wise in the sense of an intersectional understanding? The examination of these topics will be framed in anthropological and other disciplinary approaches to gift-giving.

Shopping and giving souvenirs

'Well, it's common in Malaysia to bring back gifts when people perform their *umrah*,' Sharifah once told me, making it clear that the practice of bringing back souvenirs is something very customary for Malaysian pilgrims and emphasising the relevance of gift-giving in the context of the religious journey. This importance was put in a nutshell by Farrah: 'It's good to give gifts to others, especially if it's from *haramain* [the Holy Land].'

Buying keepsakes for others back home in Malaysia is a common practice not only on pilgrimage but also on the *ziarah* stopover. When I followed the *umrah* & *ziarah* Dubai groups in Dubai on their shopping outings, I observed that clothes, dates, nuts, raisins, fridge magnets, key chains, small replicas of Burj Khalifa, mugs and prayer mats were the most popular items. Farrah talked about her shopping activities in terms of quantity when related to Mecca:

> We went to so many shopping places and, in the end, I think I ended up with 30 dresses, ya. I did not miss any of my mosques and, at the same time, when I went back, I bought souvenirs for my office mates, my family. [She begins to speak much faster and more excitedly than before.] I got only one dress, the black *abaya*, for myself; the 29 others were only for gifts. My daughter got five *abayas* from me! So, I got one and then I gave some to the staff where I work. (1 June 2017)

The amount the travellers in this study spent on souvenirs differed from individual to individual. I asked the *umrah* & *ziarah* Dubai group members about this topic after their trip via a questionnaire. The sum my respondents spent on clothes, dates, nuts, raisins, fridge magnets, key chains or prayer mats in Dubai, Mecca and/or Medina that were meant for family members, friends and colleagues ranged from 80 MYR (about 20 USD) to 3,000 MYR (about 750 USD).

What meaning is assigned to all these different souvenirs? Are some keepsakes with a special meaning? The *abaya* is, amongst other things, a very important item to bring back from *umrah* because it is a religiously connoted garment. Other items related to Islam are also purchased for distribution back in Malaysia. Farrah continued: 'And then we also brought back [from *umrah*] the *tasbih* [prayer chain]. The *tasbih* is for, you know, there are the bits with which you are glorifying the Lord 32 times . . . [T]he *tasbih* is usually for old people because they prefer the old method of glorifying the Lord.' Farrah stated that *tasbih* are especially useful for older people. The reason for this generational specification is that many young Muslims use the 'digital *tasbih*' nowadays, by which the number of glorifications of Allah is counted by pressing a button. Farrah's husband Ubaidah brought back the following from their *hajj* journey in 2002: 'What I spent money on was . . . the [physical] *Qur'an*, because, at that time, we didn't have the electronic *Al-Qur'an*, only the physical. And then cassettes, at that time, with *Qur'an* recitation, it was very popular then but no longer' (8 September 2017).

Mementos such as *tasbih*, the *Qur'an* and *Qur'anic* recitations recorded on a cassette are considered religious because these material objects are normally used for Islamic practices. Other keepsakes, however, have more of a spiritual sense than a religious meaning. Nur Sofia, the mother of Siti Sabrina, told me over our fast-breaking meal during Ramadhan: 'When we came back from our trip, we brought dates, perfume and *abayas* with us.' Farrah also referred to dates and perfume: 'I buy *ajwa* [certain type of dates] from Medina [see figure 6.1]. Because the dates that are being blessed with the Prophet's *du'a* [supplication] are the dates from Medina [aka *ajwa*]. Perhaps the dates from Medina [even] have *barakah* [God's blessing]' (1 June 2017). She went on: 'People like perfume from Mecca; they call it *minyak atar*. The Prophet [Mohamad] liked the *atar*, [and this special perfume] is called *kasturi*. So, I bought the *atar kasturi*.' These things represent the *possibility* of spirituality; their mere potential to create cosmological relationships is sufficient for the social actors here.

Kasturi perfume and *ajwa* dates from Medina obviously have an intangible, non-material value based on the spiritual senses they imply. The material objects as such do not make them valuable in the religious context, as in the case of the *tasbih* or *Qur'an*, more the additional 'something' that cannot be seen and known from the object itself but which only grows when a Muslim puts the thing (perfume or date) into a specific religious context. This is also applicable to another famous item.

Figure 6.1 *Ajwa* dates from Medina, sold in Dubai during Ramadhan, UAE, 2018.

Farish's opinion about small gifts from Mecca was: 'People mostly bring back home *zam zam* water [water from the Well of *zam zam* located within the *Masjid al-Haram* in Mecca] and fruits, the dates. These are the most important things. Everything else is just for decoration' (6 July 2017). I met Farish a week later to gain more information about the value he assigned to these nourishments. Together with Haneefah, who was his colleague at that time, we were sitting in their office at HDC. Farish followed up from our previous meeting as follows:

Farish: *Zam zam* is holy water. And it's about the value of this product, because it comes from there and you can only get it there. There is no other place in the world where you can get *zam zam* water from! The dates were the Prophet's diet. Regarding nutrition, they are high in glucose. During Ramadhan, we should take water and dates before breaking the fast.[1]

Haneefah: The Saudi government prohibits selling *zam zam* water. What you buy are only the containers; they are only 5 RM each. Every person is allowed to get two of these containers. It's illegal to sell it, otherwise people will take it for granted, it will no longer have any value.

Farish: . . . It became like a culture to bring back *zam zam* water and dates; it's a *buah tangan* [souvenir]. After coming back, you will serve it to people back home. You give them *zam zam* water together with the dates. These are valuable items, everyone knows it. (13 July 2017)

For my respondents, the value inherent in these spiritually laden souvenirs is materialised and they are not just 'decoration', as Farish termed it: he explained that when people are ill, they 'should drink *zam zam* water for purification. Or we give it to our children before they have an important exam.' The psychological belief in the power of *zam zam* water is, according to Haneefah, particularly applicable to one generation: 'Especially the older people will *niat* [formulate their intention] before they drink it . . . They *niat* to make it become effective.'

The material or non-material value the Malay Malaysian pilgrims of this study attach to the various souvenirs obviously depends on their religious embeddedness and the place they come from – similar to the meaning of the *abaya*. Since the small gifts are diverse in nature, the potpourri of what characterises the keepsakes goes beyond differentiation between religious and spiritual, material and non-material value, as we will see. Farrah, for example, raised the issue of to whom the souvenirs are distributed: 'We have 15 litres [of *zam zam* water] that we can bring back, so I put it in small, small cups and then give it to my neighbours and other families . . . Upon my return, I had lots of boxes [with dates and *zam zam* water] and I brought the boxes to my office.' Later in the conversation she said: 'My husband also brought dates for everybody. We just brought the boxes to the pantry and then said to everyone "Feel free to take!"' (8 July 2017). Neighbours, family members and office mates are embraced with *zam zam* water and dates. At first glance this might seem non-specific, particularly when it comes to colleagues: everybody and anybody can just grab them in the pantry. In contrast to dates and *zam zam* water distributed to acquaintances, the giving away of other items was bound to specific people. Farrah explained:

> The *abaya* were *cendera hati* [souvenirs] related to certain people . . . [This] is for my family and certain friends. I give it privately . . . [T]hese are people very close to me, [so] I give them something special . . . I give them a special gift separately . . . [T]he last time I went [for *umrah*], I gave an *abaya* to my sister, so, this time when I went, I gave the *abaya* to another sister. (8 July 2017)

To complement the rather vague group of receivers above, here, 'people [who] are very close' to the giver get 'something special'. These variations in gift recipients and in the items they received were depicted in the way my respondents talked about the souvenirs. Above, Farish described the souvenirs (dates and *zam zam* water) using the vernacular term '*buah tangan*', whereas Farrah used '*cendera hati*' when describing the *abaya*s she purchased for certain family members and friends. My respondents translated both expressions into English as 'souvenirs' in the context of things brought back from a journey. To complicate matters, *abaya* designer Sofea described an *abaya* when it was a gifted souvenir as '*buah tangan*'. What is the story behind these entanglements of giver, taker, gifts and the corresponding local terms? Sofea said:

> [W]hen I remember someone and I come back from Dubai and give the *abaya* from Dubai to that person I remembered as a gift, then the *abaya* is a *buah tangan* [literally: fruit in hands]. '*Buah tangan*' means that I don't want to come empty-handed to someone's house. When I visit them, I remember them and I get something for them so that I don't come empty-handed. Like I get fruits for someone when I visit him; that's why it's called '*buah tangan*', because

you have the fruits you bring in your hands, you don't come empty-handed. (15 August 2017)

In this sense, Farish used 'buah tangan' also for dates and zam zam water – what he perceived as the 'most important things'. Yet, the importance of the material things are in this regard not as relevant as the intention of distributing them. As Farrah made clear, zam zam water and dates are for everyone because as a traveller, she obviously does not want to come back to her colleagues empty-handed. The naming of the souvenirs in Bahasa Melayu varies depending on either who the gifts are meant for or the intention of gifting something.

Mawar made it similarly clear that the vernacular term used is not bound to materiality or value of objects, things or items that function as souvenirs. For her, all souvenirs from pilgrimage such as a sajada (prayer mat), tasbih (prayer chain), henna, perfume, kurma (dates), air zam zam (zam zam water) or jubah and abaya are cendera hati (literally: a gift with sentimental value [cendera] from the heart [hati]). This expression means that the gift comes right from her heart – and this expression is reasonable for her because all the souvenirs she brought back were only meant for family members, as she told me.

In the broader Malay Malaysian context, i.e. not particularly related to bringing back souvenirs aka buah tangan or cendera hati from a (pilgrimage) journey, both buah tangan and cendera hati can be translated into English as 'gift'. In fact, even more Malay terms exist for what might be called a 'gift' in a general sense in English. These peculiarities lead me to the question of how buying souvenirs on pilgrimage and giving them away upon return is embedded in forms and practices of gift-giving in the wider socio-cultural framework.

Gift-giving in Malaysia

Zamira once said: 'For me, I guess when we Malaysians go for umrah, we buy a lot of things, that's in our nature. Malaysians always want to shop. Not only for ourselves but we also bring it back home and give it away' (5 June 2017). In a similar vein, Mawar stated: 'When someone travels and brings back something, like a souvenir, this is part of our culture' (25 May 2017). Receiving and giving gifts, especially following a journey, is, according to Zamira and Mawar, something that is essentially Malay. Marilyn Strathern (1990) claims in The Gender of the Gift that exchange relationships via gifts are constitutive for the self and for society as a whole. Zamira and Mawar's assumptions and Strathern's foundational argument lead to the question of whether – and if so, how – shopping, consumption and purchasing something as a gift on the Islamic journey shape and are shaped by local cultural identifications and practices. What meaning is allocated to purchasing, bringing along and giving away things for others in the Malay Malaysian context? On what occasions do people in Malaysia get something and transform it into a *buah tangan* or *cendera hati*, i.e. into a gift? How do the Malay Malaysians of this study constitute and (re)construct their social relationships via gift-exchange and how do they conceive their cultural, religious and social identification in relation to this practice?

I joined Mawar and her husband, son, daughters, daughter-in-law and grandchildren at a *rumah terbuka* (open house) celebration in July 2017. This is a common festivity during Ramadhan where either communities and neighbourhoods or private households invite other people to public places in the former case or to their private houses in the latter. This *rumah terbuka* was organised by Mawar and her neighbours for the community. A 'lucky draw' was held: quiz questions were asked and whoever provided the correct answer was given a gift. The gifts were displayed on a table so that everyone could see them. All the gifts were wrapped in paper so the guests and I could not know what was inside. However, I could spot two food baskets which were wrapped in transparent foil and decorated with a big ribbon. I asked Mawar's eldest daughter Dewi, aged 38, about the gifts. She answered: 'These gifts from the lucky draw are *hadiah* [Malay term for 'gift']. *Hadiah* is for anyone; it has no special value. When I give a gift, for example, to him [she pointed at a man she did not know who was passing our table], it would be a *hadiah*.' Dewi added that lucky draws are very popular in Malaysia because everybody loves to receive gifts. I asked, 'On which occasions do you give gifts?' She answered: 'For example, when I visit my mum. I will bring something for her. When I'm on my way to her, I will stop by a stall to get some fruits for her, for example.' I wanted to know what she called this type of gift. 'This is *buah tangan*,' she explained, and continued:

> *buah tangan* can also be a flower bouquet when you meet at your family's or friend's house or fruits from your own farm or it can be something you cook at home and then bring to the family's or friend's house. *Buah tangan* is something small and it is for people you are very close to; you have a close relationship to. Because for other people, I would never think of bringing something for them when I visit their house. (29 July 2017)

This explanation aligns with Sofea's understanding of *buah tangan* in the sense of bringing fruits (*buah*) to a person she is visiting, as shown above. I learned that *buah tangan* is not only something specifically brought back from a (religious) journey (with its variations in meaning) but that it is something rooted in more general Malay Malaysian cultural practices. In this regional context, as both Dewi and Sofea understood it, *buah tangan* is something small that one puts special effort into because it is meant for a person with whom one has a close relationship.

In Malay Malaysian contexts, the description of a gift as *buah tangan* is not only applicable for something small that one brings and gifts to others once the giver returns home or to work (as in the case of a trip) or once the giver arrives at the taker (as in the case when a person visits a family member). *Buah tangan* are, furthermore, gifted when a taker leaves and the giver stays put. The term *buah tangan* is used in both situations because both cases refer to the situation of 'empty hands' that should be filled. When my partner Harry and I left the barbecue dinner at Haytham and Noorhaliza's house in June 2017, for example, they gave us the leftover crisps from the barbecue as '*buah tangan*' – 'You shouldn't go empty-handed!' was how Noorhaliza put it. We had a similar experience when Masjaliza, Ramli, their kids, Kartini, Harry and I left a wedding celebration in July 2017. Like all the other guests, we received a *buah tangan* upon leaving in the form of cookies and hard-boiled eggs in a small basket (*bakul telur*) – a symbol during Malay wedding feasts to welcome fertility to the newlyweds.

The second category of gifts Dewi introduced in our conversation at the lucky draw was *hadiah*. According to her, this was a present without any special value. When Masjaliza, Ramli, Kartini, Harry and I were sitting in a car heading to the wedding ceremony (*kenduri kahwin*) mentioned above, holding our *hadiah* in our hands (a casserole) – 'one family, one present', as Masjaliza put it – Masjaliza explained that *hadiah* is a general term for a gift; it designates something someone can show, something material. *Hadiah* is something wrapped or packed – in this sense, not only the gifts from the lucky draw but, for example, also a prize one can win (*hadiah* pertama [first prize], *hadiah* kedua [second prize] etc). Other gifts classified as *hadiah* can be household items, such as kitchen utensils, which are usually given for a wedding ('to reduce the bridegroom's commitment after marriage when they move into their new house', as Masjaliza explained); toys are common gifts for children's birthdays; a car or a house that parents, if they are rich, give to their children as birthday presents; or a watch or ring for the same occasion if the parents' income is much lower. A *hadiah* is also given upon retirement;

in this case, the present can be 'photographs to refresh their [the person who is retiring] memories', as Ramli said, or 'healthy food and vitamins', as Kartini, Ramli's mother-in-law, chipped in.

Continuing our discussion about gifts in Malaysia over the wedding buffet, the family introduced me to even more types of gifts in Malay Malaysian culture: *cendera mata* [*cendera*: see above, *mata*: eye] is a gift from Allah. Kartini told me that a newborn baby is a *cendera mata* as it is regarded as a gift granted by God. Subsequently, I read in one of *Ibn Ziyad*'s advertising brochures that they describe an *umrah-for-free* package that one gets when one books an *umrah* tour for 20 people as *cendera mata*. Hence, this free package is not understood as a gift from *Ibn Ziyad* to its customers but as something that Allah himself intends for that person, who can perform the *umrah* trip without having to spend anything. An additional type of gift is the *anugerah*. This present can best be translated as a 'blessing'. This blessing is either intangible, as it is equally granted by Allah – in this case, a newborn baby, for instance, is simultaneously understood as a *cendera mata* and an *anugerah*; or it is intangible and tangible at the same time: an *anugerah* is also something formally awarded, such as a doctoral degree or a medal.

The classification of gifts as *buah tangan, cendera hati, cendera mata, anugerah* and *hadiah* differ in their character (small vs big), material or non-material value (expression of close relationship vs for anyone and everyone) and religious or secular connotation (gift granted by Allah or purchased by humans). However, one further difference exists that is relevant for an understanding of gift-giving in the Malay Malaysian context: closing the link to the beginning of this section, it is the cultural background of the gift-giving practice. What Mawar and Zamira saw as Malay gift culture (bringing back mementos from pilgrimage), Nur Sofia, by contrast, regarded as the opposite: she understood these as *not* Malay. '*Hadiah* is something wrapped up, the presents you give for birthdays, newborn child . . . That's *hadiah* and that's *not* part of Malay culture' (29 July 2017). The constitutive character of giving gifts for the self and society as a whole, as Strathern (1990) noted above, apparently needs specification in its applicability.

So where does the culture of giving *hadiah* for birthdays or for a newborn child come from? What kind of gift-giving is understood as belonging to Malay customs? And how do those related practices that are regarded as non-Malay intermingle with gift-giving practices perceived as Malay? It is important to answer these questions here in order to embed Zamira's previous statement – 'when we Malaysians go for *umrah*, we buy a lot of things, that's in our nature' – into a broader context that can reveal what this 'nature' should be.

Gender equal gift-exchange

Nur Sofia said that a *hadiah*, i.e. a wrapped, material gift, is *not* part of Malay culture. Given this, I traced the cultural customs of gift-giving that my respondents perceived as Malay that go beyond the dimension of giving souvenirs from pilgrimage. Two situations offered a framework for gift-exchange that the Malay Malaysians of this study unanimously understood as *the* customary culture of gift-exchange: Malay weddings and *hari raya* (feast at the end of Ramadhan). What forms do these situations and the related gift-giving practices take and how are they characterised – especially concerning gendered, spiritual and religious notions?

In this regard, one of my conversations with Nur Sofia's mother-in-law Mawar went as follows:

Viola: For what situations do you usually give gifts?
Mawar: For marriage . . . For marriage in the *kampung* [rural areas], back then people gave milk, rice, sugar, *kopi* [coffee] and *teh* [tee]. People give 1 kilo, 1 kilo, 1 kilo. 1 kilo milk, 1 kilo rice, 1 kilo rice, 1 kilo *kopi*, 1 kilo *teh*. So they all give and at the end it is a lot to use, to cook it. People will give it to the mother if it's the child's marriage. And later on, when some of those who gave it to you get married, then you have to give the same back. Both bride and groom. So when the others marry, you also give milk, rice, sugar, *kopi* and *teh*.
Viola: What do you call these gifts?
Mawar: This is called *kutu-kutu makanan* [best translated as 'laid table composed by many contributing people'[2]]. (19 August 2017)

Mawar raised three interesting points. She introduced an additional category of gift in Malay tradition (*kutu-kutu makanan*); she then described a reciprocal form of gift-giving – an important point regarding the argument in this chapter; and she designated this practice as applicable to both men and women (groom and bride). This mutual practice includes two to three social actors and three actions: firstly, the giver(s) (people from the village) who give something; secondly, the taker (directly the bride's or groom's mother and indirectly the bride and bridegroom) who takes it; and thirdly, the bride and groom who will give the same back.

Nur Sofia summed up perfectly the functioning of the food products given upon marriage, on the one hand, and more broadly the gendered notion, on the other, by mapping out a further form of gift-exchange:

[Do] you know [that] on weddings the bride and the groom usually exchange gifts? These are the *hantaran*. Back then in the *kampung*, people give condensed milk, salt or sugar only as *hantaran*. They will decorate it and wrap it up nicely, put some flowers maybe. The friends and neighbours will come to the family and give them stuff like this to make it a *hantaran*. So, the bride's or groom's family will turn it into *hantaran* for them. Nowadays, people give very expensive things as *hantaran*, even an iPad! This is part of our culture. (29 July 2017)

While the foodstuffs are first passed to the mother (as in Mawar's description) or to other family members of the bride and the groom (as in Nur Sofia's narration), they are then handed on to the bride and groom to make it usable for them. At this point of exchange, the foodstuffs turn into wedding gifts (*hantaran*) that bride and groom give to each other. This is, again, true of both genders.

As Nur Sofia stated, the Malay practice of giving *hantaran* at a wedding still exists, but different items are involved. I observed this custom at various wedding ceremonies I attended in Malaysia, including Masjaliza and Ramli's wedding in June 2009 in Kelantan. A Malay wedding implies several ceremonies: *Merisik* (literally 'spying'), an initial form of engagement; *bertunang* (engagement); *akad nikah* (literally 'contract of coitus'), the formal marriage contract; *bersanding* (best translated as 'sitting of the bridal pair on the *pelamin* [throne]'), where the bride and groom's families offer the newlywed couple their blessings together with friends and neighbours; and *menyembut mengantu* (reception) in the groom's parents' house to welcome the bride to their family.

Hantaran are usually exchanged during the *bertunang* (engagement) and, if celebrated at all, when *merisik* happens. Nowadays *merisik* is no longer practised as widely as it used to be. This tradition has declined in particular in urban areas, where parents do not arrange marriages and couples instead choose each other. In Masjaliza and Ramli's case *merisik* was still practised because they followed the old habits in the *kampung* (village), even though they had chosen one another. Ramli's parents were 'spying' whether Masjaliza could be married. Usually, the man's parents visit the parents of the bride-to-be without their son, but in their case, Ramli came along. This was the first time he had visited

Masjaliza's house. Ramli's parents came to propose to Masjaliza's parents that Masjliza should become their daughter-in-law. Both sets of parents exchanged three *hantaran*: her parents received *kain sarung* (a piece of chequered cloth that males occasionally tie around their hips when they wear *Baju Melayu*, their traditional festive dress) for the father, one *baju* (blouse or shirt) for the mother, and *kuih* (Malay cake) for everyone. Ramli's parents received one *baju* for the father and one for the mother, and *kuih akok* (Malay cake made of coconut milk, *gula melaka* [special cane sugar from Melaka], sugar and eggs) with canned lychee. An additional part of the ceremony was that Ramli's parents gave a *cincin tanda* (proposal ring) to Masjaliza. This ring symbolised that she was now no longer allowed to accept offers from other men. 'You accept; means you are booked' is how Masjaliza described it. So this was a kind of engagement, but not yet an official engagement.

I could observe the exchange of *hantaran* during fieldwork at Masjaliza and Ramli's engagement ceremony. The number of *hantaran* given on such occasions differs from state to state, but in Masjaliza and Ramli's case they each gave seven *hantaran* to the other, as is common in Kelantan and also in its neighbouring state Terengganu. The number of *hantaran* given by each is the same, and the character is, according to my observations, very similar for both bride and groom – neither the male nor the female dominates the exchange of *hantaran* with a different (higher) number, a divergent character or varying material value of these gifts. This equal character was clear during the exchange of *hantaran* during *merisik* too.

Nowadays, the bride and groom obtain the *hantaran* themselves rather than receiving them from their family, as in Nur Sofia's narration. The couple have to pay for their *hantaran* themselves; they do not get any financial or material support from family or friends, as practised with the *kutu-kutu makanan* in the past. Masjaliza and Ramli's *hantaran*, which they had chosen together, were presented attractively, for everyone to see, on 14 trays (*dulang*) in front of the bridal couple's *pelamin* (throne). On the right-hand side, Ramli's *hantaran* for Masjaliza were displayed: *sirih junjung* (a floral arrangement made of betel) together with the engagement ring, *kuih* (Malay sweets), *baju bertandang* (a dress for the reception), *gubahan* (a folded towel that looks like a flower arrangement), *pulut* (glutinous rice), *kain bersembahyang* (literally 'prayer cloth' which is the same as a *telekung*, also known as the female prayer garment) and a *Qur'an*. Masjaliza's seven *hantaran* for Ramli were displayed opposite: *kek* (Malay cake), *buah* (fruits), perfume (from Hugo Boss), a watch (from Victorinox, worth about 2,000 RMY [about 500 USD]), *pulut* (glutinous rice), *kemeja* (shirt), *coklat* (chocolate). The type of *hantaran* exchanged and their value depend on the couple's financial situation. My respondent Fauzana, for example, was married to a millionaire (*jutawan*) and received a large, elegant, relatively expensive car as a *hantaran*.

The Malay quality of this form of gift-exchange was summarised by Syakirah, aged 46, who termed this practice *adat bersanding*, i.e. as the *Malay* form of engagement depicted via the term *adat*, and she explicitly differentiated it from Islamic traditions. This designation underlines the gender neutrality of this gift-giving practice since the Malay *adat* is basically bilateral (Ong 2003; Wazir Jahan 1995, 1992; Zainah 2001).

Conversely, the second form of gift-exchange my respondents defined as characteristically Malay is directly embedded in Islamic traditions – interestingly, a bilateral notion can similarly be observed here. Still in conversation with Nur Sofia about gift-exchange she defined as Malay, she explained:

Nur Sofia: For *hari raya* [Muslim feast at the end of Ramadhan], for example, we don't give gifts. We give money [*duit raya*; literally 'festive money', a set expression for the money presented during the *hari raya* season]. We give money to our parents and they give money to the children . . . We do not have something similar to Christmas where all people in one society exchange gifts on the same day. We do not exchange gifts; that's something Western.

Viola: So that a group of people exchanging something collectively is only on *hari raya*?

Nur Sofia: Yes, indeed. Some people also exchange gifts on *hari raya haji* [feast at the end of *hajj*] but that all Malays give gifts to someone is only on *hari raya* and it's always money. (29 July 2017)

I observed the giving of money to children (girls and boys alike) and to parents (both mother and father) on *hari raya* on several occasions. Children usually receive this festive money until they are grown up and independent. In a similar economically conceptualised vein, the wage-earning generation provides *duit raya* to their retired parents, who do not have as many financial resources as they had during their economically active life. For instance, Nur Sofia's husband, 42-year-old Raahim, who worked in the oil and gas sector, gave 500 Ringgit to his retired 64-year-old mother Mawar on *hari raya*; his 38-year-old sister Dewi, a dentist who was financially better off than her brother, gave her mother 1,000 Ringgit. Both son and daughter fulfilled this expectation. (The reason they did not give anything to their father was because he had passed away long before.)

Mawar stated in this regard that this *duit raya* she received was *cendera hati* – material value (money) coming from her son and daughter's hearts, as exemplified above. Yet, to give money is something different from giving material resources, as Sprenger (2017) points out for the Western context – material things that can potentially come, as is the case here, right from the heart. The relationship between social actors, things and services in a capitalist economy is usually expressed via money. Money alienates the thing from the producer or the giver. Through money, things get commodified, 'by which an increasing number of objects and services – and ultimately persons – become potentially exchangeable on the market' (Sprenger 2017: 2). Based on alienation, these commodities are then conveyed in short-term relationships (Sprenger 2017: 3). By contrast, gift-giving systems are configured as long-lasting bonding frameworks. Bloch and Parry (1989: 9) explain:

> [F]or us money signifies a sphere of 'economic' relationships which are inherently impersonal, transitory, amoral and calculating. There is therefore something profoundly awkward about offering it as a gift expressive of relationships which are supposed to be personal, enduring, moral and altruistic.

Sprenger and Bloch & Parry refer to capitalist, Western circumstances here and argue that in other contexts money certainly can function as a gift. My observations confirm that the distinction commonly drawn between money and gift-giving is not necessarily the case here: the giving of money is *not* exclusively characterised as being part of a marketised, short-term, impersonal exchange system. The valueless symbol of banknotes, coins and credit cards, aka money, gets its profound social value when understood in the context of the meanings, expectations, trajectories, origins, etc in which it circulates and is circulated. Giving money (*duit raya*) transforms into giving a gift here once it is embedded in cultural practices of celebrating *hari raya*, in which this has become the common form of tying or deepening social relationships with the needy (here, children and pensioners).

Social bonding through gifts – or, in this case, money – has been widely studied in anthropological research. This scholarship has predominantly described tangible gift-exchange (for example Addo and Besnier 2008; Mauss 2016 [1925]; Sprenger 2019, 2017; Werbner 1996). Mauss (2016 [1925]), in his pioneering work on gift-exchange, theorises gift-giving as a threefold process implying, first, the obligation to give; secondly, the obligation to receive; and thirdly, the obligation to reciprocate. This process is, according to Mauss, not an individual, spontaneous practice but a structurally embedded social phenomenon. Put simply, giving a gift implies an obligation to reciprocate with a counter-gift. A gift infers permanent liability, so that theoretically (and often practically) an endless exchange of objects evolves (Werbner 1996: 213). As Mauss argues, people create bonds via the objects they exchange. He terms this force that binds the receiver and giver together the *hau* of the gift. This momentum interrelates with broader social dynamics since the manner in which social actors relate to the objects and, thereby, to those they remain in an exchange-relationship with, captures and influences social transformations (Addo and Besnier 2008: 40). Hence, gifts and gift-giving practices depict, (re-)construct and (re-)constitute social relationships – a claim supported by Mawar's description of festive money as *cendera hati*.

The exchange of money during *hari raya* happens within a religious, Islamic framework and is, according to my experiences, a bilateral matter similar to gift-exchange in the context of a Malay wedding. Giving and taking *kutu-kutu makanan*, *hantaran* and *duit raya* are Malay gender-equal issues perceived as culturally or naturally Malay that form a backdrop to the practice of bringing, gifting and being gifted *buah tangan* or *cendera hati* in the sense of souvenirs from pilgrimage. Given this, this latter practice is embedded in bilateral frameworks that are true of, amongst other things, wider religious settings (*hari raya* and pilgrimage). This religious condition of the bilateral form of gift-exchange differentiates further when not only the institutional framework (Islamic festivities and rituals such as *hari raya* and pilgrimage) is operative but precisely when the social practice of giving and taking is enmeshed with Islamic connotations. A spiritual dimension then evolves.

Spiritual gift-exchange

Gift-exchange is a highly differentiated cultural practice in the Malay Malaysian context. In the above discussions, gifting systems were discussed mainly from the moment the external status quo that allows particular giving and taking situations, such as a celebration (wedding, *hari raya*) or the moment of the traveller's or pilgrim's return, begins. However, in the context of a religious journey to the Holy Land, gift-exchange begins long before that.

On 5 April 2018, I followed an *umrah* & *ziarah* Dubai group on their shopping tour through souvenir shops and the *souq* (market) area in Deira, the old town part of Dubai. Ahmad and Zulla, a married couple, both aged 38, were strolling with me through the small alleys of historical Deira. We entered a small shop containing shawls, lots of bric-a-brac and *abayas*. They bought souvenirs, mainly fridge magnets and keychains for 2–10 Dhs each. They told me that some of their friends had given them money for the trip, so they were looking for things they could bring back especially for these friends. Some friends had given them 50 RM, others 100 RM and one Chinese friend (*kawan cina*) even 1,000 RM. 'Kawan cina gets a particularly costly souvenir from us!', they commented. I could see from what they were purchasing and for whom that their Chinese friend would be the only one not getting a fridge magnet. Instead, he would be gifted a coloured metal statue in the shape of a peacock encrusted with glittering stones. The peacock could be opened and used as a box. Ahmad and Zulla spent 100 Dhs on it – the most expensive souvenir they purchased. The remainder of the 1,000 RM that Ahmad and Zulla had received from their Chinese friend was used by them – and intended by· the Chinese friend – to finance the entire journey with all its expenses. Thus, the money the pilgrims had received in advance was intended to be a form of support, and the thing they brought back in return was understood as a gift.

Obviously, some of those who stay at home give something to the traveller – which initiates an even more complex net of motivations, hopes, expectations and activities than those we have been introduced to so far. Ahmad and Zulla had received money from friends at home in Malaysia before they left for *umrah* & *ziarah* Dubai. The amount of money differed widely from friend to friend. In return for the money, they shopped for small or large souvenirs in Dubai for these friends. The amount *they* spent conversely differed too, mirroring the quantity they had received.

Ahmad and Zulla bought the keepsakes for those who had handed over money in Dubai. Other Malay Malaysians of this study bought souvenirs for exactly these kinds of people in Mecca and/or Medina. The variance in character and material value dependent upon the amount of money they had received in advance was similar in both cases. I spoke to Sharifah about this topic:

Sharifah: My uncle gave me 200 Ringgit [before I left for *umrah* & *zia-rah* Dubai], my auntie gave me 150 Ringgit.

Viola: And did they get something special from the trip?

Sharifah: Well, we gave them a frame with a picture of the *kaabah* or a plate which is made of something like steel but more colourful. We also gave them Mecca perfume. In Mecca they have their own perfume, so that's special . . . All the other people just got *sajada* [prayer mat] or bracelets from us, but the frame, plate and Mecca perfume were only for those who had given money. (19 August 2017)

The *social* and, thus, explicitly non-marketised relationship that the giving of money is part of here, as touched on already above, was given further context when Ubaidah provided an insight into the connection between the amount spent, the type of souvenir and the money received in advance:

Viola: Those people who give you money before you go, do they get something more special than others or just the same items?

Ubaidah: Depends on how much they give you. If they give you quite a bit, probably you have to give something a bit more [than to others], a better quality item for them . . . People can give you, for example, a certain amount. If they give you five times more, then you want to return back their generosity, something better . . . Surely, when they give you something of more value, they give you that because they probably feel closer to us. Because it [the amount/value you give] relates to how you feel about that person. So, to people [with whom] we don't have such a close connection, I don't think that we will give a high amount. (8 September 2017)

Ubaidah stated that social relationships determine what is given to whom and what material value attaches to gifts. The closer the social relationship, the greater the amount of money given to those who leave for pilgrimage – and, in turn, the higher the amount to be spent on those givers. This contrasts with short-term transfers that usually characterise give-and-take once money is involved: the social relationships and the bringing of gifts discussed by Ahmad, Zulla, Farrah and Ubaidah illustrate a reciprocal and, thus, long-term social relationship.

What kinds of social relationships are fostered via gifting souvenirs, especially from Muslim pilgrimage, and how are these relationships characterised? Kenny (2007) notes that keepsakes from the Holy Land represent *spiritual capital* that grows through pilgrimage for the pilgrim. Relying on Bourdieu's theory of social capital, Kenny states that spiritual capital is 'the prestige and status possessed by a person within a cultural structure' (2007: 365). That prestige and status develop through the ritual of pilgrimage. The accumulation of spiritual capital through mementos is important for a pilgrim because it 'allows for the enhancement of personal status especially with regard to piety, and alters the way an individual may be regarded by others'. She goes on: 'Spiritual capital . . . may be interpreted as a measure of enhanced piety that marks the individual as more religious, and perhaps more moral (at least theoretically), than other members of the community' (Kenny 2007: 365). Souvenirs from pilgrimage mark the prestige appropriated through pilgrimage and, thus, a pilgrim's enhanced spiritual status. Where a gift (souvenir) is given to people who have not performed pilgrimage themselves, this highlights a higher status over them and, therefore, a hierarchical relationship (see Strathern 1990). The spiritual-religious capital is *ad infinitum* part of the souvenir: '[The] spiritual presence of the person [in the sense of a 'spirit of the person', V.T.] who originally gave the gift resides within and lingers around it,' is how Almila and Inglis (2018: 160) describe it.

The social bonds that evolve between social actors through mementos from Muslim pilgrimage relate not only to gifter and giftee. As Almila and Inglis (2018: 162) argue, the tie between these individuals and the general *ummah*, i.e. the Muslim community all over the world, will also be deepened. When a pilgrim gives someone a souvenir from the Holy Land, according to the authors, the receiver is often expected to return a gift to the community that the giver (the pilgrim) represents – based on the pilgrimage experience, in this case, the Muslim community.

When Ahmad, Zulla, Farrah and Ubaidah bring back value-laden souvenirs to people who gave them money for the journey, they therefore not only thank and acknowledge them and their gift on a social level but also transmit their own experiences of the trip to those people. These experiences – here, the performance of pilgrimage – are commonly understood by my respondents as leading to a spiritually enhanced inner stance. The spiritual capital the pilgrims gift with the mementos are part of every souvenir. When pilgrims gift more sophisticated souvenirs for those who provided money beforehand, they furthermore gift the strong social bonding back.

The spiritual capital that is transmitted shows that the social relationships my respondents work hard at through gift-giving following pilgrimage are not just embedded in personal relationships in the form of friendship, kinship or solidarity. More than that, these relationships are characterised by a religious or even spiritual moment.

Allah comes along

Ubaidah emphasised the social relationship between people as relevant for the configuration of gifting money to soon-to-be pilgrims. Kenny (2007) focused on the spiritual capital that is expressed through the returned gift. Ramli revealed an additional spiritual moment as part of gift-exchange when talking about another decisive aspect for the motivation to hand over money to future pilgrims:

> I brought back a *tasbih* [prayer chain] and a *kopiah* [male Muslim cap] as a show of gratitude for those who had given me money before I went for *umrah*. It's our culture to support each other like this. Village people still don't have so many possibilities to perform *umrah*, that's why they give money to those who can go in the hope of getting *pahala* [rewards granted by Allah] for it. (14 July 2017)

According to Ramli, the custom of exchanging items (money and keepsakes), which is considered to be 'culturally Malay' by him and other respondents, is interrelated with Muslim doctrines, thoughts and practices. At a certain point in the exchange system, Allah can enter into it by granting rewards.

What is the condition for getting *pahala* from God through exchange, especially in the context of pilgrimage? This religious and spiritual setting was specified by Sofea. She talked about an item that is usually gifted in advance of pilgrimage in this regard:

Sofea: When people are going for *hajj* or *umrah*, we usually give them an *abaya* as a gift [before they leave]. In fact, we mainly give the *abaya* to others as a present [*hadiah*] when they go for *umrah* or *hajj*.

Viola: Why an *abaya*?

Sofea: Because she is a woman and she doesn't want to wear something curvy [on pilgrimage] . . . And then, when I give someone an *abaya* when she goes for *umrah* or *hajj*, I *kirim du'a*, which means I ask her to pray for me. To pray for my baby, for my wealth or my health.

Viola: And is '*kirim du'a*' only possible with an *abaya*?

Sofea: No, it can be with any other item as well. And we not only 'kirim du'a', but we also get *pahala* [rewards granted by Allah] for it. Because Allah says 'Thank you' when I give an *abaya* to someone when she goes for *hajj* or *umrah*. He says 'Thank you' because I appreciate people who go for this religious journey. (15 August 2017)

Sofea intimated that any material object (or money) can be used to generate *pahala* as part of a pilgrimage-related barter system, but the *abaya* is especially helpful in this regard as its character as a long, loose garment supports the all-important religious performance with its gendered bodily requirements (see figure 6.2). Hence, the *abaya* facilitates pilgrimage for females here and this is, according to Sofea, something Allah potentially acknowledges.

We know that the *abaya* can be very loose and simple, but what about its fashionable incarnations emphasising the female body shape, for example when an *abaya* is waisted or worn with a belt? Will Allah, according to Muslim understanding, acknowledge such an *abaya* as a gift to be used for pilgrimage performance too? During an eight-hour car journey from Kelantan to KL, I took the opportunity to ask Ramli about this issue. He got straight to the heart of it: 'For fashion, no *pahala!*' In other words, if a person gives an item of clothing to another person which is predominantly meant to decorate the body in a fashionable manner, this is not a thing that Allah can grant with rewards. He explained: 'Because *ikhlas* [sincerity] is the most important thing. Only then do we get the *pahala*, but if it's for fashion only, then no *pahala!*' (15 July 2017). The present, i.e. the object or thing, must be of a character that is in alignment with Islamic and Muslim rules and regulations.

Ramli indicated a second precondition for God becoming part of the barter system: being sincere (*ikhlas*) when one gives. This was an aspect Sofea revealed later on in her narration when she talked about further preconditions for the possibility of getting *pahala* for giving an *abaya* to a soon-to-be pilgrim:

But you must be *ikhlas* [sincere] [when you give an *abaya* to someone when she goes for *hajj* or *umrah*]! Allah doesn't say 'Thank you' when you have a bad intention [*niat*]. If you give an *abaya* to an actress, for example, and you ask her to promote the *abaya* during *umrah* or *hajj*, this is not *ikhlas*. Your *du'a* [supplication] will not be valid, you will be disqualified! Your *du'a* will not be granted. Because to promote a business is wrong; it has nothing to do with religion. It's wrong if you want her to promote your *abaya* for your wealth. But if she promotes it to increase your wealth in order to give a part of your business or your wealth to an orphanage, then you do good deeds and it's *ikhlas*. (15 August 2017)

Allah can only enter the exchange system when the intention (*niat*) of the giver is religiously reasonable. If the intention (*niat*) is not sincere

Figure 6.2 *Syariah*-compliant *abayas* offered for sale at *Souq Naif*, Dubai, UAE, 2017.

(*ikhlas*), God will not grant *pahala* for the social act (here: giving an *abaya* for pilgrimage).

So, we have seen that when someone gives money or any other useful object to a pilgrim before they set off on pilgrimage, it can imply a social connection between these people, as noted by Ubaidah above. It can develop into a transfer that is embedded in the spiritual capital of the pilgrim, as discussed by Kenny (2007). But it can also imply that the gift-exchange is intended to become part of a spiritual exchange system. In this case, the giver who does *not* perform pilgrimage benefits spiritually from the pilgrim's religious journey too; but this presupposes certain conditions of the gifter, the gift and the giftee.

So far, we have seen that the character of the item given needs to be religiously acceptable and that the relationship between the giver and the item has to fulfil a certain inner stance. But a third condition is necessary to transform the exchange into a spiritual endeavour. Farrah explained:

Farrah: [W]e believe that once you give people who go for *umrah* an *abaya*, when they go and use that to do their *umrah*, the *barakah* [God's blessing] will also flow to you. So once they wear it, you also get the *barakah*.

Viola: Why do you get the *barakah* too?

Farrah: You *can* [emphasising 'can'] get the *barakah*.

Viola: But you won't get the *barakah*, let's say, when you give them a watch or a normal shirt? Is the *barakah* only related to a religious item?

Farrah: No, anything. When you give anything for the convenience of other people [to make their life more convenient], the *barakah* will get back to you. It can be a watch. If you don't have a watch and I give you a watch, I think you can use it as an example here. Any time you use that watch and it helps you, it gives you benefits, then the *barakah* will flow back to me. (1 June 2017)

According to Farrah, the relationship between the item and the taker is an additional factor for developing the exchange into a spiritual condition. The receiver of the gifted thing must be religiously incorporated into the system with her inner stance about and utilisation of the gift. As shown with Ahmad, Zulla and their Chinese friend, and with Sharifah and Ubaidah, the gift in this context is not necessarily an object but can also be money. Regarding the receiver of money, Mawar said:

[W]hen I give money to poor people, like old ladies or orphans, then I will get *pahala*, but only if they sincerely receive it. In the case where the lady says, 'I don't like this, I don't want this,' but she takes it nevertheless, then I don't get any *pahala*. So before I give a gift I will ask the people 'What do you want? What do you need?' (19 August 2017)

Farrah explained this condition another way: 'The charity you give to others is actually for you. It's actually for you.' To give something useful (here: money) to the needy is motivated less by a social, supportive or solidary attitude and more by a desire to strengthen one's relationship with God (see Moufahim 2013: 432) – and with the imagined *ummah*, as touched on above. One's relationship with the sacred world becomes tangible through material things (money or objects) here. According to Muslim understanding, the reason why Allah rewards His believers is because basically they do not give their own wealth but Allah's wealth and, thus, follow His will to distribute wealth: '[W]ealth of the faithful is not – strictly speaking – their private property. Created as it was by God . . . A good Muslim is obliged to give because he [*sic*] has received from God' (Kochuyt 2009: 100).

That the sincere threefold relationship between giver, thing and taker can potentially provoke God's blessing (*barakah*), as Farrah termed it, or *pahala*, as Ramli and Annisa described it, does not just happen spiritually between giver, taker and Allah intangibly; it can manifest palpably in earthly life. Mawar explained this topic further:

When I give poor people food to eat or when I give them money, then I will get *pahala*, God will double you. If you give 1 Ringgit to orphans, Allah will give you double. But He doesn't give you 2 Ringgit, he will give you double in a different way, you don't know how. This will be your *rezeki*; *rezeki* is the luck coming from God. The *pahala* are for judgment day and afterlife. But *rezeki* is for the life now. For example, if you need a taxi, and you don't know how to get one, then you go outside and start walking along the road and then suddenly a taxi comes, then this is *rezeki*.[3] Because Allah will know what you say in your heart. I cooked this food for you today [she served *pisang goreng*; deep-fried bananas] because I know, Viola will come, so I think about what to cook, how to make it nice for you, so this is your *rezeki*. And I will get *rezeki* as a double back and I will also get *pahala* for afterlife. (19 August 2017)

So the luck endowed by Allah (*rezeki*) can be experienced in the form of a taxi arriving in a desperate situation or the unexpected serving of a delicious meal. Once Mawar had explained this to me, a brief incident before I had set off to her house suddenly made sense to me: I had asked her via SMS whether I should bring something for her when I came to visit. She replied: 'Your wish . . .' When I read this, I could not understand why it would make sense for her that I come with a wish. Following Mawar's explanations about *rezeki*, however, it made sense: if I come with a wish, then it will eventually come true in the form of *rezeki* because she took pains and made an effort for me, in this case by preparing a nice meal. This will flow back again to her in form of *pahala*.

Rezeki can be realised in even more subtle, non-material ways. When I met Mawar's daughter Annisa for breakfast a couple of days after my visit to her mother, we were talking about her parents' *umrah* & *ziarah* Dubai journey. I was interested to know whether Annisa had given something to her mother before she commenced the pilgrimage journey. Annisa said:

> I bought a *telekung* [female prayer garment] for her because I wanted to make sure that she feels happy when she goes there [to Dubai, Mecca and Medina]. That was the reason. I didn't want to get anything in return for it. We want to make people happy . . . As Muslims, if we make other people happy, we believe in the *ganjaran*, the *pahala*. The *ganjaran* is the price that God has promised us. And how to make people happy? Usually through giving a gift . . . In the *Qur'an*, it says that if we make people happy, Allah will give us happiness back. If we cannot afford to get a gift for someone, then even a smile is a form of *sedekah* in Islam because it's just enough to help other people, to make them happy. (26 August 2017)

Giving a gift to someone can, in the context of Muslim Malaysia, induce a highly complex spiritual situation – whereby the gift can be material or non-material, such as a single smile provoked by happiness. Annisa's statement shows an additional aspect: She emphasised 'I didn't want to get anything in return for it' and believed in the *ganjaran* and *pahala*. Both *ganjaran* and *pahala* are rewards. *Ganjaran* can be material or sentimental rewards granted by any human being. By contrast, *pahala* are believed to be awarded only by Allah. *Pahala* cannot be valued by humans, as only Allah knows how many rewards He grants. The *pahala* are relevant for the afterlife when humans are judged according to their *pahala* and *dosa* based on their deeds in earthly life. Allah can, furthermore, reward people in earthly life, not only in the afterlife, in the sense of material value (for example money) or sentimental value (for example happiness based on the good deeds a person has done). This is what people understand as *rezeki*. The *pahala* granted for these deeds then become effective in the afterlife. This principle explains why Annisa did not expect anything in return from her mother when she gave her the *telekung* as a gift. Allah is the actor who gives something back to her: *pahala* for afterlife, on the one hand, and happiness in earthly life, on the other.

Moufahim (2013: 433ff) conceptualises the rewards given by Allah for the giving of a material gift from the religious journey in the context of gift-exchange by Syrian and Iraqi pilgrims as a 'soteriological gift': a gift that is suitable for salvation. The form of granting gifts (*pahala*) shows clearly that gift-exchange here is not (only) asymmetrical or characterised by delayed exchange (see Descola 2018: 453f). It *is* asymmetrical and characterised as delayed exchange between Annisa and her mother – but Annisa gets something back from Allah immediately. Given this, this form of spiritual exchange can be regarded as a direct barter, i.e. immediate exchange.

Religion and shopping

Very little scholarship has focused on exchange systems in which intangible aspects are similarly constitutive for the giving and taking of things as tangible configurations (e.g. Belk 1996; Birchok 2020; Descola 2018: 453–89; Kenny 2007; Kochuyt 2009; Moufahim 2013; Sleebom-Faulkner 2014). While most studies on gift-exchange take the giving and taking of material objects between humans into account, Belk (1996), on the other hand, considers intangible values and symbols that can similarly be gifted under religious conditions. He questions Mauss's argument regarding the reciprocal relationship of gift-exchange by taking religious circumstances into account. Non-material gifts, such as a smile, *rezeki* (luck provoked by Allah) or *pahala*, are in Mauss's theory formation treated as marginal. Belk (1996: 59–61) focuses in particular on the 'perfect gift' that derives from religious (in his study Christian) thoughts and practices. The 'perfect gift' is 'priceless, unconstraining and immaterial' (Belk 1996: 59). The material value of the perfect gift does not count; what counts is the symbolic gesture in the sense of 'It's the thought that counts' (Belk 1996: 59). Moufahim (2013: 424) emphasises in her study of gift-giving by Shia pilgrims that this kind of 'perfect gift' differs from objects in market relations as it is characterised as a moral form of gift.

The 'perfect gift' is, in its original connotation, a material expression of 'agapic love', which is an unselfish and sacrificial love. It can characterise a relationship between humans but true agapic love comes from God, and God's gifts to mankind are, according to the New Testament of the Bible, the true and only forms of the 'perfect gift' (Belk 1996: 60). Given this, the 'perfect gift' that can be found in religious frameworks is unilateral. The incorporation of intangible or non-material gifts marks an important turning point for understanding gift-exchange as either reciprocal or one-sided – or both.

The form of gift-giving described here is often unilateral, as exemplified by Annisa's present, the *telekung*, for her mother for which she did 'not expect anything in return'. By not expecting anything in return from the recipient, the *telekung* can be regarded as a form of the 'perfect gift' exchanged between humans. Considering only the level of visible social activities, this might imply that this act of gift-giving performed by Annisa is not reciprocal. However, as I argue here, in the moment that it is given, the four preconditions described above are fulfilled, Allah enters the situation as a third honouring actor. He is the one returning the gift. We have to consider here that, according to Muslim thinking, Allah is associated with the created world and the creatures and things to be found in it through His capacity as creator. This is based on the Islamic concept of *tawhid*, i.e. the Oneness and Uniqueness of God, that 'bring[s] all things into unity and harmony' (Wadud 2009: 108). This concept implies an understanding that once two Muslims get together, Allah makes the third; when three get together, Allah makes the fourth, and so on (Wadud 2009: 108). When the prerequisites mentioned above are fulfilled during the act of giving and taking, the omnipresent God will acknowledge the activity and honour it with rewards, collected for judgment day (*qiamat*). This marks a reciprocal relationship in the spiritual system of gift-giving that depends on Allah as the third actor (Moufahim 2013: 424). In this way, a 'triadic relationship' (Kochuyt 2009: 110) results.

Nevertheless, the act of giving is still bound to the expectation that one will be honoured with *pahala* by Allah – although, according to my respondents, nobody ever knows when and how many *pahala* God grants. Acknowledging this spiritual situation of gift-exchange means, then, replacing Mauss's conceptualised obligations to give, to receive and to return with the notion of expectations, as Sprenger (2019, 2017) suggests. In this sense, giving a gift means *expecting* to receive something in return (from Allah) but does not necessarily enforce it from the human taker.

This means that the 'ethics of religious giving' (Feener and Wu 2020), which only comes into operation when all these elements are in their determined and 'correct place', depends on Allah as a third actor and, thus, on an (imagined) collective. This collective is comprised of at least the buyer, the taker (in the sense of someone who takes something back from the returner) and God – or the buyer, taker and the whole *ummah* (Muslim community) which shares the same, or at least a similar, value system. If the value system is not shared, the meaningful utility value of the taker's side will not match the level of the intention to give something in a spiritual sense with the giver's side. Through God, then, the object-exchange system becomes *totalising*[4] (see Mauss 2016 [1925]; Sprenger 2019): the obligations of giving, taking and returning are thus complied with (Descola 2018: 456).

This condition also implies that the object (here: *abaya*) evolves in its meaningfulness and functioning only once it arrives in Mecca, Medina or Dubai. Taking Sprenger's notion of *expectations* in the process of spiritual gift-giving into account, the object gets its *value* only once the gift becomes part of the collective – or at least an imagined collective. Whereas its attached value during the production process, for example in China, was distinctly non-spiritual, it receives its 'special something', as my respondents described it, at the very moment it is brought to specific places on the Arabian Peninsula. Hence, the object's value becomes transformed and transferred once Allah enters the situation as an (expected) rewarding actor. The value, which is a spiritual value in this case, only evolves as part of this imagined collective.

Given the fact that most Muslims in the world have a sense of belonging to the collective of the *ummah* and that God based on the principle of *tawhid* is always present as an additional actor, giving and taking is part of a spiritual whole. This condition of a spiritual whole is crucial for an understanding of the activity of shopping as performed by my respondents on pilgrimage. When I spoke to Annisa about shopping in a religious environment, she had this to say:

> There is a *Hadith* that says that whatever you do will be back to your intention . . . [Given this,] shopping can be an *ibadah* [surrender to God]. If the intention is to get a gift for someone and to make them happy. If you make them happy by bringing a gift and how to bring a gift? You will go shopping for it. So if you go shopping in order to get a gift for someone to make this person happy, then shopping is an *ibadah*. But if the *niat* [intention] is wrong, like you go shopping to spend all of your money and you turn poor after that, then

shopping is prohibited . . . The *niat* [intention] and the things we do must be interrelated . . . If you want to go shopping to help the needy, for example, then also your *niat* is good. Or when you buy something in a shop to help the seller, because you see that the shop is empty and he is losing his business maybe, then you have a good intention. Or if we buy something in a lot of quantity for a religious event, then we have a good *niat* [intention] and shopping goes back to *ibadah* [shopping is a surrender to God]. (26 August 2017)

As Annisa emphasised, shopping can be a religious obligation. Shopping is undertaken with Allah here. As this activity is part of a complex gift-giving culture in Muslim Malaysia, the spiritual part of shopping can turn into a sophisticated situation that involves more people than the buyer and the potential receiver. Annisa continued:

If we tell the seller that we are buying something for *sedekah* [charity], for orphans, for example, then perhaps he wants to join in, he also wants to get the *pahala* [rewards granted by Allah] and he gives us the things we want to buy for free. We are the middle person then. We and the seller do something good for the orphans. He will also enjoy the *ganjaran* [rewards]. (26 August 2017)

Annisa referred to orphans as a receiving group in this context of spiritual shopping. Farrah, however, closed the circle of *souvenir shopping* on pilgrimage as a religious act. I want to go back to my conversation with Farrah, begun in the introduction to this chapter, by putting it into the larger context of our conversation:

Farrah: [O]nce you submit, you surrender, you obey [to God], then the *ziarah* [visit, here, for example, at a market] is an *ibadah*. Shopping is a *ziarah* [a visit that can potentially invite God's blessing] and can be an *ibadah* [surrender to God] because once you shop, once you want to give charity, that is also an *ibadah*, something that you obey. You buy things and then you give charity with the things that you buy.

Viola: But must it be a gift to poorer people or can it be to anybody?

Farrah: It can be to anybody, but in the *Qur'an*, it is mentioned that the best charity you offer is to your family, and then to the orphans and then to the *miskin* [poor people] and then to the *muzaffir* [travellers].[5] And then when the family is okay, then you can give to them [to the orphans], then to them [the poor] and then to them [the travellers].

Viola: And is this also one of the reasons why you bring back all the souvenirs from the trip?

Farrah: Ya, ya. I have the intention in my heart. Even my husband also says [during the pilgrimage journey] 'Okay, buy, buy!' . . . We buy and give for charity and then people will be happy, we make people happy.[6] It is an *ibadah*. It's an instruction. (8 July 2017)

Farrah said that making people happy by means of a gift is a religious obligation. With reference to the theme of this study, she also pointed out that giving something to travellers is a religious obligation: these people are far from home and therefore are not able to rely on their own resources as much as when they are at home (Kochuyt 2009: 104). But giving to travellers, according to Farrah, is only righteous when first the family, second the orphans and third the poor have already been supported. This means that buying something for family members, for orphans (as Annisa emphasised) and for the poor are preconditions for giving something to travellers (in this case: pilgrims) with a clear and sincere conscience. Secondly, it also implies that when people give money, an *abaya* or a *telekung* to those who are about to leave for pilgrimage, as exemplified in the previous section, this act is presumably embedded in previous giving practices to family, orphans and the poor. Thirdly, and supporting what we have seen so far, people who give something to pilgrims follow a religious idea that will foster the giver's, taker's and taker's who takes from the returner (who is equal to the giver) relationship with God. As both Annisa and Farrah revealed, this means, fourthly, that where the gifts intended for pilgrims are objects and not just abstract things, such as banknotes, these must usually be bought in advance. Thus, once the shopping act is part of the intended religiously related gift-giving process, it is as much part of a spiritual barter system as the practices of giving and taking.

Females at the core

Strikingly, this barter system seems to be configured differently according to the gender of the future pilgrim. From what Farrah, Ubaidah, Sofea, Ramli and Annisa revealed, the items given vary depending on whether the person about to perform pilgrimage is female or male. Both genders (may) receive money. But females (may) obviously get an addi-tional thing, namely an *abaya* or a *telekung* to be used on pilgrimage. Annisa clearly stated in this regard that 'when people are going for *hajj* or *umrah*, we *usually* [emphasis added] give them an *abaya* as a gift'. Since an *abaya* is only meant for females, her wording 'people' needs to be specified with this gendered group of people. The sincere use of an *abaya* or a *telekung* with the appropriate intention as to usage can poten-tially provoke *pahala* and/or *barakah*.

The issue of gifting something similar that is only or especially given to *male* pilgrims was not raised in any of my conversations or interviews with women and men about gifting practices in the context of pilgrimage. Only female religious garments given to female pilgrims before they start their pilgrimage journey were mentioned. Given this, both genders can, under the conditions explained above, become part of a spiritual exchange system through money. Females, though, can poten-tially be rewarded with additional *pahala* or *barakah* in contrast to males via the gendered religious garments. Thus, females have the potential to perform pilgrimage with a more spiritual outcome than males in this regard – on the basis of what other people give them and how this thing is then contextualised. Intersectionally speaking, a situation opens up via the spiritual barter system that can accrue in the context of Muslim pilgrimage in which females can be spiritually advantaged in contrast to males. Females can acquire a specific form of *spiritual capital*, as dis-cussed by Kenny (2007), over and above that which is available to males. This form of capital can be embodied by the Malay Malaysian women of this study, once again, through the *abaya* that is brought back as a sou-venir from pilgrimage. The spiritual, the gendered and the intersectional conditions have deep repercussions for the analysis of shopping for sou-venirs on pilgrimage and bring us back to the discussion in the first part of this chapter.

Shopping as a tourist

A comparison of the different forms of gift-giving in Malay culture as described by *buah tangan*, *hadiah*, *cendera hati* and *hantaran* has shown that consuming certain religious goods on the *umrah* & *ziarah* Dubai journey as souvenirs and giving them to relatives, friends or colleagues as gifts is not specifically related to Dubai as a so-called shopping paradise or to Mecca, which has always been a trading hub. It is rather an inherent part of Malay culture. In this sense, *shopping* and *consumption* on *umrah*

& *ziarah* Dubai are rooted in Malay forms of gift-giving as well as in gift-giving as a spiritual act.

The common misunderstanding of the spiritual visit aka *ziarah* in Dubai by non-pilgrims as a mere a touristic shopping stopover – and not religiously connoted at all – is influenced by the trap of separating tourism from pilgrimage. 'Tourism' is an idea and practice that was developed during industrialisation, based on the introduction of wage work and the separation of the spheres of labour and free time (Graburn 1989: 24ff; Harrison 2001; Karenzos and Kittner 2010; Smith 1989; Urry 2002; Wang 2000). Previous scholarship discussed tourism in relation to (Muslim) pilgrimage ambivalently, either as related or separated concepts. Cultural anthropologists Victor and Edith Turner (1978: 20), for instance, combined the two practices and concepts: 'A tourist is half a pilgrim, if a pilgrim is half a tourist.' Tourists are pilgrims and vice versa, because, they claim, both groups of travellers use the same infrastructure, for example. Tourists and pilgrims book their journeys through the same travel agencies, they travel by the same carriers and stay in the same hotels. Consequently, the two types of travelling are bureaucratised in the same way.

The concept of tourism can be seen as a form of structuring the personal life cycle. In this sense, tourists can be perceived as (secular) pilgrims (Smith 1989: 4). Peter Burns (1999: 75–77) compares a touristic journey with a 'rite de passage', and thereby introduces a spiritual aspect to the concept of tourism (see Cassar and Munro 2016; Fedele 2014; Fleischer 2000). He discusses tourism as a 'modern form of religion or pilgrimage' because, on the one hand, going on holiday is a kind of ritual that confirms one's personal social status (Burns 1999: 94f). On the other hand, pilgrimage means paying tribute to cultural places in a wider sense. While Burns (1999: 77) classifies tourism 'as a ritual and sacred journey', Noel Salazar (2014: 260) emphasises the quest for authenticity in both tourism and pilgrimage (see Schlehe 2003: 34f).

In contrast to merging the concepts of tourism and pilgrimage, Kadir (1989) disconnects tourism from pilgrimage, here Muslim pilgrimage, because he considers Islam as totally separate from the idea of tourism as a leisure trip. Discussing tourism strategies and practices imported from the West as early as the 1980s, modern tourism is seen as based on consumerism and abundance, whereas Muslim travel is a reciprocal form of communication between cultures (Kadir 1989: 554). In a similar vein, Lina and Hairul (2012: 1f) understand a tourist as someone who wishes to explore new places through sightseeing trips. On the contrary, they argue, a Muslim traveller goes on a journey in order to strengthen their relationships with relatives or friends and to experience God's creations and, thus, increase their faith in Allah.

Scholars such as Kadir, Lina and Hairul reveal the widely held perception that the idea of tourism is highly enmeshed with consumption. Similar to a specific conceptualisation of tourism that developed though capitalism, consumption and shopping as ideas are dependent on particular perspectives and standpoints. Yet we have seen that both the understanding of the *ziarah* to Dubai and the act of shopping in that place are deeply rooted in a spiritual and cultural framework (see Cohen and Cohen 2015). Whereas Moufahim (2013: 422) conceptualises the activity of shopping on a religious trip as 'sacred consumption', I argue that it rather shows how 'consumption' and 'shopping' as terms and concepts are part of a capitalist background and are only partially applicable to the Muslim context of this study. Ever since the development of capitalism and consumer culture, the act of buying souvenirs on overseas trips has been conceptualised as 'shopping' (aka capitalist consumption). It has always been the norm to bring home *buah tangan, cendera hati* or *hadiah* from (religious) trips, so the act as such is nothing new – only the categorisation of it.

The importance of an awareness of how to frame socio-cultural normative orders and practices becomes clear when we compare chapters 4 and 6 of this book. In chapter 4, shopping (here: especially for *abayas*) was discussed in the context of consumption (and thus touched on middle-classness and modernity). In this chapter, the same issue has been analysed without that aspect. It becomes possible to take the same situation without (capitalist) consumption into account when considering the exchange system as a whole. Whereas in chapter 4 the relationship between buyer and object was the focus, in this chapter, buyer and object are complemented by the taker. Both analytical approaches have their merit and their place, as both show parts of the social reality of Muslim Malay Malaysian life-worlds. Bringing in the taker in this chapter has enabled a shift to the spiritually saturated framing of the same condition. Longstanding traditional concepts and practices of buying souvenirs (*buah tangan*) have turned into 'modern ones' in the course of capitalist developments.

Given this shift in understanding, this might mean that the Malay Malaysian pilgrims of this study are under the impression that they need to purify themselves of shameful practices (shopping) that were once regarded as traditional practices (bringing back *buah tangan*). The evolution of 'tourism' as a concept and practice and its related shopping activities transform Muslim Malay customs of gift-giving in the context of pilgrimage into something abnormal that suddenly needs special justification. This shift allows a further perspective that is crucial to this study: the gendered dimension of shopping in this context.

The term and activity of 'shopping' is connoted female (not only) in the context of this research (see, for example, Miller 1998). As discussed in chapter 4, Malay Malaysian women are usually the decision-makers when it comes to the location of the *ziarah* stopover. They aim for Dubai in order to shop for the *abaya*, while the men do not shop for anything in particular at all. They are not interested in the activity of purchasing, except some *buah tangan* in the form of keychains, fridge magnets and the like. The practice of shopping for something with enthusiasm, excitement and pleasure is the women's job – at least in Dubai. Shopping here means 'the longing for that coveted object' as part of 'holiday browsing', as Miller (1998: 2) puts it in his work *A Theory of Shopping*. This contrasts with everyday purchases of groceries and other essential things (Miller 1998: 2). Yet providing *buah tangan* from pilgrimage and gifting them to others *is* something essential – namely, for Malay Malaysian identity.

However, the place of purchase and the concrete character of the gift are relevant to the distinction between shopping for something as a gift and purchasing something as a gift. Considering 'shopping' as a female activity in the context of this study is, firstly, based on place: it is undertaken in Dubai. This place is regarded as a convergence between spirituality (as it is located on the Arabian Peninsula with its Islamic history) and modern tourism. Secondly, the item they predominantly shop for in only this place on the entire journey is the fashionable *abaya*, which evinces notions of modernity. Hence, female shopping is bound to the capitalist, modern realm of the journey. By contrast, the purchasing of souvenirs from pilgrimage happens especially in the *haramain*, the Holy Land, as Sharifah and Farrah mentioned at the beginning of this chapter. As we have seen, this practice is not gendered but gender-neutral: both women and men are eager to bring back *buah tangan* or *cendera hati* from the pilgrimage trip.

This finding stands in stark contrast to previous research undertaken in both Western and Malaysian contexts which argues that gift-giving is a female practice (Ajello *et al.* 2015; Areni *et al.* 1998; Cheal 1987; Fischer, E. and Arnold 1990; Md. Nor Othman *et al.* 2005). In these studies, women are understood to invest more time and effort in selecting, buying and distributing gifts – in the sense of material, non-human objects as also treated in this study – than men are. According to these scholars, some reasons for this might be that they are more responsible for expressive functions (Cheal 1987) and generally more involved in moral domestic spheres (Md. Nor Othman *et al.* 2005). However, feminist philosophical research includes symbolic forms of gift-giving such as love (O'Grady 2013) and time (Holland 2013) in the analysis and deconstructs the gendering of the concept.

The gender-equal tradition of gift-giving in Malaysia points to the condition that, I argue, tourism as part of capitalist developments brings women not only into play but even *to the core* of exchange systems in the Malaysian context. From an intersectional standpoint, *shopping*, with its modern and sometimes luxurious notions of consumption on *umrah* & *ziarah* Dubai, empowers Malay Malaysian women within the Islamic, especially orthodox and male, realm of Malaysian society. They become modern, visible, self-confident social actors not only through utilising the *abaya*, as discussed in chapter 4, but also through shopping for and gifting this garment. Women decide in this situation not only about their spiritual capital, but also about their social capital that is consolidated through gifts. Therefore, this transformative gendered social development is based on touristic and, thus, capitalist conditions and would not (necessarily) occur in common Malaysian gift-giving systems. I therefore nuance Addo and Besnier's, Mauss's, Werbner's and others' theoretical approaches of gift-giving in a specific direction: *shopping* as part of exchange systems is the situation that provokes socio-cultural transformation in Muslim Malaysia and not the complex exchange of gifts per se.

To wrap up, the most sought-after object that my respondents want to obtain on their religious journey is the *abaya*. This thing transforms into a commodity (see Sleebom-Faulkner 2014; Strathern 1990: 134–67), ready to be shopped for, and once it is bought, it can subsequently change into a gift. This transformation of the female garment also implies a status transition of the *abaya* from a short-term transferred commodified object into a long-term exchanged thing (see Sprenger 2017: 3).

This item gets it value from the place it was purchased and through the presence of God, which can be engendered during prayer or as part of a spiritual barter context. Thus, the exchange of goods, objects and barter only attains a special value when the object is part of a collective. On the spiritual scale of *Scaling Holistic Intersectionality* it becomes evident that once Allah enters the situation of object or gift-exchange – or of shopping – the value of the item is transformed and transferred. This means that when a person gives an *abaya*, for instance, to another person, that act is just a common form of exchange. Yet, when (1) the intention (*niat*) is righteous according to Muslim moral belief and thus sincere (*ikhlas*); when (2) the activity of shopping is morally proper, i.e. not excessive (see chapter 4); when (3) the thing bought meets Islamic requirements and therefore does not distract from God (simple vs fashionable *abaya*); and when (4) the taker can use the *abaya* for herself and finds it reasonable for her, then shopping (and any other form of exchange) transforms into a spiritual act.

This spiritual act is equally true of both women and men in the Malay Malaysian gift-giving context. Gift-exchange is deeply rooted in Malay cultural orders and practices and is performed similarly in terms of quantity and quality of gifts as between women and men. Yet, under the socio-cultural and political conditions of capitalism, *buying* a gift has been understood increasingly as *shopping for* a gift. Shopping has been incorporated into the idea of tourism and consumption. This transformation is parallel to a development whereby the gender equality of Muslim Malay gift-exchange has become a gendered, namely a female, activity, for example due to gendered connotations of caring for others by buying things. In this research, in fact, males do not shop for anything in particular on the consumption level of the religious journey but females are eager to go shopping for female items (*abayas*). This means that since there is nothing 'male' about shopping (in contrast to buying souvenirs), the potential spirituality of shopping is not applicable to males at all. Consequently, the spiritual scale of *Scaling Holistic Intersectionality* is only applicable here to Muslim females. Thus, gift-giving in the context of this study can be spiritual but it is gender neutral; shopping can be spiritual but it is female. The intersectional situation of female spiritual shopping allows the women of this research to enhance their spiritual stance on the pilgrimage journey in a way that is not accessible to males – specifically embodied via shopping, gifting and using the *abaya*.

Notes

1. Hannefah clarified this with: 'Dates have natural sugar. We are either supposed to eat honey or dates before breaking fast. Dates are easy to get, honey is not. So, we eat the dates. It is *sunnat* [recommended according to Islamic understanding] to eat dates.' Farish noted the similarly wholesome character of *zam zam* water: 'And *zam zam* water, similar to the dates, is also about nutrition. It gives you energy. When you are ill, you should drink it for purification. My father was not allowed to drink it, the doctor didn't allow him, because he had high blood pressure.' Haneefah said, '[Z]am zam is thicker than normal water because it contains minerals; it has more salt.'
2. '*Kutu*' literally means small insect, louse or flea; '*kutu-kutu*' is plural. '*Makanan*' means meal. In this context it means that many people contribute the food together, similar to many small insects buzzing around. They contribute the food or supplies to fund the event and its dishes. When guests bring gifts in the form of foodstuffs to the bride and groom, they, in turn, will share what was contributed. Against this backdrop, '*kutu-kutu makanan*' can best be translated as 'laid table composed by many contributing people'.

3. She chose this as an example because shortly beforehand we had been talking about how I could get from her home to the place I was staying in KL. I said that I intended to get a taxi but that I did not use Grab or Uber, the two online taxi services in KL, and that I did not have any idea how to find a common taxi in her neighbourhood. So I was worried about how to get home.
4. Interestingly, Mauss (2016 [1925]: 174f) draws explicitly on sura 64, verses 16–19 of the *Qur'an* which describes this spiritual exchange framework – but he does not acknowledge it in its own religious right. He only uses the *Qur'anic* reference to take it as an example for coeval economic circumstances.
5. On my way home from my discussion with Farrah, she sent me an SMS which read: 'Need to share with you the correct commandment [as stated in the *Qur'an*] that I am earnestly try-ing to carry out as we discussed: "They ask you (O Muhamad), what they should spend. Say, 'Whatever you spend of good is (to be) for parents and relatives and orphans and the needy and the traveller. And whatever you do of good – indeed, Allah is knowing of it.'" Al Quran, 2:215.'
6. She sent a second SMS to me on my way home: 'Al-Quran 2:261–3: When I go shopping on *umrah* and then give what I shopped to others as presents. Look for that in the *Qur'an*.' I promptly looked it up. These suras deal with giving practices to the needy, with the balancing act of getting something for the needy and thereby not becoming poor oneself, and with the prohibition of interest. Farrah related this content directly to shopping.

7
Conclusion

Setting the postcolonial stage

This book matters for researchers who study Islam and/or gender in Southeast Asia, but its relevance goes far beyond that. It is also informative for scholars researching Islam in Western Asia and North Africa, for anthropologists who are interested in issues pertaining to the globalised world in general and for academics researching gender issues in a broad sense. It shows the huge relevance of Malaysia's religious economy and the strategies of the *halal* market that are part of the reorganisation of global markets and political power across the globe. It demonstrates the increasingly relevant global relations and negotiations between Southeast Asia and the Middle East, which are challenged in this very process precisely by Malaysian strategies, approaches and practices: Malaysia is now *the* point of reference for the Gulf states when it comes to the *halal* market, for example. Shifts in power blocs and particularly South-South relations are being renegotiated and reordered by Malaysia's (and the Gulf's) presence and power. These relations are also significant in the field of mobility studies in general terms: South-South migration and South-South mobility in a broader sense are still very much neglected in academia, and this does not do justice to their importance.

Above all, this study matters for the ever-present, overheated academic and socio-political field of Islam-and-gender-issues. It intervenes into the highly ideological racist and sexist discourses and debates that have been going on for decades, particularly in Western Europe and the United States. These revolve around the gendered body and clothing and materialise in paternalistic and neo-colonial debates about the headscarf. I hope that it is clear that ethnographic work has the capacity to give way to nuanced research – in this case especially on marginalisation, power and agency. This capability of ethnography is particularly apparent when it incorporates an intersectional lens. Adopting this lens to whichever disciplinary approach can have far-reaching consequences. Sirma Bilge (2014: 176) states:

> Instead of settling intersectionality as a speciality field, [I suggest that] . . . un-disciplinary critical intersectionality [be] viewed as an epistemic *potentiality* to disrupt Eurocentric knowledge-production politics and its attendant (inter)disciplinary formations.

Eurocentric knowledge production and the quest to disrupt it forms the central backdrop to this research. Any contemporary study located in Western academia that deals with Islam, and particularly with Islam and gender, will attract criticism that is motivated by general assumptions about the secular and the religious (Mahmood 2005: 189). This is as true for individual involvement on the part of the researcher in academic or personal discussions as it is for their scientific contribution in the form of publications in broader scholarly or public debates and discourses. As Saba Mahmood (2005: 189) stated, this is embedded in 'Western imagination concerning Islam's patriarchal and misogynist qualities. Far more than issues of democracy and tolerance, the "Woman Question" has been key within the development of the Western critique of Islam'.

This socio-political and cultural situation in Western academia, polity and policies leads me and other scholars to conclude that intersectional research – be it anthropological or otherwise – should be framed by postcolonial debates. Beverly M. Weber (2015: 28) relates this necessity specifically to an intersectionality study that incorporates religion:

> In order to consider the roles of religion and faith in intersectional frameworks . . . it is first key to acknowledge, following Umut Erel, Encarnación Gutiérrez Rodríguez, Jin Haritaworn, and Christian Klesse, that intersectionality only has analytical value if it is part of an anti-racist and postcolonial socio-critical framework that accounts for the ways in which racist histories structure knowledge. (Erel *et al.*, 2007: 245)

Whether intended or not, this study is inevitably situated within a postcolonial framework. This setting evolved in the 1970s when Edward Said (1978) revealed in his ground-breaking work *Orientalism* the discriminatory and oppressive discursive practices of the 'West' (colonialist, imperialist and postcolonialist states) towards the 'Orient' (the Islamic Arabic World) which has constantly produced a binary opposition between the two regions. Fifteen years later, Lila Abu-Lughod (1983) enhanced Said's approach by bringing in a gender lens. In *Writing Women's Worlds*, she urges us from an anthropologist, feminist, Middle Eastern scholarly perspective to 'write against culture', which she understands as actively avoiding reproducing common ideas and views, namely of an exotic, sexualised and therefore gendered East (see Ali 2014: 203–98). Similarly, Fadwa El Guindi (1999: 23) argues that imaginings of 'the harem' comprising sexually available Muslim females and homophile and sexually potent Muslim males are a depiction of the violent and dominant gaze of male European colonial powers. This gaze eventually constructed images of 'veil, harem, seclusion and unbridled sexual access' as a constituted entity. This gendered vehicle for constructing and practising identities, Self and Other, and global political orders was similarly evidenced by Frantz Fanon (1965: 35–64), who emphasised in *Algeria Unveiled* that the symbol of the veil provided a means for French colonisers in Algeria to establish discourses and practices concerning the backwardness of Algerian society and the need to 'civilise' this society by occupation. On a practical level, according to Fanon, French people living in Algeria established the narrative of 'de-veiling' in order to communicate to local Algerian women that this practice would eventually liberate them.

Hence, particularly through the connection between Islam and issues of women, gender and embodiment, Western conquerors, scientists and creative artists shaped a powerful narrative of (assumed) oriental culture (Förschler 2010). This construction of the 'Oriental Other' has served as a boundary to a 'civilised' and 'enlightened' Self (Bilge 2010), which is based on sexed bodies (Bilge 2010). The image of a passive, oppressed and available Muslim woman who veils her face in public stood in contrast to European Christian bourgeois women who were constituted and constructed as modest and progressive, for example. This relation is addressed through the concept of 'Occidentalism', which forms the basis and condition for Orientalism. It refers to the construction of a more civilised, better placed and superior Self (the Occident) which enables the projection of an inferior, less civilised Other (the Orient) (Roth 2017).

This is a general overview of the last couple of centuries and is not only applicable to Western imaginations and practices towards sociocultural contexts deemed as exotic, savage and inferior. Who is regarded as 'Other' depends on who is in power – and is not limited just to discourses, debates and practices related to the Muslim world. Moreover, I do not claim that discourses in Muslim contexts or Islamic normative orders are not discriminatory against women. Additionally, state policies, orthodox Muslims and nationalist movements have time and again tried to employ both women and feminist discourses tactically. Nevertheless, following Sabah Mahmood (2005: 190), the oversimplification of the sketched framing of an 'enlightened Self' and 'an uncivilised Other' needs to be questioned.

Recently, this oversimplification has had echoes in the international exhibition *Contemporary Muslim Fashions*, which was conceptualised, realised and hosted by and in the Fine Arts Museums of San Francisco and the Museum für Angewandte Kunst in Frankfurt (see D'Alessandro and Lewis 2018) in 2018/19. Showcasing the entangled themes of Islam, Gender, Embodiment and Fashion, this exhibition represented the diverse approaches to modest fashion taken by designers, producers and consumers that has led to a distinct fashion market. Certain media representatives, anthropologists and women's rights activists, interestingly especially in Germany but not in the USA, doubted the legitimacy of this exhibition as it focused on possibilities for and self-confidence of Muslim women via their clothing rather than the constraints and oppression that they would generally face within the Muslim context (see for example ARD, 7 April 2019 and WDR, 11 April 2019).

The Gulf Wars are an additional factor that still lingers and continues to have an impact on social values, categorisations and mindsets that are based in the hierarchical orders between 'the West and the Rest', as Stuart Hall (1992) puts it. United States and Western European governments have legitimised imperialist wars in Iraq, Afghanistan and Syria since 1991, when George Bush Sr launched 'Operation Desert Storm' against the Iraqi regime. In particular, since George W. Bush Jr picked up in 2003 where his father left off in 1991 together with the United Kingdom and the so-called 'coalition of the willing' by commencing the third Gulf War, references to women's rights were centrally incorporated into the argument: they were to be (re-)established through armed intervention. In her article *Do Muslim Women Really Need Saving? Anthropological reflections on cultural relativism and its others*, Lila Abu-Lughod (2002) discusses with great clarity how women's roles are instrumentalised in armed interventions for the legitimisation of power and force over people (in this case Muslim), territory and natural resources. On the basis of colonial constellations, women's roles have been developed as a matter of negotiation of sovereignty and independence on the one side and of oppression and rule on the other.

The social and political dimensions and one's own responsibility within these prevailing conditions are wide-ranging, as Abu-Lughod (2002: 789) emphasises:

> As anthropologists, feminists, or concerned citizens, we should be wary of taking on the mantles of those 19th-century Christian

missionary women who devoted their lives to saving their Muslim sisters. One of my favorite documents from that period is a collection called *Our Moslem Sisters*, the proceedings of a conference of women missionaries held in Cairo in 1906 (Van Sommer and Zwemer 1907: 15) . . . 'This book,' it begins, 'with its sad, reiterated story of wrong and oppression is an indictment and an appeal . . . It is an appeal to Christian womanhood to right these wrongs and enlighten this darkness by sacrifice and service' (Van Sommer and Zwemer 1907: 5). One can hear uncanny echoes of their virtuous goals today, even though the language is secular, the appeals not to Jesus but to human rights or the liberal.

I myself am not free from prejudices and presuppositions. My interest in Muslim life-worlds in general and in Muslim *women's* practices, thoughts and ideological orientations in particular is strongly driven by deep respect, empathy, feminist solidarity and the allure of the unknown. However, throughout my research, I was often irritated by the decisions and social actions of my female respondents. Why do they – as powerful, self-confident, active women – decide to wear the *abaya*, which is a symbol of Islamisation in some regional and socio-political contexts? Why does wearing gloves and veils after pilgrimage make them feel so comfortable? Why do some of them find it most liberating to wear *niqab*, the face veil? My irritations have their roots in my upbringing in a western European context with all the abovementioned discourses, values, norms and power relations that implies. Even though I constantly reflect upon and distance myself from anti-Muslim discriminatory and often oppressive perspectives and social dynamics, they form the basis of my confusion regarding some of my respondents' practices.

Judging 'the Other' as an anthropologist in hierarchical ways is not a feature typical of evaluations of Islam or Muslim contexts but can be traced in many anthropological inquiries (Mahmood 2005: 190). As anthropologists, we are influenced by knowledge production as we produce knowledge, and this entangled situation is embedded in Western forms of projection (see for example Barth 2002; Mielke and Hornidge 2017; Narotzky 2005; Newhouse 2018). This is a logical outcome of us being bound to social-cultural upbringings and surroundings that leave their mark on our thinking and behaviour. Yet it is our responsibility to connect our knowledge production as academics to our research subjects' realities:

In anthropology . . . we use the ethnographic descriptions (however critical we are about how they were produced) as material for comparison, we adopt in this regard something similar to the 'suspension of disbelief' that realist fiction entails, we have to trust that there is some reference to 'real' reality in the description. Because we need to proceed in this way through communication of other works of very different kinds to think and grow in our thinking about reality. (Narotzky 2005: 49)

The research at hand is an attempt to shoulder responsibility for what we transmit to our audience. Admittedly, the Western audience at least of this ethnography will be intellectually, mentally and emotionally framed by 'secular-liberal presuppositions about the proper role religiosity should play in the constitution of a modern subjectivity, community, and polity' (Mahmood 2005: 191). To juxtapose possible presuppositions, I have tried to draw a differentiated picture of my respondents' narratives through my analytical discussions.

Going shopping with Allah: constituting and embodying a pious, modern female self

Just as my Malay Malaysian respondents travelled from Southeast Asia to the Arabian Peninsula and then returned home, I too want to come full circle, revisiting the research questions I posed in the introduction. How far do Muslim forms of travel have an impact on gendered identifications and practices, and vice versa? How does the consumption, distribution and giving of objects and goods relate to religious concepts and practices, and how is this relationship in turn connected to the category and practices of gender? What meaning do female and male Muslim actors assign to the consumer goods they acquire in Dubai, Mecca and Medina, and how is this meaning related to gendered and religious normative orders, discourses and social practices in Malaysia and its transregional connectivities to the Arabian Peninsula?

The complex answers to these questions lie, figuratively speaking, in shopping with Allah. For the Malay Malaysian women in this research, the most desired object for purchase during religious travel is the *abaya,* the female Arabic costume, as it functions as a form of negotiation and a means of representation. When women shop for this gendered garment on the religious journey, they are connected to their Lord and communicate with Him on various levels. Allah is part of their mind and guides the practical realisation of travel, rituals and consumption. Shopping and

Allah are not contradictions but innately entangled. The Malay Malaysian women in this study use the shopped-for, purchased, organised, worn, utilised, gifted and taken *abaya* as an embodiment of femininity, religiosity and spirituality. This material thing turns out to be the material exterior where embodied intersectionality, i.e. mutually dependent processes of gender and faith/spirituality, becomes transparent.

This research does not intend to articulate universally valid declarations. I wanted to understand how social actors shape their rich living environments in the social-cultural dynamics of gender, Islam, consumption and mobility, and how they position themselves within these dynamics. This research has offered a positioned and situated analysis of local and transregional transformations in which female and male social actors give and negotiate meaning, social relations and power. I hope that I have convinced my readers that *scaling* a holistically conceptualised intersectionality, as I put forward in the introduction, as a research optic offers a fruitful engagement with these social life-worlds. This proposed approach, from the intersectionality perspective, makes sense of holistic intersections in a manner that brings hierarchical relationships and the negotiations and agency therein to the fore. The anthropological perspective of the holistic intersectionality in turn gives special meaning to mutually constitutive identity formations through thick ethnographic data and consequently has the potential to question Western ways of thinking and knowledge production. Scaling a holistic intersectionality shows that hierarchical relationships, i.e. marginalisation, power and empowerment, can shift for an individual or a social group dependent upon the social sphere or, analytically speaking, the social scale.

Due to recurring patterns that emerged in the course of addressing, tackling, analysing and scaling a holistic intersectionality, the main results of this work have nevertheless proved to be generalisable. The central goal of this anthropological research was to investigate the mutually influencing gendered, spiritual and religious identifications and differentiations that social actors negotiate in the framework of social, political, economic and religious dynamics. Reconsidering the research questions posed earlier, how can the linkages between gender, Islam and consumption in the context of religious travel, which I approached with the idea of a holistic intersectionality, be summarised in the setting of the transformation processes in and connectivities between Malaysia and the Arabian Peninsula?

Based on 14 months of ethnographic fieldwork in Malaysia, the United Arab Emirates and Oman between 2013 and 2018, this study shows on an empirical level that Malay Malaysian pilgrims consume religiously connoted travel packages and, women especially, shop for (partly) spiritual, gender-specific souvenirs during the trip. The social actors draw on the commercialisation of spirituality, driven by local and global tourism and fashion industries specialised in Islamic-related products, primarily gendered garments. The main item purchased, the *abaya*, is sought after by the Malay Malaysian women in this study as it is religiously connoted and therefore regarded as especially useful for praying, but also, if it is a fashionable one, for representing a pious, modern Self. The *abaya* ultimately serves as a medium for submission to Allah – whereas males rather relate to Prophet Mohamad via their gendered Arabic dress. Other garments can be utilised by women to show devotion to their husbands which, in turn, refers back to their submission to their God. In contrast, men, in their role as fathers, show devotion to Allah through increased transmission of Islamic knowledge to their children. Since the predominant good to be consumed on *umrah* & *ziarah* Dubai is, based on these attributions and usages, the *abaya* and not any other thing, consumption on the religious journey is highly gendered. There is no similar thing to be consumed by males in order to embody, i.e. to show or to inwardly deal with, their experiences on the pilgrimage journey. Deriving from these empirical findings, this ethnographic research, which is based in feminist gender and intersectionality studies, argues on a theoretical level that gendered spirituality leads to different, reciprocally constitutive, gendered and religiously infused embodied expressions of this inner disposition and of femininity or masculinity, which eventually challenge gendered social hierarchical orders.

In order to prove the validity and coherence of these main (1) empirical and (2) theoretical findings and the usefulness of the (3) theoretical-methodological agenda to scale a holistically framed intersectionality, I want to merge and thereby explain and differentiate these three contributions in detail.

On the national and social scales it can be seen that pilgrimage in Malaysia was originally practised as an individual endeavour, but is nowadays highly controlled, regulated and marketised. State Islamisation processes have led to a deepening of Islamic belief since the 1970s, intermingled with economic development strategies that make these dynamics especially true of the Malay middle class. Products with Islamic connotations, such as clothing and travel packages, have developed as an important sector of the capitalist market in Malaysia and are desired targets for Malay middle-class (female) consumers. Gender, religion, class and mobility intersect here and bring females as part of capitalist and *halal* production and consumption processes to the core of social and economic realities.

These travel packages have an impact on notions regarding one particular form of pilgrimage: *ziarah*. Hence, on the institutional scale, i.e. the analytical level of the travel industry, religion is mutually constitutive of capitalism. *Ziarah*, in a religious sense, can have different meanings that relate to physical places within Islamic history, to the awareness of religious duties given by Allah and to the inner disposition of the specific activity labelled *ziarah*. Parts of this understanding have been transformed based on the travel industry's interventions since the 1980s. Until this decade, *ziarah* was used to describe visiting certain tombs in Mecca and Medina and, therefore, '*umrah*' and '*ziarah*' were understood as two different activities. Nowadays, *ziarah* refers to travel to other countries as well, so that *ziarah* can be part of *umrah*. When it comes to '*umrah* & *ziarah* Dubai', the practical realities of the trip lead to irritation for most travellers. Travel agents include the term *ziarah* in the package for strategic reasons, but do not realise the concept and activities of this religious endeavour. Given this, the travel industry incorporated *ziarah* as a commercialised product into their market segment. As a consequence, on the institutional scale of analysis, pilgrims' and travel agencies' needs do not match on all levels of the journey.

One need that does match, even if not fully, is shopping in Dubai. This is particularly true for women. While travel agents do not stipulate that they will bring groups to places where they can find their desired good (the *abaya*), the women in this study still found their own way to purchase it. Due to sacred landscaping in which the Arabian Peninsula is perceived as the Islamic centre and Southeast Asia as part of the Islamic margins, they require *abayas* from Dubai because of the religious, classed, fashionable notions they transmit for women. *Abayas* from Mecca and Medina, however, which are usually much simpler in style, are understood as purely religious and spiritual on the basis of the place where they are purchased.

Malay Malaysian women bring the *abayas* from the Arabian Peninsula through the transregional space to their home country and thereby create a social space in which they generate several transformation processes. For example, when they wear their *abayas* back home in Malaysia, no matter whether it comes from Dubai (fashionable) or from Mecca or Medina (simple), they challenge certain social conditions: when they wear the *abaya* in private and public spaces in Malaysia, they transcend normative spatial orders. These females appropriate and claim the public space, which has been a predominantly male Muslim space. On this transregional scale, the Malay Malaysian women in this study intervene in structures of gendered cityscapes by visibly embodying female spirituality in public spaces and thereby challenging the all-encompassing presence of male religiosity in this space (for example in mosques). On the transnational or transregional scale, we can thus observe an intersecting condition of gender and spirituality/faith that enhances women's subject positions.

Differentiating the usages of fashionable and simple *abayas* back home in Malaysia, the picture becomes more complex. On a geographic, here transregional, scale, women adopt the fashionable *abaya* from Dubai, which they unanimously perceive as modern due to its 'modern place of purchase'. Modernity forms the basis here for the socio-geographic (transregional) scale as being modern, understood here as being connected to temporal developments, appropriations and differentiation. While women can wear the *abaya*, men can wear the *kandora*, which is the male Arabic cultural garment. Men, however, usually obtain their *kandoras* not in Dubai but in the Holy Land where it represents traditional culture. Consequently, the modern dimension of the gendered garment comes into play only for females. Thus embodying a modern, pious self through the typical Arabic garment is only possible for females, not for males.

The Malay Malaysian women in this study assign further meaning to their *abayas* and utilise them in other circumstances, for example when praying. In this situation the simple *abaya* from Mecca or Medina becomes especially relevant. Based on Islamic and cultural (*adat*) ideologies, Muslim women are perceived, and perceive themselves, as inherently less chaste than men. This leads to females constantly needing to put greater effort into preparing their bodies for certain situations in which a chaste body is required. This is the case for every formal prayer situation, i.e. when communicating with God formally. In this situation, the spiritual scale grows. Since women, according to ideological assumptions, are intrinsically unable to fully attain a chaste body, they change their clothes for prayer, which men usually do not do. Females in Malaysia often put on their culturally embedded prayer garment, the *telekung*. Yet since the Malay Malaysian subjects of this study particularly understand the simple *abaya* as *syariah* compliant and therefore as an object through which they can come close to having a pure body, some of them exchange the *telekung* for the *abaya*. This special attention to the female body and its attire, and the simultaneous normality of the male praying body, marks degradation for the former and privilege for the latter.

On the intimate scale of intersectional analysis, Muslim women are also disparaged in contrast to their male fellows when it comes to the question of what gendered and religiously connoted garments from the so-called centre of Islam entail in terms of relations with Islamic history and culture. For my Malay Malaysian respondents, both *abaya* and *kandora* from the Arabian Peninsula relate to Islam, but only the garment made for males has the potential to connect the wearer directly with Prophet Mohamad and his lifestyle. My respondents believe that the Prophet wore the *kandora* himself and that he required all male Muslims in the world to follow this habit. Hence wearing the *kandora* is an embodiment of following *Sunnah*, i.e. the sayings and deeds of Prophet Mohamad, which is the second fundamental source of Islam after the *Qur'an*. Since no embodied equivalent exists to allow women and girls to follow the deeds and sayings of Prophet Mohamad, females are disadvantaged in this regard. This unequal intersectional relationship, however, does at least show common causes among both genders concerning the will or intention to connect oneself to the Islamic past by wearing traditional Arab garments.

Male privilege is furthermore evident when men strengthen their position on the family scale, particularly in their role as Muslim fathers. Based on a generally reinforced belief resulting from pilgrimage, the intersectional situation shows the role males play in this regard, as many of them begin to actively educate their children in Islamic issues. This form of parenting and childcare in turn relieves the double duties that are common for mothers in contemporary Malaysia.

Men's transformative role within their family constellations is realised in the form of social action that does not touch on issues of the body. Women's intersectional development processes on the family scale are, in contrast, situated in the realms of social actions *and* embodiment. This latter situation is highly ambiguous between submission and liberation. Both the men and women in this study deepen their belief through pilgrimage. This leads to women, in their roles as wives and equally on the family scale, showing their intensified relationship with their husband via additional garments that deactivate their *aurat*. By this means they express, amongst other things, a consciousness of being only (sexually) available to the husband, belonging to him and obeying him, as the *aurat* are those body parts that are only to be shown to the husband. This practice is embedded in a consolidated matrimony that arose out of the pilgrimage experience and hence out of a deepened submission to Allah. The family scale connects with the spiritual scale here. The intersectional effect on the family and spiritual scales alike arises out of the wider hierarchical gendered ordering of Allah first, *imam* or any other Islamic scholar second, and husband (or father) third – who women follow or submit to. Thus the women in this study simultaneously show devotion to figures perceived as male (Allah and husbands) that cannot be understood separately, but rather in a mutually constitutive and embodied manner.

This intersectional circumstance of submissive Muslim women seems to disempower them, especially from a perspective that is present in Western academia and the public sphere. Yet the entangled and parallel submission to God and to the husband needs to be considered as a twofold relationship. While women stabilise and consolidate their bonds to their husbands, they simultaneously liberate themselves and become independent due to their preconditioned devotion to God. Total submission to God means becoming free. Free to choose between different options that Allah offers in order to gain a more positive life. Thus the intersectional position as submissive, believing wives on the family scale liberates them on the spiritual scale as a consequence of spiritual enhancement through *umrah* or *hajj*.

The spiritual scale is, again, relevant for a last condition of this study in which the issues discussed above are comprehensively knitted together: shopping. The nuanced relationships between the good, object or thing and the buyer on the one hand, and the user on the other, have been demonstrated, but when considering the *comprehensive* situation of shopping, more social actors such as taker and returner appear so that the greater exchange system complements the preceding analysis of motivations and utilisations in the sphere of consumption.

Before Malay Malaysian women can wear their *abayas* from sacred landscapes to transcend social spaces, to become the embodiment of modern pious Muslim women or for formal prayer, they naturally need to acquire them. One possibility is to shop for them themselves on the journey; another is to receive them as gifts from someone who has travelled to the Arabian Peninsula. Thus shopping is central, as women predominantly shop for the *abaya* on their pilgrimage journey, but women and men purchase many other objects on their sojourn too and thereby turn them into souvenirs. Most often, these souvenirs have a religious or spiritual sense, such as prayer chains, the *Qur'an* or a certain type of dates that are perceived as the food of the Prophet Mohamad. In their form as souvenirs, my respondents either bring the items back home for themselves, or – and this is the case for most souvenirs – give them to family, friends and colleagues. To give something to someone in the Malay Malaysian context, as long as it follows practices my respondents understand as 'culturally' or 'naturally' Malay, is a spiritual act, since fostering social bonds is an Islamic requirement, and this can be achieved by giving gifts.

Gift exchange in general, and as part of a return from pilgrimage in particular, is deeply rooted in Malay cultural orders and practices. Commonly and traditionally, giving and receiving gifts in Malay Malaysia is performed for and by women and men similarly in terms of the quantity and quality of gifts. Yet under the socio-cultural and political conditions of capitalism, *buying* a gift is more and more understood as *shopping for* a gift. In a broader sense, the concept of shopping activities has been incorporated into the idea of tourism and consumption. However, the spiritual notion of buying something for others is not changed in this shift in meaning. This transformation from buying to shopping is parallel to the development of Muslim Malay gift exchange into a gendered, namely a female, activity due to gendered connotations of caring for others by buying things. In fact, the men in this research do not shop – in the sense of a consumer or even luxury purchase – for anything particular during their religious journey but females are eager to go shopping for female items (*abayas*). This means that, since shopping is not a male activity, the potential spirituality of shopping is not applicable to them. Consequently, the spiritual scale of *Scaling Holistic Intersectionality* is only applicable to Muslim females in this regard. Thus, gift-giving in the context of this study can be spiritual but it is gender neutral; shopping can be spiritual but it is female. The intersectional situation of female spiritual shopping allows the women in this study to enhance their spiritual stance on their pilgrimage journey in a way that is not accessible to males – specifically embodied via shopping, giving and using the *abaya*.

My approach of holistic intersectionality, heuristically processed by *scaling* the analysis, has guided my inquiries in this research. In its fullness, this ethnographic and anthropological research inherently considers empirically driven, local intersections. These intersections, i.e. social categories, practices, forms of belonging, norms, orders and systems, were analysed from a starting point that centres on mutually constitutive axes of identification and differentiation and their corresponding power systems. The anthropologist's holistic view has established the complexity of the gender-spirituality/faith conditions, which are better captured when researching the correlations between individual life-worlds and socio-cultural circumstances.

Without this approach, this research would have taken a different direction. In an intersectional study that lacks the holistic ethnographic perspective, sightseeing and tourism would presumably be regarded as leisure time, as part of a capitalist condition, rather than as a form of spiritual knowledge-seeking (*kembara ilmu*). Similarly, the finding that Allah's possible presence during shopping turns it into a religious obligation (*ibadah*) would potentially be missing. Incorporating female submission and devotion to male characters into a fully liberating argument for women and girls seems inconceivable for intersectional, i.e. feminist and anti-racist, scholarship.

On the other side of the coin, a study on Muslim pilgrimage, gender and consumption could contingently examine relations between women, men and/or queer and transgender people on their religious journeys and the connected shopping practices without pinpointing the interventions into and negotiations of gender hierarchies in the corresponding context. Embodied practices of communicating spiritual capital to the outside world could analytically stand for themselves – but the notion that Malay Muslim women thereby reclaim social, predominantly male, spaces could potentially be lost. The nuanced, interlinked relationship through which the gendered positions of Muslim males is strengthened due to their ability to relate to the Islamic past via traditional Arabic male dress and which also raises Muslim females' status via modern Arabic female dress could end up being absent from the analysis.

The value of scaling holistic intersectionality becomes visible through the following. Reconsidering the intersectional conditions of, first, preparing the body for formal prayer, second, liberating oneself from any limitations by securing God's total custody and, third, going shopping with Allah, it is obvious that the spiritual scale only applies to females when the specific gender lens of embodiment is part of the analysis. My female respondents deal with all three relationships via female attire and thus with an object intended to modify their gendered bodies. Thus, without the scaled intersectional analysis, the fact that spirituality is gendered and that the embodiment of it is itself simultaneously gendered and religiously infused would not be clearly visible. Scaling intersectional analysis has furthermore shown that challenging social hierarchical orders that arise out of reciprocally constitutive, gendered and religiously infused embodied practices of femininity or masculinity due to pilgrimage happens on the intimate, family, temporal, transnational and spiritual scales, but not on the institutional, social or national scales.

Given the main empirical and theoretical findings, this research contributes to our understanding of how gendered meanings and practices of spirituality and faith are redefined or reified in the process of religious travel and consumer practices. It helps to make sense of the linkages between religious markets, gender, material culture and travel in a globalised world. This book thereby informs a wider interdisciplinary debate on intersectionality, constructions and practices of identification, material religion and mobilities.

However, readers will judge whether this study helps anthropologists to be more sensitive to power structures, whether or not it will encourage intersectionality theorists and activists to be more inclusive of religious identifications and conditions, and whether it contributes to applying a more nuanced and differentiated view on gender relations that potentially differs between analytic scales.

References

Abaza, Mona (2011). Asia Imagined by the Arabs. In Kamaruzzaman Bustamam-Ahmad and Patrick Jory (eds), *Islamic Studies and Islamic Education in Contemporary Southeast Asia*, pp. 1–27. Kuala Lumpur: Yayasan Ilmuwan.

Abaza, Mona (2007). More on the Shifting Worlds of Islam. The Middle East and Southeast Asia: a troubled relationship? *The Muslim World* 97(3): 419–36.

Abaza, Mona (1996). Islam in South-east Asia: Varying impact and images of the Middle East. In Hussin Mutalib and Taj ul-Islam Hashmi (eds), *Islam, Muslims and the Modern State. Case-studies of Muslims in thirteen countries*, pp. 139–51. London: Macmillan.

Abdul Rahman Embong (ed.), *Southeast Asian Middle Classes. Prospects for social change and democratisation*, pp. 31– 45. Bangi: Penerbit Universiti Kebangsaan Malaysia.

Abu-Lughod, Lila (2002). Do Muslim Women Really Need Saving? Anthropological reflections on cultural relativism and its others. *American Anthropologist* 104(3): 783–90.

Abu-Lughod, Lila (1990). The Romance of Resistance: Tracing transformations of power through Bedouin women. *American Ethnologist* 17(1): 41–55.

Abu-Lughod, Lila (1983). *Writing Women's Worlds: Bedouin stories*. Berkeley: University of California Press.

Addo, Ping-Ann and Niko Besnier (2008). When Gifts become Commodities: Pawnshops, valuables, and shame in Tonga and the Tongan diaspora. *Journal of the Royal Anthropological Institute* 14: 39–59.

Ahmad Fauzi, Abdul Hamid (1999). Development in the Post-Colonial State: Class, capitalism and the Islamist political alternative in Malaysia. *Kajian Malaysia/Journal of Malaysian Studies* 17(2): 21–58.

Ahmad, Irfan (2018). Twentieth-Century Faces of Anthropology's Holism. *Anthropology News* 59(3).

Aiedah, Abdul Khalek (2018). Entrepreneurship and the Halal Wave in Malaysia. In Norhayati Zakaria and Kaushal Leena (eds), *Global Entrepreneurship and New Venture Creation in Sharing Economy*, pp. 191–205. Hershey: IGI Global.

Aiza, Maslan Baharudin (2014). Hajj and the Malayan Experience, 1860s–1941. *Kemanusiaan* 21(2): 79–98.

Ajello, Linell; Áine Duggan, Gail Cooper and Sudha Rao (2015). The Perfect Present: Gift giving and gender norms. *re:gender. Research, rethink, reframe*. https://www.icrw.org/publications/the-perfect-present-gift-giving-and-gender-norms/ (accessed 25 March 2023).

Al-Qasimi, Noor (2010). Immodest Modesty: Accommodating dissent and the '*abaya*-as-fashion' in the Arab Gulf States. *Journal of Middle East Women's Studies* 6(1): 46–74.

Ali, Zahra (2014). *Islamische Feminismen*. Vienna: Passagen Verlag.

Almila, Anna-Mari and David Inglis (2018). The Hijab as Gift: Mechanisms of community socialisation in the Muslim diaspora. In Rosalba Morese, Sara Palermo and Juri Nervo (eds), *Socialization. Multidimensional perspective*, pp. 155–70. London: IntechOPen.

Amira, El-Azhary Sonbol (2009). The Genesis of Family Law. How Shari'ah, custom and colonial laws influenced the development of personal status codes. In Zainah Anwar (ed.), *Wanted: Equality and Justice in the Muslim Family*, pp. 179–207. Petaling Jaya: musawah.

Ansary, Tamim (2010). *Die unbekannte Mitte der Welt: Globalgeschichte aus islamischer Sicht*. Frankfurt/Main: Campus.

Ansori, Mohammad Hasan (2009). Consumerism and the Emergence of a New Middle Class in Globalizing Indonesia. *Explorations* 9: 87–97.

Appadurai, Arjun (1996). *Modernity at Large: Cultural dimensions of globalization*. Minneapolis/London: University of Minnesota Press.

Appadurai, Arjun (1986). Introduction: commodities and the politics of value. In Arjun Appadurai (ed.), *The Social Life of Things: Commodities in cultural perspective*, pp. 3–63. Cambridge: Cambridge University Press.

Arabian Business (29 October 2018) Revealed: the UAE's growing role in the global Islamic economy. https://www.arabianbusiness.com/retail/407018-revealed-the-uaes-growing-role-in-theglobal-islamic-economy (accessed 25 March 2023).

Arabian Business (3 May 2017) UAE Challenges Malaysia for Top Destination for Muslim travellers. https://www.arabianbusiness.com/uae-challenges-malaysia-for-topdestination-for-muslim-travellers-672819.html (accessed 25 March 2023).

ARD (Titel, Thesen, Temperamente) (7 April 2019) Die Ausstellung 'Contemporary Muslim Fashions' in Frankfurt. https://www.daserste.de/information/wissenkultur/ttt/videos/ttt-07042019-contemporary-muslim-fashions-video-100.html (accessed 25 March 2023).

Areni, Charles S., Pamela Kiecker and Kay M. Palan (1998). Is it Better to Give than to Receive? Exploring gender differences in the meaning of memorable gifts. *Psychology & Marketing* 15(1): 81–109.

Asad, Talal (1986). *The Idea of an Anthropology of Islam*. Washington, DC: Center for Contemporary Arab Studies, Georgetown University.

Atia, Mona (2012). 'A Way to Paradise': Pious neoliberalism, Islam, and faith-based development. *Annals of the Association of American Geographers* 102(4): 808–27.

Azizah, Mohd and Badruddin Hj Ibrahim (2010). Muslim Wife's Rights to Maintenance: Husband's duty to maintain a working wife in Islamic law and the law in Malaysia. *IIUM Law Journal* 18(1): 103–21.

Banks, David J. (1976). Islam and Inheritance in Malaya: Culture conflict or Islamic revolution? *American Ethnologist* 3(4): 573–86.

Barlas, Asma (2015). *Believing Women in Islam: Unreading patriarchal interpretations of the Qur'an*. Austin: University of Texas Press.

Barth, Fredrik (2002). An Anthropology of Knowledge. *Current Anthropology* 43(1): February 2002.

BBC (29 July 2020) Coronavirus: Scaled back Hajj pilgrimage begins in Saudi Arabia. https://www.bbc.com/news/world-middle-east-53571886 (accessed 25 March 2023).

Behar, Ruth and Deborah A. Gordon (eds) (1995). *Women Writing Culture*. Berkeley: University of California Press.

Belk, Russell W. (1996). The Perfect Gift. In Cele Otnes and Richard F. Beltramini (eds), *Gift Giving. A research anthology*, pp. 95–84. Bowling Green: Bowling Green State University Popular Press.

Bereswill, Mechthild and Anke Neuber (2011). Organized Masculinity, Precarisation and the Gender Order. In Helma Lutz, Maria Teresa Herrera Vivar and Linda Supik (eds), *Framing Intersectionality: Debates on a multi-faceted concept in gender studies*, pp. 69–88. Surrey: Ashgate.

Bhabha, Homi (1984). Of Mimicry and Man: The ambivalence of colonial discourse. *Discipleship: A Special Issue on Psychoanalysis* (Spring 1984): 125–33.

Bianchi, Robert R. (2017). Reimagining the Hajj. *Social Sciences* 6: 36.

Bianchi, Robert R. (2016). The Hajj by Air. In Eric Tagliacozzo and Shawkat M. Toorawa (eds), *The Hajj: Pilgrimage in Islam*, pp. 131–51. Cambridge: Cambridge University Press.

Bianchi, Robert R. (2004). *Guests of God: Pilgrimage and politics in the Islamic world*. Oxford: Oxford University Press.

Bilge, Sirma (2014). Whitening Intersectionality. Evanescence of race in intersectionality scholarship. In Wulf D. Hund and Alana Lentin (eds), *Racism and Sociology*, pp. 175–205. Vienna/Berlin Lit Press.

Bilge, Sirma (2013). Intersectionality Undone: Saving intersectionality from feminist intersectionality studies. *Du Bois Review* 10(2): 405–24.

Bilge, Sirma (2010). Beyond Subordination vs. Resistance: An intersectional approach to the agency of veiled Muslim women. *Journal of Intercultural Studies* 31(1): 9–28.

Birchok, Daniel Andrew (2020). Ridwan's Conversion: *Kandoeri* giving, moral personhood, and the re-imagining of communal difference in Indonesia. *Journal of Contemporary Religion* 35(1): 71–91.

Bloch, Maurice and Jonathan Parry (1989). Introduction. In Jonathan Parry and Maurice Bloch (eds), *Money and the Morality of Exchange*, pp. 1–32. Cambridge: Cambridge University Press.

Boellstorff, Tom (2007). Queer Studies in the House of Anthropology. *Annual Review of Anthropology* 36: 17–35.

Boltanski, Luc and Ève Chiapello (2003). *Der neue Geist des Kapitalismus*. Konstanz: UVK University Press.

Bonfanti, Sara (2016). Dislocating Punjabiyat: Gendered mobilities among Indian diasporas in Italy. In Miriam Gutekunst, Andreas Hackl, Sabina Leoncini, Julia Sophia Schwarz and Irene Götz (eds), *Bounded Mobilities: Ethnographic perspectives on social hierarchies and global inequalities*, pp. 183–205. Bielefeld: transcript.

Bourdieu, Pierre (2010 [1979]) *Distinction: A social critique of the judgement of taste*. Hoboken: Taylor & Francis.

Brah, Avtar and Ann Phoenix (2004). Ain't I a Woman? Revisiting intersectionality. *Journal of International Women's Studies* 5: 75–86.

Bräunlein, Peter J. (2016). Comments on the Paper by Members of the DORISEA Network. DORISEA Working Paper 24: 20–23.

Brenner, Neil (2004). *New State Spaces: Urban governance and the rescaling of statehood*. Oxford: Oxford University Press.

Bristol-Rhys, Jane (2010). *Emirati Women: Generations of change*. New York: Columbia University Press.

Brubaker, Rogers and Frederick Cooper (2000). Beyond 'Identity'. *Theory and Society* 29(1): 1–47.

Bubandt, Nils and Ton Otto (2010). Anthropology and the Predicaments of Holism. In Ton Otto and Nils Bubandt (eds), *Experiments in Holism: Theory and practice in contemporary anthropology*, pp. 1–15. Malden: Blackwell.

Bunnell, Tim (2016). *From World City to the World in One City: Liverpool through Malay lives*. Chichester: John Wiley & Sons.

Bunnell, Tim (2004). *Malaysia, Modernity and the Multimedia Super Corridor: A critical geography of intelligent landscapes*. Abingdon: Routledge.

Burke, Edmund (2014). *The Ethnographic State: France and the invention of Moroccan Islam*. Oakland: University of California Press.

Burns, Peter (1999). *An Introduction to Tourism and Anthropology*. Abingdon: Routledge.

Butler, Judith (1993). *Bodies that Matter: On the Discursive Limits of 'Sex'*. New York: Routledge.

Butler, Judith (1990). *Gender Trouble: Feminism and the subversion of identity*. New York: Routledge.

Campbell, Colin (2004). I Shop therefore I know that I am: The metaphysical basis of modern consumerism. In Karin M. Ekström and Helene Brembeck (eds), *Elusive Consumption*, pp. 27–43. Oxford: Berg.

Carneiro, Sueli (2018). *Escritos de uma vida*. Belo Horizonte: Editorial Letramento.

Carstens, Sharon A. (2005). *Histories, Cultures, Identities: Studies in Malaysian Chinese worlds*. Singapore: NUS Press.

Cassar, George and Dane Munro (2016). Malta: A differentiated approach to the pilgrim-tourist dichotomy. *International Journal of Religious Tourism and Pilgrimage* 4(4), Article 6.

Chakrabarty, Dipesh (2000). *Provincializing Europe: Postcolonial thought and historical difference*. Princeton: Princeton University Press.

Chandler, Siobhan (2013). The Way of the Spiritual Seeker. In M. Darrol Bryant (ed.), *Ways of the Spirit: Celebrating dialogue, diversity and spirituality*, pp. 1–7. Kitchener: Pandora Press.

Chaudhuri, Mayurakshi (2014). *Gender in Motion: Negotiating Bengali social statuses across time and territories*. Miami: Florida International University.

Chaudhuri, Mayurakshi, Viola Thimm and Sarah J. Mahler (2019). Scaling Educational Policy and Practices Intersectionally: Historical and contemporary education policies, practices and effects in South and Southeast Asia. In Olena Hankivsky and Julia Jordan-Zachery (eds), *The Palgrave Handbook of Intersectionality in Public Policy*, pp. 367–85. Houndsmills: Palgrave Macmillan.

Chaudhuri, Mayurakshi, Viola Thimm and Sarah J. Mahler (2014). Gendered Geographies of Power: Their value for analyzing gender across transnational spaces. In Julia Gruhlich and Birgit Riegraf (eds), *Geschlecht und Transnationale Räume. Feministische Perspektiven auf neue Ein- und Ausschlüsse*, pp. 192–209. Münster: Westfälisches Dampfboot.

Cheal, David (1987). 'Showing Them You Love Them': Gift giving and the dialectic of intimacy. *Sociological Review* 35(1): 150–69.

Chitose, Yoshimi (1998). Female Migration and the Regional Context in Peninsular Malaysia. *Regional Development Studies: An Annual Journal of the United Nations Centre* 4: 101–17.

Chong, Terence (2005). *Modernization Trends in Southeast Asia*. Singapore: ISEAS.

CNN (29 July 2020). 'Unprecedented' Hajj begins – with 1,000 pilgrims, rather than the usual 2 million. https://edition.cnn.com/travel/article/hajj-2020-coronavirus-intl/index.html (accessed 25 March 2023).

Cohen, Eric and Scott Cohen (2015). A Mobilities Approach to Tourism from Emerging World Regions. *Current Issues in Tourism* 18(1): 11–43.

Coleman, Simon and Pauline von Hellermann (eds) (2011). *Multi-Sited Ethnography: Problems and possibilities in the translocation of research methods*. New York: Routledge.

Collier, Stephen J. and Aihwa Ong (eds) (2005). *Global Assemblages: Technology, politics, and ethics as anthropological problems*. Malden: Blackwell.

Crenshaw, Kimberlé (1989). Demarginalizing the Intersection of Race and Sex: A Black feminist critique of antidiscrimination doctrine, feminist theory and antiracist politics. *University of Chicago Legal Forum* (1): 139–67.

Curiel·Pichardo, Ochy (2014). Hacia la construcción de un feminismo decolonizado. In Yuderkys Espiñosa Miñoso, Dania Gómez Correal and Karina Ochoa Muñoz (eds), *Tejiendo de oto modo: Feminismo, epistemología y apuestas descoloniales en Abya Yala*, pp. 325–34. Popayán: editorial Universidad del Cauca.

D'Alessandro, Jill and Reina Lewis (eds) (2018). *Contemporary Muslim Fashions*. Munich; London; New York: DelMonico Books, Prestel.

D'Arcangelis, Carol-Lynne (2020). Feministische Aufrufe des Dekolonialen. Widerstand und Wiederaufleben in den Arbeiten von María Lugones und Leanne Betasamosake Simpson. *Peripherie* 157–8(1–2): 34–67.

Daily Mail, The (24 July 2017). Malaysian Children Parade in White Robes for Practice hajj. https://www.straitstimes.com/asia/se-asia/malaysian-children-parade-in-white-robes-for-practice-haj (accessed 25 March 2023).

Davis, Kathy (2008). Intersectionality as Buzzword: A sociology of science perspective on what makes a feminist theory successful. *Feminist Theory* 9: 67–85.

Degnen, Cathrine and Katharine Tyler (2017). Amongst the Disciplines: Anthropology, sociology, intersection and intersectionality. *The Sociological Review Monographs* 65(1): 35–53.

Delaney, David and Helga Leitner (1997). The Political Construction of Scale. *Political Geography* 16(2): 93–97.

Department of Statistics, Malaysia (2019). Current Population Estimates, Malaysia, 2018–2019. https://www.dosm.gov.my/v1/index.php?r=column/cthemeByCat&cat=155&bul_id=aWJZ RkJ4UEdKcUZpT2tVT090Snpydz09&menu_id=L0pheU43NWJwRWVSZklWdzQ4TlhUUT09 (accessed 25 March 2023).

Department of Statistics, Malaysia (2010). Banci penduduk dan perumahan Malaysia/ Population and Housing Census of Malaysia 2010: Taburan Penduduk dan ciri-ciri asas demografi/Population Distribution and basic demographic characteristics. http://www. statistics.gov.my/portal/download_Population/files/census2010/Taburan_Penduduk_dan_ Ciri-ciri_Asas_Demografi.pdf (accessed 25 March 2023).

Department of Statistics, Malaysia (2007). Buletin Perangkaan Sosial/Social Statistics Bulletin, November.

Department of Statistics, Malaysia (2005). Banci penduduk dan perumahan Malaysia/Population and Housing Census of Malaysia 2000: Laporan am Banci penduduk dan perumahan/General Report of the Population and Housing Census, Oktober/October 2005.

Descola, Philippe (2018). *Jenseits von Natur und Kultur*. Frankfurt/Main: Suhrkamp.

Descola, Philippe (2010). From Wholes to Collectives. Steps to an ontology of social forms. In Ton Otto and Nils Bubandt (eds), *Experiments in Holism: Theory and practice in contemporary anthropology*, pp. 209–26. Malden: Blackwell.

Desplat, Patrick A. (2012). Introduction: Representations of space, place-making and urban life in Muslim societies. In Patrick A. Desplat and Dorothea Schulz (eds), *Prayer in the City: The making of Muslim sacred places in urban life*, pp. 9–34. Bielefeld: transcript.

Desplat, Patrick A. and Dorothea Schulz (eds) (2012). *Prayer in the City: The making of Muslim sacred places in urban life*. Bielefeld: transcript.

Dick, Howard W. (1990). Further Reflections on the Middle Class. In Richard Tanter and Kenneth R. Young (eds), *The Politics of Middle Class Indonesia*, pp. 63–70. Monash papers on SEA, 19.

Dina, Zaman (2007). *I am Muslim*. Kuala Lumpur: Silverfishbooks.

Douglas, Mary and Baron Isherwood (1980). *The World of Goods: Towards an anthropology of consumption*. Harmondsworth: Penguin.

Duden, Barbara (2002). Entkörperungen in der Moderne: Zur Genese des diagnostischen (Frauen-) Körpers zwischen Nachkrieg und heute. In Ellen Kuhlmann (ed.), *Konfiguration des Menschen: Biowissenschaften als Arena der Geschlechterpolitik*, pp. 121–33. Opladen: Leske + Budrich.

Duden, Barbara (1993). *Disembodying Women: perspectives on pregnancy and the unborn.* Cambridge, MA: Harvard University Press.

Duden, Barbara (1991). *Der Frauenleib als öffentlicher Ort: vom Mißbrauch des Begriffs Leben.* Munich: Dt. Taschenbuch-Verlag.

Edwards, Jeanette and Marilyn Strathern (2000). Including our Own. In Janet Carsten (ed.), *Cultures of Relatedness. New approaches to the study of kinship*, pp. 149–66. Cambridge: Cambridge University Press.

Egholm Feldt, Jakob and Kirstine Sinclair (2011). Lived Space: Reconsidering transnationalism among Muslim minorities. In Jakob Egholm Feldt and Kirstine Sinclair (eds), *Lived Space: Reconsidering transnationalism among Muslim minorities*, pp. 7–10. Frankfurt/Main: Peter Lang.

Eisenstadt, Shmuel N. (2000). *Die Vielfalt der Moderne.* Weilerswist: Velbrück.

El Guindi, Fadwa (2005). The Veil becomes a Movement. In Haideh Moghissi (ed.), *Women and Islam. Critical concepts in sociology, Volume II*, pp. 70–91. Abingdon: Routledge.

El Guindi, Fadwa (1999). *Veil: Modesty, privacy and resistance.* Oxford: Berg.

Elg, Camilla and Sune Qvotrup Jensen (2012). The Intersectional Body – An embodiment perspective on differentiated experiences. *Sociologisk Arbejdspapir* 34. Forskningsgruppen CASTOR Institut for Sociologi og Socialt Arbejde Aalborg Universitet: Aalborg.

Ellingson, Laura L. (2006). Embodied Knowledge: Writing researchers' bodies into qualitative health research. *Qualitative Health Research* 16(2): 298–310.

Endres, Marcel, Katharina Manderscheid and Christophe Mincke (eds) (2016). *The Mobilities Paradigm: Discourses and ideologies.* London: Routledge.

Englund, Harri and James Leach (2000). Ethnography and the Meta-Narratives of Modernity. *Current Anthropology* 41(2): 225–48.

Entwistle, Joanne (2015). *The Fashioned Body: Fashion, dress and modern social theory.* Cambridge: Polity Press.

Erel, Umut, Jinthana Haritaworn, Encarnación Gutiérrez Rodríguez and Christian Klesse (2007). Intersektionalität oder Simultaneität?! – Zur Verschränkung und Gleichzeitigkeit mehrfacher Machtverhältnisse. In Jutta Hartmann, Christian Klesse, Peter Wagenknecht, Bettina Fritzsche and Kristina Hackmann (eds), *Heteronormativität. Empirische Studien zu Geschlecht, Sexualität und Macht–eine Einführung*, pp. 239–49. Wiesbaden: VS Verlag für Sozialwissenschaften.

Espiñosa Miñoso, Yuderkys (2014). Etnocentrismo y colonialidad en los feminismos latinoamericanos: complicidades y consolidación de las hegemonías feministas en el espacio transnacional. In Yuderkys Espiñosa Miñoso, Dania Gómez Correal and Karina Ochoa Muñoz (eds), *Tejiendo de oto modo: Feminismo, epistemología y apuestas descoloniales en Abya Yala*, pp. 309–24. Popayán: editorial Universidad del Cauca.

Fábos, Anita H. and Riina Isotalo (2014). Introduction. Managing Muslim mobilities: A conceptual framework. In Anita H. Fábos and Riina Isotalo (eds), *Managing Muslim Mobilities: Between spiritual geographies and the global security regime*, pp. 1–18. New York: Palgrave Macmillan.

Falah, Ghazi-Walid and Caroline Nagel (eds) (2005). *Geographies of Muslim Women: Gender, religion, and space.* New York: Guilford.

Falzon, Mark-Anthony (ed.) (2009). *Multi-Sited Ethnography: Theory, praxis and locality in contemporary research.* Farnham: Ashgate.

Fanon, Frantz (1965). *A Dying Colonialism.* New York: Grove Press.

Fedele, Anna (2014). Energy and Transformation in Alternative Pilgrimages to Catholic Shrines: Deconstructing the tourist/pilgrim divide. *Journal of Tourism and Cultural Change* 12(2): 150–65.

Feener, Michael R. and Keping Wu (2020). The Ethics of Religious Giving in Asia: Introduction. *Journal of Contemporary Religion* 35(1): 1–12.

Fischer, Eileen and Stephen J. Arnold (1990). More than a Labor of Love: Gender roles and Christmas gift shopping. *Journal of Consumer Research* 17(3): 333–45.

Fischer, Johan (2018). Forging New Malay Networks: Imagining global halal markets. *Focaal – European Journal for Anthropology* 80(1): 91–104.

Fischer, Johan (2016). Halal Activism: Networking between Islam, the state and market. *Asian Journal of Social Science* 44(1–2): 104–31.

Fischer, Johan (2011). *The Halal Frontier. Muslim consumers in a globalized market.* New York: Palgrave.

Fischer, Johan (2008). *Proper Islamic Consumption: Shopping among the Malays in modern Malaysia.* Copenhagen: NIAS.

Fleischer, Aliza (2000). The Tourist Behind the Pilgrim in the Holy Land. *Hospitality Management* 19: 311–26.

Förschler, Silke (2010). *Bilder des Harem. Medienwandel und kultureller Austausch.* Berlin: Reimer.

Foucault, Michel (2009a [1978]). *Geschichte der Gouvernementalität 1; Sicherheit, Territorium, Bevölkerung: Vorlesung am Collège de France, 1977–1978.* Frankfurt/Main: Suhrkamp.

Foucault, Michel (2009b [1979]) *Geschichte der Gouvernementalität 2; Die Geburt der Biopolitik: Vorlesung am Collège de France, 1978–1979.* Frankfurt/Main: Suhrkamp.

Foucault, Michel (2008). *Sexualität und Wahrheit, Band 2: Der Gebrauch der Lüste.* Frankfurt/Main: Suhrkamp. [reprint]

Foucault, Michel (1994). *Überwachen und Strafen: Die Geburt des Gefängnisses.* Frankfurt/Main: Suhrkamp.

Foucault, Michel (1977). *Sexualität und Wahrheit, Band 1: Der Wille zum Wissen.* Frankfurt/Main: Suhrkamp.

Francis, Matthew D.M. (2016). Why the 'Sacred' is a better Resource than 'Religion' for Understanding Terrorism. *Terrorism and Political Violence* 28(5): 912–27.

Freitag, Ulrike (2020). *A History of Jeddah. The gate to Mecca in the nineteenth and twentieth centuries.* Cambridge: Cambridge University Press.

Friedman, Jonathan (2010). Holism and the Transformation of the Contemporary Global Order. In Ton Otto and Nils Bubandt (eds), *Experiments in Holism: Theory and practice in contemporary anthropology*, pp. 227–47. Malden: Blackwell.

Frisk, Sylva (2015). Gendered Dimensions of Islamization: The case of IMAN. In Adeline Koh and Yu-Mei Balasingamchow (eds), *Women and the Politics of Representations in Southeast Asia: Engendering discourse in Singapore and Malaysia*, pp. 139–54. Abingdon: Routledge.

Frisk, Sylva (2009). *Submitting to God: Women and Islam in Urban Malaysia.* Copenhagen: NIAS.

Frith, Tabitha (2002). *Constructing Malay Muslim Womanhood in Malaysia.* Monash Asia Institute: Monash University.

Gale, Richard (2007). The Place of Islam in the Geography of Religion: Trends and intersections. *Geography Compass* 1(5): 1015–36.

Gatens, Moira (1998). Institutions, Embodiment and Sexual Difference. In Moira Gatens and Alison Mackinnon (eds), *Gender and Institutions. Welfare, work and citizenship*, pp. 1–15. Cambridge: Cambridge University Press.

Gell, Alfred (1992). *The Anthropology of Time: Cultural constructions of temporal maps and images.* Oxford: Berg.

Gielis, Ruben (2009). A Global Sense of Migrant Places: Towards a place perspective in the study of migrant transnationalism. *Global Networks* 9(2): 271–87.

Giddens, Anthony (1984). *The Constitution of Society. Outline of the theory of structuration.* Cambridge: Polity Press.

Gingrich, Andre (2008). Ethnizität für die Praxis. In Karl R. Wernhart and Werner Zips (eds), *Ethnohistorie: Rekonstruktion und Kulturkritik. Eine Einführung*, pp. 99–111. Vienna: Promedia.

Glick Schiller, Nina and Noel B. Salazar (2013). Regimes of Mobility Across the Globe. *Journal of Ethnic and Migration Studies* 39(2): 183–200.

Goh, Daniel P.S. and Philip Holden (2009). Introduction: Postcoloniality, race and multiculturalism. In Daniel P.S. Goh *et al.* (eds), *Race and Multiculturalism in Malaysia and Singapore*, pp. 1–16. Abingdon: Routledge.

Goh, Daniel P.S., Matilda Gabrielpillai, Philip Holden and Gaik Cheng Khoo (eds) (2009). *Race and Multiculturalism in Malaysia and Singapore.* Abingdon: Routledge.

Graburn, Nelson (1989). Tourism: The Sacred Journey. In Valene Smith (ed.), *Hosts and guests. The anthropology of tourism*, pp. 21–36. Philadelphia: University of Pennsylvania Press.

Graham, Mark (2014). *Anthropological Explorations in Queer Theory.* Farnham: Ashgate.

Green, Nile (2015). The *Hajj* as its Own Undoing: Infrastructure and integration on the Muslim journey to Mecca. *Past & Present* 22(1.1): 193–226.

Grosz, Elizabeth (1995). *Space, Time and Perversion.* Abingdon: Routledge.

Guardian, The (6 July 2020). Malaysian Taskforce Investigates Allegations $700m Paid to PM Najib. https://www.theguardian.com/world/2015/jul/06/malaysian-task-forceinvestigates-allegations-700m-paid-to-pm-najib (accessed 25 March 2023).

Günzel, Stephan (2006). Einleitung. In Jörg Dünne and Stephan Günzel, *Raumtheorie: Grundlagentexte aus Philosophie und Kulturwissenschaften*, pp. 19–43. Frankfurt/Main: Suhrkamp.

Gutekunst, Miriam, Andreas Hackl, Sabina Leoncini, Julia Sophia Schwarz and Irene Götz, (eds) (2016). *Bounded Mobilities: Ethnographic perspectives on social hierarchies and global inequalities*. Bielefeld: transcript.

Hahn, Hans Peter (2008). Zur Ethnologie des Konsums in Afrika. *Paideuma* 53: 199–220.

Hall, Stuart (1992). The West and the Rest: Discourse and power. In Stuart Hall and Bram Gieben (eds), *Formations of Modernity*, pp. 275–331. Cambridge: Polity Press.

Hammudah, 'Abd al-'Ati (2008). *The Family Structure in Islam*. Kuala Lumpur: The Other Press.

Hannam, Kevin, Mimi Sheller and John Urry (2006). Editorial: Mobilities, immobilities and moorings. *Mobilities* 1(1): 1–22.

Haraway, Donna (2011 [1985]). A Cyborg Manifesto. In Imre Szeman and Timothy Kaposy (eds), *Cultural Theory: An anthology*, pp. 454–71. Oxford: Wiley-Blackwell.

Haraway, Donna (1988). Situated Knowledges: The science question in feminism and the privilege of partial perspective. *Feminist Studies* 14(3): 575–99.

Harrison, David (2001). Tourism and Less Developed Countries. In David Harrison (ed.), *Tourism and the Less Developed World. Issues and case studies*, pp. 23–46. Wallingford: CABI.

Harvey, David (1969). *Explanation in Geography*. London: Arnold.

HDC (Halal Industry Development Corporation) (n.d., a). *Why Malaysia?* http://halalpark. hdcglobal.com/publisher/alias/halal_park_why_malaysia (accessed 25 March 2023).

HDC (Halal Industry Development Corporation) (n.d., b). *Halal. The new source of economic growth*. Petaling Jaya: Inhouse publishers.

Hefner, Robert W. (2001). Introduction: Multiculturalism and citizenship in Malaysia, Singapore, and Indonesia. In Robert W. Hefner (ed.), *The Politics of Multiculturalism. Pluralism and citizenship in Malaysia, Singapore, and Indonesia*, pp. 1–58. Honolulu: University of Hawai'i Press.

Henderson, Joan (2011). Religious Tourism and its Management: The Hajj in Saudi Arabia. *International Journal of Tourism Research* 13: 541–52.

Henderson, Joan (2010). Islam and Tourism. Brunei, Indonesia, Malaysia, and Singapore. In Noel Scott and Jafar Jafari (eds), *Tourism in the Muslim World*, pp. 76–89. Bingley: Emerald.

Henderson, Joan (2009). Islamic Tourism Reviewed. *Tourism Recreation Research* 34(2): 207–11.

Henderson, Joan (2003). Managing Tourism and Islam in Peninsular Malaysia. *Tourism Management* 24: 447–56.

Hermann, Elfriede (2011). Introduction: Engaging with interactions. Traditions as context-bound articulations. In Elfriede Hermann (ed.), *Changing Contexts, Shifting Meanings. Transformations of cultural traditions in Oceania*, pp. 1–19. Honolulu: University of Hawai'i Press.

Hill Collins, Patricia (2008). *Black Feminist Thought: Knowledge, consciousness, and the politics of empowerment*. New York: Routledge.

Hirschman, Charles (2016). Gender, the Status of Women, and Family Structure in Malaysia. *Malaysian Journal of Economic Studies* 53(1): 33–50.

Holbraad, Martin (2010). The Whole Beyond Holism. Gambling, divination, and ethnography in Cuba. In Ton Otto and Nils Bubandt (eds), *Experiments in Holism: Theory and practice in contemporary anthropology*, pp. 67–85. Malden: Blackwell.

Holland, Nancy J. (2013). 'Everything Comes Back to It': Woman as the gift in Derrida. In Morny Joy (ed.), *Women and the Gift. Beyond the given and all-giving*, pp. 92–100. Bloomington and Indianapolis: Indiana University Press.

Holst, Frederik (2012). *Ethnicization and Identity Construction in Malaysia*. Abingdon: Routledge.

hooks, bell (2000). *Feminist Theory: From margin to center*. London: Pluto Press.

hooks, bell (1981). *Ain't I a Woman? Black women and feminism*. Boston: South End Press.

Höpflinger, Anna-Katharina, Anne Lavanchy and Janine Dahinden (2012). Introduction: Linking gender and religion. *Women's Studies: An inter-disciplinary journal* 41(6): 615–38.

Hopwood, Derek (1998). The Culture of Modernity in Islam and the Middle East. In John Cooper, Ronald L. Nettler and Mohamed Mahmoud (eds), *Islam and Modernity. Muslim intellectuals respond*, pp. 1–9. London: I.B. Tauris.

Houben, Vincent and Mona Schrempf (2008). Introduction: Figuration and representations of modernity. In Vincent Houben and Mona Schrempf (eds), *Figurations of Modernity: Global and local representations in comparative perspective*, pp. 7–20. Frankfurt/Main: Campus.

Illouz, Eva (2009). Emotions, Imagination and Consumption: A new research agenda. *Journal of Consumer Culture* 9(3): 377–413.

ITC (Islamic Tourism Centre) (n.d.). Malaysia – The world's leading Halal hub. https://itc. gov.my/tourists/discover-the-muslim-friendly-malaysia/malaysia-the-worldsleading-halal-hub/ (accessed 25 March 2023).

Izharuddin, Alicia (2018). 'Free Hair': Narratives of unveiling and the reconstruction of self. *Signs: Journal of Women in Culture and Society* 44(1): 155–76.

Jafari, Aliakbar and Özlem Sandıkcı (eds) (2016). *Islam, Marketing and Consumption*. Abingdon: Routledge.

Jafari, Aliakbar and Ahmet Süerdem (2012). An Analysis of Material Consumption Culture in the Muslim World. *Marketing Theory* 12(1): 61–79.

Jafari, Jafar and Noel Scott (2014). Muslim World and its Tourisms. *Annals of Tourism Research* 44: 1–19.

Jamhari, Makruf (2001). The Meaning Interpreted: The concept of barakah in *ziarah*. *Studika Islamika – Indonesian Journal of Islamic Studies* 8(1): 87–128.

Jamhari, Makruf (2000). In the Center of Meaning: *Ziarah* tradition in Java. *Studika Islamika – Indonesian Journal of Islamic Studies* 7(1): 51–90.

Jamhari, Makruf (1999). *Ziarah* Traditions. In James J. Fox (ed.), *Religion and Ritual*, pp. 34–35. Singapore: Archipelago.

Jones, Carla (2010). Images of Desire. Creating virtue and value in an Indonesian Islamic lifestyle magazine. *Journal of Middle East Women's Studies* 6(3): 91–117.

Jones, Carla (2007). Fashion and faith in Urban Indonesia. *Fashion Theory* 11(2–3): 211–32.

Kadir, Din (1989). Islam and Tourism. *Annals of Tourism Research* 16: 542–63.

Kahn, Joel S. (2001). Anthropology and Modernity. *Current Anthropology* 42(5): 651–80.

Kahn, Joel S. (1996). The Middle Class as a Field of Ethnological Study. In Muhammad Ikmal Said and Zahid Emby (eds), *Malaysia. Pandangan Kritis. Esei Panghargaan untuk Syed Husin Ali*, pp. 12–33. Petaling Jaya: Persatuan Sains Social Malaysia.

Kapferer, Bruce (2010). Louis Dumont and a Holist Anthropology. In Ton Otto and Nils Bubandt (eds), *Experiments in Holism: Theory and practice in contemporary anthropology*, pp. 187–208. Malden: Blackwell.

Ken, Ivy (2008). Beyond the Intersection: A new culinary metaphor for race-class-gender studies. *Sociological Theory* 26: 152–72.

Kenneson, Philip D. (2015). What's in a Name? A brief introduction to the 'Spiritual But Not Religious'. *Liturgy* 30(3): 3–13.

Kenny, Erin (2007). Gifting Mecca: Importing spiritual capital to West Africa. *Mobilities* 2(3): 363–81.

Kessler, Clive S. (2001). Alternative Approaches, Divided Consciousness: Dualities in studying the contemporary Southeast Asian middle classes. In Abdul Rahman Embong (ed.), *Southeast Asian Middle Classes. Prospects for social change and democratisation*, pp. 31–45. Bangi: Penerbit Universiti Kebangsaan Malaysia.

Khalaf, Sulayman (2005). National Dress and the Construction of Emirati Cultural Identity. *Journal of Human Sciences* 11: 267–329.

Khaleej Times, The (23 September 2015). Global Islamic Tourism Set to Grow 11% by 2020. https://www.khaleejtimes.com/business/economy/global-islamic-tourism-set-to-grow-11-by-2020 (accessed 25 March 2023).

Kitiarsa, Pattana (ed.) (2011). *Religious Commodifications in Asia. Marketing gods*. Abingdon: Routledge.

Knapp, Gudrun-Axeli (2005). Race, Class, Gender. *European Journal of Women's Studies* 12: 249–65.

Knott, Kim (2014). *The Location of Religion: A spatial analysis*. Abingdon: Routledge.

Knudsen, Susanne V. (2006). Intersectionality – A theoretical inspiration in the analysis of minority cultures and identities in textbooks. In Éric Bruillard, Bente Aamotsbakken, Susanne V. Knudsen and Mike Horsley (eds), *Caught in the Web or Lost in the Textbook?*, pp. 61–76. Utrecht: International Association for Research on Textbooks and Educational Media.

Kochuyt, Thierry (2009). God, Gifts and Poor People: On charity in Islam. *Social Compass* 56(1): 98–116.

Kokoschka, Alina (2019). *Waren Welt Islam: Konsumkultur und Warenästhetik in Syrien 2000–2011*. Berlin: Kulturverlag Kadmos.

Kua, Kia Soong (2007). *May 13. Declassified documents on the Malaysian riots of 1969*. Kuala Lumpur: Suaram.

Kuran, Timur (2005). *Islam and Mammon: The economic predicaments of Islamism*. Princeton: Princeton University Press.

Lafaye de Micheaux, Elsa (2017). *The Development of Malaysian Capitalism: From British rule to the present day*. Petaling Jaya: SIRD.

Lamrabet, Asma (2018). *Women and Men in the Qur'an*. Cham: Palgrave Macmillan.

Lamrabet, Asma (2016). *Women in the Qur'an. An emancipatory reading*. Leicestershire: Square View.

Landweer, Hilge (1994). Generativität und Geschlecht: ein blinder Fleck in der sex/gender-Debatte. In Theresa Wobbe and Gesa Lindemann (eds), *Denkachsen: Zur theoretischen und institutionellen Rede vom Geschlecht*, pp. 147–76. Frankfurt/Main: Suhrkamp.

Latour, Bruno (1993). *We Have Never Been Modern*. New York: Harvester Wheatsheaf.

Lee, Raymond L.M. and Susan E. Ackerman (1997). *Sacred Tensions: Modernity and religious transformation in Malaysia*. Columbia: University of South Carolina Press.

Lefebvre, Henri (1991 [1974]). *The Production of Space*. Wiley: Blackwell.

Lévi-Strauss, Claude (2018 [1955]) *Traurige Tropen*. Frankfurt/Main: Suhrkamp.

Lewis, Gail (2013). Unsafe Travel: Experiencing intersectionality and feminist displacements. *Signs* 38: 869–92.

Lina, Munirah Kamarudin and Hairul Nizam Ismail (2012). Muslim Tourist's Typology in Malaysia: Perspectives and challenges. *Proceedings: Tourism and Hospitality International Conference*, 23–24 November.

Lindemann, Gesa (1993). *Das paradoxe Geschlecht. Transsexualität im Spannungsfeld von Körper, Leib und Gefühl*. Frankfurt/Main: Fischer.

Lindholm, Christina (2014). Cultural Collision: The branded *abaya*. *Fashion, Style & Popular Culture* 1(1): 45–55.

Longman, Chia (2002). Empowering and Engendering 'Religion'. A critical perspective on ethnographic holism. *Social Anthropology* 10(2): 239–48.

Lorde, Audre (1984). *Sister Outsider*. Berkeley: Ten Speed Press.

Löw, Martina (2015). Space Oddity. Raumtheorie nach dem Spatial Turn, https://www.sozialraum.de/space-oddity-raumtheorie-nach-demspatial-turn.php (accessed 25 March 2023).

Löw, Martina (2001). *Raumsoziologie*. Frankfurt/Main: Suhrkamp.

Lugones, María (2010). Toward a Decolonial Feminism. *Hypatia* 25(4): 742–59.

Lutz, Helma, Maria Teresa Herrera Vivar and Linda Supik (eds) (2011). *Framing Intersectionality: Debates on a multi-faceted concept in gender studies*. Surrey: Ashgate.

Luutz, Wolfgang (2007). Vom 'Containerraum' zur 'entgrenzten' Welt – Raumbilder als sozialwissenschaftliche Leitbilder. *Social Geography* (2): 29–45.

Luz, Nimrod (2020). Pilgrimage and Religious Tourism in Islam. *Annals of Tourism Research* 82, May, 102–915.

Mahler, Sarah J., Mayurakshi Chaudhuri and Vrushali Patil (2015). Scaling Intersectionality: Advancing feminist analysis of transnational families. *Sex Roles* 73: 100–12.

Mahler, Sarah J. and Patricia R. Pessar (2006). Gender Matters: Ethnographers bring gender from the periphery toward the core of migration studies. *International Migration Review* 40(1): 27–63.

Mahler, Sarah J. and Patricia R. Pessar (2001). Gendered Geographies of Power: Analyzing gender across transnational spaces. *Identities* 7(4): 441–59.

Mahmood, Saba (2005). *Politics of Piety: The Islamic revival and the feminist subject*. Princeton: Princeton University Press.

Malay Mail, The (04 October 2015). Big Demand for Stylish Modest Fashion as More Malaysian Muslim Women Don Hijabs. https://www.malaymail.com/news/malaysia/2015/10/04/big-demand-for-stylishmodest-fashion-as-more-malaysian-muslim-women-don-hi/981215#sthash.cVA6PhL4.dpuf (accessed 25 March 2023).

Malay Online, The (27 January 2017). Haj Quota for Pilgrims Restored to 27,900 this Year, Says Tabung Haji. http://www.themalaymailonline.com/malaysia/article/haj-quota-forpilgrims-restored-to-27900-this-year-says-tabung-haji#fO2Cp885fY2wtVOd.97 (accessed 25 March 2023).

Malaysian Digest (10 June 2016). No Favouritism in Selection of Pilgrims for Haj. http://malaysiandigest.com/frontpage/29-4-tile/615872-no-favouritism-in-selection-ofpilgrims-for-haj-th.html (accessed 25 March 2023).

Malaysian Government (1986). *The Fifth Malaysian Plan 1986–1990*. Kuala Lumpur, Economic Planning Unit, Prime Minister's Department.

Maneval, Stefan (2019). *New Islamic Urbanism. The architecture of public and private space in Jeddah, Saudi Arabia*. London: UCL Press.

Marcus, George E. (2011). Multi-Sited Ethnography: Five or six things I know about it now. In Simon Coleman and Pauline von Hellermann (eds), *Multi-Sited Ethnography: Problems and possibilities in the translocation of research methods*, pp. 16–32. New York: Routledge.

Marcus, George E. (2010). Holism and the Expectations of Critique in Post-1980s Anthropology: Notes and queries in three acts and an epilogue. In Ton Otto and Nils Bubandt (eds), *Experiments in Holism: Theory and practice in contemporary anthropology*, pp. 28–46. Malden: Blackwell.

Marcus, George E. (1995). Ethnography in/of the World System: The emergence of multi-sited ethnography. *Annual Review of Anthropology* 24: 95–117.

Marcus, George E. (1989). Imagining the Whole: Ethnography's contemporary efforts to situate itself. *Critique of Anthropology* 9(3): 7–30.

Marcus, George E. and Michael M.J. Fischer (1986). *Anthropology as Cultural Critique: An experimental moment in the human sciences*. Chicago: University of Chicago Press.

Marston, Sallie A. (2000). The Social Construction of Scale. *Progress in Human Geography* 24(2): 219–42.

Marx, Karl (1968 [1844]). Ökonomisch-philosophische Manuskripte aus dem Jahre 1844. In Karl Marx and Friedrich Engels, *Werke, Ergänzungsband, Schriften bis 1844*, 1. Teil, pp. 465–588. Berlin: Dietz.

Massey, Doreen (2001). *Space, Place, and Gender*. Minneapolis: University of Minnesota Press.

Mauss, Marcel (2016 [1925]). *Die Gabe: Form und Funktion des Austauschs in archaischen Gesellschaften*. Frankfurt/Main: Suhrkamp.

Maznah, Mohamad (2009). Politicization of Islam in Indonesia and Malaysia: Women's rights and inter-religious relations. In Theresa W. Devasahayam (ed.), *Gender Trends in Southeast Asia: Women now, women in the future*, pp. 95–110. Singapore: ISEAS.

McDonnell, Mary B. (1990). Patterns of Muslim Pilgrimage from Malaysia, 1885–1985. In Dale Eickelman and James Piscatori (eds), *Muslim Travelers*, pp. 111–30. Berkeley: University of California Press.

McGranahan, Carole (2018). Ethnography Beyond Method: The importance of an ethnographic sensibility. *Sites: new series* (15): 1–10.

Md. Nor Othman, Fon Sim Ong and Anna T.M. Teng (2005). Occasions and Motivations for Gift-Giving: A comparative study of Malay and Chinese consumers in urban Malaysia. *Asia Pacific Management Review* 10(3): 197–204.

Mead, Margaret (1935). *Sex and Temperament in Three Primitive Societies*. Abingdon: Routledge.

Mee, Wendy and Joel S. Kahn (2012). Introduction. In Wendy Mee and Joel S. Kahn (eds), *Questioning Modernity in Indonesia and Malaysia*, pp. 1–20. Singapore: NUS Press/Kyoto University Press.

Mercandante, Linda A. (2014). *Belief without Borders: Inside the minds of the spiritual but not religious*. New York: Oxford University Press.

Metcalf, Barbara D. (ed.) (1996). *Making Muslim Space in North America and Europe*. Berkeley: University of California Press.

Meyer, Birgit and Dick Houtman (2012). Introduction: Material Religion – how things matter. In Dick Houtman and Birgit Meyer (eds), *Things: Religion and the question of materiality*, pp. 1–23. New York: Fordham University Press.

Meyer, Silke and Guido Sprenger (2011). Der Blick der Kultur- und Sozialanthropologie. Sehen als Körpertechnik zwischen Wahrnehmung und Deutung. In Silke Meyer and Armin Owzar (eds), *Disziplinen der Anthropologie*, pp. 203–27. Münster: Waxmann.

Mielke, Katja and Anna-Katharina Hornidge (2017). Introduction: Knowledge production, area studies and the mobility turn. In Katja Mielke and Anna-Katharina Hornidge (eds), *Area Studies at the Crossroads*, pp. 3–26. New York: Palgrave Macmillan.

Miller, Daniel (1998). *A Theory of Shopping*. Ithaca: Cornell University Press.

Miller, Daniel (1994). *Modernity – An Ethnographic Approach: Dualism and mass consumption in Trinidad*. Oxford: Berg.

Millie, Julian (2017). *Hearing Allah's Call: Preaching and performance in Indonesian Islam*. Ithaca: Cornell University Press

Millie, Julian and Lewis Mayo (2019). Grave Visiting (*Ziyara*) in Indonesia. In Bapak Rahimi and Peyman Eshagi (eds), *Muslim Pilgrimage in the Modern World*, pp. 183–204. Chapel Hill: University of North Carolina Press.

Mir-Hosseini, Ziba (2009). Towards Gender Equality: Muslim family laws and the Shari'ah. In Zainah Anwar (ed.), *Wanted: Equality and Justice in the Muslim Family*, pp. 23–63. Petaling Jaya: musawah.

Mittermaier, Amira (2008). (Re)Imagining Space: Dreams and saint shrines in Egypt. In Georg Stauth and Samuli Schielke (eds), *Dimensions of Locality: Muslim saints, their place and space. Yearbook of the Sociology of Islam No. 8*, pp. 47–66.

Al-Fahim, Mohammed (2013). *From Rags to Riches. A story of Abu Dhabi*. Abu Dhabi: Makarem.

Mohd Asri, Zainul Abidin (2013). *Islam in Malaysia. Perceptions and facts*. Petaling Jaya: Mata Hari Books.

Mohd Faizal, M. (2013). Axiology of Pilgrimage: Malaysian Shi'ites *ziyarat* in Iran and Iraq. *Cultura. International Journal of Philosophy of Culture and Axiology* 10(1): 67–84.

Monroe, Shawnthea (2015). Preaching to the 'Spiritual But Not Religious'. *Liturgy* 30(3): 23–31.

Moors, Annelies (2012). Popularizing Islam: Muslims and materiality – Introduction. *Material Religion* 8(3): 272–9.

Möser, Cornelia (2013). Was die Intersektionalitätsdiskussion aus den feministischen Gender-Debatten in Frankreich und Deutschland lernen kann. In Vera Kallenberg, Johanna M. Müller and Jennifer Meyer (eds), *Intersectionality und Kritik: neue Perspektiven für alte Fragen*, pp. 39–58. Wiesbaden: Springer.

Moufahim, Mona (2013). Religious Gift Giving: An ethnographic account of a Muslim pilgrimage. *Marketing Theory* 13(4): 421–41.

Muhammad Khalid, Masud (2010). Islamic Modernism. In Masud Muhammad Khalid, Armando Salvatore and Martin van Bruinessen (eds), *Islam and Modernity*, pp. 237–60. Edinburgh: Edinburgh University Press.

Müller, Dominik (2014). *Islam, Politics and Youth in Malaysia: The pop-Islamist reinvention of PAS*. Abingdon: Routledge.

Muslimah Life (01 November 2015). Dubai's Trending Abaya Fashion Designers. http://www.muslimahlife.com/2015/11/dubais-trending-abaya-fashion-designers.html (accessed 25 March 2023).

Narotzky, Susana (2005). The Production of Knowledge and the Production of Hegemony: Anthropological theory and political struggles in Spain. *Journal of the World Anthropology Network* (1): 35–54.

Nasser, Noha (2003). The Space of Displacement: Making Muslim South Asian place in British neighborhoods. *Traditional Dwellings and Settlements Review* 15(1): 7–21.

New Straits Times (28 July 2020). Najib sentenced to 12 years' jail, RM210 million fine. https://www.nst.com.my/news/crime-courts/2020/07/612343/najib-sentenced-12-yearsjail-rm210-million-fine (accessed 25 March 2023).

New Straits Times (22 January 2020). Malaysian haj quota increases to 31,600. https://www.nst.com.my/news/nation/2020/01/558782/malaysian-haj-quota-increases31600 (accessed 25 March 2023).

New Straits Times (30 May 2017). dUCk's New Scarves. https://www.nst.com.my/lifestyle/flair/2017/05/244014/ducks-new-scarves (accessed 25 March 2023).

Newhouse, Léonie (2018). Other Paths, Other Destinations. Towards a manifold reading of mobility across borders. *movements. Journal for Critical Migration and Border Regime Studies* 4(1): 83–100.

Ng, Cecilia, Maznah Mohamad and tan beng hui (2007). *Feminism and the Women's Movement in Malaysia: An unsung (r)evolution*. New York: Routledge.

Nik Noriani, Nik Badlishah (2003). Marriage: Malaysia. In Nik Badlishah Nik Noriani (ed.), *Islamic Family Law and Justice for Muslim Women*, pp. 18–21. Kuala Lumpur: Sisters in Islam.

Norani, Othman (1998). Islamization and Modernization in Malaysia. Competing cultural reassertions and women's identity in a changing society. In Rick Wilford and Robert L. Miller (eds), *Women, Ethnicity and Nationalism*, pp. 170–92. Abingdon: Routledge.

O'Grady, Kathleen (2013). Melancholia, Forgiveness, and the Logic of *The Gift*. In Morny Joy (ed.), *Women and the Gift. Beyond the given and all-giving*, pp. 101–10. Bloomington: Indiana University Press.

Olsen, Torjer A. (2018). This Word is (Not?) Very Exciting: Considering intersectionality in indigenous studies. *NORA – Nordic Journal of Feminist and Gender Research* 26(3): 182–96.

Ong, Aihwa (2005). Ecologies of Expertise: Assembling flows, managing citizenship. In Stephen J. Collier and Aihwa Ong (eds), *Global Assemblages: Technology, politics, and ethics as anthropological problems*, pp. 337–53. Malden: Blackwell.

Ong, Aihwa (2003). State versus Islam: Malay families, women's bodies, and the body politic in Malaysia. In Bryan S. Turner (ed.), *Islam, Gender and the Family*, pp. 262–88. Abingdon: Routledge.

Ortbals, Candice D. and Meg E. Rincker (2009). Bodies, Research Activity, and Pregnancy in the Field. *PS: Political Science & Politics* 42(2): 315–19.

Osella, Filippo and Daromir Rudnyckyj (2017). Introduction: Assembling markets and religious moralities. In Daromir Rudnyckyj and Filippo Osella (eds), *Religion and the Morality of the Market*, pp. 1–28. Cambridge: Cambridge University Press.

Paredes, Julieta (2014). *Hilando Fino. Desde el feminismo comuniatria*. Mexico: El Rebozo.

Parray, Tauseef Ahmad (2011). Operational Concepts of Islamic Democracy – Khilafah, shura, ijma, and ijtihad. *Journal of Humanity & Islam* 1(1): 11–27.

Parvin, Manoucher and Maurie Sommer (2018). Dar al-Islam: The evolution of Muslim territoriality and its implications for conflict resolution in the Middle East. In Thijl Sunier (ed.), *Islam and Society, Vol II: Space, Place, Time: The spatial dimensions of Islam*, pp. 131–52. New York: Routledge.

Patel, David S. (2012). Concealing to Reveal: The informational role of Islamic dress. *Rationality and Society* 24(3): 295–323.

Patil, Vrushali (2013). From Patriarchy to Intersectionality: A transnational feminist assessment of how far we've really come. *Signs* 38: 847–67.

Peletz, Michael G. (1996). *Reason and Passion: Representations of gender in a Malay society*. Berkeley: University of California Press.

Peletz, Michael G. (1995). Neither Reasonable nor Responsible: Contrasting representations of masculinity in a Malay society. In Aihwa Ong and Michael G. Peletz (eds), *Bewitching Women, Pious Men: Gender and body politics in Southeast Asia*, pp. 76–123. Berkeley: University of California Press.

Petrone, Michele (2015). Devotional Texts in Ethiopian Islam: A munāğāh invoking the intercession of prophets, male and female saints and 'ulamā'. In Alessandro Bausi, Alessandro Gori and Denis Nosnitsin (eds), *International Conference Manuscripts and Texts, Languages and Contexts: The Transmission of Knowledge in the Horn of Africa. Essays in Ethiopian manuscript studies. Proceedings of the International Conference Manuscripts and Texts, Languages and Contexts: The Transmission of Knowledge in the Horn of Africa, Hamburg, 17–19 July 2014*, pp. 259–72.

Phoenix, Ann and Pamela Pattynama (2006). Intersectionality. *European Journal of Women's Studies* 13: 187–92.

Pinto, Paulo G. (2007). Pilgrimage, Commodities, and Religious Objectification: The Making of transnational Shiism between Iran and Syria. *Comparative Studies of South Asia, Africa and the Middle East* 27(1): 109–25.

Polanyi, Karl (1944). *The Great Transformation: The political and economic origins of our time*. Boston: Beacon Press.

Poria, Yaniv, Richard Butler and David Airey (2003). Tourism, Religion and Religiosity: A holy mess. *Current Issues in Tourism* 6(4): 340–63.

Prager, Laila (2013). Alawi *ziyara* Traditions and their Inter-Religious Dimensions. *The Muslim World* 103: 41–61.

Puar, Jasbir K. (2011). I would Rather be a Cyborg than a Goddess. European Institute for Progressive Cultural Politics. https://eipcp.net/transversal/0811/puar/en.html (accessed 25 March 2023).

Puar, Jasbir K. (2007). *Terrorist Assemblages: Homonationalism in queer times*. Durham, NC: Duke University Press.

Qvotrup Jensen, Sune and Camilla Elg (2010). Intersectionality as Embodiment. *Kvinder, KØn & Forskning* 30(2–3): 30–39.

Radmacher, Jason P. (2015). Pass the Peace, Please: Embracing the 'spiritual but not religious'. *Liturgy* 30:(3) 32–39.

Rahimi, Bapak and Peyman Eshagi (2019). Introduction. In Bapak Rahimi and Peyman Eshagi (eds), *Muslim Pilgrimage in the Modern World*, pp. 1–46. Chapel Hill: University of North Carolina Press.

Raj, Razaq and Nigel D. Morpeth (eds) (2007). *Religious Tourism and Pilgrimage Festivals Management*. Oxfordshire: Cabi.

Raj, Rita Karim, Rashidah Abdullah *et al.* (2003). Reproductive Rights and Reproductive Health: The Malaysian experience. In Roziah Omar and Azizah Hamzah (eds), *Women in Malaysia. Breaking boundaries*, pp. 169–85. Kuala Lumpur: Utusan.

Raj, Rita Karim, Chee Heng Leng and Rashida Shuib (2001). Between Modernization and Patriarchal Revivalism: Reproductive negotiations among women in Peninsular Malaysia. In

Rosalind P. Petchesky and Karen Judd (eds), *Negotiating Reproductive Rights: Women's perspectives across countries and cultures*, pp. 108–44. London: Zed.

Rappa, Antonio L. (2002). *Modernity and Consumption: Theory, politics, and the public in Singapore and Malaysia*. New Jersey: World Scientific.

Reader, Ian (2014). *Pilgrimage in the Marketplace*. New York: Routledge.

Rehbein, Boike and Guido Sprenger (2016). Religion and Differentiation: Three Southeast Asian configurations. *DORISEA Working Paper*, 24.

Rinallo, Diego, Linda Scott and Pauline Maclaran (eds) (2012). *Consumption and Spirituality*. Abingdon: Routledge.

Roth, Julia (2017). Feminism Otherwise: Intersectionality beyond Occidentalism. *InterDisciplines* 2: 97–122.

Roziah, Omar (2003). Negotiating their Visibility: The lives of educated and married Malay women. In Roziah Omar and Azizah Hamzah (eds), *Women in Malaysia. Breaking boundaries*, pp. 117–42. Kuala Lumpur: Utusan.

Rudnyckyj, Daromir (2019). *Beyond Debt*. Chicago: University of Chicago Press.

Rudnyckyj, Daromir (2017a). Subjects of Debt: Financial subjectification and collaborative risk in Malaysian Islamic Finance. *American Anthropologist* 119(2): 269–83.

Rudnyckyj, Daromir (2017b). Assembling Islam and Liberalism: Market freedom and the moral project of Islamic Finance. In Daromir Rudnyckyj and Filippo Osella (eds), *Religion and the Morality of the Market*, pp. 160–76. Cambridge: Cambridge University Press.

Rudnyckyj, Daromir (2013). From Wall Street to *Halal* Street: Malaysia and the globalization of Islamic Finance. *The Journal of Asian Studies* 72(4): 831–48.

Rudnyckyj, Daromir (2010). *Spiritual Economies. Islam, globalization, and the afterlife of development*. New York: Cornell University Press.

Said, Edward W. (1978). *Orientalism*. Abingdon: Routledge and Kegan Paul.

Salazar, Noel (2016). Conceptual Notes on the Freedom of Movement and Bounded Mobilities. In Miriam Gutekunst, Andreas Hackl, Sabina Leoncini, Julia Sophia Schwarz and Irene Götz (eds), *Bounded Mobilities: Ethnographic perspectives on social hierarchies and global inequalities*, pp. 284–9. Bielefeld: transcript.

Salazar, Noel (2014). To Be or Not to Be a Tourist. *Tourism Recreation Research* 39(2): 259–65.

Salem, Sara (2018). Intersectionality and its Discontents: Intersectionality as traveling theory. *European Journal of Women's Studies* 25(4): 404–18.

Salem, Sara (2013). Feminist Critique and Islamic Feminism: The question of intersectionality. *The Postcolonialist* 1(1). http://postcolonialist.com/civil-discourse/feministcritique-and-islamic-feminism-the-question-of-intersectionality/ (accessed 25 March 2023).

Sandıkcı, Özlem (2018). Religion and the Marketplace: Constructing the 'new' Muslim consumer. *Religion* 48(3): 453–73.

Sandıkcı, Özlem and Güliz Ger (2011). Islam, Consumption, and Marketing: Going beyond essentialist approaches. In Özlem Sandıkcı and Gillian Rice (eds), *Handbook of Islamic Marketing*, pp. 484–501. Cheltenham: Edward Elgar.

Sandıkcı, Özlem and Aliakbar Jafari (2013). Islamic Encounters in Consumption and Marketing. *Marketing Theory* 13(4): 410–20.

Saravanamuttu, Johan (2001). Is there a Politics of the Malaysian Middle Class? In Abdul Rahman Embong (ed.), *Southeast Asian Middle Classes. Prospects for social change and democratisation*, pp. 103–18. Bangi: Penerbit Universiti Kebangsaan Malaysia.

Sayeed, Asma (2016). Women and the Ḥajj. In Eric Tagliacozzo and Shawkat Toorawa (eds), *The Hajj: Pilgrimage in Islam*, pp. 65–84. New York: Cambridge University Press.

Schaufler, Birgit (2002). *"Schöne Frauen – Starke Männer": Zur Konstruktion von Leib, Körper und Geschlecht*. Opladen: Leske + Budrich.

Schielke, Samuli (2010). Second Thoughts About the Anthropology of Islam, or How to Make Sense of Grand Schemes in everyday life. *ZMO Working Papers* (2).

Schielke, Samuli and Georg Stauth (2008). Introduction. In Georg Stauth and Samuli Schielke (eds), *Dimensions of Locality: Muslim saints, their place and space. Yearbook of the Sociology of Islam No. 8*, pp. 7–22.

Schimmel, Annemarie (1994). *Das Thema des Weges und der Reise im Islam*. Opladen: Westdeutscher Verlag.

Schlehe, Judith (2003). Ethnologie des Tourismus: Zur Entgrenzung von Feldforschung und Reise. *Peripherie. Zeitschrift für Politik und Ökonomie in der Dritten Welt* 89(23): 31– 47.

Schroer, Markus (2006). *Räume, Orte, Grenzen: Auf dem Weg zu einer Soziologie des Raums.* Frankfurt/Main: Suhrkamp.

Scott, Noel and Jafar Jafari (eds) (2010). Introduction. Islam and tourism. In Noel Scott and Jafar Jafari (eds), *Tourism in the Muslim World*, pp. 1–13. Bingley: Emerald.

Segato, Rita (2015). *La crítica al la colonialidad en ocho ensayos. Y una antropología por demanda.* Buenos Aires: Prometeo.

Şeker, Nimet (2020). *Koran und Gender. Exegetische und hermeneutische Studien zum Geschlechterverhältnis im Koran.* Hamburg: Editio Gryphus.

Şeker, Nimet (2019). Geschlechterhierarchie, Geschlechtergerechtigkeit und androzentrische Rede im Koran. In Christian Ströbele, Tobias Specker, Amir Dziri, Muna Tatari and Theologisches Forum Christentum-Islam, *Welche Macht hat Religion? Anfragen an Christentum und Islam*, pp. 105–17. Regensburg: Pustet.

Sen, Arijit and Lisa Silverman (2014). Introduction: Embodied placemaking: an important category of critical analysis. In Arijit Sen and Lisa Silverman (eds), *Making Place: Space and embodiment in the city*, pp. 1–18. Bloomington: Indiana University Press.

Shaikh, Sa'diyya (2003). Family Planning, Contraception, and Abortion in Islam. Undertaking Khilafah. In Daniel C. Maguire (ed.), *Sacred Rights: The case for contraception and abortion in world religions*, pp. 105–43. Oxford: Oxford University Press.

Shamsul, Amri Baharuddin (2008). Islam and Cultural Diversity in Malaysia, a Mirror for Southeast Asia. In Ikuya Tokoro, Tōkyō Gaikokugo Daigaku, Ajia Afurika Gengo and Bunka Kenkyūjo (eds), *Islam and Cultural Diversity in Southeast Asia (Vol. 2)*, pp. 91–114. Tokyo: TUFS.

Sharifa, Zaleha Syed Hassan (2001). Islamisation and Urban Religious Identity: The Middle Class of Bandar Baru Bangi. In Abdul Rahman Embong (ed.), *Southeast Asian Middle Classes. Prospects for social change and democratisation*, pp. 119–38. Bangi: Penerbit Universiti Kebangsaan Malaysia.

Shields, Stephanie (2008). Gender: An intersectionality perspective. *Sex Roles* 59: 301–11.

Sisters in Islam (1991). *Are Women and Men Equal Before Allah?* Petaling Jaya: Sisters in Islam.

Slater, Don (2010). The Moral Seriousness of Consumption. *Journal of Consumer Culture* 10(2): 280–7.

Sleeboom-Faulkner, Margaret (2014). The Twenty-First-Century Gift and the Cocirculation of Things. *Anthropological Forum: A Journal of Social Anthropology and Comparative Sociology* 24(4): 323–37.

Sloane-White, Patricia (2017). *Corporate Islam: Sharia and the modern workplace.* Cambridge: Cambridge University Press.

Smith, Valene (1989). Introduction. In Valene Smith (ed.), *Hosts and Guests. The anthropology of tourism*, pp. 1–17. Philadelphia: University of Pennsylvania Press.

Sobh, Rana, Russell Belk and Justin Gressel (2014). Mimicry and Modernity in the Middle East: Fashion invisibility and young women of the Arab Gulf. *Consumption Markets & Culture* 17(4): 392–412.

Spatz, Ben (2017). Embodied Research: A methodology. *Liminalities: A Journal of Performance Studies* 13(2).

Sprenger, Guido (2019). Die konstitutiven Widersprüche der Gabe. *Paideuma: Mitteilungen zur Kulturkunde,* 65: 139–56.

Sprenger, Guido (2017). Goods and Ethnicity: Trade and bazaars in Laos from a gift perspective. *Heidelberg Ethnology Occasional Paper No. 6.*

Sprenger, Guido (2015). Idiome von Zentrum und Peripherie. Transkulturalität in einer asiatischen Grenzregion. In Jutta Ernst and Florian Freitag (eds), *Transkulturelle Dynamiken. Aktanten – Prozesse – Theorien*, pp. 227–54. Bielefeld: transcript.

Sprenger, Guido (2014). Where the Dead Go to the Market: Market and ritual as social systems in upland Southeast Asia. In Volker Gottowik (ed.), *The Magic of Modernity: Dynamics of religion in Southeast Asia*, pp. 75–90. Amsterdam: Amsterdam University Press.

Star, The (12 July 2017). PM: 1MDB has Done its Fair Share of Good. https://www.thestar.com.my/news/nation/2017/07/12/pm-1mdb-has-done-its-fair-share-of-good-people-just-unaware-of-its-contributions-says-najib (accessed 25 March 2023).

Star, The (27 August 2014). The Abaya is a Stylish Cover-up. https://www.thestar.com.my/lifestyle/women/fashion/2014/08/27/stylish-coverup (accessed 25 March 2023).

Staunæs, Dorthe (2003). Where Have all the Subjects Gone? Bringing together the concepts of intersectionality and subjectification. *Nora* 11(2): 101–10.

Stivens, Maila (2013). Family Values and Islamic Revival: Gender, rights and state moral projects in Malaysia. In Susanne Schröter (ed.), *Gender and Islam in Southeast Asia: Women's rights movements, religious resurgence and local traditions*, pp. 143–68. Leiden: Brill.

Stivens, Maila (2007). Post-modern Motherhoods and Cultural Contest in Malaysia and Singapore. In Theresa W. Devasahayam and Brenda S.A. Yeoh (eds), *Working and Mothering in Asia: Images, ideologies and identities*, pp. 29–50. Copenhagen: NIAS.

Stivens, Maila (2006). 'Family Values' and Islamic Revival: Gender, rights and state moral projects in Malaysia. *Women's Studies International Forum* 19: 354–67.

Stivens, Maila (2000). Becoming Modern in Malaysia: Women at the end of the twentieth century. In Louise Edwards and Mina Roces (eds), *Women in Asia. Tradition, modernity and globalisation*, pp. 16–38. Ann Arbor: University of Michigan Press.

Stivens, Maila (1998). Theorising Gender, Power and Modernity in Affluent Asia. In Krishna Sen and Maila Stivens (eds), *Gender and Power in Affluent Asia*, pp. 87–126. Abingdon: Routledge.

Strathern, Marilyn (1990). *The Gender of the Gift. Problems with women and problems with society in Melanesia*. Berkeley: University of California Press.

Sullins, D. Paul (2006). Gender and Religion: Deconstructing universality, constructing complexity. *American Journal of Sociology* 112(3): 838–80.

Surinder, Bhardwaj (1998). Non-*Hajj* Pilgrimage in Islam: A neglected dimension of religious circulation. *Journal of Cultural Geography* 17(2): 69–87.

Tabung Haji (n.d.,). Hajj Registration. https://www.tabunghaji.gov.my/en/hajj/general-info/hajj-registration-off (accessed 25 March 2023).

Tagliacozzo, Eric (2013). *The Longest Journey: Southeast Asians and the pilgrimage to Mecca*. Oxford: Oxford University Press.

TallyPress (13 November 2015). Malaysia's Top 10 Muslimah Fashion Brands. https://tallypress.com/malaysia-top-10s/malaysias-top-10-muslimah-fashion-brands/ (accessed 25 March 2023).

Tarlo, Emma (2010). *Visibly Muslim: Fashion, politics, faith*. London: Bloomsbury.

Tayob, Abdulkader (2018). Decolonizing the Study of Religions: Muslim intellectuals and the enlightenment project of religious studies. *Journal for the Study of Religion* 31(2): 7–35.

Thanem, Torkild and David Knights (2012). Feeling and Speaking Through our Gendered Bodies: Embodied self-reflection and research practice in organisation studies. *International Journal of Work Organisation and Emotion* 5(1): 91–108.

Thijl, Sunier (ed.) (2018). *Islam and Society, Vol II: Space, Place, Time: The spatial dimensions of Islam*. Abingdon: Routledge.

Thimm, Viola (2022). *Narrating Intersectional Perspectives Across Social Scales: Voicing Valerie*. Abingdon: Routledge.

Thimm, Viola (2021). Gendered Pilgrimage: *Hajj* and *umrah* from women's perspectives. *Journal of Contemporary Religion* 36(2): 223–41.

Thimm, Viola (2018). Muslim Mobilities and Gender: An introduction. *Social Sciences* 7(1): 5.

Thimm, Viola (2017). *Commercialising Islam in Malaysia: Ziarah at the intersection of Muslim pilgrimage and the market-driven tourism industry*. UKM Ethnic Studies Paper Series No. 56, December. Bangi: Institute of Ethnic Studies.

Thimm, Viola (2016a). 'I really love that guy!' Romantische Liebe als Weg zur Moderne im regionalen Kontext Singapurs und Malaysias. *Asien – The German Journal on Contemporary Asia* 139 2/2016: 25–43.

Thimm, Viola (2016b). 'I can give you money but there is no use. The best thing I [can] give you is education.' Negotiating Educational Migration and Gender in a Chinese Malaysian Family. *TRaNS: Trans-Regional and National Studies of Southeast Asia* 4(1): 65–84.

Thimm, Viola (2014a). *Geschlecht und Bildungsmigration: Lebensentwürfe und Weiblichkeitsbilder malaysischer Bildungsmigrantinnen in Singapur*. Bielefeld: transcript.

Thimm, Viola (2014b). 'Gendered Geographies of Power'. Ein Modell zur Analyse von Bildungsmigration und Geschlecht am Beispiel von Malaysia und Singapur. In Silker Förschler *et al.* (eds), *Verorten – Verhandeln – Verkörpern*, pp. 61–84. Bielefeld: transcript.

Thimm, Viola (2014c). Soziale Mobilität für Frauen durch bildungsmotivierte Land-Stadt-Migration: Eine Biographie aus Malaysia. *Ethnoscripts* 16(2): 27–41.

Thimm, Viola (2014d). The Female Body in Transnational Space between Malaysia and Singapore. In Kristy Buccieri (ed.), *Body Tensions: Beyond corporeality in time and space*, pp. 55–72. Oxford: ID-Press.

Thimm, Viola, Mayurakshi Chaudhuri and Sarah J. Mahler (2017). Enhancing Intersectional Analyses with Polyvocality: Making and illustrating the model. *Social Sciences* 6(2): 37.

Thornton, Robert J. (1988). The Rhetoric of Ethnographic Holism. *Cultural Anthropology* 3(3): 285–303.

Timothy, Dallen J. and Thomas Iverson (2006). Tourism and Islam: Considerations of culture and duty. In Dallen J. Timothy and Daniel H. Olsen (eds), *Tourism, Religion and Spiritual Journeys*, pp. 186–205. Abingdon: Routledge.

Timothy, Dallen J. and Daniel H. Olsen (eds) (2006). *Tourism, Religion and Spiritual Journeys*. Abingdon: Routledge.

Ting, Helen (2007). Gender Discourse in Malay Politics: Old wine in new bottle? In Edmund Terence Gomez (ed.), *Politics in Malaysia: The Malay dimension*, pp. 75–106. Abingdon: Routledge.

Tripp, Charles (2006). *Islam and the Moral Economy: The challenge of capitalism*. Cambridge: Cambridge University Press.

Tsing, Anna Lowenhaupt (2005). *Friction. An ethnography of global connection*. Princeton: Princeton University Press.

Turner, Victor and Edith Turner (1978). *Image and Pilgrimage in Christian Culture*. New York: Columbia University Press.

Ufen, Andreas (2008). Die komplexe Dynamik der Islamisierung. Der malaysische Islam im Spannungsfeld von Staat, politischer Gesellschaft und Zivilgesellschaft. In Fritz Schulze and Holger Warnk (eds), *Religion und Identität: Muslime und Nicht-Muslime in Südostasien*, pp. 111–36. Wiesbaden: Harrassowitz.

Urry, John (2002). *The Tourist Gaze*, 2nd ed. London: Sage.

Uteng, Tanu Priya and Tim Cresswell (2008). Gendered Mobilities: Towards a holistic understanding. In Tanu Priya Uteng and Tim Cresswell (eds), *Gendered Mobilities*, pp. 1–12. Aldershot: Ashgate.

van Liere, Lucien (2017). At the Threshold: A panorama for future research and challenges to religious studies. In Bob Becking, Anne-Marie Korte and Lucien van Liere (eds), *Contesting Religious Identities: Transformations, disseminations and mediations*, pp. 277–96. Leiden: Brill.

Van Sommer, Annie and Samuel Marinus Zwemer (eds) (1907). *Our Moslem Sisters: A cry of need from lands of darkness interpreted by those who heard it*. New York: Revell.

Vukonić, Boris (2010). Do We Always Understand Each Other? In Noel Scott and Jafar Jafari (eds), *Tourism in the Muslim World*, pp. 31–45. Bingley: Emerald.

Waardenburg, Jacques (1996). Some Thoughts on Modernity and Modern Muslim Thinking about Islam. In Sharifah Shifa Al-Attas (ed.), *Islam and the Challenge of Modernity*, pp. 317–50. Kuala Lumpur: ISTAC.

Wadud, Amina (2009). Islam Beyond Patriarchy through Gender Inclusive Qur'anic Analysis. In Zainah Anwar (ed.), *Wanted: Equality and Justice in the Muslim Family*, pp. 95–112. Petaling Jaya: musawah.

Wadud, Amina (2008). *Inside the Gender Jihad: Women's reform in Islam*. Oxford: Oneworld.

Wadud, Amina (2003). What's Interpretation Got to Do with it?: The relationship between theory and practice in Islamic gender reforms. In Nik Noriani Nik Badlishah (ed.), *Islamic Family Law and Justice for Muslim Women*, pp. 83–94. Kuala Lumpur: Sisters in Islam.

Wadud, Amina (1999). *Qur'an and Woman: Rereading the sacred text from a woman's perspective*. Oxford: Oxford University Press.

Wang, Nina (2000). *Tourism and Modernity: A sociological analysis*. Amsterdam: Pergamon.

Warnk, Holger (2008). 'Why are they So Afraid of Islam?' Nik Abdul Aziz Nik Mat, Abdul Hadi Awang und Nicht-Muslime in Malaysia. In Fritz Schulze and Holger Warnk (eds), *Religion und Identität: Muslime und Nicht-Muslime in Südostasien*, pp. 137–59. Wiesbaden: Harrassowitz.

Wazir Jahan, Karim (1995). Bilateralism and Gender in Southeast Asia. In Wazir Jahan Karim (ed.), *'Male' and 'Female' in Developing Southeast Asia*, pp. 35–74. Oxford: Berg

Wazir Jahan, Karim (1992). *Women and Culture. Between Malay adat and Islam*. Boulder: Westview.

WDR (Frau tv) (11 April 2019). Contemporary Muslim Fashions. Eine Ausstellung in Frankfurt sorgt für Aufregung und Proteste. https://www1.wdr.de/mediathek/video/sendungen/frau-tv/video-contemporary-muslimfashions-eine-ausstellung-in-frankfurt-sorgt-fuer-aufregung-und-proteste--100.html (accessed 25 March 2023).

Weber, Beverly M. (2015). Gender, Race, Religion, Faith? Rethinking intersectionality in German feminisms. *European Journal of Women's Studies* 22(1): 22–36.

Weller, Robert P. (2011). Asia and the Global Economies of Charisma. In Pattana Kitiarsa (ed.), *Religious Commodifications in Asia: Marketing gods*, pp. 15–30. Abingdon: Routledge.

Werbner, Pnina (1996). From Commodities to Gifts: Pakistani migrant workers in Manchester. In Alistair Rogers and Steven Vertovec (eds), *The Urban Context: Ethnicity, social networks and situational analysis*, pp. 213–36. Oxford: Berg.

Werlen, Benno (2010). *Gesellschaftliche Räumlichkeit 2: Konstruktion geografischer Wirklichkeiten*. Stuttgart: Steiner.

Werlen, Benno (2005). Raus aus dem Container: Ein sozialgeografischer Blick auf die aktuelle (Sozial)Raumdiskussion. In Projekt 'Netzwerke im Stadtteil' (ed.), *Grenzen des Sozialraums: Kritik eines Konzepts – Perspektiven für soziale Arbeit*, pp. 15–35. Wiesbaden: VS-Verlag für Sozialwissenschaften.

Werlen, Benno (1987). *Gesellschaft, Handlung und Raum: Grundlagen handlungstheoretischer Sozialgeographie*. Stuttgart: Steiner.

Wikan, Unni (1982). *Behind the Veil in Arabia: Women in Oman*. Chicago: University of Chicago Press.

Wimmer, Andreas and Nina Glick Schiller (2002). Methodological Nationalism and Beyond: Nation-state building, migration and the social sciences. *Global Networks* 2: 301–34.

Wolcott, Harry F. (2008). *Ethnography: A way of seeing*. Lanham: Altamira.

Woodhead, Linda (2013). Foreword. In Reina Lewis (ed.), *Modest Fashion: Styling Bodies, Mediating Faith*, pp. xvii–xx. London: I.B. Tauris.

Yeoh, Sen-Guan (2016). Religious Pluralism and Pilgrimage Studies in West (Peninsular) Malaysia. In Dionigi Albera and John Eade (eds), *New Pathways in Pilgrimage Studies: Global perspectives*, pp. 68–88. Abingdon: Routledge.

Yusuf, Abdul Azeez, Luqman Zakariyah, Syahirah Abdul Shukor and Ahmad Zaki Salleh (2016). Codification of Islamic Family Law in Malaysia: The contending legal intricacies. *Scientific International (Lahore)* 28(2): 1,753–62.

Yuval-Davis, Nira (2006). Intersectionality and Feminist Politics. *European Journal of Women's Studies* 13(3): 193–209.

Zainah, Anwar (2009). Introduction: Why equality and justice now. In Zainah Anwar (ed.), *Wanted: Equality and Justice in the Muslim Family*, pp. 1–9. Petaling Jaya: musawah.

Zainah, Anwar (2001). What Islam, Whose Islam? Sisters in Islam and the Struggle for Women's Rights. In Robert W. Hefner (ed.), *The Politics of Multiculturalism. Pluralism and citizenship in Malaysia, Singapore, and Indonesia*, pp. 227–52. Honolulu: University of Hawai'i Press.

Zayed, Ahmed A. (2008). Saints (*awliya'*), Public Places and Modernity in Egypt. In Georg Stauth and Samuli Schielke (eds), *Dimensions of Locality: Muslim saints, their place and space. Yearbook of the Sociology of Islam No. 8*, pp. 103–23.

Index